... to call ...
ition to ... ng
... the state ...
...vice. It was not that there
... acceptance, upon the disposal
... have had any influence,
...d what would be agreeable
... progress of affairs. If we are
...ilitary operations, 'tis not a
..., that you are one of those
...field. With such an enemy
...will not barely do their duty

...gy equal to all dangers

with very great regard.

I am dear Sir

Your obed Servant

A Hamilton

Selected Works of
Alexander Hamilton

Selected Works of
Alexander Hamilton

Word Cloud Classics

San Diego

Canterbury Classics
An imprint of Printers Row Publishing Group
10350 Barnes Canyon Road, Suite 100, San Diego, CA 92121
www.canterburyclassicsbooks.com

Printers Row Publishing Group is a division of Readerlink Distribution Services, LLC. The Canterbury Classics and Word Cloud Classics names and logos are trademarks of Readerlink Distribution Services, LLC.

All correspondence concerning the content of this book should be addressed to Canterbury Classics, Editorial Department, at the above address.

Publisher: Peter Norton
Associate Publisher: Ana Parker
Publishing/Editorial Team: April Farr, Kelly Larsen, Kathryn C. Dalby
Editorial Team: JoAnn Padgett, Melinda Allman, Dan Mansfield
Production Team: Jonathan Lopes, Rusty von Dyl

Library of Congress Cataloging-in-Publication Data

Names: Hamilton, Alexander, 1757-1804, author.
Title: Selected works of Alexander Hamilton.
Description: San Diego, CA : Canterbury Classics, 2018.
Identifiers: LCCN 2017049969 (print) | LCCN 2017051403 (ebook) |
ISBN 9781684123520 (ebook) | ISBN 9781684122912 (flexibound)
Subjects: LCSH: Hamilton, Alexander, 1757-1804. | Hamilton, Alexander,
1757-1804--Correspondence. | Hamilton, Alexander, 1757-1804--Political and
social views. | United States--History--1783-1815. | United States--Politics and
government--1801-1809. | United States--Politics and government--1783-1789.
Classification: LCC E302 (ebook) | LCC E302 .H22 2018 (print) |
DDC 973.4092--dc23
LC record available at https://lccn.loc.gov/2017049969

PRINTED IN CHINA

22 21 20 19 18 1 2 3 4 5

CONTENTS

A Note on the Text

The writings included in *Selected Works of Alexander Hamilton* are printed here as they originally appeared, with any inconsistencies in spelling, punctuation, and style retained to preserve the original flavor of Hamilton's words.

In places, portions of Hamilton's handwriting and archival copies of printed materials contained missing or indecipherable text; these instances are indicated by bracketed blank spaces: [   ].

The works included in this volume were obtained from the Alexander Hamilton Papers at Founders Online, a digital resource from the National Archives that provides the public with access to the collected writings of the founders of the United States of America.

Chronology

1755   Alexander Hamilton is born on January 11 in the British West Indies, possibly on the island of Nevis. He is the second child of Rachel Lavien and James Hamilton.

1765   James Hamilton leaves his wife and family on the island of St. Croix, and is never heard from again. Rachel Lavien opens a store in Christiansted.

1768   Rachel Lavien becomes ill and dies on February 19; her entire estate is inherited by Peter Lavien, her only legitimate child from a previous marriage. Alexander Hamilton begins work as a clerk at a mercantile firm.

1772   With the help of Hugh Knox, a minister in Christiansted, Hamilton sails to the United States to begin his education. He enrolls at a Presbyterian academy in Elizabethtown, New Jersey.

1773   Enters King's College (now Columbia University) in New York City, and begins lifelong friendships with Robert Troup and John Jay. Writes *A Full Vindication of the Measures of Congress*, a pamphlet published on December 15.

1775   Sees his first action in the Revolutionary War in August when he comes under fire from a British ship in New York Harbor.

1776   Leaves King's College without completing his studies, in order to serve as a commander in an artillery company, with the rank of captain.

1777   Becomes aide-de-camp to General George Washington, with the rank of lieutenant colonel. Forms a friendship with the Marquis de Lafayette, who joins Washington's camp in August. Spends the winter with the Continental army at Valley Forge.

1780   Begins a courtship of Elizabeth Schuyler, daughter of New York landowner Philip Schuyler. Is denied a field command by General Washington. Marries Elizabeth Schuyler on December 14.

1781   Resigns his position with General Washington during a dispute in February, but remains on the staff until April. Publishes the first of his "Continentalist" papers, outlining his plan for the powers to be given to the United States Congress. Commands a New York battalion and participates in the siege of Yorktown in September. Leaves active military service after the British surrender on October 19.

1782   The Hamiltons' first child, Philip, is born on January 22. Hamilton begins his study of the law, and is appointed a delegate to Congress by the New York state legislature.

1783   Moves with his family to New York City, where he establishes his law office.

1787   Attends the Philadelphia constitutional convention as a delegate from New York. His speech advocating for a stronger central government modeled on the British system causes his political opponents to label him as a monarchist. Publishes (anonymously) the first of the *Federalist* papers advocating for the ratification of the new U.S. Constitution.

1788   Elected as a delegate to the New York ratifying convention, where he engages in debate with Antifederalists; the Constitution is ratified by a narrow margin on July 26.

1789   Becomes the first Secretary of the Treasury, and is assigned by the House of Representatives to organize the new nation's finances.

1790   Submits a report to the House of Representatives, urging support for the establishment of a national bank.

1791   Engages in an affair with Marisa Reynolds while his wife and family are at the Schuyler home in Albany; Hamilton ends up paying blackmail to Marisa's husband James in an attempt to preserve his reputation.

1792   Hamilton's management of the U.S. Treasury is called into question when James Reynolds accuses him of misusing funds to speculate. Under questioning by other representatives, Hamilton confesses to the affair with Marisa Reynolds and to making blackmail payments with his own money.

1793   Informs President George Washington that he will resign from his position as Secretary of the Treasury in June 1794.

1794   Hamilton postpones his resignation due to the ongoing conflict between Great Britain and France, and then informs Washington in December that he will resign in early 1795.

1795   Resigns as Secretary of the Treasury on January 31, and moves with his family to New York. Resumes his law practice in New York City, but maintains unofficial role as President Washington's adviser.

1796   Continues to advise Washington, and writes the first drafts of the president's farewell address. Urges members of the Federalist Party to support John Adams and Thomas Pickney in the presidential election; Adams wins the election, and Thomas Jefferson, who finished second, is elected vice president.

1797   Publishes the "Reynolds Pamphlet," in which he details his account of the affair with Marisa Reynolds, refuting claims that he made payments to James Reynolds in order to speculate in public funds. Remains occupied with his law practice in New York City.

1798   An undeclared naval conflict breaks out between the United States and France; George Washington is appointed commander in chief by President Adams, and Hamilton agrees to serve as inspector general. Supervises the fortification of New York City and is named second in command of the army in October.

1799   Continues reorganization of the army, and drafts a plan for a national military academy. George Washington dies on December 14.

1800   Attempts to rally support among members of the Federalist Party for presidential candidate Charles Cotesworth Pinckney. Writes a pamphlet for the Federalists that claims John Adams is unfit for the presidency; when the pamphlet is leaked to the press, Hamilton's reputation is damaged and support for the Federalist Party is diminished. Presidential election results in a tie between Republican candidates Thomas Jefferson and Aaron Burr, leaving the election in the hands of the House of Representatives, which is controlled by the Federalists. Hamilton urges the Federalists to support Jefferson over Burr.

1801   Jefferson is elected president on the thirty-sixth ballot in the House of Representatives on February 17. Hamilton helps establish the New-York Evening Post newspaper, and publishes several articles critical of the Jefferson administration. His eldest son, Philip, dies after a duel fought in defense of his father's policies.

1802   Drafts a resolution for the New York legislature calling for separate ballots to elect the president and vice president, and that electors be chosen according to popular vote in districts established by Congress; this system is eventually adopted as part of the Twelfth Amendment in 1804.

1803   Helps found the Merchants' Bank in New York City, and remains involved in his private law practice.

1804   Hamilton denounces the qualifications of Aaron Burr, who had been gaining support among Republicans as a candidate for governor of New York. Burr loses the election and demands explanations from Hamilton for his conduct; Hamilton offers no apologies. On June 27, Burr challenges Hamilton to a duel, which he accepts. The duel is conducted on July 11 at Weehawken, New Jersey. Burr's pistol ball hits Hamilton, puncturing his liver and lodging in his spine. After seeing his wife and children and receiving communion, Hamilton dies on the afternoon of July 12.

To Edward Stevens

St Croix Novemr. 11th 1769

DEAR EDWARD

This just serves to acknowledge receipt of yours per Cap Lowndes which was delivered me Yesterday. The truth of Cap Lightbourn & Lowndes information is now verifyd by the Presence of your Father and Sister for whose safe arrival I Pray, and that they may convey that Satisfaction to your Soul that must naturally flow from the sight of Absent Friends in health, and shall for news this way refer you to them. As to what you say respecting your having soon the happiness of seeing us all, I wish, for an accomplishment of your hopes provided they are Concomitant with your welfare, otherwise not, tho doubt whether I shall be Present or not for to confess my weakness, Ned, my Ambition is prevalent that I contemn the grov'ling and condition of a Clerk or the like, to which my Fortune &c. condemns me and would willingly risk my life tho' not my Character to exalt my Station. Im confident, Ned that my Youth excludes me from any hopes of immediate Preferment nor do I desire it, but I mean to prepare the way for futurity. Im no Philosopher you see and may be jusly said to Build Castles in the Air. My Folly makes me ashamd and beg youll Conceal it, yet Neddy we have seen such Schemes successfull when the Projector is Constant I shall Conclude saying I wish there was a War.

I am Dr Edward Yours

ALEX HAMILTON

PS   I this moment receivd yours by William Smith and am pleasd to see you Give such Close Application to Study.

To The Royal Danish American Gazette

St. Croix, Sept. 6, 1772

HONOURED SIR,

I take up my pen just to give you an imperfect account of one of the most dreadful Hurricanes that memory or any records whatever can trace, which happened here on the 31st ultimo at night.

It began about dusk, at North, and raged very violently till ten o'clock. Then ensued a sudden and unexpected interval, which lasted about an hour. Meanwhile the wind was shifting round to the South West point, from whence it returned with redoubled fury and continued so 'till near three o'clock in the morning. Good God! what horror and destruction. Its impossible for me to describe or you to form any idea of it. It seemed as if a total dissolution of nature was taking place. The roaring of the sea and wind, fiery meteors flying about it in the air, the prodigious glare of almost perpetual lightning, the crash of the falling houses, and the ear-piercing shrieks of the distressed, were sufficient to strike astonishment into Angels. A great part of the buildings throughout the Island are levelled to the ground, almost all the rest very much shattered; several persons killed and numbers utterly ruined; whole families running about the streets, unknowing where to find a place of shelter; the sick exposed to the keeness of water and air without a bed to lie upon, or a dry covering to their bodies; and our harbours entirely bare. In a word, misery, in all its most hideous shapes, spread over the whole face of the country. A strong smell of gunpowder added somewhat to the terrors of the night; and it was observed that the rain was surprizingly salt. Indeed the water is so brackish and full of sulphur that there is hardly any drinking it.

My reflections and feelings on this frightful and melancholy occasion, are set forth in the following self-discourse.

Where now, oh! vile worm, is all thy boasted fortitude and resolution? What is become of thine arrogance and self sufficiency? Why dost thou tremble and stand aghast? How humble, how helpless, how contemptible you now appear. And for why? The jarring of elements—the discord of clouds? Oh! impotent presumptuous fool! how durst thou offend that Omnipotence, whose nod alone were sufficient to quell the destruction that hovers over thee, or crush thee into atoms? See thy wretched helpless state, and learn to know thyself. Learn to know thy best support. Despise thyself, and adore thy God. How sweet, how unutterably sweet were now, the voice of an approving conscience; Then couldst thou say, hence ye idle alarms, why do I shrink? What have I to fear? A pleasing calm suspense! A short repose from calamity to end in eternal bliss? Let the Earth rend. Let the planets forsake their course. Let the Sun be extinguished and the Heavens burst asunder. Yet what have I to dread? My staff can never be broken—in Omnipotence I trusted.

He who gave the winds to blow, and the lightnings to rage—even him have I always loved and served. His precepts have I observed. His commandments have I obeyed—and his perfections have I adored. He will snatch me from ruin. He will exalt me to the fellowship of Angels and Seraphs, and to the fullness of never ending joys.

But alas! how different, how deplorable, how gloomy the prospect! Death comes rushing on in triumph veiled in a mantle of tenfold darkness. His unrelenting scythe, pointed, and ready for the stroke. On his right hand sits destruction, hurling the winds and belching forth flames: Calamity on his left threatening famine disease and distress of all kinds. And Oh! thou wretch, look still a little further; see the gulph of eternal misery open. There mayest thou shortly plunge—the just reward of thy vileness. Alas! whither canst thou fly? Where hide thyself? Thou canst not call upon thy God; thy life has been a continual warfare with him.

Hark—ruin and confusion on every side. 'Tis thy turn next; but one short moment, even now, Oh Lord help. Jesus be merciful!

Thus did I reflect, and thus at every gust of the wind, did I conclude, 'till it pleased the Almighty to allay it. Nor did my emotions proceed either from the suggestions of too much natural fear, or a conscience over-burthened with crimes of an uncommon cast. I thank God, this was not the case. The scenes of horror exhibited around us, naturally awakened such ideas in every thinking breast, and aggravated the deformity of every failing of our lives. It were a lamentable insensibility indeed, not to have had such feelings, and I think inconsistent with human nature.

Our distressed, helpless condition taught us humility and contempt of ourselves. The horrors of the night, the prospect of an immediate, cruel death—or, as one may say, of being crushed by the Almighty in his anger—filled us with terror. And every thing that had tended to weaken our interest with him, upbraided us in the strongest colours, with our baseness and folly. That which, in a calm unruffled temper, we call a natural cause, seemed then like the correction of the Deity. Our imagination represented him as an incensed master, executing vengeance on the crimes of his servants. The father and benefactor were forgot, and in that view, a consciousness of our guilt filled us with despair.

But see, the Lord relents. He hears our prayer. The Lightning ceases. The winds are appeased. The warring elements are reconciled and all things promise peace. The darkness is dispell'd and drooping nature revives at the approaching dawn. Look back Oh! my soul, look back and tremble. Rejoice at thy deliverance, and humble thyself in the presence of thy deliverer.

Yet hold, Oh vain mortal! Check thy ill timed joy. Art thou so selfish to exult because thy lot is happy in a season of universal woe? Hast thou no feelings for the miseries of thy fellow-creatures? And art thou incapable of the soft pangs of sympathetic sorrow? Look around thee and shudder at the view. See desolation and ruin where'er thou turnest thine eye! See thy fellow-creatures pale and lifeless; their bodies mangled, their souls snatched into eternity, unexpecting. Alas! perhaps unprepared! Hark the bitter groans of distress. See sickness and infirmities exposed to the inclemencies of wind and water! See tender infancy pinched with hunger and hanging on the mothers knee for food! See the unhappy mothers anxiety. Her poverty denies relief, her breast heaves with pangs of maternal pity, her heart is bursting, the tears gush down her cheeks. Oh sights of woe! Oh distress unspeakable! My heart bleeds, but I have no power to solace! O ye, who revel in affluence, see the afflictions of humanity and bestow your superfluity to ease them. Say not, we have suffered also, and thence withold your compassion. What are your sufferings compared to those? Ye have still more than enough left. Act wisely. Succour the miserable and lay up a treasure in Heaven.

I am afraid, Sir, you will think this description more the effort of imagination than a true picture of realities. But I can affirm with the greatest truth, that there is not a single circumstance touched upon, which I have not absolutely been an eye witness to.

Our General has issued several very salutary and humane regulations, and both in his publick and private measures, has shewn himself *the Man*.

A Full Vindication of the Measures of the Congress, &c.

New-York 1774

FRIENDS AND COUNTRYMEN,

It was hardly to be expected that any man could be so presumptuous, as openly to controvert the equity, wisdom, and authority of the measures, adopted by the congress: an assembly truly respectable on every account! Whether we consider the characters of the men, who composed it; the number, and dignity of their constituents, or the important ends for which they were appointed. But, however improbable such a degree of presumption might have seemed, we find there are some, in whom it exists. Attempts are daily making to diminish the influence of their decisions, and prevent the salutary effects, intended by them. The impotence of such insidious efforts is evident from the general indignation they are treated with; so that no material ill-consequences can be dreaded from them. But lest they should have a tendency to mislead, and prejudice the minds of a few; it cannot be deemed altogether useless to bestow some notice upon them.

And first, let me ask these restless spirits, whence arises that violent antipathy they seem to entertain, not only to the natural rights of mankind; but to common sense and common modesty. That they are enemies to the natural rights of mankind is manifest, because they wish to see one part of their species enslaved by another. That they have an invincible aversion to common sense is apparent in many respects: They endeavour to persuade us, that the absolute sovereignty of parliament does not imply our absolute slavery; that it is a Christian duty to submit to be plundered of all we have, merely because some of our fellow-subjects are wicked enough to require it of us, that slavery, so far from being a great evil, is a great blessing; and even, that our contest with Britain is founded entirely upon the petty duty of 3 pence per pound on East India tea; whereas the whole world knows, it is built upon this interesting question, whether the inhabitants of Great-Britain have a right to dispose of the lives and properties of the inhabitants of America, or not? And lastly, that these men have discarded all pretension to common modesty, is clear from hence, first, because they, in the plainest terms, call an august body of men, famed for their patriotism and abilities, fools or knaves, and of course the people whom they represented cannot be exempt from the same opprobrious appellations; and secondly, because they set themselves up as standards of wisdom and probity, by contradicting and censuring the public voice in favour of those men.

A little consideration will convince us, that the congress instead of having "ignorantly misunderstood, carelessly neglected, or basely betrayed the interests of the colonies," have, on the contrary, devised and recommended the only effectual means to secure the freedom, and establish the future prosperity of America upon a solid basis. If we are not free and happy hereafter, it must proceed from the want of integrity and resolution, in executing what they have concerted; not from the temerity or impolicy of their determinations.

Before I proceed to confirm this assertion by the most obvious arguments, I will premise a few brief remarks. The only distinction between freedom and slavery consists in this: In the former state, a man is governed by the laws to which he has given his consent, either in person, or by his representative: In the latter, he is governed by the will of another. In the one case his life and property are his own, in the other, they depend upon the pleasure of a master. It is easy to discern which of these two states is preferable. No man in his senses can hesitate in choosing to be free, rather than a slave.

That Americans are intitled to freedom, is incontestible upon every rational principle. All men have one common original: they participate in one common nature, and consequently have one common right. No reason can be assigned why one man should exercise any power, or pre-eminence over his fellow creatures more than another; unless they have voluntarily vested him with it. Since then, Americans have not by any act of their's impowered the British Parliament to make laws for them, it follows they can have no just authority to do it.

Besides the clear voice of natural justice in this respect, the fundamental principles of the English constitution are in our favour. It has been repeatedly demonstrated, that the idea of legislation, or taxation, when the subject is not represented, is inconsistent with *that*. Nor is this all, our charters, the express conditions on which our progenitors relinquished their native countries, and came to settle in this, preclude every claim of ruling and taxing us without our assent.

Every subterfuge that sophistry has been able to invent, to evade or obscure this truth, has been refuted by the most conclusive reasonings; so that we may pronounce it a matter of undeniable certainty, that the pretensions of Parliament are contradictory to the law of nature, subversive of the British constitution, and destructive of the faith of the most solemn compacts.

What then is the subject of our controversy with the mother country? It is this, whether we shall preserve that security to our lives and properties, which the law of nature, the genius of the British constitution, and our charters afford us; or whether we shall resign them into the hands of the British House of Commons, which is no more privileged to dispose of them than the Grand Mogul? What can actuate those men, who labour to delude any of us into an opinion, that the object of contention between the parent state and the colonies is only three pence duty upon tea? or that the commotions in America originate in a plan, formed by some turbulent men to erect it into a republican government? The parliament claims a right to tax us in all cases whatsoever: Its late acts are in virtue of that claim. How ridiculous then is it to affirm, that we are quarrelling for the trifling sum of three pence a pound on tea; when it is evidently the principle against which we contend.

The design of electing members to represent us in general congress, was, that the wisdom of America might be collected in devising the most proper and expedient means to repel this atrocious invasion of our rights. It has been accordingly done. Their decrees are binding upon all, and demand a religious observance.

We did not, especially in this province, circumscribe them by any fixed boundary, and therefore as they cannot be said to have exceeded the limits of their authority, their act must be esteemed the act of their constituents. If it should be objected, that they have not answered the end of their election; but have fallen upon an improper and ruinous mode of proceeding: I reply, by asking, Who shall be the judge? Shall any individual oppose his private sentiment to the united counsels of men, in whom America has reposed so high a confidence? The attempt must argue no small degree of arrogance and self-sufficiency.

Yet this attempt has been made, and it is become in some measure necessary to vindicate the conduct of this venerable assembly from the aspersions of men, who are their adversaries, only because they are foes to America.

When the political salvation of any community is depending, it is incumbent upon those who are set up as its guardians, to embrace such measures, as have justice, vigour, and a probabilty of success to recommend them: If instead of this, they take those methods which are in themselves feeble, and little likely to succeed; and may, through a defect in vigour, involve the community in still greater danger; they may be justly considered as its betrayers. It is not enough in times of eminent peril to use only possible means of preservation: Justice and sound policy dictate the use of probable means.

The only scheme of opposition, suggested by those, who have been, and are averse from a non-importation and non-exportation agreement, is, by REMONSTRANCE and PETITION. The authors and abettors of this scheme, have never been able to *invent* a single argument to prove the likelihood of its succeeding. On the other hand, there are many standing facts, and valid considerations against it.

In the infancy of the present dispute, we had recourse to this method only. We addressed the throne in the most loyal and respectful manner, in a legislative capacity; but what was the consequence? Our address was treated with contempt and neglect. The first American congress did the same, and met with similar treatment. The total repeal of the stamp act, and the partial repeal of the revenue acts took place, not because the complaints of America were deemed just and reasonable; but because these acts were found to militate against the commercial interests of Great Britain: This was the declared motive of the repeal.

These instances are sufficient for our purpose; but they derive greater validity and force from the following:

The legal assembly of Massachusetts Bay, presented, not long since, a most humble, dutiful, and earnest petition to his Majesty, requesting the dismission of a governor, highly odious to the people, and whose misrepresentations they regarded as one chief source of all their calamities. Did they succeed in their request? No, it was treated with the greatest indignity, and stigmatized as "a seditious, vexatious, and scandalous libel."

I know the men I have to deal with will acquiesce in this stigma.

Will they also dare to calumniate the noble and spirited petition that came from the Mayor and Aldermen of the city of London? Will they venture to justify that unparalelled stride of power, by which popery and arbitrary dominion were established in Canada? The citizens of London remonstrated against it; they signified its repugnancy to the principles of the revolution; but like ours, their complaints were unattended to. From thence we may learn how little dependence ought to be placed on this method of obtaining the redress of grievances.

There is less reason now than ever to expect deliverance, in this way, from the hand of oppression. The system of slavery, fabricated against America, cannot at this time be considered as the effect of inconsideration and rashness. It is the offspring of mature deliberation. It has been fostered by time, and strengthened by every artifice human subtilty is capable of. After the claims of parliament had lain dormant for awhile, they are again resumed and prosecuted with more than common ardour. The Premier has advanced too far to recede with safety: He is deeply interested to execute his purpose, if possible: we know he has declared, that he will never desist, till he has brought America to his feet; and we may conclude, nothing but necessity will induce him to abandon his aims. In common life, to retract an error even in the beginning, is no easy task. Perseverance confirms us in it, and rivets the difficulty; but in a public station, to have been in an error, and to have persisted in it, when it is detected, ruins both reputation and fortune. To this we may add, that disappointment and opposition inflame the minds of men, and attach them, still more, to their mistakes.

What can we represent which has not already been represented? what petitions can we offer, that have not already been offered? The rights of America, and the injustice of parliamentary pretensions have been clearly and repeatedly stated, both in and out of parliament. No new arguments can be framed to operate in our favour. Should we even resolve the errors of the ministry and parliament into the fallibility of human understanding, if they have not yet been convinced, we have no prospect of being able to do it by any thing further we can say. But if we impute their conduct to a wicked thirst of domination and disregard to justice, we have no hope of prevailing with them to alter it, by expatiating on our rights, and suing to their compassion for relief; especially since we have found, by various experiments, the inefficacy of such methods.

Upon the whole, it is morally certain, this mode of opposition would be fruitless and defective. The exigency of the times requires vigorous and probable remedies; not weak and improbable. It would therefore be the extreme of folly to place any confidence in, much less, confine ourselves wholly to it.

This being the case, we can have no resource but in a restriction of our trade, or in a resistance *vi & armis*. It is impossible to conceive any other alternative. Our congress, therefore, have imposed what restraint they thought necessary. Those, who condemn or clamour against it, do nothing more, nor less, than advise us to be slaves.

I shall now examine the principal measures of the congress, and vindicate them fully from the charge of injustice or impolicy.

Were I to argue in a philosophical manner, I might say, the obligation to a mutual intercourse in the way of trade with the inhabitants of Great-Britain, Ireland and the West-Indies is of the *imperfect* kind. There is no law, either of nature, or of the civil society in which we live, that obliges us to purchase, and make use of the products and manufactures of a different land, or people. It is indeed a dictate of humanity to contribute to the support and happiness of our fellow creatures and more especially those who are allied to us by the ties of blood, interest, and mutual protection; but humanity does not require us to sacrifice our own security and welfare to the convenience, or advantage of others. Self preservation is the first principle of our nature. When our lives and properties are at stake, it would be foolish and unnatural to refrain from such measures as might preserve them, because they would be detrimental to others.

But we are justified upon another principle besides this. Though the manufacturers of Great Britain and Ireland, and the Inhabitants of the West Indies are not chargeable with any actual crime towards America, they may, in a political view, be esteemed criminal. In a civil society, it is the duty of each particular branch to promote, not only the good of the whole community, but the good of every other particular branch: If one part endeavours to violate the rights of another, the rest ought to assist in preventing the injury: When they do not, but remain neutral, they are deficient in their duty, and may be regarded, in some measure, as accomplices.

The reason of this is obvious, from the design of civil society, which is, that the united strength of the several members might give stability and security to the whole body, and each respective member; so that one part cannot encroach upon another, without becoming a common enemy, and eventually endangering the safety and happiness of all the other parts.

Since then the persons who will be distressed by the methods we are using for our own protection, have by their neutrality first committed a breach of an obligation, similar to that which bound us to consult their emolument, it is plain, the obligation upon us is annulled, and we are blameless in what we are about to do.

With respect to the manufacturers of Great Britain, they are criminal in a more particular sense. Our oppression arises from that member of the great body politic, of which they compose a considerable part. So far as their influence has been wanting to counteract the iniquity of their rulers, so far they acquiesced in it, and are to be deemed confederates in their guilt. It is impossible to exculpate a people, that suffers its rulers to abuse and tyrannize over others.

It may not be amiss to add, that we are ready to receive with open arms, any who may be sufferers by the operation of our measures, and recompense them with every blessing our country affords to honest industry. We will receive them as brethren, and make them sharers with us in all the advantages we are struggling for.

From these plain and indisputable principles, the mode of opposition we have chosen is reconcileable to the strictest maxims of Justice. It remains now to be examined, whether it has also the sanction of good policy.

To render it agreeable to good policy, three things are requisite. First, that the necessity of the times require it: Secondly, that it be not the probable source of greater evils, than those it pretends to remedy: And lastly, that it have a probability of success.

That the necessity of the times demands it needs but little elucidation. We are threatened with absolute slavery; it has been proved, that resistance by means of REMONSTRANCE and PETITION, would not be efficacious, and of course, that a restriction on our trade, is the only peaceable method, in our power, to avoid the impending mischief: It follows therefore, that such a restriction is necessary.

That it is not the probable source of greater evils than those it pretends to remedy, may easily be determined. The most abject slavery, which comprehends almost every species of human misery, is what it is designed to prevent.

The consequences of the means are a temporary stagnation of commerce, and thereby a deprivation of the luxuries and some of the conveniencies of life. The necessaries, and many of the conveniencies, our own fertile and propitious soil affords us.

No person, that has enjoyed the sweets of liberty, can be insensible of its infinite value, or can reflect on its reverse, without horror and detestation. No person, that is not lost to every generous feeling of humanity, or that is not stupidly blind to his own interest, could bear to offer himself and posterity as victims at the shrine of despotism, in preference to enduring the short lived inconveniencies that may result from an abridgment, or even entire suspension of commerce.

Were not the disadvantages of slavery too obvious to stand in need of it, I might enumerate and describe the tedious train of calamities, inseparable from it. I might shew that it is fatal to religion and morality; that it tends to debase the mind, and corrupt its noblest springs of action. I might shew, that it relaxes the sinews of industry, clips the wings of commerce, and introduces misery and indigence in every shape.

Under the auspices of tyranny, the life of the subject is often sported with; and the fruits of his daily toil are consumed in oppressive taxes, that serve to gratify the ambition, avarice and lusts of his superiors. Every court minion riots in the spoils of the honest labourer, and despises the hand by which he is fed. The page of history is replete with instances that loudly warn us to beware of slavery.

Rome was the nurse of freedom. She was celebrated for her justice and lenity; but in what manner did she govern her dependent provinces? They were made the continual scene of rapine and cruelty. From thence let us learn, how little confidence is due to the wisdom and equity of the most exemplary nations.

Should Americans submit to become the vassals of their fellow-subjects in Great Britain, their yoke will be peculiarly grievous and intolerable. A vast majority of mankind is intirely biassed by motives of self-interest. Most men are glad to remove any burthens off themselves, and place them upon the necks of their neighbours. We cannot therefore doubt, but that the British Parliament, with a view to the ease and advantage of itself, and its constituents, would oppress and grind the Americans as much as possible. Jealousy would concur with selfishness; and for fear of the future independence of America, if it should be permitted to rise to too great a height of splendor and opulence, every method would be taken to drain it of its wealth and restrain its prosperity. We are already suspected of aiming at independence, and that is one principal cause of the severity we experience. The same cause will always operate against us, and produce an uniform severity of treatment.

The evils which may flow from the execution of our measures, if we consider them with respect to their extent and duration, are comparatively nothing. In all human probability they will scarcely be felt. Reason and experience teach us, that the consequences would be too fatal to Great Britain to admit of delay. There is an immense trade between her and the colonies. The revenues arising from thence are prodigious. The consumption of her manufactures in these colonies supplies the means of subsistence to a vast number of her most useful inhabitants. The experiment we have made heretofore, shews us of how much importance our commercial connexion is to her; and gives us the highest assurance of obtaining immediate redress by suspending it.

From these considerations it is evident, she must do something decisive. She must either listen to our complaints, and restore us to a peaceful enjoyment of our violated rights; or she must exert herself to enforce her despotic claims by fire and sword. To imagine she would prefer the latter, implies a charge of the grossest infatuation of madness itself. Our numbers are very considerable; the courage of Americans has been tried and proved. Contests for liberty have ever been found the most bloody, implacable and obstinate. The disciplined troops Great Britain could send against us, would be but few, Our superiority in number would over balance our inferiority in discipline. It would be a hard, if not an impracticable task to subjugate us by force.

Besides, while Great Britain was engaged in carrying on an unnatural war against us, her commerce would be in a state of decay. Her revenues would be decreasing. An armament, sufficient to enslave America, would put her to an insupportable expence.

She would be laid open to the attacks of foreign enemies. Ruin, like a deluge, would pour in from every quarter. After lavishing her blood and treasure to reduce us to a state of vassalage, she would herself become a prey to some triumphant neighbour.

These are not imaginary mischiefs. The colonies contain above three millions of people. Commerce flourshes with the most rapid progress throughout them. This commerce Great-Britain has hitherto regulated to her own advantage. Can we think the annihilation of so exuberant a source of wealth, a matter of trifling import. On the contrary, must it not be productive of the most disastrous effects? It is evident it must. It is equally evident, that the conquest of so numerous a people, armed in the animating cause of liberty could not be accomplished without an inconceivable expence of blood and treasure.

We cannot therefore suspect Great-Britain to be capable of such frantic extravagance as to hazard these dreadful consequences; without which she must necessarily desist from her unjust pretensions, and leave us in the undisturbed possession of our privileges.

Those, who affect to ridicule the resistance America might make to the military force of Great-Britain, and represent its humiliation as a matter the most easily to be achieved, betray, either a mind clouded by the most irrational prejudices, or a total ignorance of human nature. However, it must be the wish of every honest man never to see a trial.

But should we admit a possibility of a third course, as our pamphleteer supposes, that is, the endeavouring to bring us to a compliance by putting a stop to our whole trade: Even this would not be so terrible as he pretends. We can live without trade of any kind. Food and clothing we have within ourselves. Our climate produces cotton, wool, flax and hemp, which, with proper cultivation would furnish us with summer apparel in abundance. The article of cotton indeed would do more, it would contribute to defend us from the inclemency of winter. We have sheep, which, with due care in improving and increasing them, would soon yield a sufficiency of wool. The large quantity of skins, we have among us, would never let us want a warm and comfortable suit. It would be no unbecoming employment for our daughters to provide silks of their own country. The silk-worm answers as well here as in any part of the world. Those hands, which may be deprived of business by the cessation of commerce, may be occupied in various kinds of manufactures and other internal improvements. If by the necessity of the thing, manufactures should once be established and take root among us, they will pave the way, still more, to the future grandeur and glory of America, and by lessening its need of external commerce, will render it still securer against the encroachments of tyranny.

It is however, chimerical to imagine that the circumstances of Great-Britain will admit of such a tardy method of subjecting us, for reasons, which have been already given, and which shall be corroborated by others equally forcible.

I come now to consider the last and principal ingredient that constitutes the policy of a measure, which is a probability of success. I have been obliged to anticipate this part of my subject, in considering the second requisite, and indeed what I have already said seems to me to leave no room for doubting, that the means we have used will be successful, but I shall here examine the matter more thoroughly, and endeavour to evince it more fully.

The design of the Congress in their proceedings, it cannot, and need not be desired, was either, by a prospect of the evil consequences, to influence the ministry to give up their enterprize; or should they prove inflexible, to affect the inhabitants of Great-Britain, Ireland and the West-Indies in such a manner, as to rouse them from their state of neutrality, and engage them to unite with us in opposing the lawless hand of tyranny, which is extended to ravish our liberty from us, and might soon be extended for the same purpose against them.

The FARMER mentions, as one probable consequence of our measures, "clamours, discord, confusion, mobs, riots, insurrections, rebellions in Great-Britain, Ireland and the West-Indies;" though at the same time that he thinks *it is*, he also thinks *it is not* a probable consequence. For my part, without hazarding any such seeming contradictions, I shall, in a plain way, assert, that I verily believe a non-importation and non-exportation will effect all the purposes they are intended for.

It is no easy matter to make any tolerably exact estimate of the advantages that acrue to Great-Britain, Ireland and the West-Indies from their commercial intercourse with the colonies, nor indeed is it necessary. Every man, the least acquainted with the state and extent of our trade, must be convinced, it is the source of immense revenues to the parent state, and gives employment and bread to a vast number of his Majesty's subjects. It is impossible but that a suspension of it for any time, must introduce beggary and wretchedness in an eminent degree, both in England and Ireland; and as to the West-India plantations, they could not possibly subsist without us. I am the more confident of this, because I have a pretty general acquaintance with their circumstances and dependencies.

We are told, "that it is highly improbable, we shall succeed in distressing the people of Great-Britain, Ireland and the West-Indies, so far as to oblige them to join with us in getting the acts of Parliament, which we complain of, repealed: The first distress (it is said) will fall on ourselves; it will be more severely felt by us, than any part of all his Majesty's dominions, and will affect us the longest. The fleets of Great-Britain command respect throughout the globe. Her influence extends to every part of the earth. Her manufactures are equal to any: Superior to most in the world. Her wealth is great. Her people enterprizing and persevering in their attempts to extend, and enlarge, and protect her trade. The total loss of our trade will be felt only for a time. Her merchants would turn their attention another way: New sources of trade and wealth would be opened: New schemes pursued. She would soon find a vent for all her manufactures in spite of all we could do. Our malice would hurt only ourselves. Should our schemes distress some branches of her trade, it would be only for a time; and there is ability and humanity enough in the nation to relieve those, that are distressed by us, and put them in some other way of getting their living."

The omnipotence and all sufficiency of Great-Britain may be pretty good topics for her passionate admirers to exercise their declamatory powers upon, for amusement and trial of skill; but they ought not to be proposed to the world as matters of truth and reality. In the calm, unprejudiced eye of reason, they are altogether visionary. As to her wealth, it is notorious that she is oppressed with a heavy national debt, which it requires the utmost policy and œconomy ever to discharge. Luxury has arrived to a great pitch; and it is an universal maxim that luxury indicates the declension of a state. Her subjects are loaded with the most enormous taxes: All circumstances agree in declaring their distress. The continual emigrations, from Great-Britain and Ireland, to the continent, are a glaring symptom, that those kingdoms are a good deal impoverished.

The attention of Great-Britain has hitherto been constantly awake to expand her commerce. She has been vigilant to explore every region, with which it might be her interest to trade. One of the principal branches of her commerce is with the colonies. These colonies, as they are now settled and peopled, have been the work of near two centuries: They are blessed with every advantage of soil, climate and situation. They have advanced with an almost incredible rapidity. It is therefore an egregious piece of absurdity to affirm, that the loss of our trade would be felt for a time (which must signify a short time.) No new schemes could be pursued that would not require, at least, as much time to repair the loss of our trade, as was spent in bringing it to its present degree of perfection, which is near two centuries. Nor can it be reasonably imagined, that the total and sudden loss of so extensive and lucrative a branch, would not produce the most violent effects to a nation that subsists entirely upon its commerce.

It is said, "there is ability and humanity enough in the nation to relieve those that are distressed by us; and to put them into some other way of getting their living." I wish the gentleman had obliged his readers so much, as to have pointed out this other way; I must confess, I have racked my brains to no purpose to discover it, and am fully of opinion it is purely ideal. Besides the common mechanic arts, which are subservient to the ordinary uses of life, and which are the instruments of commerce; know no other ways in time of peace, in which men can be employed, except in agriculture and the liberal arts. Persons employed in the mechanic arts, are those, whom the abridgment of commerce would immediately affect, and as to such branches as might be less affected, they are already sufficiently stocked with workmen, and could give bread to no more; not only so, but I can't see by what legerdemain, a weaver, or clothier could be at once converted into a carpenter or black-smith. With respect to agriculture, the lands of Great Britain and Ireland have been long ago distributed and taken up; nor do they require any additional labourers to till them; so that there could be no employment in this way. The liberal arts cannot maintain those who are already devoted to them; not to say, it is more than probable, the generality of mechanics, would make but indifferent philosophers, poets, painters and musicians.

What poor shifts is sophistry obliged to have recourse to! we are threatened with the resentment of those against whom our measures will operate. It is said, that "instead of conciliating, we shall alienate the affections of the people of Great-Britain, of friends, we shall make them our enemies;" and further, that "we shall excite the resentment of the government at home against us, which will do us no good, but, on the contrary, much harm."

Soon after, we are told that "we shall probably raise the resentment of the Irish and West-Indians: The passions of human nature" it is said, "are much the same in all countries. If they find us disposed wantonly to distress them, to serve our own purposes, they will look out for some method to do without us: will they not look elsewhere for a supply of those articles, they used to take from us? They would deserve to be despised for their meanness did they not."

To these objections I reply, first with respect to the inhabitants of Great-Britain, that if they are our friends, as is supposed, and as we have reason to believe; they cannot, without being destitute of rationality, be incensed against us for using the only peaceable and probable means, in our power, to preserve our invaded rights: They know by their own experience how fruitless remonstrances and petitions are: They know, we have tried them over and over to no purpose: They know also, how dangerous to their liberties, the loss of ours must be. What then could exite their resentment if they have the least regard to common justice? The calamities, that threaten them, proceed from the weakness, or wickedness of their own rulers; which compels us to take the measures we do. The insinuation, that we *wantonly* distress them to serve our own purposes, is futile and unsupported by a single argument. I have shewn, we could have no other resource; nor can they think our conduct such, without a degree of infatuation, that it would be impossible to provide against, and therefore useless to consult. It is most reasonable to believe, they will revenge the evils they may feel on the true authors of them, on an aspiring and ill-judging ministry; not on us, who act out of a melancholy necessity, and are the innocent causes in self-defence.

With respect to the ministry, it is certain, that any thing, which has a tendency to frustrate their designs, will not fail to excite their displeasure; but since we have nothing to expect from their justice and lenity, it can be no objection to a measure, that it tends to stir up their resentment. But their resentment (it is often said) may ruin us. The impossibility of doing that, without at the same time, ruining Great-Britain, is a sufficient security.

The same may be said with regard to the Irish and the West-Indians, which has been said concerning the people of Great-Britain. The Irish, in particular, by their own circumstances will be taught to sympathise with us, and commend our conduct. Justice will direct their resentment to its proper objects.

It is true self-love will prompt both the Irish and the West-Indians to take every method in their power, to escape the miseries they are in danger of; but what methods can they take? "The Irish (it is said) may be supplied with flax-seed from Holland, the Baltic, and the river St.

Lawrence: Canada produces no inconsiderable quantity already." And as to the West-Indies, "they produce now many of the necessaries of life. The quantity may be easily increased. Canada will furnish them with many articles they now take from us; flour, lumber, horses, &c. Georgia, the Floridas, and the Mississippi abound in lumber: Nova Scotia in fish."

The Dutch are rivals to the English in their commerce. They make large quantities of fine linens, gause, laces, &c. which require the flax to be picked before it comes to seed; for which reason, it is not in their power to raise much more seed than they want for their own use. Ireland has always had the surplus from them. They could, if they were ever so willing, enlarge their usual supplies but very little. It is indeed probable they may withold them. They may choose to improve the occasion for the advancement of their own trade: They may take advantage of the scarcity of materials in Ireland, to increase and put off their own manufactures.

The Baltic has ever supplied Ireland with its flax, and she has been able to consume that, with all she could derive from other quarters.

As to Canada, I am well informed it could at present afford, but a very inconsiderable quantity. It has had little encouragement, hitherto, to raise that article, and of course has not much attended to it. The instances mentioned, of seed being "bought up there at a low price, brought to New-York, and sold to the Irish factors at a great advance," does not prove there is any quantity raised there. Its cheapness proceeds from there being no demand for it; and where there was no demand, there was no inducement to cultivate it.

Upon the whole, it appears, that the supplies of flax-seed, which Ireland might draw elsewhere, could be trifling in comparison with those received from us, and not at all equivalent to her wants. But if this were not the case, if she might procure a sufficiency without our help, yet could she not do without us. She would want purchasers for her linens after they were manufactured; and where could she find any so numerous and wealthy as we are? I must refer it to the profound sagacity of Mr. A. W. Farmer, to explore them, it is too arduous a task for me.

Much less could the West-Indies subsist independent of us. Notwithstanding the continual imports from hence, there is seldom or ever, in any of the islands, a sufficient stock of provisions to last six months, which may give us an idea, how great the consumption is. The necessaries they produce within themselves, when compared with the consumption, are scarcely worth mentioning. Very small portions of the lands are appropriated to the productions of such necessaries, indeed it is too valuable to admit of it. Nor could the quantity be increased to any material degree, without applying the whole of the land to it. It is alledged, that Canada will furnish them with "flour, lumber, horses, &c. and that Georgia, the Floridas and Mississipi abound in lumber; Nova Scotia in fish." These countries have been all-along carrying on a trade to the West-Indies, as well as we; and can it be imagined that alone, they will be able to supply them tolerably? The Canadians have been indolent, and have not improved their country as they ought to have done. The wheat they raise at present, over and above what they have occasion for themselves, would be found to go but little way among the islands. Those, who think the contrary, must have mistaken notions of them. They must be unapprized of the number of souls they contain: Almost every 150 or 200 acres of land, exclusive of populous towns, comprehend a hundred people. It is not a small quantity of food that will suffice for so many. Ten or fifteen years diligence, I grant, might enable Canada to perform what is now expected from her; but, in the mean time, the West-Indians might have the satisfaction of starving.

To suppose the best, which is, that by applying their canelands to the purpose of procuring sustenance, they may preserve themselves from starving: still the consequences must be very serious or pernicious. The wealthy planters would but ill relish the loss of their crops, and such of them as were considerably in debt would be ruined. At any rate, the revenues of Great-Britain would suffer a vast diminution.

The FARMER, I am inclined to hope, builds too much upon the present disunion of Canada, Georgia, the Floridas, the Mississippi, and Nova Scotia from other colonies. A little time, I trust, will awaken them from their slumber, and bring them to a proper sense of their indiscretion. I please myself with the flattering prospect, that they will, ere long, unite in one indissoluble chain with the rest of the colonies. I cannot believe they will persist in such a conduct as must exclude them from the secure enjoyment of those heaven-descended immunities we are contending for.

There is one argument I have frequently heard urged, which it may be of some use to invalidate. It is this, that if the mother country should be inclined to an accommodation of our disputes, we have by our rash procedure thrown an insurmountable obstacle in her way; we have made it disgraceful to her to comply with our requisitions, because they are proposed in a hostile manner.

Our present measures, I have proved, are the only peaceable ones we could place the least confidence in. They are the least exceptionable, upon the score of irritating Great-Britain, of any our circumstances would permit. The congress have petitioned his Majesty for the redress of grievances. They have, no doubt, addressed him in the most humble, respectful and affectionate terms; assured him, of their own loyalty, and fidelity and of the loyalty and fidelity of his American subjects in general; endeavoured to convince him, that we have been misrepresented and abused; and expressed an earnest desire to see an amicable termination of the unhappy differences now existing. Can a pretext be wanting, in this case, to preserve the dignity of this parent state, and yet remove the complaints of the colonies? How easy would it be to overlook our particular agreements, and grant us redress in consequence of our petitions? It is easy to perceive there would be no difficulty in this respect.

I have omitted many considerations, which might be adduced to shew the impolicy of Great-Britains, delaying to accommodate matters, and attempting to enforce submission by cutting off all external sources of trade. To say all the subject allows, would spin out this piece to an immoderate length; I shall, therefore, content myself with mentioning only three things more. First, it would be extremely hurtful to the commerce of Great-Britain to drive us to the necessity of laying a regular foundation for manufactories of our own; which, if once established, could not easily, if at all, be undermined, or abolished. Secondly, it would be very expensive to the nation to maintain a fleet for the purpose of blocking up our ports, and destroying our trade: nor could she interrupt our intercourse with foreign climes without, at the same time, retrenching her own revenues; for she must then lose the duties and customs upon the articles we are wont to export to, and import from them. Added to this, it would not be prudent to risk the displeasure of those nations, to whom our trade is useful and beneficial. And lastly, a perseverance in ill-treatment would naturally beget such deep-rooted animosities in America, as might never be eradicated; and which might operate to the prejudice of the empire to the latest period.

Thus have I clearly proved, that the plan of opposition concerted by our congress is perfectly consonant with justice and sound policy; and will, in all human probability, secure our freedom against the assaults of our enemies.

But, after all, it may be demanded why they have adopted a non-exportation; seeing many arguments tend to shew that a non-importation alone would accomplish the end desired?

I answer, that the continuance of our exports is the only thing which could lessen, or retard the efficacy of a non-importation. It is not indeed probable it should do that to any great degree; but it was adviseable to provide against every possible obstruction. Besides this, the prospect of its taking place, and of the evils attendant upon it, will be a prevailing motive with the ministry to abandon their malignant schemes. It will also serve to convince them, that we are not afraid of putting ourselves to any inconveniencies, sooner than be the victims of their lawless ambition.

The execution of this measure has been wisely deferred to a future time, because we have the greatest reason to think affairs will be settled without it, and because its consequences would be too fatal to be justified by any thing but absolute necessity. This necessity there will be, should not our disputes terminate before the time allotted for its commencement.

Before I conclude this part of my address, I will answer two very singular interrogatories proposed by the Farmer, "Can we think (says he) to threaten, and bully, and frighten the supreme government of the nation into a compliance with our demands? Can we expect to force submission to our peevish and petulant humours, by exciting clamours and riots in England?" No, gentle Sir. We neither desire, nor endeavour to threaten, bully, or frighten any persons into a compliance with our demands. We have no peevish and petulant humours to be submitted to. All we aim at, is to convince your high and mighty masters, the ministry, that we are not such asses as to let them ride us as they please. We are determined to shew them, that we know the value of freedom; nor shall their rapacity extort, that inestimable jewel from us, without a manly and virtuous struggle. But for your part, sweet Sir! tho' we cannot much applaud your wisdom, yet we are compelled to admire your valour, which leads you to hope you may be able to *swear*, threaten, bully and frighten all America into a compliance with your sinister designs.

When properly accoutered and armed with your formidable hiccory cudgel, what may not the ministry expect from such a champion? alas! for the poor committee gentlemen, how I tremble when I reflect on the many wounds and scars they must receive from your tremendous arm! Alas! for their supporters and abettors; a very large part indeed of the continent; but what of that? they must all be soundly drubbed with that confounded hiccory cudgel; for surely you would not undertake to drub one of them, without knowing yourself able to treat all their friends and adherents in the same manner; since 'tis plain you would bring them all upon your back.

I am now to address myself in particular to the Farmers of New-York.

MY GOOD COUNTRYMEN,

The reason I address myself to you, in particular, is, because I am one of your number, or connected with you in interest more than with any other branch of the community. I love to speak the truth, and would scorn to prejudice you in favour of what I have to say, by taking upon me a fictitious character as other people have done. I can venture to assure you, the true writer of the piece signed A. W. FARMER, is not in reality a Farmer. He is some ministerial emissary, that has assumed the name to deceive you, and make you swallow the intoxicating potion he has prepared for you. But I have a better opinion of you than to think he will be able to succeed. I am persuaded you love yourselves and children better than to let any designing men cheat you out of your liberty and property, to serve their own purposes. You would be a disgrace to your ancestors, and the bitterest enemies to yourselves and to your posterity, if you did not act like men, in protecting and defending those rights you have hitherto enjoyed.

I say, my friends, I do not address you in particular, because I have any greater connexion with you, than with other people. I despise all false pretentions, and mean arts. Let those have recourse to dissimulation and falshood, who can't defend their cause without it. 'Tis my maxim to let the plain naked truth speak for itself; and if men won't listen to it, 'tis their own fault: they must be contented to suffer for it. I am neither merchant, nor farmer. I address you, because I wish well to my country, and of course to you, who are one chief support of it; and because an attempt has been made to lead you astray in particular. You are the men too who would lose most should you be foolish enough to counteract the prudent measures our worthy congress has taken for the preservation of our liberties. Those, who advise you to do it, are not your friends, but your greatest foes. They would have you made slaves, that they may pamper themselves with the fruits of your honest labour. 'Tis the Farmer who is most oppressed in all countries where slavery prevails.

You have seen how clearly I have proved, that a non-importation and non-exportation are the only peaceable means in our power to save ourselves from the most dreadful state of slavery. I have shewn there is not the least hope, to be placed in any thing else. I have confuted all the principal cavils raised by the pretended Farmer, and I hope, before I finish, to satisfy you, that he has attempted to frighten you with the prospect of evils, which will never happen. This indeed I have, in a great measure, done already, by making appear the great probability, I may almost say certainty, that our measures will procure us the most speedy redress.

Are you willing then to be slaves without a single struggle? Will you give up your freedom, or, which is the same thing, will you resign all security for your life and property, rather than endure some small present inconveniencies? Will you not take a little trouble to transmit the advantages you now possess to those, who are to come after you? I cannot doubt it. I would not suspect you of so much baseness and stupidity, as to suppose the contrary.

Pray who can tell me why a farmer in America, is not as honest and good a man, as a farmer in England? or why has not the one as good a right to what he has earned by his labour, as the other? I can't, for my life, see any distinction between them. And yet it seems the English farmers are to be governed and taxed by their own Assembly, or Parliament; and the American farmers are not. The former are to choose their own Representatives from among themselves, whose interest is connected with theirs, and over whom they have proper controul. The latter are to be loaded with taxes by men three thousand miles off; by men, who have no interest, or connexions among them; but whose interest it will be to burden them as much as possible; and over whom they cannot have the least restraint. How do you like this doctrine my friends? Are you ready to own the English farmers for your masters? Are you willing to acknowledge their right to take your property from you, and when they please? I know you scorn the thought. You had rather die, than submit to it.

But some people try to make you believe, we are disputing about the foolish trifle of three pence duty upon tea. They may as well tell you, that black is white. Surely you can judge for yourselves. Is a dispute, whether the Parliament of Great-Britain shall make what laws, and impose what taxes they please upon us, or not; I say, is this a dispute about three pence duty upon tea? The man that affirms it, deserves to be laughed at.

It is true, we are denying to pay the duty upon tea; but it is not for the value of the thing itself. It is because we cannot submit to that, without acknowledging the principle upon which it is founded, and that principle is *a right to tax us in all cases whatsoever*.

You have, heretofore experienced the benefit of being taxed by your own Assemblies only. Your burdens are so light, that you scarcely feel them. You'd soon find the difference if you were once to let the Parliament have the management of these matters.

How would you like to pay four shillings a year, out of every pound your farms are worth, to be squandered, (at least a great part of it) upon ministerial tools and court sycophants? What would you think of giving a tenth part of the yearly products of your lands to the clergy? Would you not think it very hard to pay 10s. sterling per annum, for every wheel of your waggons and other carriages, a shilling or two for every pane of glass in your houses, and two or three shillings for every one of your hearths? I might mention taxes upon your mares, cows, and many other things; but those I have already mentioned are sufficient. Methinks I see you stare, and hear you ask how you could live, if you were to pay such heavy taxes? Indeed my friends I can't tell you. You are to look out for that, and take care you do not run yourselves in the way of danger, by following the advice of those, who want to betray you. This you may depend upon, if ever you let the Parliament carry its point, you will have these and more to pay. Perhaps before long, your tables, and chairs, and platters, and dishes, and knives and forks, and every thing else would be taxed. Nay, I don't know but they would find means to tax you for every child you got, and for every kiss your daughters received from their sweet-hearts, and God knows, that would soon ruin you. The people of England would pull down the Parliament House, if their present heavy burdens were not transferred from them to you. Indeed there is no reason to think the Parliament would have any inclination to spare you: The contrary is evident.

But being ruined by taxes is not the worst you have to fear. What security would you have for your lives? How can any of you be sure you would have the free enjoyment of your religion long? would you put your religion in the power of any set of men living? Remember civil and religious liberty always go together, if the foundation of the one be sapped, the other will fall of course.

Call to mind one of our sister colonies, Boston. Reflect upon the situation of Canada, and then tell me whether you are inclined to place any confidence in the justice and humanity of the parliament. The port of Boston is blocked up, and an army planted in the town. An act has been passed to alter its charter, to prohibit its assemblies, to license the murder of its inhabitants, and to convey them from their own country to Great Britain, to be tried for their lives. What was all this for? Just because a small number of people, provoked by an open and dangerous attack upon their liberties, destroyed a parcel of Tea belonging to the East India Company. It was not public but private property they destroyed. It was not the act of the whole province, but the act of a part of the citizens; instead of trying to discover the perpetrators, and commencing a legal prosecution against them; the parliament of Great-Britain interfered in an unprecedented manner, and inflicted a punishment upon a whole province, "untried, unheard, unconvicted of any crime." This may be justice, but it looks so much like cruelty, that a man of a humane heart would be more apt to call it by the latter, than the former name.

The affair of Canada, if possible, is still worse. The English laws have been superceded by the French laws. The Romish faith is made the established religion of the land, and his Majesty is placed at the head of it. The free exercise of the protestant faith depends upon the pleasure of the Governor and Council. The subject is divested of the right of trial by jury, and an innocent man may be imprisoned his whole life, without being able to obtain any trial at all. The parliament was not contented with introducing arbitrary power and popery in Canada, with its former limits, but they have annexed to it the vast tracts of land that surround all the colonies.

Does not your blood run cold, to think an English parliament should pass an act for the establishment of arbitrary power and popery in such an extensive country? If they had had any regard to the freedom and happiness of mankind, they would never have done it. If they had been friends to the protestant cause, they would never have provided such a nursery for its great enemy: They would not have given such encouragement to popery. The thought of their conduct, in this particular shocks me. It must shock you too my friends. Beware of trusting yourselves to men, who are capable of such an action! They may as well establish popery in New-York and the other colonies as they did in Canada. They had no more right to do it there than here.

Is it not better, I ask, to suffer a few present inconveniencies, than to put yourselves in the way of losing every thing that is precious. Your lives, your property, your religion are all at stake. I do my duty. I warn you of your danger. If you should still be so mad, as to bring destruction upon yourselves; if you should still neglect what you owe to God and man, you cannot plead ignorance in your excuse. Your consciences will reproach you for your folly, and your children's children will curse you.

You are told, the schemes of our Congress will ruin you. You are told, they have not considered your interest; but have neglected, or betrayed you. It is endeavoured to make you look upon some of the wisest and best men in the America, as rogues and rebels. What will not wicked men attempt! They will scruple nothing, that may serve their purposes. In truth, my friends, it is very unlikely any of us shall suffer much; but let the worst happen, the farmers will be better off, than other people.

Many of those that made up the Congress have large possessions in land, and may, therefore be looked upon as farmers themselves. Can it be supposed, they would be careless about the farmer's interest, when they could not injure that, without injuring themselves? You see the absurdity of such a supposition.

The merchants and a great part of the tradesmen get their living by commerce. These are the people that would be hurt most, by putting a stop to it. As to the farmers, "they furnish food for the merchant and mechanic; the raw materials for most manufactures are the produce of their industry." The merchants and mechanics are already dependent upon the farmers for their food, and if the non-importation should continue any time, they would be dependent upon them for their cloaths also.

It is a false assertion, that the merchants have imported more than usual this year. That report has been raised by your enemies to poison your minds with evil suspicions. If our disputes be not settled within eighteen months, the goods we have among us will be consumed; and then the materials for making cloaths must be had from you. Manufactures must be promoted with vigour, and a high price will be given for your wool, flax and hemp. It will be your interest to pay the greatest care and attention to your sheep. Increase and improve the breed as much as possible: *Kill them sparingly*, and such only as will not be of use towards the increase and improvement of them. In a few months we shall know what we have to trust to. If matters be not accommodated by spring, enlarge the quantity of your flax and hemp. You will experience the benefit of it. All those articles will be very much wanted: They will bring a great deal higher price than they used to do. And while you are supplying the wants of the community, you will be enriching yourselves.

Should we hereafter, find it necessary to stop our exports, you can apply more of your land to raising flax and hemp, and less of it to wheat, rye, &c. By which means, you will not have any of those latter articles to lie upon hand. There will be a consumption for as much of the former as you can raise, and the great demand they will be in, will make them very profitable to you.

Patience good Mr. Critic! *Kill them sparingly, I said*, what objection have you to the phrase? You'll tell me, it is not *classical*; but I affirm it is, and if you will condescend to look into Mr. Johnson's dictionary, you will find I have his authority for it. Pray then, for the future, *spare* your wit, upon such occasions, otherwise the world will not be disposed to *spare* its ridicule. And though the man that *spares* nobody does not deserve to be *spared* himself, yet will I *spare* you, for the present, and proceed to things of more importance.

Pardon me, my friends, for taking up your time with this digression; but I could not forbear stepping out of the way a little, to shew the world, I am as able a critic, and as good a punster as Mr. Farmer. I now return to the main point with pleasure.

It is insinuated, "That the bustle about non-importation, &c. has its rise, not from patriotism, but selfishness;" and is only made by the merchants, that they may get a high price for their goods.

By this time, I flatter myself you are convinced, that we are not disputing about trifles. It has been clearly proved to you, that we are contending for every thing dear in life, and that the measures adopted by the congress, are the only ones which can save us from ruin. This is sufficient to confute that insinuation. But to confirm it, let me observe to you, that the merchants have not been the foremost to bring about a non-importation. All the members of the congress were unanimous in it; and *many* of them were not merchants. The warmest advocates for it, every where, are not concerned in trade, and, as I before remarked, the traders will be the principal sufferers, if it should continue any time.

But it is said it will not continue, because, "when the stores are like to become empty, they will have weight enough to break up the agreement." I don't think they would attempt it; but if they should, it is impossible a few mercenary men could have influence enough to make the whole body of people give up the only plan their circumstances admit of for the preservation of their rights, and, of course, to forfeit all they have been so long striving to secure. The making of a non-importation agreement did not depend upon the merchants; neither will the breaking of it depend upon them. The congress have provided against the breach of the non-importation, by the non-consumption agreement. They have resolved for themselves and us their constituents, "not to purchase, or use any East-India Tea whatsoever; nor any goods, wares, or merchandize, from Great-Britain or Ireland, imported after the first of December, nor molasses, &c. from the West Indies, nor wine from Madeira, or the Western Islands, nor foreign Indigo." If we do not purchase or use these things, the merchant will have no inducement to import them.

Hence you may perceive the reason of a non-consumption agreement. It is to put it out of the power of dishonest men, to break the non importation. *Is this a slavish regulation?* Or is it a hardship upon us to submit to it? Surely not. Every sensible, every good man must approve of it. Whoever tries to disaffect you to it, ought to meet with your contempt.

Take notice, my friends, how these men are obliged to contradict themselves. In one place you are told, that all the bustle about non-importation, &c. has its rise, not from patriotism, but from selfishness, "or, in other words, that it is made by the merchants to get a higher price for their goods." In another place it is said, that all we are doing is instigated by some turbulent men, who want to establish a republican form of government among us.

The Congress is censured for appointing committees to carry their measures into execution, and directing them "to establish such further regulations, as they may think proper for that purpose." Pray, did we not appoint our Delegates to make regulations for us? What signified making them, if they did not provide some persons to see them executed? Must a few bad men be left to do what they please, contrary to the general sense of the people, without any persons to controul them, or to look into their behaviour and mark them out to the public? The man that desires to screen his knavery from the public eye, will answer yes; but the honest man, that is determined to do nothing hurtful to his country, and who is conscious his actions will bear the light, will heartily answer no.

The high prices of goods are held up to make you dissatisfied with the non-importation. If the argument on this head were true, it would be much better to subject yourselves to that disadvantage, for a time, than to bring upon yourselves all the mischiefs I have pointed out to you. Should you submit to claims of the Parliament, you will not only be oppressed with the taxes upon your lands, &c. which I have already mentioned; but you will have to pay heavy taxes upon all the goods we import from Great-Britain. Large duties will be laid upon them at home; and the merchants, of course, will have a greater price for them, or it would not be worth their while to carry on trade. The duty laid upon paper, glass, painter's colours, &c. was a beginning of this kind. The present duty upon tea is preparatory to the imposition of duties upon all other articles. Do you think the Parliament would make such a serious matter of three pence a pound upon tea, if it intended to stop there? It is absurd to imagine it. You would soon find your mistake if you did. For fear of paying somewhat a higher price to the merchants for a year or two, you would have to pay an endless list of taxes, within and without, as long as you live, and your children after you.

But I trust, there is no danger that the prices of goods will rise much, if at all. The same congress that put a stop to the importation of them, has also forbid raising the prices of them. The same committee that is to regulate the one, is also to regulate the other. All care will be taken to give no cause of dissatisfaction. Confide in the men whom you, and the rest of the continent have chosen the guardians of our common liberties. They are men of sense and virtue. They will do nothing but what is really necessary for the security of your lives and properties.

A sad pother is made too about prohibiting the exportation of sheep, without excepting weathers. The poor Farmer is at a mighty loss to know how weathers can improve, or increase the breed. Truly I am not such a conjurer, as to be able to inform him; but if you please, my friends, I can give you two pretty good reasons, why the congress has not excepted weathers. One is, that for some time, we shall have occasion for all the wool we can raise; so that it would be imprudent to export sheep of any kind: and the other is, that, if you confine yourself chiefly to killing weathers, as you ought to do, you will have none to export. The gentleman who made the objection, must have known these things, as well as myself; but he loves to crack a jest, and could not pass by so fair an opportunity.

He takes notice of the first of these reasons himself; but in order to weaken its force, cries, "let me ask you, brother farmers, which of you would keep a flock of sheep, barely, for the sake of their wool?" To this he answers, "not one of you. If you cannot sell your sheep to advantage, at a certain age, you cannot keep them to any profit." He thinks, because he calls you brother farmers, that he can cajole you into believing what he pleases; but you are not the fools he takes you for. You know what is for your own interest better than he can tell you. And we all know, that in a little time, if our affairs be not settled, the demand for wool will be very great. You will be able to obtain such a price, as will make it worth your while to bestow the greatest attention upon your sheep.

In another place, this crafty writer tells you, that, "from the day our exports, from this province are stopped, the farmers may date the commencement of their ruin." He asks, "will the shop-keeper give you his goods? will the weaver, shoe-maker, black-smith, carpenter work for you without pay?" I make no doubt, you are satisfied, from what I have said, that we shall never have occasion to stop our exports; but if things turn out contrary to our expectation, and it should become necessary to take that step, you will find no difficulty in getting what you want from the merchants and mechanics. They will not be able to do without you, and, consequently, they cannot refuse to supply you with what you stand in need of from them. Where will the merchants and mechanics get food and materials for clothing, if not from the farmer? And if they are dependent upon you, for those two grand supports of life, how can they withold what they have from you?

I repeat it (my friends) we shall know, how matters are like to be settled by the spring. If our disputes be not terminated to our satisfaction by that time, it will be your business to plant large parts of your lands with flax and hemp. Those articles will be wanted for manufactures, and they will yield you a greater profit than any thing else. In the interim, take good care of your sheep.

I heartily concur with the farmer, in condemning all illicit trade. Perjury is, no doubt, a most heineous and detestable crime; and for my part, I had rather suffer any thing, than have my wants relieved at the expence of truth and integrity. I know, there are many pretended friends to liberty, who will take offence at this declaration; but I speak the sentiments of my heart without reserve. I do not write for a party. I should scorn to be of any. All I say, is from a disinterested regard to the public weal.

The congress, I am persuaded, were of the same opinion: They, like honest men, have, as much as was in their power, provided against this kind of trade, by agreeing to use no East-India tea whatever, after the first day of March next.

I shall now consider what has been said, with respect to the payment of debts, and stopping of the courts of justice. Let what will happen, it will be your own faults, if you are not able to pay your debts. I have told you, in what manner you may make as much out of your lands as ever: by bestowing more of your attention upon raising flax and hemp, and less upon other things. Those articles (as I have more than once observed) will be in the highest demand: There will be no doing without them; and, of course, you will be able to get a very profitable price for them. How can it be, that the farmers should be at a loss for money to pay their debts, at a time, when the whole community must buy, not only their food, but all the materials for their cloaths from them? You have no reason to be uneasy on that account.

As to the courts of justice, no violence can, or will be used to shut them up; but, if it should be found necessary, we may enter into solemn agreement to cease from all litigations at law, except in particular cases. We may regulate law suits, in such a manner, as to prevent any mischief that might arise from them. Restrictions may be laid on to hinder merciless creditors, from taking advantage of the times, to oppress and ruin their debtors but, at the same time, not to put it in the power of the debtors, *wantonly*, to withold their just dues from their creditors, when they are able to pay them. The law ruins many a good honest family. Disputes may be settled in a more friendly way; one or two virtuous neighbours may be chosen by each party to decide them. If the next congress should think any regulations concerning the courts of justice requisite, they will make them; and proper persons will be appointed to carry them into execution, and to see, that no individuals deviate from them. It will be your duty to elect persons, whose fidelity and zeal for your interest you can depend upon, to represent you in *that* congress; which is to meet at Philadelphia, in May ensuing.

The Farmer cries, "tell me not of delegates, congresses committees, mobs, riots, insurrections, associations; a plague on them all. Give me the steady, uniform, unbiassed influence of the courts of justice. I have been happy under their protection, and I trust in God, I shall be so again."

I say, tell me not of the British Commons, Lords, ministry, ministerial tools, placemen, pensioners, parasites. I scorn to let my life and property depend upon the pleasure of any of them. Give me the steady, uniform, unshaken security of constitutional freedom; give me the right to be tried by a jury of my own neighbours, and to be taxed by my own representatives only. What will become of the law and courts of justice without this? The shadow may remain, but the substance will be gone. I would die to preserve the law upon a solid foundation; but take away liberty, and the foundation is destroyed.

The last thing I shall take notice of, is the complaint of the Farmer, that the congress will not allow you "a dish of tea to please your wives with, nor a glass of Madeira to cheer your spirits, nor a spoonful of molasses, to sweeten your butter milk with." You would have a right to complain, if the use of these things had been forbidden to you alone; but it has been equally forbidden to all sorts of people. The members of the congress themselves are no more permitted to please their wives with a dish of tea, or to cheer their spirits with a glass of wine, or to sweeten their butter milk with a spoonful of molasses, than you are. They are upon a footing with you in this respect.

By him! but, with your leave, my friends, we'll try, if we can, to do without swearing. I say, it is enough to make a man mad, to hear such ridiculous quibbles offered instead of sound argument; but so it is, the piece I am writing against contains nothing else.

When a man grows warm, he has a confounded itch for swearing. I have been going, above twenty times, to rap out an oath, *by him that made me*, but I have checked myself, with this reflection, that it is rather *unmannerly*, to treat him that made us with so much freedom.

Thus have I examined and confuted, all the cavils and objections, of any consequence, stated by this Farmer. I have only passed over such things, as are of little weight, the fallacy of which will easily appear. I have shewn, that the congress have neither "ignorantly misunderstood, carelessly neglected, nor basely betrayed you;" but that they have desired and recommended the *only* effectual means to preserve your invaluable privileges. I have proved, that their measures cannot fail of success; but will procure the most speedy relief for us. I have also proved, that the farmers are the people who would suffer least, should we be obliged to carry all our measures into execution.

Will you then, my friends, allow yourselves, to be duped by this artful enemy? will you follow his advices, disregard the authority of your congress, and bring ruin on yourselves and posterity? will you act in such a manner as to deserve the hatred and resentment of all the rest of America? I am sure you will not. I should be sorry to think, any of my countrymen would be so mean, so blind to their own interest, so lost to every generous and manly feeling.

The sort of men I am opposing give you fair words, to persuade you to serve their own turns; but they think and speak of you in common in a very disrespectful manner. I have heard some of their party talk of you, as the most ignorant and mean-spirited set of people in the world. They say, that you have no sense of honour or generosity; that you don't care a farthing about your country, children or any body else, but yourselves; and that you are so ignorant, as not to be able to look beyond the present; so that if you can once be persuaded to believe the measures of your congress will involve you in some little present perplexities, you will be glad to do any thing to avoid them; without considering the much greater miseries that await you at a little distance off. This is the character they give of you. Bad men are apt to paint others like themselves. For my part, I will never entertain such an opinion of you, unless you should verify their words, by wilfully falling into the pit they have prepared for you. I flatter myself you will convince them of their error, by shewing the world, you are capable of judging what is right and left, and have resolution to pursue it.

All I ask is, that you will judge for yourselves. I don't desire you to take my opinion or any man's opinion, as the guide of your actions. I have stated a number of plain arguments; I have supported them with several well-known facts: It is your business to draw a conclusion and act accordingly.

I caution you, again and again, to beware of the men who advise you to forsake the plain path, marked out for you by the congress. They only mean to deceive and betray you. Our representatives in general assembly cannot take any wiser or better course to settle our differences, than our representatives in the continental congress have taken. If you join with the rest of America in the same common measure, you will be sure to preserve your liberties inviolate; but if you separate from them, and seek for redress alone, and unseconded, you will certainly fall a prey to your enemies, and repent your folly as long as you live.

May God give you wisdom to see what is your true interest, and inspire you with becoming zeal for the cause of virtue and mankind.

A FRIEND TO AMERICA.

To John Jay

New York Novem 26. 1775

DEAR SIR

I take the liberty to trouble you with some remarks on a matter which to me appears of not a little importance; doubting not that you will use your influence in Congress to procure a remedy for the evil I shall mention, if you think the considerations I shall urge are of that weight they seem in my judgment to possess.

You will probably ere this reaches you have heard of the late incursion made into this city by a number of horsemen from New England under the command of Capt Sears, who took away Mr. Rivington's types, and a Couteau or two. Though I am fully sensible how dangerous and pernicious Rivington's press has been, and how detestable the character of the man is in every respect, yet I cannot help disapproving and condemning this step.

In times of such commotion as the present, while the passions of men are worked up to an uncommon pitch there is great danger of fatal extremes. The same state of the passions which fits the multitude, who have not a sufficient stock of reason and knowlege to guide them, for opposition to tyranny and oppression, very naturally leads them to a contempt and disregard of all authority. The due medium is hardly to be found among the more intelligent, it is almost impossible among the unthinking populace. When the minds of these are loosened from their attachment to ancient establishments and courses, they seem to grow giddy and are apt more or less to run into anarchy. These principles, too true in themselves, and confirmed to me both by reading and my own experience, deserve extremely the attention of those, who have the direction of public affairs. In such tempestuous times, it requires the greatest skill in the political pilots to keep men steady and within proper bounds, on which account I am always more or less alarmed at every thing which is done of mere will and pleasure, without any proper authority. Irregularities I know are to be expected, but they are nevertheless dangerous and ought to be checked, by every prudent and moderate mean. From these general maxims, I disapprove of the irruption in question, as serving to cherish a spirit of disorder at a season when men are too prone to it of themselves.

Moreover, New England is very populous and powerful. It is not safe to trust to the virtue of any people. Such proceedings will serve to produce and encourage a spirit of encroachment and arrogance in them. I like not to see potent neighbours indulged in the practice of making inroads at pleasure into this or any other province.

You well know too, sir, that antipathies and prejudices have long subsisted between this province and New England. To this may be attributed a principal part of the disaffection now prevalent among us. Measures of the present nature, however they may serve to intimidate, will secretly revive and increase those ancient animosities, which though smothered for a while will break out when there is a favorable opportunity.

Besides this, men coming from a neighbouring province to chastise the notorious friends of the ministry here, will hold up an idea to our ennemies not very advantageous to our affairs. They will imagine that the New Yorkers are totally, or a majority of them, disaffected to the American cause, which makes the interposal of their neighbours necessary: or that such violences will breed differences and effect that which they have been so eagerly wishing, a division and qurrelling among ourselves. Every thing of such an aspect must encourage their hopes.

Upon the whole the measure is condemned, by all the cautious and prudent among the whigs, and will evidently be productive of secret jealousy and ill blood if a stop is not put to things of the kind for the future.

All the good purposes that could be expected from such a step will be answered; and many ill consequences will be prevented if your body gently interposes a check for the future. Rivington will be intimidated & the tories will be convinced that the other colonies will not tamely see the general cause betrayed by the Yorkers. A favourable idea will be impressed of your justice & impartiality in discouraging the encroachments of any one province on another; and the apprehensions of prudent men respecting the ill-effects of an ungoverned spirit in the people of New England will be quieted. Believe me sir it is a matter of consequence and deserves serious attention

The tories it is objected by some are growing insolent and clamorous: It is necessary to repress and overawe them. There is truth in this; but the present remedy is a bad one. Let your body station in different parts of the province most tainted, with the ministerial infection, a few regiments of troops, raised in Philadelphia the Jerseys or any other province except New England. These will suffice to strengthen and support the Whigs who are still I flatter myself a large majority and to suppress the efforts of the tories. The pretence for this would be plausible. There is no knowing how soon the Ministry may make an attempt upon New York. There is reason to believe they will not be long before they turn their attention to it. In this there will be some order & regularity, and no grounds of alarm to our friends.

I am sir with very great Esteem— Your most hum servant

A. HAMILTON

To John Jay

DEAR SIR,

Col Laurens, who will have the honor of delivering you this letter, is on his way to South Carolina, on a project, which I think, in the present situation of affairs there, is a very good one and deserves every kind of support and encouragement. This is to raise two three or four batalions of negroes; with the assistance of the government of that state, by contributions from the owners in proportion to the number they possess. If you should think proper to enter upon the subject with him, he will give you a detail of his plan. He wishes to have it recommended by Congress to the state; and, as an inducement, that they would engage to take those batalions into Continental pay.

It appears to me, that an expedient of this kind, in the present state of Southern affairs, is the most rational, that can be adopted, and promises very important advantages. Indeed, I hardly see how a sufficient force can be collected in that quarter without it; and the enemy's operations there are growing infinitely serious and formidable. I have not the least doubt, that the negroes will make very excellent soldiers, with proper management; and I will venture to pronounce, that they cannot be put in better hands than those of Mr. Laurens. He has all the zeal, intelligence, enterprise, and every other qualification requisite to succeed in such an undertaking. It is a maxim with some great military judges, that with sensible officers soldiers can hardly be too stupid; and on this principle it is thought that the Russians would make the best troops in the world, if they were under other officers than their own. The King of Prussia is among the number who maintain this doctrine and has a very emphatical saying on the occasion, which I do not exactly recollect. I mention this, because I frequently hear it objected to the scheme of embodying negroes that they are too stupid to make soldiers. This is so far from appearing to me a valid objection that I think their want of cultivation (for their natural faculties are probably as good as ours) joined to that habit of subordination which they acquire from a life of servitude, will make them sooner became soldiers than our White inhabitants. Let officers be men of sense and sentiment, and the nearer the soldiers approach to machines perhaps the better.

I foresee that this project will have to combat much opposition from prejudice and self-interest. The contempt we have been taught to entertain for the blacks, makes us fancy many things that are founded neither in reason nor experience; and an unwillingness to part with property of so valuable a kind will furnish a thousand arguments to show the impracticability or pernicious tendency of a scheme which requires such a sacrifice. But it should be considered, that if we do not make use of them in this way, the enemy probably will; and that the best way to counteract the temptations they will hold out will be to offer them ourselves. An essential part of the plan is to give them their freedom with their muskets. This will secure their fidelity, animate their courage, and I believe will have a good influence upon those who remain, by opening a door to their emancipation. This circumstance, I confess, has no small weight in inducing me to wish the success of the project; for the dictates of humanity and true policy equally interest me in favour of this unfortunate class of men.

When I am on the subject of Southern affairs, you will excuse the liberty I take, in saying, that I do not think measures sufficiently vigorous are persuing for our defence in that quarter. Except the few regular troops of South Carolina, we seem to be relying wholly on the militia of that and the two neighbouring states. These will soon grow impatient of service and leave our affairs in a very miserable situation. No considerable force can be uniformly kept up by militia—to say nothing of many obvious and well known inconveniences, that attend this kind of troops. I would beg leave to suggest, Sir, that no time ought to be lost in making a draft of militia to serve a twelve month from the States of North and South Carolina and Virginia. But South Carolina being very weak in her population of whites may be excused from the draft on condition of furnishing the black batalions. The two others may furnish about 3,500 men and be exempted on that account from sending any succours to this army. The states to the Northward of Virginia will be fully able to give competent supplies to the army here; and it will require all the force and exertions of the three states I have mentioned to withstand the storm which has arisen and is increasing in the South.

The troops drafted must be thrown into batalions and officered in the best manner we can. The supernumerary officers may be made use of as far as they will go.

If arms are wanted for these troops and no better way of supplying them is to be found, we should endeavour to levy a contribution of arms upon the militia at large. Extraordinary exigencies demand extraordinary means. I fear this Southern business will become a very *grave* one.

With the truest respect & esteem I am Sir Your most Obed servant
ALEX HAMILTON

Want of time to copy it, will apologise for sending this letter in its present state.

Head Quarters March 14th. 79

To John Laurens

Cold in my professions, warm in my friendships, I wish, my Dear Laurens, it might be in my power, by action rather than words, to convince you that I love you. I shall only tell you that 'till you bade us Adieu, I hardly knew the value you had taught my heart to set upon you. Indeed, my friend, it was not well done. You know the opinion I entertain of mankind, and how much it is my desire to preserve myself free from particular attachments, and to keep my happiness independent on the caprice of others. You should not have taken advantage of my sensibility to steal into my affections without my consent. But as you have done it and as we are generally indulgent to those we love, I shall not scruple to pardon the fraud you have committed, on condition that for my sake, if not for your own, you will always continue to merit the partiality, which you have so artfully instilled into me.

I have received your two letters one from Philadelphia the other from Chester. I am pleased with your success, so far, and I hope the favourable omens, that precede your application to the Assembly may have as favourable an issue, provided the situation of affairs should require it which I fear will be the case. But both for your country's sake and for my own I wish the enemy may be gone from Georgia before you arrive and that you may be obliged to return and share the fortunes of your old friends. In respect to the Commission, which you received from Congress, all the world must think your conduct perfectly right. Indeed your ideas upon this occasion seem not to have their wonted accuracy; and you have had scruples, in a great measure, without foundation. By your appointment as Aide De Camp to the Commander in Chief, you had as much the rank of Lieutenant Colonel, as any officer in the line—your receiving a commission as Lieutenant Colonel from the date of that appointment, does not in the least injure or interfere with one of them; unless by virtue of it you are introduced into a particular regiment in violation of the right of succession; which is not the case at present neither is it a necessary consequence. As you were going to command a batalion, it was proper you should have a commission; and if this commission had been dated posterior to your appointment as Aide De Camp, I should have considered it as derogatory to your former rank, to mine, and to that of the whole corps. The only thing I see wrong in the affair is this—Congress by their conduct, both on the former and present occasion, appear to have intended to confer a privilege, an honor, a mark of distinction, a something upon you; which they withold from other Gentlemen in the family. This carries with it an air of preference, which, though we can all truly say, we love your character, and admire your military merit, cannot fail to give some of us uneasy sensations. But in this, my Dear J I wish you to understand me well. The blame, if there is any, falls wholly upon Congress. I repeat it, your conduct has been perfectly right and even laudable; you rejected the offer when you ought to have rejected it; and you accepted it when you ought to have accepted it; and let me add with a degree of overscrupulous delicacy. It was necessary to your project; your project was the public good; and *I* should have done the same. In hesitating, you have refined upon the refinements of generosity.

There is a total stagnation of news here, political and military. Gates has refused the Indian command. Sullivan is come to take it. The former has lately given a fresh proof of his impudence, his folly and his rascality. *'Tis no great matter;* but a peculiarity in the case prevents my saying *what*.

I anticipate by sympathy the pleasure you must feel from the sweet converse of your dearer self in the inclosed letters. I hope they may be recent. They were brought out of New York by General Thompson delivered to him there by a Mrs. Moore not long from England, *soi-disante parente de Madame votre épouse*. She speaks of a daughter of yours, well when she left England, perhaps [   ].

And Now my Dear as we are upon the subject of wife, I empower and command you to get me one in Carolina. Such a wife as I want will, I know, be difficult to be found, but if you succeed, it will be the stronger proof of your zeal and dexterity. Take her description—She must be young, handsome (I lay most stress upon a good shape) sensible (a little learning will do), well bred (but she must have an aversion to the word *ton*) chaste and tender (I am an enthusiast in my notions of fidelity and fondness) of some good nature, a great deal of generosity (she must neither love money nor scolding, for I dislike equally a termagent and an œconomist). In politics, I am indifferent what side she may be of; I think I have arguments that will easily convert her to mine. As to religion a moderate stock will satisfy me. She must believe in god and hate a saint. But as to fortune, the larger stock of that the better. You know my temper and circumstances and will therefore pay special attention to this article in the treaty. Though I run no risk of going to Purgatory for my avarice; yet as money is an essential ingredient to happiness in this world—as I have not much of my own and as I am very little calculated to get more either by my address or industry; it must needs be, that my wife, if I get one, bring at least a sufficiency to administer to her own extravagancies. NB You will be pleased to recollect in your negotiations that I have no invincible antipathy to the *maidenly beauties* & that I am willing to take the *trouble* of them upon myself.

If you should not readily meet with a lady that you think answers my description you can only advertise in the public papers and doubtless you will hear of many competitors for most of the qualifications required, who will be glad to become candidates for such a prize as I am. To excite their emulation, it will be necessary for you to give an account of the lover—his *size*, make, quality of mind and *body*, achievements, expectations, fortune, &c. In drawing my picture, you will no doubt be civil to your friend; mind you do justice to the length of my nose and don't forget, that I [   ].

After reviewing what I have written, I am ready to ask myself what could have put it into my head to hazard this Jeu *de follie.* Do I want a wife? No—I have plagues enough without desiring to add to the number that *greatest of all;* and if I were silly enough to do it, I should take care how I employ a proxy. Did I mean to show my wit? If I did, I am sure I have missed my aim. Did I only intend to frisk? In this I have succeeded, but I have done more. I have gratified my feelings, by lengthening out the only kind of intercourse now in my power with my friend. Adieu

Yours.

A HAMILTON

P.S—Fleury shall be taken care of. All the family send their love. In this join the General & Mrs. Washington & what is best, tis not in the stile of ceremony but sincerity.

April 1779

To John Laurens

Jany 8t.

I had written the enclosed and was called off. Some ruffian hand has treated it in the manner you see. I have no time to copy it. I shall take up the story where I left it.

Another reason for believing the destination is your way, is that Governor Martin and divers others refugees of Georgia South and North Carolina are said to have gone in the fleet. You will have a busy time; acquit yourselves well. We hope however that some late violent winds will drown them all on their way. There is no other military news.

Believe me my Dr Laurens I am not insensible of the first mark of your affection in recommending me to your friends for a certain commission. However your partiality may have led you to overrate my qualifications that very partiality must endear you to me; and all the world will allow that your struggles and scruples upon the occasion deserve the envy of men of vertue. I am happy you placed the matter upon the footing you did, because I hope it will ultimately engage you to accept the appointment. Had it fallen to my lot, I should have been flattered by such a distinction but I should have felt all your embarrassments.

Of this however I need have no apprehension. Not one of the four in nomination but would stand a better chance than myself; and yet my vanity tells me they do not all merit a preference. But I am a stranger in this country. I have no property here, no connexions. If I have talents and integrity, (as you say I have) these are justly deemed very spurious titles in these enlightened days, when unsupported by others more solid; and were it not for your example, I should be inclined in considering the composition of a certain body, to suppose that three fourths of them are mortal enemies to the first and three fourths of the other fourth have a laudable contempt for the last.

Adieu God preserve and prosper you

A HAMILTON

I have strongly sollicited leave to go to the Southward. It could not be refused; but arguments have been used to dissuade me from it, which however little weight they may have had in my judgment gave law to my feelings. I am chagrined and unhappy but I submit. In short Laurens I am disgusted with every thing in this world but yourself and *very* few more honest fellows and I have no other wish than as soon as possible to make a brilliant exit. 'Tis a weakness; but I feel I am not fit for this terrestreal Country.

All the Lads embrace you. The General sends his love. Write to him as often as you can.

1780

To Eliȝabeth Schuyler

Impatiently My Dearest have I been expecting the return of your father to bring me a letter from my charmer with the answers you have been good enough to promise me to the little questions asked in mine by him. I long to see the workings of my Betseys heart, and I promise my self I shall have ample gratification to my fondness in the sweet familiarity of her pen. She will there I hope paint me her feelings without reserve—even in those tender moments of pillowed retirement, when her soul abstracted from every other object, delivers itself up to Love and to me—yet with all that delicacy which suits the purity of her mind and which is so conspicuous in whatever she does.

It is now a week my Betsey since I have heard from you. In that time I have written you twice. I think it will be adviseable in future to number our letters, for I have reason to suspect they do not all meet with fair play. This is number one.

Meade just comes in and interrupts me by sending his love to you. He tells you he has written a long letter to his widow asking her opinion of the propriety of quitting the service; and that if she does not disapprove it, he will certainly take his final leave after the campaign. You see what a fine opportunity she has to be enrolled in the catalogue of heroines, and I dare say she will set you an example of fortitude and patriotism. I know too you have so much of the Portia in you, that you will not be out done in this line by any of your sex, and that if you saw me inclined to quit the service of your country, you would dissuade me from it. I have promised you, you recollect, to conform to your wishes, and I persist in this intention. It remains with you to show whether you are a *Roman* or an *American wife*.

Though I am not sanguine in expecting it, I am not without hopes this Winter will produce a peace and then you must submit to the mortification of enjoying more domestic happiness and less fame. This I know you will not like, but we cannot always have things as we wish.

The affairs of England are in so bad a plight that if no fortunate events attend her this campaign, it would seem impossible for her to proceed in the war. But she is an obstinate old dame, and seems determined to ruin her whole family, rather than to let Miss America go on flirting it with her new lovers, with whom, as giddy young girls often do, she eloped in contempt of her mothers authority. I know you will be ready to justify her conduct and to tell me the ill treatment she received was enough to make any girl of spirit act in the same manner. But I will one day cure you of these refractory notions about the right of resistance, (of which I foresee you will be apt to make a very dangerous application), and teach you the great advantage and absolute necessity of implicit obedience.

But now we are talking of times to come, tell me my pretty damsel have you made up your mind upon the subject of housekeeping? Do you soberly relish the pleasure of being a poor mans wife? Have you learned to think a home spun preferable to a brocade and the rumbling of a waggon wheel to the musical rattling of a coach and six? Will you be able to see with perfect composure your old acquaintances flaunting it in gay life, tripping it along in elegance and splendor, while you hold an humble station and have no other enjoyments than the sober comforts of a good wife? Can you in short be an Aquileia and chearfully plant turnips with me, if fortune should so order it? If you cannot my Dear we are playing a comedy of all in the wrong, and you should correct the mistake before we begin to act the tragedy of the unhappy couple.

I propose you a set of new questions my lovely girl; but though they are asked with an air of levity, they merit a very serious consideration, for on their being resolved in the affirmative stripped of all the colorings of a fond imagination our happiness may absolutely depend. I have not concealed my circumstances from my Betsey; they are far from splendid; they may possibly even be worse than I expect, for every day brings me fresh proof of the knavery of those to whom my little affairs are entrusted. They have already filed down what was in their hands more than one half, and I am told they go on diminishing it, 'till I *fear* they will reduce it below my *former fears*. An indifference to property enters into my character too much, and what affects me now as my Betsey is concerned in it, I should have laughed at or not thought of at all a year ago. But I have thoroughly examined my own heart. Beloved by you, I can be happy in any situation, and can struggle with every embarrassment of fortune with patience and firmness. I cannot however forbear entreating you to realize our union on the dark side and satisfy, without deceiving yourself, how far your affection for me can make you happy in a privation of those elegancies to which you have been accustomed. If fortune should smile upon us, it will do us no harm to have been prepared for adversity; if she frowns upon us, by being prepared, we shall encounter it without the chagrin of disappointment. Your future rank in life is a perfect lottery; you may move in an exalted you may move in a very humble sphere; the last is most probable; examine well your heart. And in doing it, don't figure to yourself a cottage in romance, with the spontaneous bounties of nature courting you to enjoyment. Don't imagine yourself a shepherdess, your hair embroidered with flowers a crook in your hand tending your flock under a shady tree, by the side of a cool fountain, your faithful shepherd sitting near and entertaining you with gentle tales of love. These are pretty dreams and very apt to enter into the heads of lovers when they think of a connection without the advantages of fortune. But they must not be indulged. You must apply your situation to real life, and think how you should feel in scenes of which you may find examples every day. So far My Dear Betsey as the tenderest affection can compensate for other inconveniences in making your estimate, you cannot give too large a credit for this article. My heart overflows with every thing for you, that admiration, esteem and love can inspire. *I would this moment give the world to be near you only to kiss your sweet hand*. Believe what I say to be truth and imagine what are my feelings when I say it. Let it awake your sympathy and let our hearts melt in a prayer to be soon united, never more to be separated.

Adieu loveliest of your sex

AH

Instead of inclosing your letter to your father I inclose his to you because I do not know whether he may not be on his way here. If he is at home he will tell you the military news. If he has set out for camp, you may open and read my letters to him. The one from Mr. Mathews you will return by the first opportunity.

August 1780

To James Duane

Dr. Sir

Agreeably to your request and my promise I sit down to give you my ideas of the defects of our present system, and the changes necessary to save us from ruin. They may perhaps be the reveries of a projector rather than the sober views of a politician. You will judge of them, and make what use you please of them.

The fundamental defect is a want of power in Congress. It is hardly worth while to show in what this consists, as it seems to be universally acknowleged, or to point out how it has happened, as the only question is how to remedy it. It may however be said that it has originated from three causes—an excess of the spirit of liberty which has made the particular states show a jealousy of all power not in their own hands; and this jealousy has led them to exercise a right of judging in the last resort of the measures recommended by Congress, and of acting according to their own opinions of their propriety or necessity, a diffidence in Congress of their own powers, by which they have been timid and indecisive in their resolutions, constantly making concessions to the states, till they have scarcely left themselves the shadow of power; a want of sufficient means at their disposal to answer the public exigencies and of vigor to draw forth those means; which have occasioned them to depend on the states individually to fulfil their engagements with the army, and the consequence of which has been to ruin their influence and credit with the army, to establish its dependence on each state separately rather than on them, that is rather than on the whole collectively.

It may be pleaded, that Congress had never any definitive powers granted them and of course could exercise none—could do nothing more than recommend. The manner in which Congress was appointed would warrant, and the public good required, that they should have considered themselves as vested with full power *to preserve the republic from harm*. They have done many of the highest acts of sovereignty, which were always chearfully submitted to—the declaration of independence, the declaration of war, the levying an army, creating a navy, emitting money, making alliances with foreign powers, appointing a dictator &c. &c.—all these implications of a complete sovereignty were never disputed, and ought to have been a standard for the whole conduct of Administration. Undefined powers are discretionary powers, limited only by the object for which they were given—in the present case, the independence and freedom of America. The confederation made no difference; for as it has not been generally adopted, it had no operation. But from what I recollect of it, Congress have even descended from the authority which the spirit of that act gives them, while the particular states have no further attended to it than as it suited their pretensions and convenience. It would take too much time to enter into particular instances, each of which separately might appear inconsiderable; but united are of serious import. I only mean to remark, not to censure.

But the confederation itself is defective and requires to be altered; it is neither fit for war, nor peace. The idea of an uncontrolable sovereignty in each state, over its internal police, will defeat the other powers given to Congress, and make our union feeble and precarious. There are instances without number, where acts necessary for the general good, and which rise out of the powers given to Congress must interfere with the internal police of the states, and there are as many instances in which the particular states by arrangements of internal police can effectually though indirectly counteract the arrangements of Congress. You have already had examples of this for which I refer you to your own memory.

The confederation gives the states individually too much influence in the affairs of the army; they should have nothing to do with it. The entire formation and disposal of our military forces ought to belong to Congress. It is an essential cement of the union; and it ought to be the policy of Congress to destroy all ideas of state attachments in the army and make it look up wholly to them. For this purpose all appointments promotions and provisions whatsoever ought to be made by them. It may be apprehended that this may be dangerous to liberty. But nothing appears more evident to me, than that we run much greater risk of having a weak and disunited federal government, than one which will be able to usurp upon the rights of the people. Already some of the lines of the army would obey their states in opposition to Congress notwithstanding the pains we have taken to preserve the unity of the army—if any thing would hinder this it would be the personal influence of the General, a melancholy and mortifying consideration.

The forms of our state constitutions must always give them great weight in our affairs and will make it too difficult to bend them to the persuit of a common interest, too easy to oppose whatever they do not like and to form partial combinations subversive of the general one. There is a wide difference between our situation and that of an empire under one simple form of government, distributed into counties provinces or districts, which have no legislatures but merely magistratical bodies to execute the laws of a common sovereign. Here the danger is that the sovereign will have too much power to oppress the parts of which it is composed. In our case, that of an empire composed of confederated states each with a government completely organised within itself, having all the means to draw its subjects to a close dependence on itself—the danger is directly the reverse. It is that the common sovereign will not have power sufficient to unite the different members together, and direct the common forces to the interest and happiness of the whole.

The leagues among the old Grecian republics are a proof of this. They were continually at war with each other, and for want of union fell a prey to their neighbours. They frequently held general councils, but their resolutions were no further observed than as they suited the interests and inclinations of all the parties and at length, they sunk intirely into contempt.

The Swiss-cantons are another proof of the doctrine. They have had wars with each other which would have been fatal to them, had not the different powers in their neighbourhood been too jealous of one-another and too equally matched to suffer either to take advantage of their quarrels. That they have remained so long united at all is to be attributed to their weakness, to their poverty, and to the cause just mentioned. These ties will not exist in America; a little time hence, some of the states will be powerful empires, and we are so remote from other nations that we shall have all the leisure and opportunity we can wish to cut each others throats.

The Germanic corps might also be cited as an example in favour of the position.

The United provinces may be thought to be one against it. But the family of the stadtholders whose authority is interwoven with the whole government has been a strong link of union between them. Their physical necessities and the habits founded upon them have contributed to it. Each province is too inconsiderable by itself to undertake any thing. An analysis of their present constitutions would show that they have many ties which would not exist in ours; and that they are by no means a proper mode for us.

Our own experience should satisfy us. We have felt the difficulty of drawing out the resources of the country and inducing the states to combine in equal exertions for the common cause. The ill success of our last attempt is striking. Some have done a great deal, others little or scarcely any thing. The disputes about boundaries &c. testify how flattering a prospect we have of future tranquillity, if we do not frame in time a confederacy capable of deciding the differences and compelling the obedience of the respective members.

The confederation too gives the power of the purse too intirely to the state legislatures. It should provide perpetual funds in the disposal of Congress—by a land tax, poll tax, or the like. All imposts upon commerce ought to be laid by Congress and appropriated to their use, for without certain revenues, a government can have no power; that power, which holds the purse strings absolutely, must rule. This seems to be a medium, which without making Congress altogether independent will tend to give reality to its authority.

Another defect in our system is want of method and energy in the administration. This has partly resulted from the other defect, but in a great degree from prejudice and the want of a proper executive. Congress have kept the power too much into their own hands and have meddled too much with details of every sort. Congress is properly a deliberative corps and it forgets itself when it attempts to play the executive. It is impossible such a body, numerous as it is, constantly fluctuating, can ever act with sufficient decision, or with system. Two thirds of the members, one half the time, cannot know what has gone before them or what connection the subject in hand has to what has been transacted on former occasions. The members, who have been more permanent, will only give information, that promotes the side they espouse, in the present case, and will as often mislead as enlighten. The variety of business must distract, and the proneness of every assembly to debate must at all times delay.

Lately Congress, convinced of these inconveniences, have gone into the measure of appointing boards. But this is in my opinion a bad plan. A single man, in each department of the administration, would be greatly preferable. It would give us a chance of more knowlege, more activity, more responsibility and of course more zeal and attention. Boards partake of a part of the inconveniencies of larger assemblies. Their decisions are slower their energy less their responsibility more diffused. They will not have the same abilities and knowlege as an administration by single men. Men of the first pretensions will not so readily engage in them, because they will be less conspicuous, of less importance, have less opportunity of distinguishing themselves. The members of boards will take less pains to inform themselves and arrive to eminence, because they have fewer motives to do it. All these reasons conspire to give a preference to the plan of vesting the great executive departments of the state in the hands of individuals. As these men will be of course at all times under the direction of Congress, we shall blend the advantages of a monarchy and republic in our constitution.

A question has been made, whether single men could be found to undertake these offices. I think they could, because there would be then every thing to excite the ambition of candidates. But in order to this Congress by their manner of appointing them and the line of duty marked out must show that they are in earnest in making these offices, offices of real trust and importance.

I fear a little vanity has stood in the way of these arrangements, as though they would lessen the importance of Congress and leave them nothing to do. But they would have precisely the same rights and powers as heretofore, happily disencumbered of the detail. They would have to inspect the conduct of their ministers, deliberate upon their plans, originate others for the public good—only observing this rule that they ought to consult their ministers, and get all the information and advice they could from them, before they entered into any new measures or made changes in the old.

A third defect is the fluctuating constitution of our army. This has been a pregnant source of evil; all our military misfortunes, three fourths of our civil embarrassments are to be ascribed to it. The General has so fully enumerated the mischief of it in a late letter of the [ ] to Congress that I could only repeat what he has said, and will therefore refer you to that letter.

The imperfect and unequal provision made for the army is a fourth defect which you will find delineated in the same letter. Without a speedy change the army must dissolve; it is now a mob, rather than an army, without cloathing, without pay, without provision, without morals, without discipline. We begin to hate the country for its neglect of us; the country begins to hate us for our oppressions of them. Congress have long been jealous of us; we have now lost all confidence in them, and give the worst construction to all they do. Held together by the slenderest ties we are ripening for a dissolution.

The present mode of supplying the army—by state purchases—is not one of the least considerable defects of our system. It is too precarious a dependence, because the states will never be sufficiently impressed with our necessities. Each will make its own ease a primary object, the supply of the army a secondary one. The variety of channels through which the business is transacted will multiply the number of persons employed and the opportunities of embezzling public money. From the popular spirit on which most of the governments turn, the state agents, will be men of less character and ability, nor will there be so rigid a responsibility among them as there might easily be among those in the employ of the continent, of course not so much diligence care or economy. Very little of the money raised in the several states will go into the Continental treasury, on pretence, that it is all exhausted in providing the quotas of supplies, and the public will be without funds for the other demands of governments. The expence will be ultimately much greater and the advantages much smaller. We actually feel the insufficiency of this plan and have reason to dread under it a ruinous extremity of want.

These are the principal defects in the present system that now occur to me. There are many inferior ones in the organization of particular departments and many errors of administration which might be pointed out; but the task would be troublesome and tedious, and if we had once remedied those I have mentioned the others would not be attended with much difficulty.

I shall now propose the remedies, which appear to me applicable to our circumstances, and necessary to extricate our affairs from their present deplorable situation.

The first step must be to give Congress powers competent to the public exigencies. This may happen in two ways, one by resuming and exercising the discretionary powers I suppose to have been originally vested in them for the safety of the states and resting their conduct on the candor of their country men and the necessity of the conjuncture: the other by calling immediately a convention of all the states with full authority to conclude finally upon a general confederation, stating to them beforehand explicity the evils arising from a want of power in Congress, and the impossibily of supporting the contest on its present footing, that the delegates may come possessed of proper sentiments as well as proper authority to give to the meeting. Their commission should include a right of vesting Congress with the whole or a proportion of the unoccupied lands, to be employed for the purpose of raising a revenue, reserving the jurisdiction to the states by whom they are granted.

The first plan, I expect will be thought too bold an expedient by the generality of Congress; and indeed their practice hitherto has so rivetted the opinion of their want of power, that the success of this experiment may very well be doubted.

I see no objection to the other mode, that has any weight in competition with the reasons for it. The Convention should assemble the 1st of November next, the sooner, the better; our disorders are too violent to admit of a common or lingering remedy. The reasons for which I require them to be vested with plenipotentiary authority are that the business may suffer no delay in the execution, and may in reality come to effect. A convention may agree upon a confederation; the states individually hardly ever will. We must have one at all events, and a vigorous one if we mean to succeed in the contest and be happy hereafter. As I said before, to engage the states to comply with this mode, Congress ought to confess to them plainly and unanimously the impracticability of supporting our affairs on the present footing and without a solid coercive union. I ask that the Convention should have a power of vesting the whole or a part of the unoccupied land in Congress, because it is necessary that body should have some property as a fund for the arrangements of finance; and I know of no other kind that can be given them.

The confederation in my opinion should give Congress complete sovereignty; except as to that part of internal police, which relates to the rights of property and life among individuals and to raising money by internal taxes. It is necessary, that every thing, belonging to this, should be regulated by the state legislatures. Congress should have complete sovereignty in all that relates to war, peace, trade, finance, and to the management of foreign affairs, the right of declaring war of raising armies, officering, paying them, directing their motions in every respect, of equipping fleets and doing the same with them, of building fortifications arsenals magazines &c. &c., of making peace on such conditions as they think proper, of regulating trade, determining with what countries it shall be carried on, granting indulgencies laying prohibitions on all the articles of export or import, imposing duties granting bounties & premiums for raising exporting importing and applying to their own use the product of these duties, only giving credit to the states on whom they are raised in the general account of revenues and expences, instituting Admiralty courts &c., of coining money, establishing banks on such terms, and with such privileges as they think proper, appropriating funds and doing whatever else relates to the operations of finance, transacting every thing with foreign nations, making alliances offensive and defensive, treaties of commerce, &c. &c.

The confederation should provide certain perpetual revenues, productive and easy of collection, a land tax, poll tax or the like, which together with the duties on trade and the unlocated lands would give Congress a substantial existence, and a stable foundation for their schemes of finance. What more supplies were necessary should be occasionally demanded of the states, in the present mode of quotas.

The second step I would recommend is that Congress should instantly appoint the following great officers of state—A secretary for foreign affairs—a President of war—A President of Marine—A Financier—A President of trade; instead of this last a board of Trade may be preferable as the regulations of trade are slow and gradual and require prudence and experience (more than other qualities), for which boards are very well adapted.

Congress should choose for these offices, men of the first abilities, property and character in the continent—and such as have had the best opportunities of being acquainted with the several branches. General Schuyler (whom you mentioned) would make an excellent President of War, General McDougall a very good President of Marine. Mr. Robert Morris would have many things in his favour for the department of finance. He could by his own personal influence give great weight to the measures he should adopt. I dare say men equally capable may be found for the other departments.

I know not, if it would not be a good plan to let the Financier be President of the Board of trade; but he should only have a casting voice in determining questions there. There is a connection between trade and finance, which ought to make the director of one acquainted with the other; but the Financier should not direct the affairs of trade, because for the sake of acquiring reputation by increasing the revenues, he might adopt measures that would depress trade. In what relates to finance he should be alone.

These offices should have nearly the same powers and functions as those in France analogous to them, and each should be chief in his department, with subordinate boards composed of assistant clerks &c. to execute his orders.

In my opinion a plan of this kind would be of inconceivable utility to our affairs; its benefits would be very speedily felt. It would give new life and energy to the operations of government. Business would be conducted with dispatch method and system. A million of abuses now existing would be corrected, and judicious plans would be formed and executed for the public good.

Another step of immediate necessity is to recruit the army for the war, or at least for three years. This must be done by a mode similar to that which is practiced in Sweeden. There the inhabitants are thrown into classes of sixteen, and when the sovereign wants men each of these classes must furnish one. They raise a fixed sum of money, and if one of the class is willing to become a soldier, he receives the money and offers himself a volunteer; if none is found to do this, a draft is made and he on whom the lot falls receives the money and is obliged to serve. The minds of the people are prepared for a thing of this kind; the heavy bounties they have been obliged to pay for men to serve a few months must have disgusted them with this mode, and made them desirous of another, that will once for all answer the public purposes, and obviate a repetition of the demand. It ought by all means to be attempted, and Congress should frame a general plan and press the execution upon the states. When the confederation comes to be framed, it ought to provide for this by a fundamental law, and hereafter there would be no doubt of the success. But we cannot now wait for this; we want to replace the men whose times of service will expire the 1st of January, for then, without this, we shall have no army remaining and the enemy may do what they please. The General in his letter already quoted has assigned the most substantial reasons for paying immediate attention to this point.

Congress should endeavour, both upon their credit in Europe, and by every possible exertion in this country, to provide cloathing for their officers, and should abolish the whole system of state supplies. The making good the depreciation of the currency and all other compensations to the army should be immediately taken up by Congress, and not left to the states; if they would have the accounts of depreciation liquidated, and governmental certificates given for what is due in specie or an equivalent to specie, it would give satisfaction; appointing periodical settlements for future depreciation.

The placing the officers upon half pay during life would be a great stroke of policy, and would give Congress a stronger tie upon them, than any thing else they can do. No man, that reflects a moment, but will prefer a permanent provision of this kind to any temporary compensation, nor is it opposed to economy; the difference between this and between what has been already done will be insignificant. The benefit of it to the widows should be confined to those whose husbands die during the war. As to the survivors, not more than one half on the usual calculation of mens lives will exceed the seven years for which the half pay is already established. Besides this whatever may be the visionary speculations of some men at this time, we shall find it indispensable after the war to keep on foot a considerable body of troops; and all the officers retained for this purpose must be deducted out of the half pay list. If any one will take the pains to calculate the expence on these principles, I am persuaded he will find the addition of expence from the establishment proposed, by no means a national object.

The advantages of securing the attachment of the army to Congress, and binding them to the service by substantial ties are immense. We should then have discipline, an army in reality, as well as in name. Congress would then have a solid basis of authority and consequence, for to me it is an axiom that in our constitution an army is essential to the American union.

The providing of supplies is the pivot of every thing else (though a well constituted army would not in a small degree conduce to this, by giving consistency and weight to government). There are four ways all which must be united—a foreign loan, heavy pecuniary taxes, a tax in kind, a bank founded on public and private credit.

As to a foreign loan I dare say, Congress are doing every thing in their power to obtain it. The most effectual way will be to tell France that without it, we must make terms with great Britain. This must be done with plainness and firmness, but with respect and without petulance, not as a menace, but as a candid declaration of our circumstances. We need not fear to be deserted by France. Her interest and honor are too deeply involved in our fate; and she can make no possible compromise. She can assist us, if she is convinced it is absolutely necessary, either by lending us herself or by becoming our surety or by influencing Spain. It has been to me astonishing how any man could have doubted at any period of our affairs of the necessity of a foreign loan. It was self evident, that we had not a fund of wealth in this country, capable of affording revenues equal to the expences. We must then create artificial revenues, or borrow; the first was done, but it ought to have been foreseen, that the expedient could not last; and we should have provided in time for its failure.

Here was an error of Congress. I have good reason to believe, that measures were not taken in earnest early enough, to procure a loan abroad. I give you my honor that from our first outset, I thought as I do now and wished for a foreign loan not only because I foresaw it would be essential but because I considered it as a tie upon the nation from which it was derived and as a mean to prop our cause in Europe.

Concerning the necessity of heavy pecuniary taxes I need say nothing, as it is a point in which everybody is agreed; nor is there any danger, that the product of any taxes raised in this way will over burthen the people, or exceed the wants of the public. Indeed if all the paper in circulation were drawn annually into the treasury, it would neither do one, nor the other.

As to a tax in kind, the necessity of it results from this principle—that the money in circulation is not a sufficient representative of the productions of the country, and consequently no revenues raised from it as a medium can be a competent representative of that part of the products of the country, which it is bound to contribute to the support of the public. The public therefore to obtain its due or satisfy its just demands and its wants must call for a part of those products themselves. This is done in all those countries which are not commercial, in Russia, Prussia, Denmark Sweden &c. and is peculiarly necessary in our case.

Congress in calling for specific supplies seem to have had this in view; but their intention has not been answered. The states in general have undertaken to furnish the supplies by purchase, a mode as I have observed, attended with every inconvenience and subverting the principle on which the supplies were demanded—the insufficiency of our circulating medium as a representative for the labour and commodities of the Country. It is therefore necessary that Congress should be more explicit, should form the outlines of a plan for a tax in kind, and recommend it to the states, as a measure of absolute necessity.

The general idea I have of a plan, is that a respectable man should be appointed by the state in each county to collect the taxes and form magazines, that Congress should have in each state an officer to superintend the whole and that the state collectors should be subordinate and responsible to them. This Continental superintendent might be subject to the general direction of the Quarter Master General, or not, as might be deemed best; but if not subject to him, he should be obliged to make monthly returns to the President at War, who should instruct him what proportion to deliver to the Quarter Master General. It may be necessary that the superintendents should sometimes have power to dispose of the articles in their possession on public account; for it would happen that the contributions in places remote from the army could not be transported to the theatre of operations without too great expence, in which case it would be eligible to dispose of them and purchase with the money so raised in the countries near the immediate scene of war.

I know the objections which may be raised to this plan—its tendency to discourage industry and the like; but necessity calls for it; we cannot proceed without it, and less evils must give place to greater. It is besides practiced with success in other countries, and why not in this? It may be said, the examples cited are from nations under despotic governments and that the same would not be practicable with us; but I contend where the public good is evidently the object more may be effected in governments like ours than in any other. It has been a constant remark that free countries have ever paid the heaviest taxes. The obedience of a free people to general laws however hard they bear is ever more perfect than that of slaves to the arbitrary will of a prince. To this it may be added that Sweden was always a free government, and is so now in a great degree, notwithstanding the late revolution.

How far it may be practicable to erect a bank on the joint credit of the public and of individuals can only be certainly determined by the experiment; but it is of so much importance that the experiment ought to be fully tried. When I saw the subscriptions going on to the bank established for supplying the army, I was in hopes it was only the embryo of a more permanent and extensive establishment. But I have reason to believe I shall be disappointed. It does not seem to be at all conducted on the true principles of a bank. The directors of it are purchasing with their stock instead of bank notes as I expected; in consequence of which it must turn out to be a mere subscription of a particular sum of money for a particular purpose.

Paper credit never was long supported in any country, on a national scale, where it was not founded on the joint basis of public and private credit. An attempt to establish it on public credit alone in France under the auspices of Mr. Law had nearly ruined the kingdom; we have seen the effects of it in America, and every successive experiment proves the futility of the attempt. Our new money is depreciating almost as fast as the old, though it has in some states as real funds as paper money ever had. The reason is, that the monied men have not an immediate interest to uphold its credit. They may even in many ways find it their interest to undermine it. The only certain manner to obtain a permanent paper credit is to engage the monied interest immediately in it by making them contribute the whole or part of the stock and giving them the whole or part of the profits.

The invention of banks on the modern principle originated in Venice. There the public and a company of monied men are mutually concerned. The Bank of England unites public authority and faith with private credit; and hence we see what a vast fabric of paper credit is raised on a visionary basis. Had it not been for this, England would never have found sufficient funds to carry on her wars; but with the help of this she has done, and is doing wonders. The bank of Amsterdam is on a similar foundation.

And why can we not have an American bank? Are our monied men less enlightened to their own interest or less enterprising in the persuit? I believe the fault is in our government which does not exert itself to engage them in such a scheme. It is true, the individuals in America are not very rich, but this would not prevent their instituting a bank; it would only prevent its being done with such ample funds as in other countries. Have they not sufficient confidence in the government and in the issue of the cause? Let the Government endeavour to inspire that confidence, by adopting the measures I have recommended or others equivalent to them. Let it exert itself to procure a solid confederation, to establish a good plan of executive administration, to form a permanent military force, to obtain at all events a foreign loan. If these things were in a train of vigorous execution, it would give a new spring to our affairs; government would recover its respectability and individuals would renounce their diffidence.

The object I should propose to myself in the first instance from a bank would be an auxiliary mode of supplies; for which purpose contracts should be made between Government and the bank on terms liberal and advantageous to the latter. Every thing should be done in the first instance to encourage the bank; after it gets well established it will take care of itself and government may make the best terms it can for itself.

The first step to establishing the bank will be to engage a number of monied men of influence to relish the project and make it a business. The subscribers to that lately established are the fittest persons that can be found; and their plan may be interwoven.

The outlines of my plan would be to open subscriptions in all the states for the stock, which we will suppose to be one million of pounds. Real property of every kind, as well as specie should be deemed good stock, but at least a fourth part of the subscription should be in specie or plate. There should be one great company in three divisions in Virginia, Philadelphia, and at Boston or two at Philadelphia and Boston. The bank should have a right to issue bank notes bearing two per Cent interest for the whole of their stock; but not to exceed it. These notes may be payable every three months or oftener, and the faith of government must be pledged for the support of the bank. It must therefore have a right from time to time to inspect its operations, and must appoint inspectors for the purpose.

The advantages of the bank may consist in this, in the profits of the contracts made with government, which should bear interest to be annually paid in specie, in the loan of money at interest say six per Cent, in purchasing lives by annuities as practiced in England &c. The benefit resulting to the company is evident from the consideration, that they may employ in circulation a great deal more money than they have specie in stock, on the credit of the real property which they will have in other use; this money will be employed either in fulfilling their contracts with the public by which also they will gain a profit, or in loans at an advantageous interest or in annuities.

The bank may be allowed to purchase plate and bullion and coin money allowing government a part of the profit. I make the bank notes bear interest to obtain a readie currency and to induce the holders to prefer them to specie to prevent too great a run upon the bank at any time beyond its ability to pay.

If Government can obtain a foreign loan it should lend to the bank on easy terms to extend its influence and facilitate a compliance with its engagements. If government could engage the states to raise a sum of money in specie to be deposited in bank in the same manner, it would be of the greatest consequence. If government could prevail on the enthusiasm of the people to make a contribution in plate for the same purpose it would be a master stroke. Things of this kind sometimes succeed in popular contests; and if undertaken with address; I should not despair of its success; but I should not be sanguine.

The bank may be instituted for a term of years by way of trial and the particular privilege of coining money be for a term still shorter. A temporary transfer of it to a particular company can have no inconvenience as the government are in no condition to improve this resource nor could it in our circumstances be an object to them, though with the industry of a knot of individuals it might be.

A bank of this kind even in its commencement would answer the most valuable purposes to government and to the proprietors; in its progress the advantages will exceed calculation. It will promote commerce by furnishing a more extensive medium which we greatly want in our circumstances. I mean a more extensive valuable medium. We have an enormous nominal one at this time; but it is only a name.

In the present unsettled state of things in this country, we can hardly draw inferences from what has happened in others, otherwise I should be certain of the success of this scheme; but I think it has enough in its favour to be worthy of trial.

I have only skimmed the surface of the different subjects I have introduced. Should the plans recommended come into contemplation in earnest and you desire my further thoughts, I will endeavour to give them more form and particularity. I am persuaded a solid confederation a permanent army a reasonable prospect of subsisting it would give us treble consideration in Europe and produce a peace this winter.

If a Convention is called the minds of all the states and the people ought to be prepared to receive its determinations by sensible and popular writings, which should conform to the views of Congress. There are epochs in human affairs, when *novelty* even is useful. If a general opinion prevails that the old way is bad, whether true or false, and this obstructs or relaxes the operation of the public service, a change is necessary if it be but for the sake of change. This is exactly the case now. 'Tis an universal sentiment that our present system is a bad one, and that things do not go right on this account. The measure of a Convention would revive the hopes of the people and give a new direction to their passions, which may be improved in carrying points of substantial utility. The Eastern states have already pointed out this mode to Congress; they ought to take the hint and anticipate the others.

And, in future, My Dear Sir, two things let me recommend, as fundamental rules for the conduct of Congress—to attach the army to them by every motive, to maintain an air of authority (not domineering) in all their measures with the states. The manner in which a thing is done has more influence than is commonly imagined. Men are governed by opinion; this opinion is as much influenced by appearances as by realities; if a Government appears to be confident of its own powers, it is the surest way to inspire the same confidence in others; if it is diffident, it may be certain, there will be a still greater diffidence in others, and that its authority will not only be distrusted, controverted, but contemned.

I wish too Congress would always consider that a kindness consists as much in the manner as in the thing: the best things done hesitatingly and with an ill grace lose their effect, and produce disgust rather than satisfaction or gratitude. In what Congress have at any time done for the army, they have commonly been too late: They have seemed to yield to importunity rather than to sentiments of justice or to a regard to the accommodation of their troops. An attention to this idea is of more importance than it may be thought. I who have seen all the workings and progress of the present discontents, am convinced, that a want of this has not been among the most inconsiderable causes.

You will perceive My Dear Sir this letter is hastily written and with a confidential freedom, not as to a member of Congress, whose feelings may be sore at the prevailing clamours; but as to a friend who is in a situation to remedy public disorders, who wishes for nothing so much as truth, and who is desirous of information, even from those less capable of judging than himself. I have not even time to correct and copy and only enough to add that I am very truly and affectionately D Sir Your most Obed ser

A. HAMILTON

Liberty Pole
Sept. 3d 1780

To Elizabeth Schuyler

Sepr 25

In the midst of my letter, I was interrupted by a scene that shocked me more than any thing I have met with—the discovery of a treason of the deepest dye. The object was to sacrifice West Point. General Arnold had sold himself to André for this purpose. The latter came but in disguise and in returning to New York was detected. Arnold hearing of it immediately fled to the enemy. I went in persuit of him but was much too late, and I could hardly regret the disappointment, when on my return, I saw an amiable woman frantic with distress for the loss of a husband she tenderly loved—a traitor to his country and to his fame, a disgrace to his connections. It was the most affecting scene I ever was witness to. She for a considerable time intirely lost her senses. The General went up to see her and she upbraided him with being in a plot to murder her child; one moment she raved; another she melted into tears; sometimes she pressed her infant to her bosom and lamented its fate occasioned by the imprudence of its father in a manner that would have pierced insensibility itself. All the sweetness of beauty, all the loveliness of innocence, all the tenderness of a wife and all the fondness of a mother showed themselves in her appearance and conduct. We have every reason to believe she was intirely unacquainted with the plan, and that her first knowlege of it was when Arnold went to tell her he must banish himself from his Country and from her forever. She instantly fell into a convulsion and he left her in that situation.

This morning she is more composed. I paid her a visit and endeavoured to sooth her by every method in my power, though you may imagine she is not easily to be consoled. Added to her other distresses, She is very apprehensive the resentment of her country will fall upon her (who is only unfortunate) for the guilt of her husband. I have tried to persuade her, her apprehensions are ill founded; but she has too many proofs of the illiberality of the state to which she belongs to be convinced. She received us in bed, with every circumstance that could interest our sympathy. Her sufferings were so eloquent that I wished myself her brother, to have a right to become her defender. As it is, I have entreated her to enable me to give her proofs of my friendship.

Could I forgive Arnold for sacrificing his honor reputation and duty I could not forgive him for acting a part that must have forfieted the esteem of so fine a woman. At present she almost forgets his crime in his misfortune, and her horror at the guilt of the traitor is lost in her love of the man. But a virtuous mind cannot long esteem a base one, and time will make her despise, if it cannot make her hate.

Indeed my angelic Betsey, I would not for the world do any thing that would hazard your esteem. 'Tis to me a jewel of inestimable price & I think you may rely I shall never make you blush.

I thank you for all the goodness of which your letters are expressive, and I entreat you my lovely girl to believe that my tenderness for you every day increases and that no time or circumstances can abate it. I quarrel with the hours that they do not fly more rapidly and give us to each other.

1780

To Elizabeth Schuyler

Since my last to you, I have received your letters No. 3 & 4; the others are yet on the way. Though it is too late to have the advantage of novelty, to comply with my promise, I send you my account of Arnold's affair; and to justify myself to your sentiments, I must inform you that I urged a compliance with Andre's request to be shot and I do not think it would have had an ill effect; but some people are only sensible to motives of policy, and sometimes from a narrow disposition mistake it. When André's tale comes to be told, and present resentment is over, the refusing him the privilege of choosing the manner of death will be branded with too much obduracy.

It was proposed to me to suggest to him the idea of an exchange for Arnold; but I knew I should have forfieted his esteem by doing it, and therefore declined it. As a man of honor he could not but reject it and I would not for the world have proposed to him a thing, which must have placed me in the unamiable light of supposing him capable of a meanness, or of not feeling myself the impropriety of the measure. I confess to you I had the weakness to value the esteem of a *dying* man; because I reverenced his merit.

I fear you will admire the picture so much as to forget the painter. I wished myself possessed of André's accomplishments for your sake; for I would wish to charm you in every sense. You cannot conceive my avidity for every thing that would endear me more to you. I shall never be satisfied with giving you pleasure, and I am mortified that I do not unite in myself every valuable and agreeable qualification. I do not my love affect modesty. I am conscious of the advantages I possess. I know I have talents and a good heart; but why am I not handsome? Why have I not every acquirement that can embellish human nature? Why have I not fortune, that I might hereafter have more leisure than I shall have to cultivate those improvements for which I am not entirely unfit?

Tis not the vanity of excelling others, but the desire of pleasing my Betsey that dictates these wishes. In her eyes I should wish to be the first the most amiable the most accomplished of my sex; but I will make up all I want in love.

Two days since, the bundle directed to your papa was delivered to me. I beg you to present my affectionate compliments with it to your mama.

I am in very good health and shall be in very good spirits when I meet my Betsey.

Adieu

A HAMILTON

How is your little sister? Is she as sprightly as ever? Does she set so much value upon a certain kiss as she seemed to do when we entered the carriage at Hartford? I forgot to tell you that she fell in love there with an old man of fifty.

October 2, 1780

To Margarita Schuyler

Because your sister has the talent of growing more amiable every day, or because I am a fanatic in love, or both—or if you prefer another interpretation, because I have address enough to be a good dissembler, she fancies herself the happiest woman in the world, and would need persuade all her friends to embark with her in the matrimonial voyage. But I pray you do not let her advice have so much influence as to make you matrimony-mad. 'Tis a very good thing when their stars unite two people who are fit for each other, who have souls capable of relishing the sweets of friendship, and sensibilities. The conclusion of the sentence I trust to your fancy. But its a dog of life when two dissonant tempers meet, and 'tis ten to one but this is the case. When therefore I join her in advising you to marry, I add be cautious in the choice. Get a man of sense, not ugly enough to be pointed at—with some good-nature—a few grains of feeling—a little taste—a little imagination—and above all a good deal of decision to keep you in order; for that I foresee will be no easy task. If you can find one with all these qualities, willing to marry you, marry him as soon as you please.

I must tell you in confidence that I think I have been very fortunate.

January 21, 1781

To Philip Schuyler

Head Quarters New Windsor Feby 18, 81

MY DEAR SIR.

Since I had the pleasure of writing you last an unexpected change has taken place in my situation. I am no longer a member of the General's family. This information will surprise you , and the manner of the change will surprise you more.—Two day ago The General and I passed each other on the stairs. He told me he wanted to speak to me, I answered that I would wait upon him immediately. I went below and delivered Mr. Tilghman a letter to be sent to The Commissary containing an order of a pressing and interesting nature, Returning to The General, I was stopped in the way Marquis De la Fayette and we conversed together about a minute on a matter of business. He can testify how impatient I was to get back and that I left him in a manner which but for our intimacy would have been more than abrupt. Instead of finding the General as usual in his room, I met him at the head of the stairs, where accosting me in a very angry tone, "Col Hamilton (said he), you have kept me waiting at the head of the stairs these ten minutes. I must tell you Sir you treat me with disrespect." I replied without petulancy, but with decision "I am not conscious of it Sir, but since you have thought it necessary to tell me so we part" "Very well Sir (said he) if it be your choice" or something to this effect and we separated.

I sincerely believe my absence which gave so much umbrage did not last two minutes.

In less than an hour after, Tilghman came to me in the Generals name assuring me of his great confidence in my abilities, integrity usefulness &c, and of his desire in a candid conversation to heal, a difference which could not have happened but in a moment of passion. I requested Mr. Tilghman to tell him 1. that I had taken my resolution in a manner not to be revoked: 2. that as a conversation could serve no other purpose than to produce explanations mutually disagreeable, though I certainly would not refuse an interview if he desired it yet I should be happy he would permit me to decline it 4. that however I did not wish to distress him or the public business, by quitting him before he could derive other assistance by the return of some of the Gentlemen who were absent: 3. that though determined to leave the family, the same principles which had kept me so long in it would continue to direct my conduct towards him when out of it. 5. And that in the mean time it depended on him to let our behaviour to each other be the same as if nothing had happened.

He consented to decline the conversation and thanked me for my offer of continuing my aid, in the manner I had mentioned.

Thus we stand. I wait Mr. Humphrey's return from the Eastward and may perhaps be induced to wait the return of Mr. Harrison from Virginia.

I have given you so particular a detail of our difference from the desire I have to justify myself in your opinion.

Perhaps you may think I was precipitate in rejecting the overture made by the general to an accommodation. I assure you My Dr Sir it was not the effect of resentment, it was the deliberate result of maxims I had long formed for the government of my own conduct.

I always disliked the office of an Aide de Camp as having in it a kind of personal dependance. I refused to serve in this capacity with two Major General's at an early period of the war. Infected however with the enthusiasm of the times, an idea of the Generals character which experience soon taught me to be unfounded overcame my scruples and induced me to *accept his invitation* to enter into his family. I believe you know the place I held in The Generals confidence and councils of which will make it the more extraordinary to you to learn that for three years past I have felt no friendship for him and have professed none. The truth is our own dispositions are the opposites of each other & the pride of my temper would not suffer me to profess what I did not feel. Indeed when advances of this kind have been made to me on his part, they were received in a manner that showed at least I had no inclination to court them, and that I wished to stand rather upon a footing of military confidence than of private attachment. You are too good a judge of human nature not to be sensible how this conduct in me must have operated on a man to whom all the world is offering incense. With this key you will easily unlock the present mystery. At the end of the war I may say many things to you concerning which I shall impose upon myself 'till then inviolable silence.

The General is a very honest man. His competitors have slender abilities and less integrity. His popularity has often been essential to the safety of America, and is still of great importance to it. These considerations have influenced my past conduct respecting him, and will influence my future. I think it is necessary he should be supported.

His estimation in your mind, whatever may be its amounts, I am persuaded has been formed on principles which a circumstance like this cannot materially affect; but if I thought it could diminish your friendship for him, I should almost forego the motives that urge me to justify myself to you. I wish what I have said to make no other impression than to satisfy you I have not been in the wrong. It is also said in confidence, for as a public knowlege of the breach would in many ways have an ill effect. it will probably be the policy of both sides to conceal it and cover the separation with some plausible pretext. I am importuned by such friends as are privy to the affair, to listen to a reconciliation: but my resolution is unalterable.

As I cannot think of quitting the army during the war, I have a project of re-entering into the artillery, by taking Lieutenant-Colonel Forrest's place, who is desirous of retiring on half pay. I have not however made up my mind upon this head, as I should be obliged to come in the youngest Lt Col instead of the eldest, which I ought to have been by natural succession had I remained in the corps; and at the same time to resume studies relative to the profession which, to avoid inferiority, must be laborious.

If a handsome command for the campaign in the light infantry should offer itself, I shall ballance between this and the artillery. My situation in the latter would be more solid and permanent; but as I hope the war will not last long enough to make it progressive, this consideration has the less force. A command for the campaign would leave me the winter to prosecute studies relative to my future career in life. With respect to the former, I have been materially the worse for going into his family.

I have written to you on this subject with all the freedom and confidence to which you have a right and with an assurance of the interest you take in all that concerns me.

Very sincerely & Affectionately I am Dr Sir Yr. most Obed

A HAMILTON

To Major James McHenry

I have, Dear Mac, several of your letters. I shall soon have time enough to write my friends as often as they please.

The Great man and I have come to an open rupture. Proposals of accomodation have been made on his part but rejected. I pledge my honor to you that he will find me inflexible. He shall for once at least repent his ill-humour. Without a shadow of reason and on the slightest ground, he charged me in the most affrontive manner with treating him with disrespect. I answered very decisively—"Sir I am not conscious of it but since you have thought it necessary to tell me so, we part." I wait till more help arrives. At present there is besides myself only Tilghman, who is just recovering from a fit of illness the consequence of too close application to business.

We have often spoken freely our sentiments to each other. Except to a very few friends our difference will be a secret; therefore be silent. I shall continue to support a popularity that has been essential, is still useful.

Adieu my friend. May the time come when characters may be known in their true light.

AH

Madame sends her friendship to you.

February 18, 1781

The Continentalist No. III

Fishkill, New York, August 9, 1781

The situation of these states is very unlike that of the United Provinces. Remote as we are from Europe, in a little time, we should fancy ourselves out of the reach of attempts from abroad, and in full liberty, at our leisure and convenience, to try our strength at home. This might not happen at once; but if the FOEDERAL GOVERNMENT SHOULD LOSE ITS AUTHORITY, it would CERTAINLY FOLLOW. Political societies, in close neighbourhood, must either be strongly united under one government, or there will infallibly exist emulations and quarrels. This is in human nature; and we have no reason to think ourselves wiser, or better, than other men. Some of the larger states, a small number of years hence, will be in themselves populous, rich and powerful, in all those circumstances calculated to inspire ambition and nourish ideas of separation and independence. Though it will ever be their true interest to preserve the union, their vanity and self importance, will be very likely to overpower that motive, and make them seek to place themselves at the head of particular confederacies independent of the general one. A schism once introduced, competitions of boundary and rivalships of commerce will easily afford pretexts for war. European powers may have inducements for fomenting these divisions and playing us off against each other. But without such a disposition in them, if separations once take place, we shall, of course, embrace different interests and connections. The particular confederacies, leaguing themselves with rival nations, will naturally be involved in their disputes; into which they will be the more readily tempted by the hope of making acquisitions upon each other, and upon the colonies of the powers with whom they are respectively at enmity.

WE ALREADY SEE SYMPTOMS OF THE EVILS TO BE APPREHENDED. In the midst of a war for our existence as a nation; in the midst of dangers too serious to be trifled with, some of the states have evaded, or refused, compliance with the demands of Congress in points of the greatest moment to the common safety. If they act such a part at this perilous juncture, what are we to expect in a time of peace and security? Is it not to be feared, that the resolutions of Congress would soon become like the decisions of the Greek amphyctions, or like the edicts of a German diet?

But as these evils are at a little distance, we may perhaps be insensible and short sighted enough to disregard them. There are others that threaten our immediate safety. Our whole system is in disorder; our currency depreciated, till in many places it will hardly obtain a circulation at all, public credit at its lowest ebb, our army deficient in numbers, and unprovided with every thing, the government, in its present condition, unable to command the means to pay, clothe, or feed their troops, the enemy making an alarming progress in the southern states, lately in complete possession of two of them, though now in part rescued by the genius and exertions of a General without an army, a force under Cornwallis still formidable to Virginia.

We ought to blush to acknowledge, that this is a true picture of our situation, when we reflect, that the enemy's whole force in the United States, including their American levies and the late reinforcement, is little more than fourteen thousand effective men; that our population, by recent examination, has been found to be greater, than at the commencement of the war; that the quantity of our specie has also increased, that the country abounds with all the necessaries of life, and has a sufficiency of foreign commodities, with a considerable and progressive commerce; that we have beyond comparison a better stock of warlike materials, than when we began the contest, and an ally as willing as able to supply our further wants: And that we have, on the spot, five thousand auxiliary troops, paid and subsisted by that ally, to assist in our defence.

Nothing but a GENERAL DISAFFECTION of the PEOPLE, or MISMANAGEMENT in their RULERS, can account for the figure we make, and for the distresses and perplexities we experience, contending against so small a force.

Our enemies themselves must now be persuaded, that the first is not the cause; and WE KNOW it is not. The most decided attachment of the people could alone have made them endure, without a convulsion, the successive shocks in our currency, added to the unavoidable inconveniences of war. There is perhaps not another nation in the world, that would have shown equal patience and perseverance in similar circumstances. The enemy have now tried the temper of almost every part of America; and they can hardly produce in their ranks a thousand men, who without their arts and seductions have voluntarily joined their standard. The miseries of a rigorous captivity, may perhaps have added half as many more to the number of the American levies, at this time in their armies. This small accession of force is the more extraordinary, as they have at some periods, been apparently in the full tide of success, while every thing wore an aspect tending to infuse despondency into the people of this country. This has been remarkably the case in the southern states. They for a time had almost undisturbed possession of two of them; and Cornwallis, after overruning a great part of a third; after two victorious battles, only brought with him into Virginia, about two hundred tories. In the state where he thought himself so well established, that he presumptuously ventured to assure the minister, there was not a rebel left, a small body of Continental troops, have been so effectually seconded by the militia of that vanquished country, as to have been able to capture a number of his troops more than equal to their own, and to repossess the principal part of the state.

As in the explanation of our embarrassments nothing can be alledged to the disaffection of the people, we must have recourse to the other cause of IMPOLICY and MISMANAGEMENT in their RULERS.

Where the blame of this may lie is not so much the question as what are the proper remedies; yet it may not be amiss to remark, that too large a share has fallen upon Congress. That body is no doubt chargeable with mistakes; but perhaps its greatest has been too much readiness to make concessions of the powers implied in its original trust. This is partly to be attributed to an excessive complaisance to the spirit, which has evidently actuated a majority of the states, a desire of monopolizing all power in themselves. Congress have been responsible for the administration of affairs, without the means of fulfilling that responsibility.

It would be too severe a reflection upon us to suppose, that a disposition to make the most of the friendship of others, and to exempt ourselves from a full share of the burthens of the war has had any part in the backwardness, which has appeared in many of the states, to confer powers and adopt measures adequate to the exigency. Such a sentiment would neither be wise, just, generous, nor honorable; nor do I believe the accusation would be well founded, yet our conduct makes us liable to a suspicion of this sort. It is certain, however, that too sanguine expectations from Europe have unintentionally relaxed our efforts, by diverting a sense of danger, and begetting an opinion, that the inequality of the contest would make every campaign the last.

We did not consider how difficult it must be to exhaust the resources of a nation circumstanced like that of Great Britain; whose government has always been distinguished for energy, and its people for enthusiasm. Nor did we, in estimating the superiority of our friends make sufficient allowance for that want of concert, which will ever characterise the operations of allies, or for the immense advantage to the enemy, of having their forces, though inferior, under a single direction. Finding the rest of Europe either friendly, or pacific, we never calculated the contingencies, which might alter that disposition; nor reflected that the death* of a single prince, the change or caprice of a single minister, was capable of giving a new face to the whole system.

We are at this time more sanguine than ever. The war with the Dutch, we believe, will give such an addition of force to our side, as will make the superiority irresistible. No person can dispute this, if things remain in their present state; but the extreme disparity of the contest is the very reason, why this cannot be the case. The neutral powers will either effect a particular, or a general accommodation, or they will take their sides. There are three suppositions to be made: one, that there will be a compromise between the united provinces and England; for which we are certain the mediation of Austria and Russia have been offered; another, a pacification between all the belligerent powers, for which we have reason to believe the same mediation has been offered; the third, a rejection of the terms of mediation and a more general war.

---

* The death of the Empress Queen has actually produced a change: Her politics, if not friendly to our connections, were at least pacific: and while she lived no hostile interference of the House of Austria was to be expected. The Emperor, her son, by her death, left more at liberty to pursue his inclinations, averse to the aggrandisement of France, of course afraid of the abasement of England, has given several indications of an unfriendly disposition. It should be a weighty consideration with us, that among the potentates which we look upon as amicable, three of the principal ones are at a very advanced stage of life. The King of Spain, the King of Prussia, and the Empress of Russia. We know not what may be the politics of successors.

Either of these suppositions is a motive for exertion. The first will place things in the same, probably in a worse situation, than before the declaration of the war against Holland. The composing of present differences may be accompanied with a revival of ancient connections; and at least would be productive of greater caution and restraint in a future intercourse with us.

The second, it is much to be dreaded, would hazard a dismemberment of a part of these states; and we are bound in honor, in duty and in interest, to employ every effort to dispossess the enemy of what they hold. A natural basis of the negociation, with respect to this continent, will be, that each party shall retain what it possesses at the conclusion of the treaty, qualified perhaps by a cession of particular points for an equivalent elsewhere. It is too delicate to dwell on the motives to this apprehension; but if such a compromise sometimes terminates the disputes of nations originally independent, it will be less extraordinary where one party was originally under the dominion of the other.

If we are determined, as we ought to be with the concurrence of our allies, not to accept such a condition, then we ought to prepare for the third event, a more general and more obstinate war.

Should this take place, a variety of new interests will be involved, and the affairs of America MAY CEASE TO BE OF PRIMARY IMPORTANCE. In proportion as the objects and operations of the war become complicated and extensive, the final success must become uncertain; and in proportion as the interests of others in our concerns may be weakened, or supplanted by more immediate interests of their own, ought our attention to ourselves, and exertions in our own behalf to be awakened and augmented.

We ought therefore, not only to strain every nerve for complying with the requisitions, to render the present campaign as decisive as possible; but we ought without delay, to ENLARGE THE POWERS OF CONGRESS. Every plan of which, this is not the foundation, will be illusory. The separate exertions of the states will never suffice. Nothing but a well-proportioned exertion of the resources of the whole, under the direction of a Common Council, with power sufficient to give efficacy to their resolutions, can preserve us from being a CONQUERED PEOPLE now, or can make us a HAPPY PEOPLE hereafter.

The New-York Packet, and the American Advertiser, August 9, 1781

To George Washington

SIR

Flattering myself that your knowlege of me will induce you to receive the observations I make as dictated by a regard to the public good, I take the liberty to suggest to you my ideas on some matters of delicacy and importance. I view the present juncture as a very interesting one. I need not observe how far the temper and situation of the army make it so. The state of our finances was perhaps never more critical. I am under injunctions which will not permit me to disclose some facts that would at once demonstrate this position, but I think it probable you will be possessed of them through another channel. It is however certain that there has scarcely been a period of the revolution which called more for wisdom and decision in Congress. Unfortunately for us we are a body not governed by reason or foresight but by circumstances. It is probable we shall not take the proper measures, and if we do not a few months may open an embarrassing scene. This will be the case whether we have peace or a continuance of the war.

If the war continues it would seem that the army must in June subsist itself to *defend the* country; if peace should take place it *will* subsist itself to *procure justice to itself.* It appears to be a prevailing opinion in the army that the disposition to recompence their services will cease with the necessity for them, and that if they once lay down their arms, they will part with the means of obtaining justice. It is to be lamented that appearances afford too much ground for their distrust.

It becomes a serious inquiry what will be the true line of policy. The claims of the army urged with moderation, but with firmness, may operate on those weak minds which are influenced by their apprehensions more than their judgments; so as to produce a concurrence in the measures which the exigencies of affairs demand. They may add weight to the applications of Congress to the several states. So far an useful turn may be given to them. But the difficulty will be to keep a *complaining* and *suffering* army within the bounds of moderation.

This Your Excellency's influence must effect. In order to it, it will be adviseable not to discountenance their endeavours to procure redress, but rather by the intervention of confidential and prudent persons, *to take the direction of them*. This however must not appear: it is of moment to the public tranquillity that Your Excellency should preserve the confidence of the army without losing that of the people. This will enable you in case of extremity to guide the torrent, and bring order perhaps even good, out of confusion. 'Tis a part that requires address; but 'tis one which your own situation as well as the welfare of the community points out.

I will not conceal from Your Excellency a truth which it is necessary you should know. An idea is propagated in the army that delicacy carried to an extreme prevents your espousing its interests with sufficient warmth. The falsehood of this opinion no one can be better acquainted with than myself; but it is not the less mischievous for being false. Its tendency is to impair that influence, which you may exert with advantage, should any commotions unhappily ensue, to moderate the pretensions of the army and make their conduct correspond with their duty.

The great *desideratum* at present is the establishment of general funds, which alone can do justice to the Creditors of the United States (of whom the army forms the most meritorious class), restore public credit and supply the future wants of government. This is the object of all men of sense; in this the influence of the army, properly directed, may cooperate.

The intimations I have thrown out will suffice to give Your Excellency a proper conception of my sentiments. You will judge of their reasonableness or fallacy; but I persuade myself you will do justice to my motives.

I have the honor to be With great respect Your Excellencys Most Obedt servt.

ALEX HAMILTON

General Knox has the confidence of the army & is a man of sense. I think he may be safely made use of. Situated as I am Your Excellency will feel the confidential nature of these observations.

Philadelphia
Feby. 13th, 1783

To James Hamilton

New York, June 22, 1785.

MY DEAR BROTHER:

I have received your letter of the 31st of May last, which, and one other, are the only letters I have received from you in many years. I am a little surprised you did not receive one which I wrote to you about six months ago. The situation you describe yourself to be in gives me much pain, and nothing will make me happier than, as far as may be in my power, to contribute to your relief. I will cheerfully pay your draft upon me for fifty pounds sterling, whenever it shall appear. I wish it was in my power to desire you to enlarge the sum; but though my future prospects are of the most flattering kind my present engagements would render it inconvenient to me to advance you a larger sum. My affection for you, however, will not permit me to be inattentive to your welfare, and I hope time will prove to you that I feel all the sentiment of a brother. Let me only request of you to exert your industry for a year or two more where you are, and at the end of that time I promise myself to be able to invite you to a more comfortable settlement in this Country. Allow me only to give you one caution, which is to avoid if possible getting in debt. Are you *married* or *single*? If the *latter*, it is my wish for many reasons it may be agreeable to you to continue in that state.

But what has become of our dear father? It is an age since I have heared from him or of him, though I have written him several letters. Perhaps, alas! he is no more, and I shall not have the pleasing opportunity of contributing to render the close of his life more happy than the progress of it. My heart bleeds at the recollection of his misfortunes and embarrassments. Sometimes I flatter myself his brothers have extended their support to him, and that he now enjoys tranquillity and ease. At other times I fear he is suffering in indigence. I entreat you, if you can, to relieve me from my doubts, and let me know how or where he is, if alive, if dead, how and where he died. Should he be alive inform him of my inquiries, beg him to write to me, and tell him how ready I shall be to devote myself and all I have to his accommodation and happiness.

I do not advise your coming to this country at present, for the war has also put things out of order here, and people in your business find a subsistence difficult enough. My object will be, by-and-by, to get you settled on a farm.

Believe me always your affectionate friend and brother,

ALEX. HAMILTON.

Constitutional Convention: Plan of Government

I   The Supreme Legislative Power of the United States of America to be vested in two distinct bodies of men—the one to be called the *Assembly* the other the *senate;* who together shall form the Legislature of the United States, with power to pass all *laws whatsoever*, subject to the *negative* hereafter mentioned.

II   The Assembly to consist of persons elected *by the People* to serve for three years.

III   The Senate to consist of persons elected to serve during *good behaviour*. Their election to be made by *Electors* chosen for that purpose by the People. In order to this The States to be divided into election districts. On the death removal or resignation of any senator his place to be filled out of the district from which he came.

IV   The Supreme Executive authority of the United States to be vested in a *governor* to be elected to serve *during good behaviour.* His election to be made by *Electors* chosen by *electors* chosen by the people in the election districts aforesaid or by electors chosen for that purpose by the respective legislatures—provided that if an election be not made within a limited time the President of the Senate shall be the Governor. The Governor to have *a negative* upon all laws about to be passed and to have the execution of all laws passed—to be the Commander in Chief of the land and naval forces and of the Militia of the United States—to have the direction of war, when authorised or began—to have with the *advice* and *approbation* of the Senate the power of making all treaties—to have the appointment of the *heads or chief* officers of the departments of finance war and foreign affairs—to have the *nomination* of all other officers (ambassadors to foreign nations included) subject to the approbation or rejection of the Senate—to have the power of pardoning all offences but *treason*, which he shall not pardon without the approbation of the Senate.

V   On the death resignation or removal of the Governor his authorities to be exercised by the President of the Senate.

VI   The Senate to have the sole power of *declaring war*—the power of advising and approving all treaties—the power of approving or rejecting all appointments of officers except the heads or chiefs of the departments of finance war and foreign affairs.

VII   The Supreme Judicial authority of the United States to be vested in twelve Judges, to hold their offices during good behaviour with adequate and permanent salaries. This Court to have original jurisdiction in all causes of capture and an appellative jurisdiction (from the Courts of the several states) in all causes in which the revenues of the general government or the citizens of foreign nations are concerned.

VIII   The Legislature of the United States to have power to institute Courts in each state for the determination of all causes of capture and of all matters relating to their revenues, or in which the citizens of foreign nations are concerned.

IX   The Governor Senators and all Officers of the United States to be liable to impeachment for mal and corrupt conduct, and upon conviction to be removed from office and disqualified for holding any place of trust or profit. All impeachments to be tried by a Court to consist of the judges of the Supreme Court chief or Senior Judge of the superior Court of law of each state—provided that such judge hold his place during good behaviour and have a permanent salary.

X   All laws of the particular states contrary to the constitution or laws of the United States to be utterly void. And the better to prevent such laws being passed the Governor or President of each state shall *be appointed by the general government* and shall have a *negative* upon the laws about to be passed in the state of which he is governor or President.

XI   No state to have any forces land or naval—and the *Militia* of all the states to be under the sole and *exclusive direction* of the United States *the officers* of which to be appointed and commissioned by them.

c. June 18, 1787

Speech in the Constitutional Convention on a Plan of Government

James Madison's Version

MR. HAMILTON, had been hitherto silent on the business before the Convention, partly from respect to others whose superior abilities age & experience rendered him unwilling to bring forward ideas dissimilar to theirs, and partly from his delicate situation with respect to his own State, to whose sentiments as expressed by his Colleagues, he could by no means accede. The crisis however which now marked our affairs, was too serious to permit any scruples whatever to prevail over the duty imposed on every man to contribute his efforts for the public safety & happiness. He was obliged therefore to declare himself unfriendly to both plans. He was particularly opposed to that from N. Jersey, being fully convinced, that no amendment of the Confederation, leaving the States in possession of their Sovereignty could possibly answer the purpose. On the other hand he confessed he was much discouraged by the amazing extent of Country in expecting the desired blessings from any general sovereignty that could be substituted. As to the powers of the Convention, he thought the doubts started on that subject had arisen from distinctions & reasonings too subtle. A *federal* Govt. he conceived to mean an association of independent Communities into one. Different Confederacies have different powers, and exercise them in different ways. In some instances the powers are exercised over collective bodies; in others over individuals, as in the German Diet—&

among ourselves in cases of piracy. Great latitude therefore must be given to the signification of the term. The plan last proposed departs itself from the *federal* idea, as understood by some, since it is to operate eventually on individuals. He agreed moreover with the Honble gentleman from Va. (Mr. R.) that we owed it to our Country, to do on this emergency whatever we should deem essential to its happiness. The States sent us here to provide for the exigences of the Union. To rely on & propose any plan not adequate to these exigences, merely because it was not clearly within our powers, would be to sacrifice the means to the end. It may be said that the *States* can not *ratify* a plan not within the purview of the article of Confederation providing for alterations & amendments. But may not the States themselves in which no constitutional authority equal to this purpose exists in the Legislatures, have had in view a reference to the people at large. In the Senate of N. York, a proviso was moved, that no act of the Convention should be binding untill it should be referred to the people & ratified; and the motion was lost by a single voice only, the reason assigned agst. it being, that it might possibly be found an inconvenient shackle.

The great question is what provision shall we make for the happiness of our Country? He would first make a comparative examination of the two plans—prove that there were essential defects in both—and point out such changes as might render a *national one*, efficacious. The great & essential principles necessary for the support of Government are 1. an active & constant interest in supporting it. This principle does not exist in the States in favor of the federal Govt. They have evidently in a high degree, the esprit de corps. They constantly pursue internal interests adverse to those of the whole. They have their particular debts—their particular plans of finance &c. All these when opposed to, invariably prevail over the requisitions & plans of Congress. 2. The love of power. Men love power. The same remarks are applicable to this principle. The States have constantly shewn a disposition rather to regain the powers delegated by them than to part with more, or to give effect to what they had parted with. The ambition of their demagogues is known to hate the controul of the Genl. Government. It may be remarked too that the Citizens have not that anxiety to prevent a dissolution of the Genl. Govt. as of the particular Govts. A dissolution of the latter would be fatal; of the former would still leave the purposes of Govt. attainable to a considerable degree. Consider what such a State as Virga. will be in a few years, a few compared with the life of nations. How strongly will it feel its importance & self-sufficiency? 3. An habitual attachment of the people. The whole force of this tie is on the side of the State Govt. Its sovereignty is immediately before the eyes of the people: its protection is immediately enjoyed by them. From its hand distributive justice, and all those acts which familiarize & endear Govt. to a people, are dispensed to them. 4. *Force* by which may be understood a *coertion of laws* or *coertion of arms*. Congs. have not the former except in few cases. In particular States, this coercion is nearly sufficient; tho' he held it in most cases, not entirely so. A certain portion of military force is absolutely necessary in large communities. Masss. is now feeling this necessity & making provision for it. But how can this force be exerted on the States collectively. It is impossible. It amounts to a war between the parties. Foreign powers also will not be idle spectators. They will interpose, the confusion will increase, and a dissolution of the Union will ensue. 5. *influence*. he did not mean corruption, but a dispensation of those regular honors & emoluments, which produce an attachment to the Govt. Almost all the weight of these is on the side of the States; and must continue so as long as the States continue to exist. All the passions then we see, of avarice, ambition, interest, which govern most individuals, and all public bodies, fall into the current of the States, and do not flow in the stream of the Genl. Govt. The former therefore will generally be an overmatch for the Genl. Govt. and render any confederacy, in its very nature precarious. Theory is in this case fully confirmed by experience. The Amphyctionic Council had it would seem ample powers for general purposes. It had in particular the power of fining and using force agst. delinquent members. What was the consequence. Their decrees were mere signals of war. The Phocian war is a striking example of it. Philip at length taking advantage of their disunion, and insinuating himself into their Councils, made himself master of their fortunes. The German Confederacy affords another lesson. The authority of Charlemagne seemed to be as great as could be necessary. The great feudal chiefs however, exercising their local sovereignties, soon felt the spirit & found the means of, encroachments, which reduced the imperial authority to a nominal sovereignty. The Diet has succeeded, which tho' aided by a Prince at its head, of great authority independently of his imperial attributes, is a striking illustration of the weakness of

Confederated Governments. Other examples instruct us in the same truth. The Swiss cantons have scarce any Union at all, and have been more than once at war with one another. How then are all these evils to be avoided? only by such a compleat sovereignty in the general Governmt. as will turn all the strong principles & passions above mentioned on its side. Does the scheme of N. Jersey produce this effect? does it afford any substantial remedy whatever? On the contrary it labors under great defects, and the defect of some of its provisions will destroy the efficacy of others. It gives a direct revenue to Congs. but this will not be sufficient. The balance can only be supplied by requisitions: which experience proves can not be relied on. If States are to deliberate on the mode, they will also deliberate on the object of the supplies, and will grant or not grant as they approve or disapprove of it. The delinquency of one will invite and countenance it in others. Quotas too must in the nature of things be so unequal as to produce the same evil. To what standard will you resort? Land is a fallacious one. Compare Holland with Russia: France or Engd. with other countries of Europe. Pena. with N. Carola. will the relative pecuniary abilities in those instances, correspond with the relative value of land. Take numbers of inhabitants for the rule and make like comparison of different countries, and you will find it to be equally unjust. The different degrees of industry and improvement in different Countries render the first object a precarious measure of wealth. Much depends too on *situation*. Cont. N. Jersey & N. Carolina, not being commercial States & contributing to the wealth of the commercial ones, can never bear quotas assessed by the ordinary rules of proportion. They will & must fail in their duty, their example will be followed, and the Union itself be dissolved. Whence then is the national revenue to be drawn? from Commerce? even from exports which notwithstanding the common opinion are fit objects of moderate taxation, from excise, &c &c. These tho' not equal, are less unequal than quotas. Another destructive ingredient in the plan, is that equality of suffrage which is so much desired by the small States. It is not in human nature that Va. & the large States should consent to it, or if they did that they shd. long abide by it. It shocks too much the ideas of Justice, and every human feeling. Bad principles in a Govt. tho slow are sure in their operation, and will gradually destroy it. A doubt has been raised whether Congs. at present have a right to keep Ships or troops in time of peace. He leans to the negative. Mr. Ps. plan provides no remedy. If the powers proposed were adequate, the organization of Congs. is such that they could never be properly & effectually exercised. The members of Congs. being chosen by the States & subject to recall, represent all the local prejudices. Should the powers be found effectual, they will from time to time be heaped on them, till a tyrannic sway shall be established. The general power whatever be its form if it preserves itself, must swallow up the State powers. Otherwise it will be swallowed up by them. It is agst. all the principles of a good Government to vest the requisite powers in such a body as Congs. Two Sovereignties can not co-exist within the same limits. Giving powers to Congs. must eventuate in a bad Govt. or in no Govt. The plan of N. Jersey therefore will not do. What then is to be done? Here he was embarrassed. The extent of the Country to be governed, discouraged him. The expence of a general Govt. was also formidable; unless there were such a diminution of expence on the side of the State Govts. as the case would admit. If they were extinguished, he was persuaded that great œconomy might be obtained by substituting a general Govt. He did not mean however to shock the public opinion by proposing such a measure. On the other hand he saw no *other* necessity for declining it. They are not necessary for any of the great purposes of commerce, revenue, or agriculture. Subordinate authorities he was aware would be necessary. There must be district tribunals: corporations for local purposes. But cui bono, the vast & expensive apparatus now appertaining to the States. The only difficulty of a serious nature which occurred to him, was that of drawing representatives from the extremes to the center of the Community. What inducements can be offered that will suffice? The moderate wages for the 1st. branch would only be a bait to little demagogues. Three dollars or thereabouts he supposed would be the utmost. The Senate he feared from a similar cause, would be filled by certain undertakers who wish for particular offices under the Govt. This view of the subject almost led him to despair that a Republican Govt. could be established over so great an extent. He was sensible at the same time that it would be unwise to propose one of any other form. In his private opinion he had no scruple in declaring, supported as he was by the opinions of so many of the wise & good, that the British Govt. was the best in the world: and that he doubted much whether any thing short of it would do in America. He hoped Gentlemen of different opinions would bear with him in this, and begged them to recollect the change of opinion on this subject which had taken place and was still going on. It was once thought that the power of Congs. was amply sufficient to secure the end of their institution. The error was now seen by every one. The members most tenacious of republicanism, he observed, were as loud as any in declaiming agst. the vices of democracy. This progress of the public mind led him to anticipate the time, when others as well as himself would join in the praise bestowed by Mr. Neckar on the British Constitution, namely, that it is the only Govt. in the world "which unites public strength with individual security." In every community where industry is encouraged, there will be a division of it into the few & the many. Hence separate interests will arise. There will be debtors & creditors &c. Give all power to the many, they will oppress the few. Give all power to the few, they will oppress the many. Both therefore ought to have power, that each may defend itself agst. the other. To the want of this check we owe our paper money, instalment laws &c. To the proper adjustment of it the British owe the excellence of their Constitution. Their house of Lords is a most noble institution. Having nothing to hope for by a change, and a sufficient interest by means of their property, in being faithful to the national interest, they form a permanent barrier agst. every pernicious innovation, whether attempted on the part of the Crown or of the Commons. No temporary Senate will have the firmness eno' to answer the purpose. The Senate (of Maryland) which seems to be so much appealed to, has not yet been sufficiently tried. Had the people been unanimous & eager, in the late appeal to them on the subject of a paper emission they would have yielded to the torrent. Their acquiescing in such an appeal is a proof of it. Gentlemen differ in their opinions concerning the necessary checks, from the different estimates they form of the human passions. They suppose seven years a sufficient period to give the senate an adequate firmness, from not duly considering the amazing violence & turbulence of the democratic spirit. When a great object of Govt. is pursued, which seizes the popular passions, they spread like wild fire, and become irresistable. He appealed to the gentlemen from the N. England States whether experience had not there verified the remark. As to the Executive, it seemed to be admitted that no good one could be established on Republican principles. Was not this giving up the merits of the question: for can there be a good Govt. without a good Executive.

The English model was the only good one on this subject. The Hereditary interest of the King was so interwoven with that of the Nation, and his personal emoluments so great, that he was placed above the danger of being corrupted from abroad—and at the same time was both sufficiently independent and sufficiently controuled, to answer the purpose of the institution at home. one of the weak sides of Republics was their being liable to foreign influence & corruption. Men of little character, acquiring great power become easily the tools of intermedling Neibours. Sweeden was a striking instance. The French & English had each their parties during the late Revolution which was effected by the predominant influence of the former. What is the inference from all these observations? That we ought to go as far in order to attain stability and permanency, as republican principles will admit. Let one branch of the Legislature hold their places for life or at least during good behaviour. Let the Executive also be for life. He appealed to the feelings of the members present whether a term of seven years, would induce the sacrifices of private affairs which an acceptance of public trust would require, so so as to ensure the services of the best Citizens. On this plan we should have in the Senate a permanent will, a weighty interest, which would answer essential purposes. But is this a Republican Govt., it will be asked? Yes if all the Magistrates are appointed, and vacancies are filled, by the people, or a process of election originating with the people. He was sensible that an Executive constituted as he proposed would have in fact but little of the power and independence that might be necessary. On the other plan of appointing him for 7 years, he thought the Executive ought to have but little power. He would be ambitious, with the means of making creatures; and as the object of his ambition wd. be to *prolong* his power, it is probable that in case of a war, he would avail himself of the emergence, to evade or refuse a degradation from his place. An Executive for life has not this motive for forgetting his fidelity, and will therefore be a safer depository of power. It will be objected probably, that such an Executive will be an *elective Monarch*, and will give birth to the tumults which characterize that form of Govt. He wd. reply that *Monarch* is an indefinite term. It marks not either the degree or duration of power. If this Executive Magistrate wd. be a monarch for life—the other propd. by the Report from the Comtte of the whole, wd. be a monarch for seven years. The circumstance of being elective was also applicable to both. It had been observed by judicious writers that elective monarchies wd. be the best if they could be guarded agst. the *tumults* excited by the ambition and intrigues of competitors. He was not sure that tumults were an inseparable evil. He rather thought this character of Elective Monarchies had been taken rather from particular cases than from general principles. The election of Roman Emperors was made by the *Army*. In *Poland* the election is made by great rival *princes* with independent power, and ample means, of raising commotions. In the German Empire, the appointment is made by the Electors & Princes, who have equal motives & means, for exciting cabals & parties. Might not such a mode of election be devised among ourselves as will defend the community agst. these effects in any dangerous degree? Having made these observations he would read to the Committee a sketch of a plan which he shd. prefer to either of those under consideration. He was aware that it went beyond the ideas of most members. But will such a plan be adopted out of doors? In return he would ask will the people adopt the other plan? At present they will adopt neither. But he sees the Union dissolving or already dissolved—he sees evils operating in the States which must soon cure the people of their fondness for democracies—he sees that a great progress has been already made & is still going on in the public mind. He thinks therefore that the people will in time be unshackled from their prejudices; and whenever that happens, they will themselves not be satisfied at stopping where the plan of Mr. R. wd. place them, but be ready to go as far at least as he proposes. He did not mean to offer the paper he had sketched as a proposition to the Committee. It was meant only to give a more correct view of his ideas, and to suggest the amendments which he should probably propose to the plan of Mr. R. in the proper stages of its future discussion. He read his sketch in the words following: towit . . ."

On these several articles he entered into explanatory observations corresponding with the principles of his introductory reasoning.

Robert Yates's Version

Mr. Hamilton. To deliver my sentiments on so important a subject, when the first characters in the union have gone before me, inspires me with the greatest diffidence, especially when my own ideas are so materially dissimilar to the plans now before the committee. My situation is disagreeable, but it would be criminal not to come forward on a question of such magnitude. I have well considered the subject, and am convinced that no amendment of the confederation can answer the purpose of a good government, so long as state sovereignties do, in any shape, exist; and I have great doubts whether a national government on the Virginia plan can be made effectual. What is federal? An association of several independent states into one. How or in what manner this association is formed, is not so clearly distinguishable. We find the diet of Germany has in some instances the power of legislation on individuals. We find the United States of America have it in an extensive degree in the cases of piracies.

Let us now review the powers with which we are invested. We are appointed for the *sole* and *express* purpose of revising the confederation, and to *alter* or *amend* it, so as to render it effectual for the purposes of a good government. Those who suppose it must be federal, lay great stress on the terms *sole* and *express*, as if these words intended a confinement to a federal government; when the manifest import is no more than that the institution of a good government must be the *sole* and *express* object of your deliberations. Nor can we suppose an annihilation of our powers by forming a national government, as many of the states have made in their constitutions no provision for any alteration; and thus much I can say for the state I have the honor to represent, that when our credentials were under consideration in the senate, some members were for inserting a restriction in the powers, to prevent an encroachment on the constitution: it was answered by others, and thereupon the resolve carried on the credentials, that it might abridge some of the constitutional powers of the state, and that possibly in the formation of a new union it would be found necessary. This appears reasonable, and therefore leaves us at liberty to form such a national government as we think best adapted for the good of the whole. I have therefore no difficulty as to the extent of our powers, nor do I feel myself restrained in the exercise of my judgment under them. We can only propose and recommend—the power of ratifying or rejecting is still in the states. But on this great question I am still greatly embarrassed. I have before observed my apprehension of the inefficacy of either plan, and I have great doubts whether a more energetic government can pervade this wide and extensive country. I shall now show, that both plans are materially defective.

1. A good government ought to be constant, and ought to contain an active principle.

2. Utility and necessity.

3. An habitual sense of obligation.

4. Force.

5. Influence.

I hold it, that different societies have all different views and interests to pursue, and always prefer local to general concerns. For example: New-York legislature made an external compliance lately to a requisition of congress; but do they not at the same time counteract their compliance by gratifying the local objects of the state so as to defeat their concession? And this will ever be the case. Men always love power, and states will prefer their particular concerns to the general welfare; and as the states become large and important, will they not be less attentive to the general government? What, in process of time will Virginia be? She contains now half a million inhabitants—in twenty-five years she will double the number. Feeling her own weight and importance, must she not become indifferent to the concerns of the union? And where, in such a situation, will be found national attachment to the general government?

By *force*, I mean the *coercion* of law and the coercion of arms. Will this remark apply to the power intended to be vested in the government to be instituted by either plan? A delinquent must be compelled to obedience by force of arms. How is this to be done? If you are unsuccessful, a dissolution of your government must be the consequence; and in that case the individual legislatures will reassume their powers; nay, will not the interest of the states be thrown into the state governments?

By *influence*, I mean the regular weight and support it will receive from those who will find it their interest to support a government intended to preserve the peace and happiness of the community of the whole. The state governments, by either plan, will exert the means to counteract it. They have their state judges and militia all combined to support their state interests; and these will be influenced to oppose a national government. Either plan is therefore precarious. The national government cannot long exist when opposed by such a weighty rival. The experience of ancient and modern confederacies evince this point, and throw considerable light on the subject. The amphyctionic council of Greece had a right to require of its members troops, money and the force of the country. Were they obeyed in the exercise of those powers? Could they preserve the peace of the greater states and republics? or where were they obeyed? History shows that their decrees were disregarded, and that the stronger states, regardless of their power, gave law to the lesser.

Let us examine the federal institution of Germany. It was instituted upon the laudable principle of securing the independency of the several states of which it was composed, and to protect them against foreign invasion. Has it answered these good intentions? Do we not see that their councils are weak and distracted, and that it cannot prevent the wars and confusions which the respective electors carry on against each other? The Swiss cantons, or the Helvetic union, are equally inefficient.

Such are the lessons which the experience of others affords us, and from whence results the evident conclusion that all federal governments are weak and distracted. To avoid the evils deducible from these observations, we must establish a general and national government, completely sovereign, and annihilate the state distinctions and state operations; and unless we do this, no good purpose can be answered. What does the Jersey plan propose? It surely has not this for its object. By this we grant the regulation of trade and a more effectual collection of the revenue, and some partial duties. These, at five or ten per cent, would only perhaps amount to a fund to discharge the debt of the corporation.

Let us take a review of the variety of important objects, which must necessarily engage the attention of a national government. You have to protect your rights against Canada on the north, Spain on the south, and your western frontier against the savages. You have to adopt necessary plans for the settlement of your frontiers, and to institute the mode in which settlements and good government are to be made.

How is the expense of supporting and regulating these important matters to be defrayed? By requisition on the states, according to the Jersey plan? Will this do it? We have already found it ineffectual. Let one state prove delinquent, and it will encourage others to follow the example; and thus the whole will fail. And what is the standard to quota among the states their respective proportions? Can lands be the standard? How would that apply between Russia and Holland? Compare Pennsylvania with North-Carolina, or Connecticut with

New-York. Does not commerce or industry in the one or other make a great disparity between these different countries, and may not the comparative value of the states from these circumstances, make an unequal disproportion when the data is numbers? I therefore conclude that either system would ultimately destroy the confederation, or any other government which is established on such fallacious principles. Perhaps imposts, taxes on specific articles, would produce a more equal system of drawing a revenue.

Another objection against the Jersey plan is, the unequal representation. Can the great States consent to this? If they did it would eventually work its own destruction. How are forces to be raised by the Jersey plan? By quotas? Will the states comply with the requisition? As much as they will with the taxes.

Examine the present confederation, and it is evident they can raise no troops nor equip vessels before war is actually declared. They cannot therefore take any preparatory measure before an enemy is at your door. How unwise and inadequate their powers! and this must ever be the case when you attempt to define powers. Something will always be wanting. Congress, by being annually elected, and subject to recall, will ever come with the prejudices of their states rather than the good of the union. Add therefore additional powers to a body thus organized, and you establish a *sovereignty* of the worst kind, consisting of a single body. Where are the checks? None. They must either prevail over the state governments, or the prevalence of the state governments must end in their dissolution. This is a conclusive objection to the Jersey plan.

Such are the insuperable objections to both plans: and what is to be done on this occasion? I confess I am at a loss. I foresee the difficulty on a consolidated plan of drawing a representation from so extensive a continent to one place. What can be the inducements for gentlemen to come 600 miles to a national legislature? The expense would at least amount to £100,000. This however can be no conclusive objection if it eventuates in an extinction of state governments. The burthen of the latter would be saved, and the expense then would not be great. State distinctions would be found unnecessary, and yet I confess, to carry government to the extremities, the state governments reduced to corporations, and with very limited powers, might be necessary, and the expense of the national government become less burthensome.

Yet, I confess, I see great difficulty of drawing forth a good representation. What, for example, will be the inducements for gentlemen of fortune and abilities to leave their houses and business to attend annually and long? It cannot be the wages; for these, I presume, must be small. Will not the power, therefore, be thrown into the hands of the demagogue or middling politician, who, for the sake of a small stipend and the hopes of advancement, will offer himself as a candidate, and the real men of weight and influence, by remaining at home, add strength to the state governments? I am at a loss to know what must be done; I despair that a republican form of government can remove the difficulties. Whatever may be my opinion, I would hold it however unwise to change that form of government. I believe the British government forms the best model the world ever produced, and such has been its progress in the minds of the many, that this truth gradually gains ground. This government has for its object *public strength* and *individual security*. It is said with us to be unattainable. If it was once formed it would maintain itself. All communities divide themselves into the few and the many. The first are the rich and well born, the other the mass of the people. The voice of the people has been said to be the voice of God; and however generally this maxim has been quoted and believed, it is not true in fact. The people are turbulent and changing; they seldom judge or determine right. Give therefore to the first class a distinct, permanent share in the government. They will check the unsteadiness of the second, and as they cannot receive any advantage by a change, they therefore will ever maintain good government. Can a democratic assembly, who annually revolve in the mass of the people, be supposed steadily to pursue the public good? Nothing but a permanent body can check the imprudence of democracy. Their turbulent and uncontrouling disposition requires checks. The senate of New-York, although chosen for four years, we have found to be inefficient. Will, on the Virginia plan, a continuance of seven years do it? It is admitted, that you cannot have a good executive upon a democratic plan. See the excellency of the British executive. He is placed above temptation. He can have no distinct interests from the public welfare. Nothing short of such an executive can be efficient. The weak side of a republican government is the danger of foreign influence. This is unavoidable, unless it is so constructed as to bring forward its first characters in its support. I am therefore for a general government, yet would wish to go the full length of republican principles.

Let one body of the legislature be constituted during good behaviour or life.

Let one executive be appointed who dares execute his powers.

It may be asked is this a republican system? It is strictly so, as long as they remain elective.

And let me observe, that an executive is less dangerous to the liberties of the people when in office during life, than for seven years.

It may be said, this constitutes an elective monarchy? Pray, what is a monarchy? May not the governors of the respective states be considered in that light? But by making the executive subject to impeachment, the term monarchy cannot apply. These elective monarchs have produced tumults in Rome, and are equally dangerous to peace in Poland; but this cannot apply to the mode in which I would propose the election. Let electors be appointed in each of the states to elect the executive— (*Here Mr. H. produced his plan, a copy whereof is hereunto annexed,*) to consist of two branches—and I would give them the unlimited power of passing all laws without exception. The assembly to be elected for three years by the people in districts—the senate to be elected by the electors to be chosen for that purpose by the people, and to remain in office during life. The executive to have the power of negativing all laws—to make war or peace, with the advice of the senate—to make treaties with their advice, but to have the sole direction of all military operations, and to send ambassadors and appoint all military officers, and to pardon all offenders, treason excepted, unless by advice of the senate. On his death or removal, the president of the senate to officiate, with the same powers, until another is elected. Supreme judicial officers to be appointed by the executive and senate. The legislature to appoint courts in each state, so as to make the state governments unnecessary to it.

All state laws to be absolutely void which contravene the general laws. An officer to be appointed in each state to have a negative on all state laws. All the militia and the appointment of officers to be under the national government.

I confess that this plan and that from Virginia are very remote from the idea of the people. Perhaps the Jersey plan is nearest their expectation. But the people are gradually ripening in their opinions of government— they begin to be tired of an excess of democracy—and what even is the Virginia plan, but *pork still, with a little change of the sauce.*

June 18, 1787

To George Washington

Dr. Sir.

In my passage through the Jerseys and since my arrival here I have taken particular pains to discover the public sentiment and I am more and more convinced that this is the critical opportunity for establishing the prosperity of this country on a solid foundation. I have conversed with men of information not only of this City but from different parts of the state; and they agree that there has been an astonishing revolution for the better in the minds of the people. The prevailing apprehension among thinking men is that the Convention, from a fear of shocking the popular opinion, will not go far enough. They seem to be convinced that a strong well mounted government will better suit the popular palate than one of a different complexion. Men in office are indeed taking all possible pains to give an unfavourable impression of the Convention; but the current seems to be running strongly the other way.

A plain but sensible man, in a conversation I had with him yesterday, expressed himself nearly in this manner. The people begin to be convinced that their "excellent form of government" as they have been used to call it, will not answer their purpose; and that they must substitute something not very remote from that which they have lately quitted.

These appearances though they will not warrant a conclusion that the people are yet ripe for such a plan as I advocate, yet serve to prove that there is no reason to despair of their adopting one equally energetic, if the Convention should think proper to propose it. They serve to prove that we ought not to allow too much weight to objections drawn from the supposed repugnancy of the people to an efficient constitution. I confess I am more and more inclined to believe that former habits of thinking are regaining their influence with more rapidity than is generally imagined.

Not having compared ideas with you, Sir, I cannot judge how far our sentiments agree; but as I persuade myself the genuineness of my representations will receive credit with you, my anxiety for the event of the deliberations of the Convention induces me to make this communication of what appears to be the tendency of the public mind. I own to you Sir that I am seriously and deeply distressed at the aspect of the Councils which prevailed when I left Philadelphia. I fear that we shall let slip the golden opportunity of rescuing the American empire from disunion anarchy and misery. No motley or feeble measure can answer the end or will finally receive the public support. Decision is true wisdom and will be not less reputable to the Convention than salutary to the community.

I shall of necessity remain here ten or twelve days; if I have reason to believe that my attendance at Philadelphia will not be mere waste of time, I shall after that period rejoin the Convention.

I remain with sincere esteem Dr Sir Yr. Obed serv

A HAMILTON

July 3d. 87

Conjectures About the New Constitution

The new constitution has in favour of its success these circumstances—a very great weight of influence of the persons who framed it, particularly in the universal popularity of General Washington—the good will of the commercial interest throughout the states which will give all its efforts to the establishment of a government capable of regulating protecting and extending the commerce of the Union—the good will of most men of property in the several states who wish a government of the union able to protect them against domestic violence and the depredations which the democratic spirit is apt to make on property; and who are besides anxious for the respectability of the nation—the hopes of the Creditors of the United States that a general government possessing the means of doing it will pay the debt of the Union—a strong belief in the people at large of the insufficiency of the present confederation to preserve the existence of the Union and of the necessity of the union to their safety and prosperity; of course a strong desire of a change and a predisposition to receive well the propositions of the Convention.

Against its success is to be put the dissent of two or three important men in the Convention; who will think their characters pleged to defeat the plan—the influence of many *inconsiderable* men in possession of considerable offices under the state governments who will fear a diminution of their consequence, power and emolument by the establishment of the general government and who can hope for nothing there—the influence of some *considerable* men in office possessed of talents and popularity who partly from the same motives and partly from a desire of *playing a part* in a convulsion for their own aggrandisement will oppose the quiet adoption of the new government—(some considerable men out of office, from motives of ambition may be disposed to act the same part)—add to these causes the disinclination of the people to taxes, and of course to a strong government—the opposition of all men much in debt who will not wish to see a government established one object of which is to restrain the means of cheating Creditors—the democratical jealousy of the people which may be alarmed at the appearance of institutions that may seem calculated to place the power of the community in few hands and to raise a few individuals to stations of great preeminence—and the influence of some foreign powers who from different motives will not wish to see an energetic government established throughout the states.

In this view of the subject it is difficult to form any judgment whether the plan will be adopted or rejected. It must be essentially a matter of conjecture. The present appearances and all other circumstances considered the probability seems to be on the side of its adoption.

But the causes operating against its adoption are powerful and there will be nothing astonishing in the Contrary.

If it do not finally obtain, it is probable the discussion of the question will beget such struggles animosities and heats in the community that this circumstance conspiring with the *real necessity* of an essential change in our present situation will produce civil war. Should this happen, whatever parties prevail it is probable governments very different from the present in their principles will be established. A dismemberment of the Union and monarchies in different portions of it may be expected. It may however happen that no civil war will take place; but several republican confederacies be established between different combinations of the particular states.

A reunion with Great Britain, from universal disgust at a state of commotion, is not impossible, though not much to be feared. The most plausible shape of such a business would be the establishment of a son of the present monarch in the supreme government of this country with a family compact.

If the government be adopted, it is probable general Washington will be the President of the United States. This will insure a wise choice of men to administer the government and a good administration. A good administration will conciliate the confidence and affection of the people and perhaps enable the government to acquire more consistency than the proposed constitution seems to promise for so great a Country. It may then triumph altogether over the state governments and reduce them to an intire subordination, dividing the larger states into smaller districts. The *organs* of the general government may also acquire additional strength.

If this should not be the case, in the course of a few years, it is probable that the contests about the boundaries of power between the particular governments and the general government and the *momentum* of the larger states in such contests will produce a dissolution of the Union. This after all seems to be the most likely result.

But it is almost arrogance in so complicated a subject, depending so intirely on the incalculable fluctuations of the human passions, to attempt even a conjecture about the event.

It will be Eight or Nine months before any certain judgment can be formed respecting the adoption of the Plan.

c. late September 1787

The Federalist No. 1

TO THE PEOPLE OF THE STATE OF NEW YORK.

After an unequivocal experience of the inefficacy of the subsisting Fœderal Government, you are called upon to deliberate on a new Constitution for the United States of America. The subject speaks its own importance; comprehending in its consequences, nothing less than the existence of the UNION, the safety and welfare of the parts of which it is composed, the fate of an empire, in many respects, the most interesting the world. It has been frequently remarked, that it seems to have been reserved to the people of this country, by their conduct and example, to decide the important question, whether societies of men are really capable or not, of establishing good government from reflection and choice, or whether they are forever destined to depend, for their political constitutions, on accident and force. If there be any truth in the remark, the crisis, at which we are arrived, may with propriety be regarded as the æra in which that decision is to be made; and a wrong election of the part we shall act, may, in this view, deserve to be considered as the general misfortune of mankind.

This idea will add the inducements of philanthropy to those of patriotism to heighten the sollicitude, which all considerate and good men must feel for the event. Happy will it be if our choice should be directed by a judicous estimate of our true interests, unperplexed and unbiassed by considerations not connected with the public good. But this is a thing more ardently to be wished, than seriously to be expected. The plan offered to our deliberations, affects too many particular interests, innovates upon too many local institutions, not to involve in its discussion a variety of objects foreign to its merits, and of views, passions and prejudices little favourable to the discovery of truth.

Among the most formidable of the obstacles which the new Constitution will have to encounter, may readily be distinguished the obvious interest of a certain class of men in every State to resist all changes which may hazard a diminution of the power, emolument and consequence of the offices they hold under the State-establishments— and the perverted ambition of another class of men, who will either hope to aggrandise themselves by the confusions of their country, or will flatter themselves with fairer prospects of elevation from the subdivision of the empire into several partial confederacies, than from its union under one government.

It is not, however, my design to dwell upon observations of this nature. I am well aware that it would be disingenuous to resolve indiscriminately the opposition of any set of men (merely because their situations might subject them to suspicion) into interested or ambitious views: Candour will oblige us to admit, that even such men may be actuated by upright intentions; and it cannot be doubted, that much of the opposition which has made its appearance, or may hereafter make its appearance, will spring from sources, blameless at least, if not respectable, the honest errors of minds led astray by preconceived jealousies and fears. So numerous indeed and so powerful are the causes, which serve to give a false bias to the judgment, that we upon many occasions, see wise and good men on the wrong as well as on the right side of questions, of the first magnitude to society. This circumstance, if duly attended to, would furnish a lesson of moderation of those, who are ever so much persuaded of their being in the right, in any controversy. And a further reason for caution, in this respect, might be drawn from the reflection, that we are not always sure, that those who advocate the truth are influenced by purer principles than their antagonists. Ambition, avarice, personal animosity, party opposition, and many other motives, not more laudable than these, are apt to operate as well upon those who support as upon those who oppose the right side of a question. Were there not even these inducements to moderation, nothing could be more illjudged than that intolerant spirit, which has, at all times, characterised political parties. For, in politics as in religion, it is equally absurd to aim at making proselytes by fire and sword. Heresies in either can rarely be cured by persecution.

And yet however just these sentiments will be allowed to be, we have already sufficient indications, that it will happen in this as in all former cases of great national discussion. A torrent of angry and malignant passions will be let loose. To judge from the conduct of the opposite parties, we shall be led to conclude, that they will mutually hope to evince the justness of their opinions, and to increase the number of their converts by the loudness of their declamations, and by the bitterness of their invectives. An enlightened zeal for the energy and efficiency of government will be stigmatised, as the off-spring of a temper fond of despotic power and hostile to the principles of liberty. An overscrupulous jealousy of danger to the rights of the people, which is more commonly the fault of the head than of the heart, will be represented as mere pretence and artifice; the bait for popularity at the expence of public good. It will be forgotten, on the one hand, that jealousy is the usual concomitant of violent love, and that the noble enthusiasm of liberty is too apt to be infected with a spirit of narrow and illiberal distrust. On the other hand, it will be equally forgotten, that the vigour of government is essential to the security of liberty; that, in the contemplation of a sound and well informed judgment, their interest can never be separated; and that a dangerous ambition more often lurks behind the specious mask of zeal for the rights of the people, than under the forbidding appearance of zeal for the firmness and efficiency of government. History will teach us, that the former has been found a much more certain road to the introduction of despotism, than the latter, and that of those men who have overturned the liberties of republics the greatest number have begun their carreer, by paying an obsequious court to the people, commencing Demagogues and ending Tyrants.

In the course of the preceeding observations I have had an eye, my Fellow Citizens, to putting you upon your guard against all attempts, from whatever quarter, to influence your decision in a matter of the utmost moment to your welfare by any impressions other than those which may result from the evidence of truth. You will, no doubt, at the same time, have collected from the general scope of them that they proceed from a source not unfriendly to the new Constitution. Yes, my Countrymen, I own to you, that, after having given it an attentive consideration, I am clearly of opinion, it is your interest to adopt it. I am convinced, that this is the safest course for your liberty, your dignity, and your happiness. I effect not reserves, which I do not feel. I will not amuse you with an appearance of deliberation, when I have decided. I frankly acknowledge to you my convictions, and I will freely lay before you the reasons on which they are founded. The consciousness of good intentions disdains ambiguity. I shall not however multiply professions on this head. My motives must remain in the depository of my own breast: My arguments will be open to all, and may be judged of by all. They shall at least be offered in a spirit, which will not disgrace the cause of truth.

I propose in a series of papers to discuss the following interesting particulars—*The utility of the UNION to your political prosperity—The insufficiency of the present Confederation to preserve that Union—The necessity of a government at least equally energetic with the one proposed to the attainment of this object—The conformity of the proposed constitution to the true principles of republican government—Its analogy to your own state constitution*—and lastly, *The additional security, which its adoption will afford to the preservation of that species of government, to liberty and to property.*

In the progress of this discussion I shall endeavour to give a satisfactory answer to all the objections which shall have made their appearance that may seem to have any claim to your attention.

It may perhaps be thought superfluous to offer arguments to prove the utility of the UNION, a point, no doubt, deeply engraved on the hearts of the great body of the people in every state, and one, which it may be imagined has no adversaries. But the fact is, that we already hear it whispered in the private circles of those who oppose the new constitution, that the Thirteen States are of too great extent for any general system, and that we must of necessity resort to separate confederacies of distinct portions of the whole.* This doctrine will, in all probability, be gradually propagated, till it has votaries enough to countenance an open avowal of it. For nothing can be more evident, to those who are able to take an enlarged view of the subject than the alternative of an adoption of the new Constitution, or a dismemberment of the Union. It will therefore be of use to begin by examining the advantages of that Union, the certain evils and the probable dangers, to which every State will be exposed from its dissolution. This shall accordingly constitute the subject of my next address.

PUBLIUS.

The Independent Journal, October 27, 1787

The Federalist No. 15

TO THE PEOPLE OF THE STATE OF NEW-YORK.

In the course of the preceding papers, I have endeavoured, my Fellow Citizens, to place before you in a clear and convincing light, the importance of Union to your political safety and happiness. I have unfolded to you a complication of dangers to which you would be exposed should you permit that sacred knot which binds the people of America together to be severed or dissolved by ambition or by avarice, by jealousy or by misrepresentation. In the sequel of the inquiry, through which I propose to accompany you, the truths intended to be inculcated will receive further confirmation from facts and arguments hitherto unnoticed. If the road, over which you will still have to pass, should in some places appear to you tedious or irksome, you will recollect, that you are in quest of information on a subject the most momentous which can engage the attention of a free people: that the field through which you have to travel is in itself spacious, and that the difficulties of the journey have been unnecessarily increased by the mazes with which sophistry has beset the way. It will be my aim to

---

* The same idea, tracing the arguments to their consequences, is held out in several of the late publications against the New Constitution.

remove the obstacles to your progress in as compendious a manner, as it can be done, without sacrificing utility to dispatch.

In pursuance of the plan, which I have laid down for the discussion of the subject, the point next in order to be examined is the "insufficiency of the present confederation to the preservation of the Union." It may perhaps be asked, what need is there of reasoning or proof to illustrate a position, which is not either controverted or doubted; to which the understandings and feelings of all classes of men assent; and which in substance is admitted by the opponents as well as by the friends of the New Constitution? It must in truth be acknowledged that however these may differ in other respects, they in general appear to harmonise in this sentiment at least, that there are material imperfections in our national system, and that something is necessary to be done to rescue us from impending anarchy. The facts that support this opinion are no longer objects of speculation. They have forced themselves upon the sensibility of the people at large, and have at length extorted from those, whose mistaken policy has had the principal share in precipitating the extremity, at which we are arrived, a reluctant confession of the reality of those defects in the scheme of our Fœderal Government, which have been long pointed out and regretted by the intelligent friends of the Union.

We may indeed with propriety be said to have reached almost the last stage of national humiliation. There is scarcely any thing that can wound the pride, or degrade the character of an independent nation, which we do not experience. Are there engagements to the performance of which we are held by every tie respectable among men? These are the subjects of constant and unblushing violation. Do we owe debts to foreigners and to our own citizens contracted in a time of imminent peril, for the preservation of our political existence? These remain without any proper or satisfactory provision for their discharge. Have we valuable territories and important posts in the possession of a foreign power, which by express stipulations ought long since to have been surrendered? These are still retained, to the prejudice of our interests not less than of our rights. Are we in a condition to resent, or to repel the aggression? We have neither troops nor treasury nor government.* Are we even in a condition to remonstrate with dignity? The just imputations on our own faith, in respect to the same treaty,

* I mean for the Union.

ought first to be removed. Are we entitled by nature and compact to a free participation in the navigation of the Mississippi? Spain excludes us from it. Is public credit an indispensable resource in time of public danger? We seem to have abandoned its cause as desperate and irretrievable. Is commerce of importance to national wealth? Ours is at the lowest point of declension. Is respectability in the eyes of foreign powers a safe guard against foreign encroachments? The imbecility of our Government even forbids them to treat with us: Our ambassadors abroad are the mere pageants of mimic sovereignty. Is a violent and unnatural decrease in the value of land a symptom of national distress? The price of improved land in most parts of the country is much lower than can be accounted for by the quantity of waste land at market, and can only be fully explained by that want of private and public confidence, which are so alarmingly prevalent among all ranks and which have a direct tendency to depreciate property of every kind. Is private credit the friend and patron of industry? That most useful kind which relates to borrowing and lending is reduced within the narrowest limits, and this still more from an opinion of insecurity than from the scarcity of money. To shorten an enumeration of particulars which can afford neither pleasure nor instruction it may in general be demanded, what indication is there of national disorder, poverty and insignificance that could befal a community so peculiarly blessed with natural advantages as we are, which does not form a part of the dark catalogue of our public misfortunes?

This is the melancholy situation, to which we have been brought by those very maxims and councils, which would now deter us from adopting the proposed constitution; and which not content with having conducted us to the brink of a precipice, seem resolved to plunge us into the abyss, that awaits us below. Here, my Countrymen, impelled by every motive that ought to influence an enlightened people, let us make a firm stand for our safety, our tranquillity, our dignity, our reputation. Let us at last break the fatal charm which has too long seduced us from the paths of felicity and prosperity.

It is true, as has been before observed, that facts too stubborn to be resisted have produced a species of general assent to the abstract proposition that there exist material defects in our national system; but the usefulness of the concession, on the part of the old adversaries of fœderal measures, is destroyed by a strenuous opposition to a remedy, upon the only principles, that can give it a chance of success. While they admit that the Government of the United States is destitute of energy; they contend against conferring upon it those powers which are requisite to supply that energy: They seem still to aim at things repugnant and irreconcilable—at an augmentation of Fœderal authority without a diminution of State authority—at sovereignty in the Union and complete independence in the members. They still in fine seem to cherish with blind devotion the political monster of an *imperium in imperio*. This renders a full display of the principal defects of the confederation necessary, in order to shew, that the evils we experience do not proceed from minute or partial imperfections, but from fundamental errors in the structure of the building which cannot be amended otherwise than by an alteration in the first principles and main pillars of the fabric.

The great and radical vice in the construction of the existing Confederation is in the principle of LEGISLATION for STATES or GOVERNMENTS, in their CORPORATE or COLLECTIVE CAPACITIES and as contradistinguished from the INDIVIDUALS of whom they consist. Though this principle does not run through all the powers delegated to the Union; yet it pervades and governs those, on which the efficacy of the rest depends. Except as to the rule of apportionment, the United States have an indefinite discretion to make requisitions for men and money; but they have no authority to raise either by regulations extending to the individual citizens of America. The consequence of this is, that though in theory their resolutions concerning those objects are laws, constitutionally binding on the members of the Union, yet in practice they are mere recommendations, which the States observe or disregard at their option.

It is a singular instance of the capriciousness of the human mind, that after all the admonitions we have had from experience on this head, there should still be found men, who object to the New Constitution for deviating from a principle which has been found the bane of the old; and which is in itself evidently incompatible with the idea of GOVERNMENT; a principle in short which if it is to be executed at all must substitute the violent and sanguinary agency of the sword to the mild influence of the Magistracy.

There is nothing absurd or impracticable in the idea of a league or alliance between independent nations, for certain defined purposes precisely stated in a treaty; regulating all the details of time, place, circumstance and quantity; leaving nothing to future discretion; and depending for its execution on the good faith of the parties. Compacts of this kind exist among all civilized nations subject to the usual vicissitudes of peace and war, of observance and non observance, as the interests or passions of the contracting powers dictate. In the early part of the present century, there was an epidemical rage in Europe for this species of compacts; from which the politicians of the times fondly hoped for benefits which were never realised. With a view to establishing the equilibrium of power and the peace of that part of the world, all the resources of negotiation were exhausted, and triple and quadruple alliances were formed; but they were scarcely formed before they were broken, giving an instructive but afflicting lesson to mankind how little dependence is to be placed on treaties which have no other sanction than the obligations of good faith; and which oppose general considerations of peace and justice to the impulse of any immediate interest and passion.

If the particular States in this country are disposed to stand in a similar relation to each other, and to drop the project of a general DISCRETIONARY SUPERINTENDENCE, the scheme would indeed be pernicious, and would entail upon us all the mischiefs that have been enumerated under the first head; but it would have the merit of being at least consistent and practicable. Abandoning all views towards a confederate Government, this would bring us to a simple alliance offensive and defensive; and would place us in a situation to be alternately friends and enemies of each other as our mutual jealousies and rivalships nourished by the intrigues of foreign nations should prescribe to us.

But if we are unwilling to be placed in this perilous situation; if we will still adhere to the design of a national government, or which is the same thing of a superintending power under the direction of a common Council, we must resolve to incorporate into our plan those ingredients which may be considered as forming the characteristic difference between a league and a government; we must extend the authority of the union to the persons of the citizens,—the only proper objects of government.

Government implies the power of making laws. It is essential to the idea of a law, that it be attended with a sanction; or, in other words, a penalty or punishment for disobedience. If there be no penalty annexed to disobedience, the resolutions or commands which pretend to be laws will in fact amount to nothing more than advice or recommendation. This penalty, whatever it may be, can only be inflicted in two ways; by the agency of the Courts and Ministers of Justice, or by military force; by the COERTION of the magistracy, or by the COERTION of arms. The first kind can evidently apply only to men—the last kind must of necessity be employed against bodies politic, or communities or States. It is evident, that there is no process of a court by which their observance of the laws can in the last resort be enforced. Sentences may be denounced against them for violations of their duty; but these sentences can only be carried into execution by the sword. In an association where the general authority is confined to the collective bodies of the communities that compose it, every breach of the laws must involve a state of war, and military execution must become the only instrument of civil obedience. Such a state of things can certainly not deserve the name of government, nor would any prudent man choose to commit his happiness to it.

There was a time when we were told that breaches, by the States, of the regulations of the fœderal authority were not to be expected—that a sense of common interest would preside over the conduct of the respective members, and would beget a full compliance with all the constitutional requisitions of the Union. This language at the present day would appear as wild as a great part of what we now hear from the same quarter will be thought, when we shall have received further lessons from that best oracle of wisdom, experience. It at all times betrayed an ignorance of the true springs by which human conduct is actuated, and belied the original inducements to the establishment of civil power. Why has government been instituted at all? Because the passions of men will not conform to the dictates of reason and justice, without constraint. Has it been found that bodies of men act with more rectitude or greater disinterestedness than individuals? The contrary of this has been inferred by all accurate observers of the conduct of mankind; and the inference is founded upon obvious reasons. Regard to reputation has a less active influence, when the infamy of a bad action is to be divided among a number, than when it is to fall singly upon one. A spirit of faction which is apt to mingle its poison in the deliberations of all bodies of men, will often hurry the persons of whom they are composed into improprieties and excesses, for which they would blush in a private capacity.

In addition to all this, there is in the nature of sovereign power an impatience of controul, that disposes those who are invested with the exercise of it, to look with an evil eye upon all external attempts to restrain or direct its operations. From this spirit it happens that in every political association which is formed upon the principle of uniting in a common interest a number of lesser sovereignties, there will be found a kind of excentric tendency in the subordinate or inferior orbs, by the operation of which there will be a perpetual effort in each to fly off from the common center. This tendency is not difficult to be accounted for. It has its origin in the love of power. Power controuled or abridged is almost always the rival and enemy of that power by which it is controuled or abriged. This simple proposition will teach us how little reason there is to expect, that the persons, entrusted with the administration of the affairs of the particular members of a confederacy, will at all times be ready, with perfect good humour, and an unbiassed regard to the public weal, to execute the resolutions or decrees of the general authority. The reverse of this results from the constitution of human nature.

If therefore the measures of the confederacy cannot be executed, without the intervention of the particular administrations, there will be little prospect of their being executed at all. The rulers of the respective members, whether they have a constitutional right to do it or not, will undertake to judge of the propriety of the measures themselves. They will consider the conformity of the thing proposed or required to their immediate interests or aims, the momentary conveniences or inconveniences that would attend its adoption. All this will be done, and in a spirit of interested and suspicious scrutiny, without that knowledge of national circumstances and reasons of state, which is essential to a right judgment, and with that strong predilection in favour of local objects, which can hardly fail to mislead the decision. The same process must be repeated in every member of which the body is constituted; and the execution of the plans, framed by the councils of the whole, will always fluctuate on the discretion of the ill-informed and prejudiced opinion of every part. Those who have been conversant in the proceedings of popular assemblies; who have seen how difficult it often is, when there is no exterior pressure of circumstances, to bring them to harmonious resolutions on important points, will readily conceive how impossible it must be to induce a number of such assemblies, deliberating at a distance from each other, at different times, and under different impressions, long to cooperate in the same views and pursuits.

In our case, the concurrence of thirteen distinct sovereign wills is requisite under the confederation to the complete execution of every important measure, that proceeds from the Union. It has happened as was to have been foreseen. The measures of the Union have not been executed; and the delinquencies of the States have step by step matured themselves to an extreme; which has at length arrested all the wheels of the national government, and brought them to an awful stand. Congress at this time scarcely possess the means of keeping up the forms of administration; 'till the States can have time to agree upon a more substantial substitute for the present shadow of a fœderal government. Things did not come to this desperate extremity at once. The causes which have been specified produced at first only unequal and disproportionate degrees of compliance with the requisitions of the Union. The greater deficiencies of some States furnished the pretext of example and the temptation of interest to the complying, or to the least delinquent States. Why should we do more in proportion than those who are embarked with us in the same political voyage? Why should we consent to bear more than our proper share of the common burthen? These were suggestions which human selfishness could not withstand, and which even speculative men, who looked forward to remote consequences, could not, without hesitation, combat. Each State yielding to the persuasive voice of immediate interest and convenience has successively withdrawn its support, 'till the frail and tottering edifice seems ready to fall upon our heads and to crush us beneath its ruins.

PUBLIUS.
The Independent Journal, December 1, 1787

The Federalist No. 35

Before we proceed to examine any other objections to an indefinite power of taxation in the Union, I shall make one general remark; which is, that if the jurisdiction of the national government in the article of revenue should be restricted to particular objects, it would naturally occasion an undue proportion of the public burthens to fall upon those objects. Two evils would spring from this source, the oppression of particular branches of industry, and an unequal distribution of the taxes, as well among the several States as among the citizens of the same State.

Suppose, as has been contended for, the fœderal power of taxation were to be confined to duties on imports, it is evident that the government, for want of being able to command other resources, would frequently be tempted to extend these duties to an injurious excess. There are persons who imagine that this can never be carried to too great a length; since the higher they are, the more it is alleged they will tend to discourage an extravagant consumption, to produce a favourable balance of trade, and to promote domestic manufactures. But all extremes are pernicious in various ways. Exorbitant duties on imported articles would beget a general spirit of smuggling; which is always prejudicial to the fair trader, and eventually to the revenue itself: They tend to render other classes of the community tributary in an improper degree to the manufacturing classes to whom they give a premature monopoly of the markets: They sometimes force industry out of its more natural channels into others in which it flows with less advantage. And in the last place they oppress the merchant, who is often obliged to pay them himself without any retribution from the consumer. When the demand is equal to the quantity of goods at market, the consumer generally pays the duty; but when the markets happen to be overstocked, a great proportion falls upon the merchant, and sometimes not only exhausts his profits, but breaks in upon his capital. I am apt to think that a division of the duty between the seller and the buyer more often happens than is commonly imagined. It is not always possible to raise the price of a commodity, in exact proportion to every additional imposition laid upon it. The merchant especially, in a country of small commercial capital, is often under a necessity of keeping prices down, in order to a more expeditious sale.

The maxim that the consumer is the payer, is so much oftener true than the reverse of the proposition, that it is far more equitable the duties on imports should go into a common stock, than that they should redound to the exclusive benefit of the importing States. But it is not so generally true as to render it equitable that those duties should form the only national fund. When they are paid by the merchant, they operate as an additional tax upon the importing State; whose citizens pay their proportion of them in the character of consumers. In this view they are productive of inequality among the States; which inequality would be encreased with the encreased extent of the duties. The confinement of the national revenues to this species of imposts, would be attended with inequality, from a different cause between the manufacturing and the non-manufacturing States. The States which can go furthest towards the supply of their own wants, by their own manufactures, will not, according to their numbers of wealth, consume so great a proportion of imported articles, as those States which are not in the same favourable situation; they would not therefore in this mode alone contribute to the public treasury in a ratio to their abilities. To make them do this, it is necessary that recourse be had to excises; the proper objects of which are particular kinds of manufactures. New-York is more deeply interested in these considerations than such of her citizens as contend for limiting the power of the Union to external taxation can be aware of—New-York is an importing State, and is not likely speedily to be to any great extent a manufacturing State. She would of course suffer in a double light from restraining the jurisdiction of the Union to commercial imposts.

So far as these observations tend to inculcate a danger of the import duties being extended to an injurious extreme it may be observed, conformably to a remark made in another part of these papers, that the interest of the revenue itself would be a sufficient guard against such an extreme. I readily admit that this would be the case as long as other resources were open; but if the avenues to them were closed HOPE stimulated by necessity would beget experiments fortified by rigorous precautions and additional penalties; which for a time would have the intended effect, till there had been leisure to contrive expedients to elude these new precautions. The first success would be apt to inspire false opinions; which it might require a long course of subsequent experience to correct. Necessity, especially in politics, often occasions false hopes, false reasonings and a system of measures, correspondently erroneous. But even if this supposed excess should not be a consequence of the limitation of the fœderal power of taxation the inequalities spoken of would still ensue, though not in the same degree, from the other causes that have been noticed. Let us now return to the examination of objections—

One, which if we may judge from the frequency of its repetition seems most to be relied on, is that the house of representatives is not sufficiently numerous for the reception of all the different classes of citizens; in order to combine the interests and feelings of every part of the community, and to produce a due sympathy between the representative body and its constituents. This argument presents itself under a very specious and seducing form; and is well calculated to lay hold of the prejudices to those to whom it is addressed. But when we come to dissect it with attention it will appear to be made up of nothing but fair sounding words. The object it seems to aim at is in the first place impracticable, and in the sense in which it is contended for is unnecessary. I reserve for another place the discussion of the question which relates to the sufficiency of the representative body in respect to numbers; and shall content myself with examining here the particular use which has been made of a contrary supposition in reference to the immediate subject of our inquiries.

The idea of an actual representation of all classes of the people by persons of each class is altogether visionary. Unless it were expressly provided in the Constitution that each different occupation should send one or more members the thing would never take place in practice. Mechanics and manufacturers will always be inclined with few exceptions to give their votes to merchants in preference to persons of their own professions or trades. Those discerning citizens are well aware that the mechanic and manufacturing arts furnish the materials of mercantile enterprise and industry. Many of them indeed are immediately connected with the operations of commerce. They know that the merchant is their natural patron and friend; and they are aware that however great the confidence they may justly feel in their own good sense, their interests can be more effectually promoted by the merchant than by themselves. They are sensible that their habits in life have not been such as to give them those acquired endowments, without which in a deliberative assembly the greatest natural abilities are for the most part useless; and that the influence and weight and superior acquirements of the merchants render them more equal to a contest with any spirit which might happen to infuse itself into the public councils unfriendly to the manufacturing and trading interests. These considerations and many others that might be mentioned prove, and experience confirms it, that artisans and manufacturers will commonly be disposed to bestow their votes upon merchants and those whom they recommend. We must therefore consider merchants as the natural representatives of all these classes of the community.

With regard to the learned professions, little need be observed; they truly form no distinct interest in society; and according to their situation and talents will be indiscriminately the objects of the confidence and choice of each other and of other parts of the community.

Nothing remains but the landed interest; and this in a political view and particularly in relation to taxes I take to be perfectly united from the wealthiest landlord to the poorest tenant. No tax can be laid on land which will not affect the proprietor of millions of acres as well as the proprietor of a single acre. Every land-holder will therefore have a common interest to keep the taxes on land as low as possible; and common interest may always be reckoned upon as the surest bond of sympathy. But if we even could suppose a distinction of interest between the opulent land-holder and the middling farmer, what reason is there to conclude that the first would stand a better chance of being deputed to the national legislature than the last? If we take fact as our guide and look into our own senate and assembly we shall find that moderate proprietors of land prevail in both; nor is this less the case in the senate which consists of a smaller number than in the Assembly, which is composed of a greater number. Where the qualifications of the electors are the same, whether they have to choose a small or a large number their votes will fall upon those in whom they have most confidence; whether these happen to be men of large fortunes or of moderate property or of no property at all.

It is said to be necessary that all classes of citizens should have some of their own number in the representative body, in order that their feelings and interests may be the better understood and attended to. But we have seen that this will never happen under any arrangement that leaves the votes of the people free. Where this is the case, the representative body, with too few exceptions to have any influence on the spirit of the government, will be composed of land-holders, merchants, and men of the learned professions. But where is the danger that the interests and feelings of the different classes of citizens will not be understood or attended to by these three descriptions of men? Will not the land-holder know and feel whatever will promote or injure the interests of landed property? and will he not from his own interest in that species of property be sufficiently prone to resist every attempt to prejudice or incumber it? Will not the merchant understand and be disposed to cultivate as far as may be proper the interests of the mechanic and manufacturing arts to which his commerce is so nearly allied? Will not the man of the learned profession, who will feel a neutrality to the rivalships between the different branches of industry, be likely to prove an impartial arbiter between them, ready to promote either, so far as it shall appear to him conducive to the general interests of the society?

If we take into the account the momentary humors or dispositions which may happen to prevail in particular parts of the society, and to which a wise administration will never be inattentive, is the man whose situation leads to extensive inquiry and information less likely to be a competent judge of their nature, extent and foundation than one whose observation does not travel beyond the circle of his neighbours and acquaintances? Is it not natural that a man who is a candidate for the favour of the people and who is dependent on the suffrages of his fellow-citizens for the continuance of his public honors should take care to inform himself of their dispositions and inclinations and should be willing to allow them their proper degree of influence upon his conduct. This dependence, and the necessity of being bound himself and his posterity by the laws to which he gives his assent are the true, and they are the strong chords of sympathy between the representatives and the constituent.

There is no part of the administration of government that requires extensive information and a thorough knowledge of the principles of political economy so much as the business of taxation. The man who understands those principles best will be least likely to resort to oppressive expedients, or to sacrifice any particular class of citizens to the procurement of revenue. It might be demonstrated that the most productive system of finance will always be the least burthensome. There can be no doubt that in order to a judicious exercise of the power of taxation it is necessary that the person in whose hands it is should be acquainted with the general genius, habits and modes of thinking of the people at large and with the resources of the country. And this is all that can be reasonably meant by a knowledge of the interests and feelings of the people. In any other sense the proposition has either no meaning, or an absurd one. And in that sense let every considerate citizen judge for himself where the requisite qualification is most likely to be found.

PUBLIUS.

The Independent Journal, January 5, 1788

The Federalist No. 70

TO THE PEOPLE OF THE STATE OF NEW-YORK.

There is an idea, which is not without its advocates, that a vigorous executive is inconsistent with the genius of republican government. The enlightened well wishers to this species of government must at least hope that the supposition is destitute of foundation; since they can never admit its truth, without at the same time admitting the condemnation of their own principles. Energy in the executive is a leading character in the definition of good government. It is essential to the protection of the community against foreign attacks: It is not less essential to the steady administration of the laws, to the protection of property against those irregular and high handed combinations, which sometimes interrupt the ordinary course of justice to the security of liberty against the enterprises and assaults of ambition, of faction and of anarchy. Every man the least conversant in Roman story knows how often that republic was obliged to take refuge in the absolute power of a single man, under the formidable title of dictator, as well against the intrigues of ambitious individuals, who aspired to the tyranny, and the seditions of whole classes of the community, whose conduct threatened the existence of all government, as against the invasions of external enemies, who menaced the conquest and destruction of Rome.

There can be no need however to multiply arguments or examples on this head. A feeble executive implies a feeble execution of the government. A feeble execution is but another phrase for a bad execution: And a government ill executed, whatever it may be in theory, must be in practice a bad government.

Taking it for granted, therefore, that all men of sense will agree in the necessity of an energetic executive; it will only remain to inquire, what are the ingredients which constitute this energy—how far can they be combined with those other ingredients which constitute safety in the republican sense? And how far does this combination characterise the plan, which has been reported by the convention?

The ingredients, which constitute energy in the executive, are first unity, secondly duration, thirdly an adequate provision for its support, fourthly competent powers.

The circumstances which constitute safety in the republican sense are, Ist. a due dependence on the people, secondly a due responsibility.

Those politicians and statesmen, who have been the most celebrated for the soundness of their principles, and for the justness of their views, have declared in favor of a single executive and a numerous legislature. They have with great propriety considered energy as the most necessary qualification of the former, and have regarded this as most applicable to power in a single hand; while they have with equal propriety considered the latter as best adapted to deliberation and wisdom, and best calculated to conciliate the confidence of the people and to secure their privileges and interests.

That unity is conducive to energy will not be disputed. Decision, activity, secrecy, and dispatch will generally characterise the proceedings of one man, in a much more eminent degree, than the proceedings of any greater number; and in proportion as the number is increased, these qualities will be diminished.

This unity may be destroyed in two ways; either by vesting the power in two or more magistrates of equal dignity and authority; or by vesting it ostensibly in one man, subject in whole or in part to the controul and co-operation of others, in the capacity of counsellors to him. Of the first the two consuls of Rome may serve as an example; of the last we shall find examples in the constitutions of several of the states. New-York and New-Jersey, if I recollect right, are the only states, which have entrusted the executive authority wholly to single men.* Both these methods of destroying the unity of the executive have their partisans; but the votaries of an executive council are the most

* New-York has no council except for the single purpose of appointing to offices; New-Jersey has a council, whom the governor may consult. But I think from the terms of the constitution their resolutions do not bind him.

numerous. They are both liable, if not to equal, to similar objections; and may in most lights be examined in conjunction.

The experience of other nations will afford little instruction on this head. As far however as it teaches any thing, it teaches us not to be inamoured of plurality in the executive. We have seen that the Achæans on an experiment of two Præetors, were induced to abolish one. The Roman history records many instances of mischiefs to the republic from the dissentions between the consuls, and between the military tribunes, who were at times substituted to the consuls. But it gives us no specimens of any peculiar advantages derived to the state, from the circumstance of the plurality of those magistrates. That the dissentions between them were not more frequent, or more fatal, is matter of astonishment; until we advert to the singular position in which the republic was almost continually placed and to the prudent policy pointed out by the circumstances of the state, and pursued by the consuls, of making a division of the government between them. The Patricians engaged in a perpetual struggle with the Plebeians for the preservation of their antient authorities and dignities; the consuls, who were generally chosen out of the former body, were commonly united by the personal interest they had in the defence of the privileges of their order. In addition to this motive of union, after the arms of the republic had considerably expanded the bounds of its empire, it became an established custom with the consuls to divide the administration between themselves by lot; one of them remaining at Rome to govern the city and its environs; the other taking the command in the more distant provinces. This expedient must no doubt have had great influence in preventing those collisions and rivalships, which might otherwise have embroiled the peace of the republic.

But quitting the dim light of historical research, and attaching ourselves purely to the dictates of reason and good sense, we shall discover much greater cause to reject than to approve the idea of plurality in the executive, under any modification whatever.

Wherever two or more persons are engaged in any common enterprize or pursuit, there is always danger of difference of opinion. If it be a public trust or office in which they are cloathed with equal dignity and authority, there is peculiar danger of personal emulation and even animosity. From either and especially from all these causes, the most bitter dissentions are apt to spring. Whenever these happen, they lessen the respectability, weaken the authority, and distract the plans and operations of those whom they divide. If they should unfortunately assail the supreme executive magistracy of a country, consisting of a plurality of persons, they might impede or frustrate the most important measures of the government, in the most critical emergencies of the state. And what is still worse, they might split the community into the most violent and irreconcilable factions, adhering differently to the different individuals who composed the magistracy.

Men often oppose a thing merely because they have had no agency in planning it, or because it may have been planned by those whom they dislike. But if they have been consulted and have happened to disapprove, opposition then becomes in their estimation an indispensable duty of self love. They seem to think themselves bound in honor, and by all the motives of personal infallibility to defeat the success of what has been resolved upon, contrary to their sentiments. Men of upright, benevolent tempers have too many opportunities of remarking with horror, to what desperate lengths this disposition is sometimes carried, and how often the great interests of society are sacrificed to the vanity, to the conceit and to the obstinacy of individuals, who have credit enough to make their passions and their caprices interesting to mankind. Perhaps the question now before the public may in its consequences afford melancholy proofs of the effects of this despicable frailty, or rather detestable vice in the human character.

Upon the principles of a free government, inconveniencies from the source just mentioned must necessarily be submitted to in the formation of the legislature; but it is unnecessary and therefore unwise to introduce them into the constitution of the executive. It is here too that they may be most pernicious. In the legislature, promptitude of decision is oftener an evil than a benefit. The differences of opinion, and the jarrings of parties in that department of the government, though they may sometimes obstruct salutary plans, yet often promote deliberations and circumspection; and serve to check excesses in the majority. When a resolution too is once taken, the opposition must be at an end. That resolution is a law, and resistance to it punishable. But no favourable circumstances palliate or atone for the disadvantages of dissention in the executive department. Here they are pure and unmixed. There is no point at which they cease to operate. They serve to embarrass and weaken the execution of the plan or measure, to which they relate, from the first step to the final conclusion of it. They constantly counteract those qualities in the executive, which are the most necessary ingredients in its composition, vigour and expedition, and this without any counterballancing good. In the conduct of war, in which the energy of the executive is the bulwark of the national security, every thing would be to be apprehended from its plurality.

It must be confessed that these observations apply with principal weight to the first case supposed, that is to a plurality of magistrates of equal dignity and authority; a scheme the advocates for which are not likely to form a numerous sect: But they apply, though not with equal, yet with considerable weight, to the project of a council, whose concurrence is made constitutionally necessary to the operations of the ostensible executive. An artful cabal in that council would be able to distract and to enervate the whole system of administration. If no such cabal should exist, the mere diversity of views and opinions would alone be sufficient to tincture the exercise of the executive authority with a spirit of habitual feebleness and delatoriness.

But one of the weightiest objections to a plurality in the executive, and which lies as much against the last as the first plan, is that it tends to conceal faults, and destroy responsibility. Responsibility is of two kinds, to censure and to punishment. The first is the most important of the two; especially in an elective office. Man, in public trust, will much oftener act in such a manner as to render him unworthy of being any longer trusted, than in such a manner as to make him obnoxious to legal punishment. But the multiplication of the executive adds to the difficulty of detection in either case. It often becomes impossible, amidst mutual accusations, to determine on whom the blame or the punishment of a pernicious measure, or series of pernicious measures ought really to fall. It is shifted from one to another with so much dexterity, and under such plausible appearances, that the public opinion is left in suspense about the real author. The circumstances which may have led to any national miscarriage or misfortune are sometimes so complicated, that where there are a number of actors who may have had different degrees and kinds of agency, though we may clearly see upon the whole that there has been mismanagement, yet it may be impracticable to pronounce to whose account the evil which may have been incurred is truly chargeable.

"I was overruled by my council. The council were so divided in their opinions, that it was impossible to obtain any better resolution on the point." These and similar pretexts are constantly at hand, whether true or false. And who is there that will either take the trouble or incur the odium of a strict scrutiny into the secret springs of the transaction? Should there be found a citizen zealous enough to undertake the unpromising task, if there happen to be a collusion between the parties concerned, how easy is it to cloath the circumstances with so much ambiguity, as to render it uncertain what was the precise conduct of any of those parties?

In the single instance in which the governor of this state is coupled with a council, that is in the appointment to offices, we have seen the mischiefs of it in the view now under consideration. Scandalous appointments to important offices have been made. Some cases indeed have been so flagrant, that ALL PARTIES have agreed in the impropriety of the thing. When enquiry has been made, the blame has been laid by the governor on the members of the council; who on their part have charged it upon his nomination: While the people remain altogether at a loss to determine by whose influence their interests have been committed to hands so unqualified, and so manifestly improper. In tenderness to individuals, I forbear to descend to particulars.

It is evident from these considerations, that the plurality of the executive tends to deprive the people of the two greatest securities they can have for the faithful exercise of any delegated power; first, the restraints of public opinion, which lose their efficacy as well on account of the division of the censure attendant on bad measures among a number, as on account of the uncertainty on whom it ought to fall; and secondly, the opportunity of discovering with facility and clearness the misconduct of the persons they trust, in order either to their removal from office, or to their actual punishment, in cases which admit of it.

In England the king is a perpetual magistrate; and it is a maxim, which has obtained for the sake of the public peace, that he is unaccountable for his administration, and his person sacred. Nothing therefore can be wiser in that kingdom than to annex to the king a constitutional council, who may be responsible to the nation for the advice they give. Without this there would be no responsibility whatever in the executive department; an idea inadmissible in a free government. But even there the king is not bound by the resolutions of his council, though they are answerable for the advice they give. He is the absolute master of his own conduct, in the exercise of his office; and may observe or disregard the council given to him at his sole discretion.

But in a republic, where every magistrate ought to be personally responsible for his behaviour in office, the reason which in the British constitution dictates the propriety of a council not only ceases to apply, but turns against the institution. In the monarchy of Great-Britain, it furnishes a substitute for the prohibited responsibility of the chief magistrate; which serves in some degree as a hostage to the national justice for his good behaviour. In the American republic it would serve to destroy, or would greatly diminish the intended and necessary responsibility of the chief magistrate himself.

The idea of a council to the executive, which has so generally obtained in the state constitutions, has been derived from that maxim of republican jealousy, which considers power as safer in the hands of a number of men than of a single man. If the maxim should be admitted to be applicable to the case, I should contend that the advantage on that side would not counterballance the numerous disadvantages on the opposite side. But I do not think the rule at all applicable to the executive power. I clearly concur in opinion in this particular with a writer whom the celebrated Junius pronounces to be "deep, solid and ingenious," that, "the executive power is more easily confined when it is one:"* That it is far more safe there should be a single object for the jealousy and watchfulness of the people; and in a word that all multiplication of the executive is rather dangerous than friendly to liberty.

A little consideration will satisfy us, that the species of security sought for in the multiplication of the executive is unattainable. Numbers must be so great as to render combination difficult; or they are rather a source of danger than of security. The united credit and influence of several individuals must be more formidable to liberty than the credit and influence of either of them separately. When power therefore is placed in the hands of so small a number of men, as to admit of their interests and views being easily combined in a common enterprise, by an artful leader, it becomes more liable to abuse and more dangerous when abused, than if it be lodged in the hands of one man; who from the very circumstance of his being alone will be more narrowly watched and more readily suspected, and who cannot unite so great a mass of influence as when he is associated with others. The Decemvirs of Rome,

* De Lome.

whose name denotes their number,* were more to be dreaded in their usurpation than any ONE of them would have been. No person would think of proposing an executive much more numerous than that body, from six to a dozen have been suggested for the number of the council. The extreme of these numbers is not too great for an easy combination; and from such a combination America would have more to fear, than from the ambition of any single individual. A council to a magistrate, who is himself responsible for what he does, are generally nothing better than a clog upon his good intentions; are often the instruments and accomplices of his bad, and are almost always a cloak to his faults.

I forbear to dwell upon the subject of expence; though it be evident that if the council should be numerous enough to answer the principal end, aimed at by the institution, the salaries of the members, who must be drawn from their homes to reside at the seat of government, would form an item in the catalogue of public expenditures, too serious to be incurred for an object of equivocal utility.

I will only add, that prior to the appearance of the constitution, I rarely met with an intelligent man from any of the states, who did not admit as the result of experience, that the UNITY of the Executive of this state was one of the best of the distinguishing features of our constitution.

PUBLIUS.
The Independent Journal, March 15, 1788

To James Madison

Some days since I wrote to you, My Dear Sir, inclosing a letter from a Mr. V Der Kemp &c.

I then mentioned to you that the question of a majority for or against the constitution would depend upon the County of Albany. By the latter accounts from that quarter I fear much that the issue there has been against us.

As Clinton is truly the leader of his party, and is inflexibly obstinate I count little on overcoming opposition by reason. Our only chances will be the previous ratification by nine states, which may shake the firmness of his followers; and a change in the sentiments of the people

* Ten.

which have been for some time travelling towards the constitution, though the first impressions made by every species of influence and artifice were too strong to be eradicated in time to give a decisive turn to the elections. We shall leave nothing undone to cultivate a favourable disposition in the citizens at large.

The language of the Antifœderalists is that if all the other states adopt, New York ought still to hold out. I have the most direct intelligence, but in a manner, which forbids a public use being made of it, that Clinton has in several conversations declared his opinion of the *inutility* of the UNION. Tis an unhappy reflection, that the friends to it should by quarrelling for straws among themselves promote the designs of its adversaries.

We think here that the situation of your state is critical. Let me know what you now think of it. I believe you meet nearly at the time we do. It will be of vast importance that an exact communication should be kept up between us at that period; and the moment *any decisive* question is taken, if favourable, I request you to dispatch an express to me with pointed orders to make all possible diligence, by changing horses &c. All expences shall be thankfully and liberally paid.

I executed your commands respecting the first vol of the Fœderalist. I sent 40 of the common copies & twelve of the finer ones addressed to the care of Governor Randolph. The Printer announces the second vol in a day or two, when an equal number of the two kinds shall also be forwarded. He informs that the Judicial department trial by jury bill of rights &c. is discussed in some additional papers which have not yet appeared in the Gazettes.

I remain with great sincerity & attachment

New York May 19. 1788

The Federalist No. 78

To the People of the State of New-York.

We proceed now to an examination of the judiciary department of the proposed government.

In unfolding the defects of the existing confederation, the utility and necessity of a federal judicature have been clearly pointed out. It is the less necessary to recapitulate the considerations there urged; as the propriety of the institution in the abstract is not disputed: The only questions which have been raised being relative to the manner of constituting it, and to its extent. To these points therefore our observations shall be confined.

The manner of constituting it seems to embrace these several objects—1st. The mode of appointing the judges—2d. The tenure by which they are to hold their places—3d. The partition of the judiciary authority between different courts, and their relations to each other.

First. As to the mode of appointing the judges: This is the same with that of appointing the officers of the union in general, and has been so fully discussed in the two last numbers, that nothing can be said here which would not be useless repetition.

Second. As to the tenure by which the judges are to hold their places: This chiefly concerns their duration in office; the provisions for their support; and the precautions for their responsibility.

According to the plan of the convention, all the judges who may be appointed by the United States are to hold their offices *during good behaviour*, which is conformable to the most approved of the state constitutions; and among the rest, to that of this state. Its propriety having been drawn into question by the adversaries of that plan, is no light symptom of the rage for objection which disorders their imaginations and judgments. The standard of good behaviour for the continuance in office of the judicial magistracy is certainly one of the most valuable of the modern improvements in the practice of government. In a monarchy it is an excellent barrier to the despotism of the prince: In a republic it is a no less excellent barrier to the encroachments and oppressions of the representative body. And it is the best expedient which can be devised in any government, to secure a steady, upright and impartial administration of the laws.

Whoever attentively considers the different departments of power must perceive, that in a government in which they are separated from each other, the judiciary, from the nature of its functions, will always be the least dangerous to the political rights of the constitution; because it will be least in a capacity to annoy or injure them. The executive not only dispenses the honors, but holds the sword of the community. The legislature not only commands the purse, but prescribes the rules by which the duties and rights of every citizen are to be regulated. The judiciary on the contrary has no influence over either the sword or the purse, no direction either of the strength or of the wealth of the society, and can take no active resolution whatever. It may truly be said to have neither force nor will, but merely judgment; and must ultimately depend upon the aid of the executive arm even for the efficacy of its judgments.

This simple view of the matter suggests several important consequences. It proves incontestibly that the judiciary is beyond comparison the weakest of the three departments of power;* that it can never attack with success either of the other two; and that all possible care is requisite to enable it to defend itself against their attacks. It equally proves, that though individual oppression may now and then proceed from the courts of justice, the general liberty of the people can never be endangered from that quarter; I mean, so long as the judiciary remains truly distinct from both the legislative and executive. For I agree that "there is no liberty, if the power of judging be not separated from the legislative and executive powers."† And it proves, in the last place, that as liberty can have nothing to fear from the judiciary alone, but would have every thing to fear from its union with either of the other departments; that as all the effects of such an union must ensue from a dependence of the former on the latter, notwithstanding a nominal and apparent separation; that as from the natural feebleness of the judiciary, it is in continual jeopardy of being overpowered, awed or influenced by its coordinate branches; and that as nothing can contribute so much to its firmness and independence, as permanency in office, this quality may therefore be justly regarded as an indispensable ingredient in its constitution; and in a great measure as the citadel of the public justice and the public security.

The complete independence of the courts of justice is peculiarly essential in a limited constitution. By a limited constitution I understand one which contains certain specified exceptions to the legislative authority; such for instance as that it shall pass no bills of attainder, no *ex post facto* laws, and the like. Limitations of this kind can be preserved in practice no other way than through the medium of the courts of justice; whose duty it must be to declare all acts contrary to the manifest tenor

---

* The celebrated Montesquieu speaking of them says, "of the three powers above mentioned, the JUDICIARY is next to nothing." Spirit of Laws, vol. I, page 186.
† Idem. page 181.

of the constitution void. Without this, all the reservations of particular rights or privileges would amount to nothing.

Some perplexity respecting the right of the courts to pronounce legislative acts void, because contrary to the constitution, has arisen from an imagination that the doctrine would imply a superiority of the judiciary to the legislative power. It is urged that the authority which can declare the acts of another void, must necessarily be superior to the one whose acts may be declared void. As this doctrine is of great importance in all the American constitutions, a brief discussion of the grounds on which it rests cannot be unacceptable.

There is no position which depends on clearer principles, than that every act of a delegated authority, contrary to the tenor of the commission under which it is exercised, is void. No legislative act therefore contrary to the constitution can be valid. To deny this would be to affirm that the deputy is greater than his principal; that the servant is above his master; that the representatives of the people are superior to the people themselves; that men acting by virtue of powers may do not only what their powers do not authorise, but what they forbid.

If it be said that the legislative body are themselves the constitutional judges of their own powers, and that the construction they put upon them is conclusive upon the other departments, it may be answered, that this cannot be the natural presumption, where it is not to be collected from any particular provision in the constitution. It is not otherwise to be supposed that the constitution could intend to enable the representatives of the people to substitute their *will* to that of their constituents. It is far more rational to suppose that the courts were designed to be an intermediate body between the people and the legislature, in order, among other things, to keep the latter within the limits assigned to their authority. The interpretation of the laws is the proper and peculiar province of the courts. A constitution is in fact, and must be, regarded by the judges as a fundamental law. It therefore belongs to them to ascertain its meaning as well as the meaning of any particular act proceeding from the legislative body. If there should happen to be an irreconcileable variance between the two, that which has the superior obligation and validity ought of course to be preferred; or in other words, the constitution ought to be preferred to the statute, the intention of the people to the intention of their agents.

Nor does this conclusion by any means suppose a superiority of the judicial to the legislative power. It only supposes that the power of the people is superior to both; and that where the will of the legislature declared in its statutes, stands in opposition to that of the people declared in the constitution, the judges ought to be governed by the latter, rather than the former. They ought to regulate their decisions by the fundamental laws, rather than by those which are not fundamental.

This exercise of judicial discretion in determining between two contradictory laws, is exemplified in a familiar instance. It not uncommonly happens, that there are two statutes existing at one time, clashing in whole or in part with each other, and neither of them containing any repealing clause or expression. In such a case, it is the province of the courts to liquidate and fix their meaning and operation: So far as they can by any fair construction be reconciled to each other; reason and law conspire to dictate that this should be done: Where this is impracticable, it becomes a matter of necessity to give effect to one, in exclusion of the other. The rule which has obtained in the courts for determining their relative validity is that the last in order of time shall be preferred to the first. But this is mere rule of construction, not derived from any positive law, but from the nature and reason of the thing. It is a rule not enjoined upon the courts by legislative provision, but adopted by themselves, as consonant to truth and propriety, for the direction of their conduct as interpreters of the law. They thought it reasonable, that between the interfering acts of an *equal* authority, that which was the last indication of its will, should have the preference.

But in regard to the interfering acts of a superior and subordinate authority, of an original and derivative power, the nature and reason of the thing indicate the converse of that rule as proper to be followed. They teach us that the prior act of a superior ought to be prefered to the subsequent act of an inferior and subordinate authority; and that, accordingly, whenever a particular statute contravenes the constitution, it will be the duty of the judicial tribunals to adhere to the latter, and disregard the former.

It can be of no weight to say, that the courts on the pretence of a repugnancy, may substitute their own pleasure to the constitutional intentions of the legislature. This might as well happen in the case of two contradictory statutes; or it might as well happen in every adjudication upon any single statute. The courts must declare the sense of the law; and if they should be disposed to exercise *will* instead of *judgment*, the consequence would equally be the substitution of their pleasure to that of the legislative body. The observation, if it proved any thing, would prove that there ought to be no judges distinct from that body.

If then the courts of justice are to be considered as the bulwarks of a limited constitution against legislative encroachments, this consideration will afford a strong argument for the permanent tenure of judicial offices, since nothing will contribute so much as this to that independent spirit in the judges, which must be essential to the faithful performance of so arduous a duty.

This independence of the judges is equally requisite to guard the constitution and the rights of individuals from the effects of those ill humours which the arts of designing men, or the influence of particular conjunctures, sometimes disseminate among the people themselves, and which, though they speedily give place to better information and more deliberate reflection, have a tendency in the mean time to occasion dangerous innovations in the government, and serious oppressions of the minor party in the community. Though I trust the friends of the proposed constitution will never concur with its enemies* in questioning that fundamental principle of republican government, which admits the right of the people to alter or abolish the established constitution whenever they find it inconsistent with their happiness; yet it is not to be inferred from this principle, that the representatives of the people, whenever a momentary inclination happens to lay hold of a majority of their constituents incompatible with the provisions in the existing constitution, would on that account be justifiable in a violation of those provisions; or that the courts would be under a greater obligation to connive at infractions in this shape, than when they had proceeded wholly from the cabals of the representative body. Until the people have by some solemn and authoritative act annulled or changed the established form, it is binding upon themselves collectively, as well as individually; and no presumption, or even knowledge of their sentiments, can warrant their representatives in a departure from it, prior to such an act. But it is easy to see that it would require an uncommon portion of fortitude in the judges to do their duty as faithful guardians of the constitution, where legislative invasions of it had been instigated by the major voice of the community.

But it is not with a view to infractions of the constitution only that

* Vide Protest of the minority of the convention of Pennsylvania, Martin's speech, &c.

the independence of the judges may be an essential safeguard against the effects of occasional ill humours in the society. These sometimes extend no farther than to the injury of the private rights of particular classes of citizens, by unjust and partial laws. Here also the firmness of the judicial magistracy is of vast importance in mitigating the severity, and confining the operation of such laws. It not only serves to moderate the immediate mischiefs of those which may have been passed, but it operates as a check upon the legislative body in passing them; who, perceiving that obstacles to the success of an iniquitous intention are to be expected from the scruples of the courts, are in a manner compelled by the very motives of the injustice they meditate, to qualify their attempts. This is a circumstance calculated to have more influence upon the character of our governments, than but few may be aware of. The benefits of the integrity and moderation of the judiciary have already been felt in more states than one; and though they may have displeased those whose sinister expectations they may have disappointed, they must have commanded the esteem and applause of all the virtuous and disinterested. Considerate men of every description ought to prize whatever will tend to beget or fortify that temper in the courts; as no man can be sure that he may not be to-morrow the victim of a spirit of injustice, by which he may be a gainer to-day. And every man must now feel that the inevitable tendency of such a spirit is to sap the foundations of public and private confidence, and to introduce in its stead, universal distrust and distress.

That inflexible and uniform adherence to the rights of the constitution and of individuals, which we perceive to be indispensable in the courts of justice, can certainly not be expected from judges who hold their offices by a temporary commission. Periodical appointments, however regulated, or by whomsoever made, would in some way or other be fatal to their necessary independence. If the power of making them was committed either to the executive or legislature, there would be danger of an improper complaisance to the branch which possessed it; if to both, there would be an unwillingness to hazard the displeasure of either; if to the people, or to persons chosen by them for the special purpose, there would be too great a disposition to consult popularity, to justify a reliance that nothing would be consulted but the constitution and the laws.

There is yet a further and a weighty reason for the permanency of the judicial offices; which is deducible from the nature of the qualifications they require. It has been frequently remarked with great propriety, that a voluminous code of laws is one of the inconveniences necessarily connected with the advantages of a free government. To avoid an arbitrary discretion in the courts, it is indispensable that they should be bound down by strict rules and precedents, which serve to define and point out their duty in every particular case that comes before them; and it will readily be conceived from the variety of controversies which grow out of the folly and wickedness of mankind, that the records of those precedents must unavoidably swell to a very considerable bulk, and must demand long and laborious study to acquire a competent knowledge of them. Hence it is that there can be but few men in the society, who will have sufficient skill in the laws to qualify them for the stations of judges. And making the proper deductions for the ordinary depravity of human nature, the number must be still smaller of those who unite the requisite integrity with the requisite knowledge. These considerations apprise us, that the government can have no great option between fit characters; and that a temporary duration in office, which would naturally discourage such characters from quitting a lucrative line of practice to accept a seat on the bench, would have a tendency to throw the administration of justice into hands less able, and less well qualified to conduct it with utility and dignity. In the present circumstances of this country, and in those in which it is likely to be for a long time to come, the disadvantages on this score would be greater than they may at first sight appear; but it must be confessed that they are far inferior to those which present themselves under the other aspects of the subject.

Upon the whole there can be no room to doubt that the convention acted wisely in copying from the models of those constitutions which have established *good behaviour* as the tenure of their judicial offices in point of duration; and that so far from being blameable on this account, their plan would have been inexcuseably defective if it had wanted this important feature of good government. The experience of Great Britain affords an illustrious comment on the excellence of the institution.

PUBLIUS.
The Federalist, May 28, 1788

The Federalist No. 84

To the People of the State of New-York.

In the course of the foregoing review of the constitution I have taken notice of, and endeavoured to answer, most of the objections which have appeared against it. There however remain a few which either did not fall naturally under any particular head, or were forgotten in their proper places. These shall now be discussed; but as the subject has been drawn into great length, I shall so far consult brevity as to comprise all my observations on these miscellaneous points in a single paper.

The most considerable of these remaining objections is, that the plan of the convention contains no bill of rights. Among other answers given to this, it has been upon different occasions remarked, that the constitutions of several of the states are in a similar predicament. I add, that New-York is of this number. And yet the opposers of the new system in this state, who profess an unlimited admiration for its constitution, are among the most intemperate partizans of a bill of rights. To justify their zeal in this matter, they alledge two things; one is, that though the constitution of New-York has no bill of rights prefixed to it, yet it contains in the body of it various provisions in favour of particular privileges and rights, which in substance amount to the same thing; the other is, that the constitution adopts in their full extent the common and statute law of Great-Britain, by which many other rights not expressed in it are equally secured.

To the first I answer, that the constitution proposed by the convention contains, as well as the constitution of this state, a number of such provisions.

Independent of those, which relate to the structure of the government, we find the following: Article I. section 3. clause 7. "Judgment in cases of impeachment shall not extend further than to removal from office, and disqualification to hold and enjoy any office of honour, trust or profit under the United States; but the party convicted shall nevertheless be liable and subject to indictment, trial, judgment and punishment, according to law." Section 9. of the same article, clause 2. "The privilege of the writ of *habeas corpus* shall not be suspended, unless when in cases of rebellion or invasion the public safety may require it." Clause 3. "No bill of attainder or *ex post facto* law shall be passed." Clause 7. "No title of nobility shall be granted by the United States: And no person holding any office of profit or trust under them, shall, without the consent of congress, accept of any present, emolument, office or title, of any kind whatever, from any king, prince or foreign state." Article III. section 2. clause 3. "The trial of all crimes, except in cases of impeachment, shall be by jury; and such trial shall be held in the state where the said crimes shall have been committed; but when not committed within any state, the trial shall be at such place or places as the congress may by law have directed." Section 3, of the same article, "Treason against the United States shall consist only in levying war against them, or in adhering to their enemies, giving them aid and comfort. No person shall be convicted of treason unless on the testimony of two witness to the same overt act, or on confession in open court." And clause 3, of the same section. "The congress shall have power to declare the punishment of treason, but no attainder of treason shall work corruption of blood, or forfeiture, except during the life of the person attainted."

It may well be a question whether these are not upon the whole, of equal importance with any which are to be found in the constitution of this state. The establishment of the writ of *habeas corpus*, the prohibition of *ex post facto* laws, and of TITLES OF NOBILITY, *to which we have no corresponding provisions in our constitution*, are perhaps greater securities to liberty and republicanism than any it contains. The creation of crimes after the commission of the fact, or in other words, the subjecting of men to punishment for things which, when they were done, were breaches of no law, and the practice of arbitrary imprisonments have been in all ages the favourite and most formidable instruments of tyranny. The observations of the judicious Blackstone* in reference to the latter, are well worthy of recital. "To bereave a man of life (says he) or by violence to confiscate his estate, without accusation or trial, would be so gross and notorious an act of despotism, as must at once convey the alarm of tyranny throughout the whole nation; but confinement of the person by secretly hurrying to goal, where his sufferings are unknown or forgotten, is a less public, a less striking, and therefore *a more dangerous engine* of arbitrary government." And as a remedy for this fatal evil, he is every where peculiarly emphatical in his

* Vide Blackstone's Commentaries, vol. I, page 136.

encomiums on the *habeas corpus* act, which in one place he calls "the BULWARK of the British constitution."*

Nothing need be said to illustrate the importance of the prohibition of titles of nobility. This may truly be denominated the corner stone of republican government; for so long as they are excluded, there can never be serious danger that the government will be any other than that of the people.

To the second, that is, to the pretended establishment of the common and statute law by the constitution, I answer, that they are expressly made subject "to such alterations and provisions as the legislature shall from time to time make concerning the same." They are therefore at any moment liable to repeal by the ordinary legislative power, and of course have no constitutional sanction. The only use of the declaration was to recognize the ancient law, and to remove doubts which might have been occasioned by the revolution. This consequently can be considered as no part of a declaration of rights, which under our constitutions must be intended as limitations of the power of the government itself.

It has been several times truly remarked, that bills of rights are in their origin, stipulations between kings and their subjects, abridgments of prerogative in favor of privilege, reservations of rights not surrendered to the prince. Such was MAGNA CHARTA, obtained by the Barons, sword in hand, from king John. Such were the subsequent confirmations of that charter by subsequent princes. Such was the *petition of right* assented to by Charles the First, in the beginning of his reign. Such also was the declaration of right presented by the lords and commons to the prince of Orange in 1688, and afterwards thrown into the form of an act of parliament, called the bill of rights. It is evident, therefore, that according to their primitive signification, they have no application to constitutions professedly founded upon the power of the people, and executed by their immediate representatives and servants. Here, in strictness, the people surrender nothing, and as they retain every thing, they have no need of particular reservations. "WE THE PEOPLE of the United States, to secure the blessings of liberty to ourselves and our posterity, do *ordain* and *establish* this constitution for the United States of America." Here is a better recognition of popular rights than volumes of those aphorisms which make the principal figure in several of our

* Vide Blackstone's Commentaries, vol. IV, page 438.

state bills of rights, and which would sound much better in a treatise of ethics than in a constitution of government.

But a minute detail of particular rights is certainly far less applicable to a constitution like that under consideration, which is merely intended to regulate the general political interests of the nation, than to a constitution which has the regulation of every species of personal and private concerns. If therefore the loud clamours against the plan of the convention on this score, are well founded, no epithets of reprobation will be too strong for the constitution of this state. But the truth is, that both of them contain all, which in relation to their objects, is reasonably to be desired.

I go further, and affirm that bills of rights, in the sense and in the extent in which they are contended for, are not only unnecessary in the proposed constitution, but would even be dangerous. They would contain various exceptions to powers which are not granted; and on this very account, would afford a colourable pretext to claim more than were granted. For why declare that things shall not be done which there is no power to do? Why for instance, should it be said, that the liberty of the press shall not be restrained, when no power is given by which restrictions may be imposed? I will not contend that such a provision would confer a regulating power; but it is evident that it would furnish, to men disposed to usurp, a plausible pretence for claiming that power. They might urge with a semblance of reason, that the constitution ought not to be charged with the absurdity of providing against the abuse of an authority, which was not given, and that the provision against restraining the liberty of the press afforded a clear implication, that a power to prescribe proper regulations concerning it, was intended to be vested in the national government. This may serve as a specimen of the numerous handles which would be given to the doctrine of constructive powers, by the indulgence of an injudicious zeal for bills of rights.

On the subject of the liberty of the press, as much has been said, I cannot forbear adding a remark or two: In the first place, I observe that there is not a syllable concerning it in the constitution of this state, and in the next, I contend that whatever has been said about it in that of any other state, amounts to nothing. What signifies a declaration that "the liberty of the press shall be inviolably preserved?" What is the liberty of the press? Who can give it any definition which would not leave the utmost latitude for evasion? I hold it to be impracticable;

and from this, I infer, that its security, whatever fine declarations may be inserted in any constitution respecting it, must altogether depend on public opinion, and on the general spirit of the people and of the government.* And here, after all, as intimated upon another occasion, must we seek for the only solid basis of all our rights.

There remains but one other view of this matter to conclude the point. The truth is, after all the declamation we have heard, that the constitution is itself in every rational sense, and to every useful purpose, A BILL OF RIGHTS. The several bills of rights, in Great Britain, form its constitution, and conversely the constitution of each state is its bill of rights. And the proposed constitution, if adopted, will be the bill of rights of the union. Is it one object of a bill of rights to declare and specify the political privileges of the citizens in the structure and administration of the government? This is done in the most ample and precise manner in the plan of the convention, comprehending various precautions for the public security, which are not to be found in any of the state constitutions. Is another object of a bill of rights to define certain immunities and modes of proceeding, which are relative to personal and private concerns? This we have seen has also been attended to, in a variety of cases, in the same plan. Adverting therefore to the substantial meaning of a bill of rights, it as absurd to allege that it is not to be found in the work of the convention. It may be said that it does not go far enough, though it will not be easy to make this appear; but it can with no propriety be contended that there is no such thing. It certainly must be immaterial what mode is observed as to the order of declaring the rights of the citizens, if they are to be found in any part of the instrument which establishes the government. And hence it must

* To show that there is a power in the constitution by which the liberty of the press may be affected, recourse has been had to the power of taxation. It is said that duties may be laid upon the publications so high as to amount to a prohibition. I know not by what logic it could be maintained that the declarations in the state constitutions, in favour of the freedom of the press, would be a constitutional impediment to the imposition of duties upon publications by the state legislatures. It cannot certainly be pretended that any degree of duties, however low, would be an abridgment of the liberty of the press. We know that newspapers are taxed in Great-Britain, and yet it is notorious that the press nowhere enjoys greater liberty than in that country. And if duties of any kind may be laid without a violation of that liberty, it is evident that the extent must depend on legislative discretion, regulated by public opinion; so that after all, general declarations respecting the liberty of the press will give it no greater security than it will have without them. The same invasions of it may be effected under the state constitutions which contain those declarations through the means of taxation, as under the proposed constitution which has nothing of the kind. It would be quite as significant to declare that government ought to be free, that taxes ought not to be excessive, &c., as that the liberty of the press ought not to be restrained.

be apparent that much of what has been said on this subject rests merely on verbal and nominal distinctions, which are entirely foreign from the substance of the thing.

Another objection, which has been made, and which from the frequency of its repetition it is to be presumed is relied on, is of this nature: It is improper (say the objectors) to confer such large powers, as are proposed, upon the national government; because the seat of that government must of necessity be too remote from many of the states to admit of a proper knowledge on the part of the constituent, of the conduct of the representative body. This argument, if it proves any thing, proves that there ought to be no general government whatever. For the powers which it seems to be agreed on all hands, ought to be vested in the union, cannot be safely intrusted to a body which is not under every requisite controul. But there are satisfactory reasons to shew that the objection is in reality not well founded. There is in most of the arguments which relate to distance a palpable illusion of the imagination. What are the sources of information by which the people in Montgomery county must regulate their judgment of the conduct of their representatives in the state legislature? Of personal observation they can have no benefit. This is confined to the citizens on the spot. They must therefore depend on the information of intelligent men, in whom they confide—and how must these men obtain their information? Evidently from the complection of public measures, from the public prints, from correspondences with their representatives, and with other persons who reside at the place of their deliberation. This does not apply to Montgomery county only, but to all the counties, at any considerable distance from the seat of government.

It is equally evident that the same sources of information would be open to the people, in relation to the conduct of their representatives in the general government; and the impediments to a prompt communication which distance may be supposed to create, will be overballanced by the effects of the vigilance of the state governments. The executive and legislative bodies of each state will be so many centinels over the persons employed in every department of the national administration; and as it will be in their power to adopt and pursue a regular and effectual system of intelligence, they can never be at a loss to know the behaviour of those who represent their constituents in the national councils, and can readily communicate the same knowledge to the people. Their disposition to apprise the community of whatever may prejudice its interests from another quarter, may be relied upon, if it were only from the rivalship of power. And we may conclude with the fullest assurance, that the people, through that channel, will be better informed of the conduct of their national representatives, than they can be by any means they now possess of that of their state representatives.

It ought also to be remembered, that the citizens who inhabit the country at and near the seat of government, will in all questions that affect the general liberty and prosperity, have the same interest with those who are at a distance; and that they will stand ready to sound the alarm when necessary, and to point out the actors in any pernicious project. The public papers will be expeditious messengers of intelligence to the most remote inhabitants of the union.

Among the many extraordinary objections which have appeared against the proposed constitution, the most extraordinary and the least colourable one, is derived from the want of some provision respecting the debts due to the United States. This has been represented as a tacit relinquishment of those debts, and as a wicked contrivance to screen public defaulters. The newspapers have teemed with the most inflammatory railings on this head; and yet there is nothing clearer than that the suggestion is entirely void of foundation, and is the offspring of extreme ignorance or extreme dishonesty. In addition to the remarks I have made upon the subject in another place, I shall only observe, that as it is a plain dictate of common sense, so it is also an established doctrine of political law, that *"States neither lose any of their rights, nor are discharged from any of their obligations by a change in the form of their civil government."**

The last objection of any consequence which I at present recollect, turns upon the article of expence. If it were even true that the adoption of the proposed government would occasion a considerable increase of expence, it would be an objection that ought to have no weight against the plan. The great bulk of the citizens of America, are with reason convinced that union is the basis of their political happiness. Men of sense of all parties now, with few exceptions, agree that it cannot be preserved under the present system, nor without radical alterations; that new and extensive powers ought to be granted

---

* Vide Rutherford's Institutes, vol. 2. book II. chap. x. sec. xiv, and xv.—Vide also Grotius, book II, chap. ix, sect. viii, and ix.

to the national head, and that these require a different organization of the federal government, a single body being an unsafe depository of such ample authorities. In conceding all this, the question of expence must be given up, for it is impossible, with any degree of safety, to narrow the foundation upon which the system is to stand. The two branches of the legislature are in the first instance, to consist of only sixty-five persons, which is the same number of which congress, under the existing confederation, may be composed. It is true that this number is intended to be increased; but this is to keep pace with the increase of the population and resources of the country. It is evident, that a less number would, even in the first instance, have been unsafe; and that a continuance of the present number would, in a more advanced stage of population, be a very inadequate representation of the people.

Whence is the dreaded augmentation of expence to spring? One source pointed out, is the multiplication of offices under the new government. Let us examine this a little.

It is evident that the principal departments of the administration under the present government, are the same which will be required under the new. There are now a secretary at war, a secretary for foreign affairs, a secretary for domestic affairs, a board of treasury consisting of three persons, a treasurer, assistants, clerks, &c. These offices are indispensable under any system, and will suffice under the new as well as under the old. As to ambassadors and other ministers and agents in foreign countries, the proposed constitution can make no other difference, than to render their characters, where they reside, more respectable, and their services more useful. As to persons to be employed in the collection of the revenues, it is unquestionably true that these will form a very considerable addition to the number of federal officers; but it will not follow, that this will occasion an increase of public expence. It will be in most cases nothing more than an exchange of state officers for national officers. In the collection of all duties, for instance, the persons employed will be wholly of the latter description. The states individually will stand in no need of any for this purpose. What difference can it make in point of expence, to pay officers of the customs appointed by the state, or those appointed by the United States? There is no good reason to suppose, that either the number or the salaries of the latter, will be greater than those of the former.

Where then are we to seek for those additional articles of expence which are to swell the account to the enormous size that has been represented to us? The chief item which occurs to me, respects the support of the judges of the United States. I do not add the president, because there is now a president of congress, whose expences may not be far, if any thing, short of those which will be incurred on account of the president of the United States. The support of the judges will clearly be an extra expence, but to what extent will depend on the particular plan which may be adopted in practice in regard to this matter. But it can upon no reasonable plan amount to a sum which will be an object of material consequence.

Let us now see what there is to counterballance any extra expences that may attend the establishment of the proposed government. The first thing that presents itself is, that a great part of the business, which now keeps congress sitting through the year, will be transacted by the president. Even the management of foreign negociations will naturally devolve upon him according to general principles concerted with the senate, and subject to their final concurrence. Hence it is evident, that a portion of the year will suffice for the session of both the senate and the house of representatives: We may suppose about a fourth for the latter, and a third or perhaps a half for the former. The extra business of treaties and appointments may give this extra occupation to the senate. From this circumstance we may infer, that until the house of representatives shall be increased greatly beyond its present number, there will be a considerable saving of expence from the difference between the constant session of the present, and the temporary session of the future congress.

But there is another circumstance, of great importance in the view of the economy. The business of the United States has hitherto occupied the state legislatures as well as congress. The latter has made requisitions which the former have had to provide for. Hence it has happened that the sessions of the state legislatures have been protracted greatly beyond what was necessary for the execution of the mere local business of the states. More than half their time has been frequently employed in matters which related to the United States. Now the members who compose the legislatures of the several states amount to two thousand and upwards; which number has hitherto performed what under the new system will be done in the first instance by sixty-five persons, and probably at no future period by above a fourth or a fifth of that number. The congress under the proposed government will do all the business of the United

States themselves, without the intervention of the state legislatures, who thenceforth will have only to attend to the affairs of their particular states, and will not have to sit in any proportion as long as they have heretofore done. This difference, in the time of the sessions of the state legislatures, will be all clear gain, and will alone form an article of saving, which may be regarded as an equivalent for any additional objects of expence that may be occasioned by the adoption of the new system.

The result from these observations is, that the sources of additional expence from the establishment of the proposed constitution are much fewer than may have been imagined, that they are counterbalanced by considerable objects of saving, and that while it is questionable on which side the scale will preponderate, it is certain that a government less expensive would be incompetent to the purposes of the union.

PUBLIUS.
The Federalist, May 28, 1788

New York Ratifying Convention: Third Speech of June 21

Francis Child's Version

THE HON. MR. HAMILTON. Mr. Chairman I rise to take notice of the observations of the hon. member from Ulster. I imagine the objections he has stated, are susceptible of a complete and satisfactory refutation. But before I proceed to this, I shall attend to the arguments advanced by the gentlemen from Albany and Dutchess. These arguments have been frequently urged, and much confidence has been placed in their strength: The danger of corruption has been dwelt upon with peculiar emphasis, and presented to our view in the most heightened and unnatural colouring: Events, merely possible have been magnified by distempered imagination into inevitable realities; and the most distant and doubtful conjectures have been formed into a serious and infallible prediction. In the same spirit, the most fallacious calculations have been made: The lowest possible quorum has been contemplated as the number to transact important business; and a majority of these to decide in all cases on questions of infinite moment. Allowing, for the present, the propriety and truth of these apprehensions, it would be easy, in comparing the two constitutions, to prove that the chances of corruption under the new, are much fewer that those to which the old one is exposed. Under the old confederation, the important powers of declaring war, making peace, &c. can be exercised by nine states. On the presumption that the smallest constitutional number will deliberate and decide, those interesting powers will be committed to fewer men, under the ancient than under the new government. In the former, eighteen members, in the latter, not less than twenty-four may determine all great questions. Thus on the principles of the gentlemen, the fairer prospect of safety is clearly visible in the new government. That we may have the fullest conviction of the truth of this position, it ought to be suggested, as a decisive argument, that it will ever be the interest of the several states to maintain, under the new government, an ample representation: For, as every member has a vote, the relative influence and authority of each state will be in proportion to the number of representatives she has in Congress. There is not therefore a shadow of probability, that the number of acting members in the general legislature, will be ever reduced to a bare quorum; especially as the expence of their support is to be defrayed from a federal treasury: But under the existing confederation, as each state has but one vote, it will be a matter of indifference, on the score of influence, whether she delegates two or six representatives: And the maintenance of them forming a striking article in the state expenditures, will forever prove a capital inducement to retain or withdraw from the federal legislature, those delegates which her selfishness may too often consider as superfluous.

There is another source of corruption, in the old government, which the proposed plan is happily calculated to remedy. The concurrence of nine states, as has been observed, is necessary to pass resolves the most important, and on which, the safety of the republic may depend. If these nine states are at any time assembled, a foreign enemy, by dividing a state and gaining over and silencing a single member, may frustrate the most indispensible plan of national policy, and totally prevent a measure, essential to the welfare or existence of the empire. Here, then, we find a radical, dangerous defect, which will forever embarrass and obstruct the machine of government; and suspend our fate on the uncertain virtue of an individual. What a difference between the old and new constitution strikes our view! In the one, corruption must embrace a majority; in the other, her poison administered to a single man, may render the efforts of a majority totally vain. This mode of corruption is still more dangerous, as its operations are more secret and imperceptible: The exertions of active villainy are commonly accompanied with circumstances, which tend to its own exposure: But this negative kind of guilt has so many plausible apologies as almost to elude suspicion.

In all reasonings on the subject of corruption, much use has been made of the examples furnished by the British house of commons. Many mistakes have arisen from fallacious comparisons between our government and theirs. It is time, that the real state of this matter should be explained. By far the greatest part of the house of commons is composed of representatives of towns or boroughs: These towns had antiently no voice in parliament; but on the extension of commercial wealth and influence, they were admitted to a seat. Many of them are in the possession and gift of the king; and from their dependence on him, and the destruction of the right of free election, they are stigmatized with the appellation of rotten boroughs. This is the true source of the corruption, which has so long excited the severe animadversion of zealous politicians and patriots. But the knights of the shire, who form another branch of the house of commons, and who are chosen from the body of the counties they represent, have been generally esteemed a virtuous and incorruptible set of men. I appeal, Sir, to the history of that house: This will shew us, that the rights of the people have been ever very safely trusted to their protection; that they have been the ablest bulwarks of the British commons; and that in the conflict of parties, by throwing their weight into one scale or the other, they have uniformly supported and strengthened the constitutional claims of the people. Notwithstanding the cry of corruption that has been perpetually raised against the house of commons, it has been found, that that house, sitting at first without any constitutional authority, became, at length, an essential member of the legislature, and have since, by regular gradations, acquired new and important accessions of privilege: That they have, on numerous occasions, impaired the overgrown prerogative, and limited the incroachments of monarchy.

An honorable member from Dutchess, (*Mr. Smith*) has observed, that the delegates from New-York, (for example) can have very little information of the local circumstances of Georgia or South Carolina, except from the representatives of those states; and on this ground, insists upon the expediency of an enlargment of the representation; since, otherwise, the majority must rely too much on the information of a few. In order to determine whether there is any weight in this reasoning, let us consider the powers of the national government, and compare them with the objects of state legislation. The powers of the new government are general, and calculated to embrace the aggregate interest of the Union, and the general interest of each state, so far as it stands in relation to the whole. The object of the state governments is to provide for their internal interests, as unconnected with the United States, and as composed of minute parts or districts. A particular knowledge, therefore, of the local circumstances of any state, as they may vary in different districts, is unnecessary for the federal representative. As he is not to represent the interests or local wants of the county of Dutchess or Montgomery; neither is it necessary that he should be acquainted with their particular resources: But in the state governments, as the laws regard the interests of the people, in all their various minute divisions; it is necessary, that the smallest interests should be represented. Taking these distinctions into view, I think it must appear evident, that one discerning and intelligent man will be as capable of understanding and representing the general interests of a state, as twenty; because, one man can be as fully acquainted with the general state of the commerce, manufactures, population, production and common resources of a state, which are the proper objects of federal legislation. It is to be presumed, that few men originally possess a complete knowledge of the circumstances of other states; They must rely, therefore, on the information, to be collected from the representatives of those states: And if the above reasoning be just, it appears evident, I imagine, that this reliance will be as secure as can be desired.

Sir, in my experience of public affairs, I have constantly remarked, in the conduct of members of Congress, a strong and uniform attachment to the interests of their own state: These interests have, on many occasions, been adhered to, with an undue and illiberal pertinacity; and have too often been preferred to the welfare of the Union. This attachment has given birth to an unaccommodating spirit of party, which has frequently embarrassed the best measures: It is by no means, however, an object of surprize. The early connections we have formed;

the habits and prejudices in which we have been bred, fix our affection so strongly, that no future objects of association can easily eradicate them: This, together with the entire and immediate dependence the representative feels on his constituent, will generally incline him to prefer the particular before the public good.

The subject, on which this argument of a small representation has been most plausibly used, is taxation. As to internal taxation, in which the difficulty principally rests, it is not probable, that any general regulation will originate in the national legislature. If Congress in times of great danger and distress, should be driven to this resource, they will undoubtedly adopt such measures, as are most conformable to the laws and customs of each state: They will take up your own codes and consult your own systems: This is a source of information which cannot mislead, and which will be equally accessible to every member. It will teach them the most certain, safe and expeditious mode of laying and collecting taxes in each state. They will appoint the officers of revenue agreeably to the spirit of your particular establishments; or they will make use of your own.

Sir, the most powerful obstacle to the members of Congress betraying the interests of their constituents, is the state legislatures themselves; who will be standing bodies of observation, possessing the confidence of the people, jealous of federal encroachments, and armed with every power to check the first essays of treachery. They will institute regular modes of enquiry: The complicated domestic attachments, which subsist between the state legislators and their electors, will ever make them vigilant guardians of the people's rights: Possessed of the means, and the disposition of resistance, the spirit of opposition will be easily communicated to the people; and under the conduct of an organized body of leaders, will act with weight and system. Thus it appears, that the very structure of the confederacy affords the surest preventives from error, and the most powerful checks to misconduct.

Sir, there is something in an argument, that has been urged, which, if it proves any thing, concludes against all union and all government; it goes to prove, that no powers should be entrusted to any body of men, because they may be abused. This is an argument of possibility and chance; one that would render useless all reasonings upon the probable operation of things, and defeat the established principles of natural and moral causes. It is a species of reasoning, sometimes used to excite popular jealousies, but is generally discarded by wise and discerning men. I do not suppose that the honorable member who advanced the idea, had any such design: He, undoubtedly, would not wish to extend his argument to the destruction of union or government; but this, Sir, is its real tendency. It has been asserted, that the interests, habits and manners of the Thirteen States are different; and hence it is inferred, that no general free government can suit them. This diversity of habits, &c. has been a favorite theme with those who are disposed for a division of our empire; and like many other popular objections, seems to be founded on fallacy. I acknowledge, that the local interests of the states are in some degree various; and that there is some difference in their habits and manners: But this I will presume to affirm; that, from New-Hampshire to Georgia, the people of America are as uniform in their interests and manners, as those of any established in Europe. This diversity, to the eye of a speculatist, may afford some marks of characteristic discrimination, but cannot form an impediment to the regular operation of those general powers, which the Constitution gives to the united government. Were the laws of the union to new-model the internal police of any state; were they to alter, or abrogate at a blow, the whole of its civil and criminal institutions; were they to penetrate the recesses of domestic life, and controul, in all respects, the private conduct of individuals, there might be more force in the objection: And the same constitution, which was happily calculated for one state, might sacrifice the wellfare of another. Though the difference of interests may create some difficulty and apparent partiality, in the first operations of government, yet the same spirit of accommodation, which produced the plan under discussion, would be exercised in lessening the weight of unequal burthens. Add to this that, under the regular and gentle influence of general laws, these varying interests will be constantly assimilating, till they embrace each other, and assume the same complexion.

June 21, 1788

To George Washington

New York September 1788

DEAR SIR

Your Excellency's friendly and obliging letter of the 28th Ulto. came safely to hand. I thank you for your assurance of seconding my application to General Morgan. The truth of that affair is, that he purchased the watch for a trifle of a British soldier, who plundered Major Cochran at the moment of his fall at York Town.

I should be deeply pained my Dear Sir if your scruples in regard to a certain station should be matured into a resolution to decline it; though I am neither surprised at their existence nor can I but agree in opinion that the caution you observe in deferring an ultimate determination is prudent. I have however reflected maturely on the subject and have come to a conclusion, (in which I feel no hesitation) that every public and personal consideration will demand from you an acquiescence in what will *certainly* be the unanimous wish of your country. The absolute retreat which you meditated at the close of the late war was natural and proper. Had the government produced by the revolution gone on in a *tolerable* train, it would have been most adviseable to have persisted in that retreat. But I am clearly of opinion that the crisis which brought you again into public view left you no alterative but to comply—and I am equally clear in the opinion that you are by that act *pledged* to take a part in the execution of the government. I am not less convinced that the impression of this necessity of your filling the station in question is so universal that you run no risk of any uncandid imputation, by submitting to it. But even if this were not the case, a regard to your own reputation as well as to the public good, calls upon you in the strongest manner to run that risk.

It cannot be considered as a compliment to say that on your acceptance of the office of President the success of the new government in its commencement may materially depend. Your agency and influence will be not less important in preserving it from the future attacks of its enemies than they have been in recommending it in the first instance to the adoption of the people. Independent of all considerations drawn from this source the point of light in which you stand at home and abroad will make an infinite difference in the respectability with which the government will begin its operations in the alternative of your being or not being at the head of it. I forbear to urge considerations which might have a more personal application. What I have said will suffice for the inferences I mean to draw.

First—In a matter so essential to the well being of society as the prosperity of a newly instituted government a citizen of so much consequence as yourself to its success has no option but to lend his services if called for. Permit me to say it would be inglorious in such a situation not to hazard the glory however great, which he might have previously acquired.

Secondly. Your signature to the proposed system pledges your judgment for its being such an one as upon the whole was worthy of the public approbation. If it should miscarry (as men commonly decide from success or the want of it) the blame will in all probability be laid on the system itself. And the framers of it will have to encounter the disrepute of having brought about a revolution in government, without substituting any thing that was worthy of the effort. They pulled down one Utopia, it will be said, to build up another. This view of the subject, if I mistake not my dear Sir will suggest to your mind greater hazard to that fame, which must be and ought to be dear to you, in refusing your future aid to the system than in affording it. I will only add that in my estimate of the matter that aid is indispensable.

I have taken the liberty to express these sentiments to lay before you my view of the subject. I doubt not the considerations mentioned have fully occurred to you, and I trust they will finally produce in your mind the same result, which exists in mine. I flatter myself the frankness with which I have delivered myself will not be displeasing to you. It has been prompted by motives which you would not disapprove.

I remain My Dear Sir With the sincerest respect and regard Your Obd & hum serv

A HAMILTON

The letter inclosed in yours was immediately forwarded.

To George Washington

Dr. Sir

In conformity to the intimation you were pleased to honor me with on [   ] evening last I have reflected on the etiquette proper to be observed by the President and now submit the ideas which have occurred to me on the subject.

The public good requires as a primary object that the dignity of the office should be supported. Whatever is essential to this ought to be pursued though at the risk of partial or momentary dissatisfaction. But care will be necessary to avoid extensive disgust or discontent. Men's minds are prepared for a pretty high tone in the demeanour of the Executive; but I doubt whether for so high a tone as in the abstract might be desireable. The notions of equality are yet in my opinion too general and too strong to admit of such a distance being placed between the President and other branches of the government as might even be consistent with a due proportion. The following plan will I think steer clear of extremes and involve no very material inconveniences.

I The President to have a levee day once a week for receiving visits. An hour to be fixed at which it shall be understood that he will appear and consequently that the visitors are previously to be assembled. The President to remain half an hour, in which time he may converse cursorily on indifferent subjects with such persons as shall strike his attention, and at the end of that half hour disappear. Some regulation will be hereafter necessary to designate those who may visit. A mode of introduction through particular officers will be indispensable. No visits to be returned.

II The President to accept no invitations: and to give formal entertainments only twice or four times a year on the anniversaries of important events in the revolution. If twice, the day of the declaration of Independence, and that of the inauguration of the President, which completed the organization of the Constitution, to be preferred; if four times, the day of the treaty of alliance with france & that of the definitive treaty with Britain to be added. The members of the two houses of the legislature Principal officers of the Government Foreign ministers and other distinguished strangers only to be invited. The numbers form in my mind an objection—

But there may be separate tables in separate rooms. This is practiced in some European Courts. I see no other method in which foreign Ministers can with propriety be included in any attentions of the table which the President may think fit to pay.

III The President on the levée days either by himself or some Gentleman of his household to give informal invitations to family dinners on the days of invitation. Not more than six or eight to be invited at a time & the matter to be confined essentially to members of the legislature and other official characters. The President never to remain long at table.

I think it probable that the last article will not correspond with the ideas of most of those with whom Your Excellency may converse but on pretty mature reflection I believe it will be necessary to remove the idea of too immense an inequality, which I fear would excite dissatisfaction and cabal. The thing may be so managed as neither to occasion much waste of time, nor to infringe on dignity.

It is an important point to consider what persons may have access to Your Excellency on business. The heads of departments will of course have this privilege. Foreign Ministers of some descriptions will also be intitled to it. In Europe I am informed ambassadors only have direct access to the Chief Magistrate. Something very *near* what prevails there would in my opinion be right. The distinction of rank between diplomatic characters requires attention and the door of access ought not to be too wide to that class of persons. I have thought that the members of the Senate should also have a right of *individual* access on matters relative to the *public administration*. In England & France Peers of the realm have this right. We have none such in this Country, but I believe that it will be satisfactory to the people to know that there is some body of men in the state who have a right of continual communication with the President. It will be considered as a safeguard against secret combinations to deceive him.

I have asked myself—will not the representatives expect the same privilege and be offended if they are not allowed to participate with the Senate? There is sufficient danger of this, to merit consideration. But there is a reason for the distinction in the constitution. The Senate are coupled with the President in certain executive functions; treaties and appointments. This makes them in a degree his constitutional counsellors and gives them a *peculiar* claim to the right of access.

On the whole, I think the discrimination will be proper & may be hazarded.

I have chosen this method of communication, because I understood Your Excellency, that it would be most convenient to you. The unstudied and unceremonious manner of it will I hope not render it the less acceptable. And if in the execution of your commands at any time I consult frankness and simplicity more than ceremony or profession, I flatter myself you will not on that account distrust the sincerity of the assurance I now give of my cordial wishes for your personal happiness and the success of your administration. I have the honor to be with the highest respect

Your Excellency's Most Obedient & humble servant

May 5, 1789

To Marquis de Lafayette

New York October 6th. 1789

MY DEAR MARQUIS

I have seen with a mixture of Pleasure and apprehension the Progress of the events which have lately taken Place in your Country. As a friend to mankind and to liberty I rejoice in the efforts which you are making to establish it while I fear much for the final success of the attempts, for the fate of those I esteem who are engaged in it, and for the danger in case of success of innovations greater than will consist with the real felicity of your Nation. If your affairs still go well, when this reaches you, you will ask why this foreboding of ill, when all the appearences have been so much in your favor. I will tell you; I dread disagreements among those who are now united (which will be likely to be improved by the adverse party) about the nature of your constitution; I dread the vehement character of your people, whom I fear you may find it more easy to bring on, than to keep within Proper bounds, after you have put them in motion; I dread the interested refractoriness of your nobles, who cannot all be gratified and who may be unwilling to submit to the requisite sacrifices. And I dread the reveries of your Philosophic politicians who appear in the moment to have great influence and who being mere speculatists may aim at more refinement than suits either with human nature or the composition of your Nation.

These my dear Marquis are my apprehensions. My wishes for your personal success and that of the cause of liberty are incessant. Be virtuous amidst the Seductions of ambition, and you can hardly in any event be unhappy. You are combined with a great and good man; you will anticipate the name of Neckar. I trust you and he will never cease to harmonize.

You will, I presume, have heard before this gets to hand, that I have been appointed to the head of the Finances of this Country: this event I am sure will give you Pleasure. In undertaking the task, I hazard much, but I thought it an occasion that called upon me to hazard. I have no doubt that the reasonable expectation of the public may be satisfied, if I am properly supported by the Legislature, and in this respect, I stand at present on the most encouraging footing.

The debt due to France will be among the first objects of my attention. Hitherto it has been from necessity neglected. The Session of Congress is now over. It has been exhausted in the organization of the Government, and in a few laws of immediate urgency respecting navigation and commercial Imposts. The subject of the debt foreign and domestic has been referred to the next session which will commence the first Monday in January with an instruction to me to prepare and report a Plan comprehending an adequate Provision for the support of the Public Credit. There were many good reasons for a temporary adjournment.

From this sketch you will perceive that I am not in a situation to address any thing officially to your administration; but I venture to say to you, as my friend, that if the installments of the Principal of the debt could be suspended for a few years, it would be a valuable accommodation to the United States. In this suggestion I contemplate a speedy payment of the arrears of *interest* now due, and effectual Provision for the punctual payment of future interest as it arises. Could an arrangement of this sort meet the approbation of your Government, it would be best on every account that the offer should come unsolicited as a fresh mark of good will.

I wrote you last by Mr. De Warville. I presume you received my letter. As it touched some delicate issues I should be glad to know its fate.

Your with unalterable   esteem and affection

ALEXANDER HAMILTON

P. S. The latest accounts from France have abated some of my apprehensions. The abdications of priviledges patronised by your Nobility in the States General are truly noble, and bespeak a Patriotic and magnanimous policy, which promises good both to them and their Country.

To Henry Lee

MY DEAR FRIEND

I have just received your letter of the 16th instant.

I am sure you are sincere when you say, you would not subject me to an impropriety. Nor do I know that there would be any in my answering your queries. But you remember the saying with regard to Caesar's Wife. I think the spirit of it applicable to every man concerned in the administration of the finances of a Country. With respect to the Conduct of such men—*Suspicion* is ever eagle eyed, And the most innocent things are apt to be misinterpreted.

Be assured of the affection & friendship of Yr.

A HAMILTON

New York December 1st 1789

Report Relative to a Provision for the Support of Public Credit

Treasury Department, January 9, 1790.

The Secretary of the Treasury, in obedience to the resolution of the House of Representatives, of the twenty-first day of September last, has, during the recess of Congress, applied himself to the consideration of a proper plan for the support of the Public Credit, with all the attention which was due to the authority of the House, and to the magnitude of the object.

In the discharge of this duty, he has felt, in no small degree, the anxieties which naturally flow from a just estimate of the difficulty of the task, from a well-founded diffidence of his own qualifications for executing it with success, and from a deep and solemn conviction of the momentous nature of the truth contained in the resolution under which his investigations have been conducted, "That an *adequate* provision for the support of the Public Credit, is a matter of high importance to the honor and prosperity of the United States."

With an ardent desire that his well-meant endeavors may be conducive to the real advantage of the nation, and with the utmost deference to the superior judgment of the House, he now respectfully submits the result of his enquiries and reflections, to their indulgent construction.

In the opinion of the Secretary, the wisdom of the House, in giving their explicit sanction to the proposition which has been stated, cannot but be applauded by all, who will seriously consider, and trace through their obvious consequences, these plain and undeniable truths.

That exigencies are to be expected to occur, in the affairs of nations, in which there will be a necessity for borrowing.

That loans in times of public danger, especially from foreign war, are found an indispensable resource, even to the wealthiest of them.

And that in a country, which, like this, is possessed of little active wealth, or in other words, little monied capital, the necessity for that resource, must, in such emergencies, be proportionably urgent.

And as on the one hand, the necessity for borrowing in particular emergencies cannot be doubted, so on the other, it is equally evident, that to be able to borrow upon *good terms*, it is essential that the credit of a nation should be well established.

For when the credit of a country is in any degree questionable, it never fails to give an extravagant premium, in one shape or another, upon all the loans it has occasion to make. Nor does the evil end here; the same disadvantage must be sustained upon whatever is to be bought on terms of future payment.

From this constant necessity of *borrowing* and *buying dear*, it is easy to conceive how immensely the expences of a nation, in a course of time, will be augmented by an unsound state of the public credit.

To attempt to enumerate the complicated variety of mischiefs in the whole system of the social œconomy, which proceed from a neglect of the maxims that uphold public credit, and justify the solicitude manifested by the House on this point, would be an improper intrusion on their time and patience.

In so strong a light nevertheless do they appear to the Secretary, that on their due observance at the present critical juncture, materially depends, in his judgment, the individual and aggregate prosperity of the citizens of the United States; their relief from the embarrassments they now experience; their character as a People; the cause of good government.

If the maintenance of public credit, then, be truly so important, the next enquiry which suggests itself is, by what means it is to be effected? The ready answer to which question is, by good faith, by a punctual performance of contracts. States, like individuals, who observe their engagements, are respected and trusted: while the reverse is the fate of those, who pursue an opposite conduct.

Every breach of the public engagements, whether from choice or necessity, is in different degrees hurtful to public credit. When such a necessity does truly exist, the evils of it are only to be palliated by a scrupulous attention, on the part of the government, to carry the violation no farther than the necessity absolutely requires, and to manifest, if the nature of the case admits of it, a sincere disposition to make reparation, whenever circumstances shall permit. But with every possible mitigation, credit must suffer, and numerous mischiefs ensue. It is therefore highly important, when an appearance of necessity seems to press upon the public councils, that they should examine well its reality, and be perfectly assured, that there is no method of escaping from it, before they yield to its suggestions. For though it cannot safely be affirmed, that occasions have never existed, or may not exist, in which violations of the public faith, in this respect, are inevitable; yet there is great reason to believe, that they exist far less frequently than precedents indicate; and are oftenest either pretended through levity, or want of firmness, or supposed through want of knowledge. Expedients might often have been devised to effect, consistently with good faith, what has been done in contravention of it. Those who are most commonly creditors of a nation, are, generally speaking, enlightened men; and there are signal examples to warrant a conclusion, that when a candid and fair appeal is made to them, they will understand their true interest too well to refuse their concurrence in such modifications of their claims, as any real necessity may demand.

While the observance of that good faith, which is the basis of public credit, is recommended by the strongest inducements of political expediency, it is enforced by considerations of still greater authority. There are arguments for it, which rest on the immutable principles of moral obligation. And in proportion as the mind is disposed to contemplate, in the order of Providence, an intimate connection between public virtue and public happiness, will be its repugnancy to a violation of those principles.

This reflection derives additional strength from the nature of the debt of the United States. It was the price of liberty. The faith of America has been repeatedly pledged for it, and with solemnities, that give peculiar force to the obligation. There is indeed reason to regret that it has not hitherto been kept; that the necessities of the war, conspiring with inexperience in the subjects of finance, produced direct infractions; and that the subsequent period has been a continued scene of negative violation, or non-compliance. But a diminution of this regret arises from the reflection, that the last seven years have exhibited an earnest and uniform effort, on the part of the government of the union, to retrieve the national credit, by doing justice to the creditors of the nation; and that the embarrassments of a defective constitution, which defeated this laudable effort, have ceased.

From this evidence of a favorable disposition, given by the former government, the institution of a new one, cloathed with powers competent to calling forth the resources of the community, has excited correspondent expectations. A general belief, accordingly, prevails, that the credit of the United States will quickly be established on the firm foundation of an effectual provision for the existing debt. The influence, which this has had at home, is witnessed by the rapid increase, that has taken place in the market value of the public securities. From January to November, they rose thirty-three and a third per cent, and from that period to this time, they have risen fifty per cent more. And the intelligence from abroad announces effects proportionably favourable to our national credit and consequence.

It cannot but merit particular attention, that among ourselves the most enlightened friends of good government are those, whose expectations are the highest.

To justify and preserve their confidence; to promote the encreasing respectability of the American name; to answer the calls of justice; to restore landed property to its due value; to furnish new resources both to agriculture and commerce; to cement more closely the union of the states; to add to their security against foreign attack; to establish public order on the basis of an upright and liberal policy. These are the great and invaluable ends to be secured, by a proper and adequate provision, at the present period, for the support of public credit.

To this provision we are invited, not only by the general considerations, which have been noticed, but by others of a more particular nature. It will procure to every class of the community some important advantages, and remove some no less important disadvantages.

The advantage to the public creditors from the increased value of that part of their property which constitutes the public debt, needs no explanation.

But there is a consequence of this, less obvious, though not less true, in which every other citizen is interested. It is a well known fact, that in countries in which the national debt is properly funded, and an object of established confidence, it answers most of the purposes of money. Transfers of stock or public debt are there equivalent to payments in specie; or in other words, stock, in the principal transactions of business, passes current as specie. The same thing would, in all probability happen here, under the like circumstances.

The benefits of this are various and obvious.

First. Trade is extended by it; because there is a larger capital to carry it on, and the merchant can at the same time, afford to trade for smaller profits; as his stock, which, when unemployed, brings him in an interest from the government, serves him also as money, when he has a call for it in his commercial operations.

Secondly. Agriculture and manufactures are also promoted by it: For the like reason, that more capital can be commanded to be employed in both; and because the merchant, whose enterprize in foreign trade, gives to them activity and extension, has greater means for enterprize.

Thirdly. The interest of money will be lowered by it; for this is always in a ratio, to the quantity of money, and to the quickness of circulation. This circumstance will enable both the public and individuals to borrow on easier and cheaper terms.

And from the combination of these effects, additional aids will be furnished to labour, to industry, and to arts of every kind.

But these good effects of a public debt are only to be looked for, when, by being well funded, it has acquired an *adequate* and *stable* value. Till then, it has rather a contrary tendency. The fluctuation and insecurity incident to it in an unfunded state, render it a mere commodity, and a precarious one. As such, being only an object of occasional and particular speculation, all the money applied to it is so much diverted from the more useful channels of circulation, for which the thing itself affords no substitute: So that, in fact, one serious inconvenience of an unfunded debt is, that it contributes to the scarcity of money.

This distinction which has been little if at all attended to, is of the greatest moment. It involves a question immediately interesting to every part of the community; which is no other than this—Whether the public debt, by a provision for it on true principles, shall be rendered a *substitute* for money; or whether, by being left as it is, or by being provided for in such a manner as will wound those principles, and destroy confidence, it shall be suffered to continue, as it is, a pernicious drain of our cash from the channels of productive industry.

The effect, which the funding of the public debt, on right principles, would have upon landed property, is one of the circumstances attending such an arrangement, which has been least adverted to, though it deserves the most particular attention. The present depreciated state of that species of property is a serious calamity. The value of cultivated lands, in most of the states, has fallen since the revolution from 25 to 50 per cent. In those farthest south, the decrease is still more considerable. Indeed, if the representations, continually received from that quarter, may be credited, lands there will command no price, which may not be deemed an almost total sacrifice.

This decrease, in the value of lands, ought, in a great measure, to be attributed to the scarcity of money. Consequently whatever produces an augmentation of the monied capital of the country, must have a proportional effect in raising that value. The beneficial tendency of a funded debt, in this respect, has been manifested by the most decisive experience in Great-Britain.

The proprietors of lands would not only feel the benefit of this increase in the value of their property, and of a more prompt and better sale, when they had occasion to sell; but the necessity of selling would be, itself, greatly diminished. As the same cause would contribute to the facility of loans, there is reason to believe, that such of them as are indebted, would be able through that resource, to satisfy their more urgent creditors.

It ought not however to be expected, that the advantages, described as likely to result from funding the public debt, would be instantaneous.

It might require some time to bring the value of stock to its natural level, and to attach to it that fixed confidence, which is necessary to its quality as money. Yet the late rapid rise of the public securities encourages an expectation, that the progress of stock to the desireable point, will be much more expeditious than could have been foreseen. And as in the mean time it will be increasing in value, there is room to conclude, that it will, from the outset, answer many of the purposes in contemplation. Particularly it seems to be probable, that from creditors, who are not themselves necessitous, it will early meet with a ready reception in payment of debts, at its current price.

Having now taken a concise view of the inducements to a proper provision for the public debt, the next enquiry which presents itself is, what ought to be the nature of such a provision? This requires some preliminary discussions.

It is agreed on all hands, that that part of the debt which has been contracted abroad, and is denominated the foreign debt, ought to be provided for, according to the precise terms of the contracts relating to it. The discussions, which can arise, therefore, will have reference essentially to the domestic part of it, or to that which has been contracted at home. It is to be regretted, that there is not the same unanimity of sentiment on this part, as on the other.

The Secretary has too much deference for the opinions of every part of the community, not to have observed one, which has, more than once, made its appearance in the public prints, and which is occasionally to be met with in conversation. It involves this question, whether a discrimination ought not to be made between original holders of the public securities, and present possessors, by purchase. Those who advocate a discrimination are for making a full provision for the securities of the former, at their nominal value; but contend, that the latter ought to receive no more than the cost to them, and the interest: And the idea is sometimes suggested of making good the difference to the primitive possessor.

In favor of this scheme, it is alledged, that it would be unreasonable to pay twenty shillings in the pound, to one who had not given more for it than three or four. And it is added, that it would be hard to aggravate the misfortune of the first owner, who, probably through necessity, parted with his property at so great a loss, by obliging him to contribute to the profit of the person, who had speculated on his distresses.

The Secretary, after the most mature reflection on the force of this argument, is induced to reject the doctrine it contains, as equally unjust and impolitic, as highly injurious, even to the original holders of public securities; as ruinous to public credit.

It is inconsistent with justice, because in the first place, it is a breach of contract; in violation of the rights of a fair purchaser.

The nature of the contract in its origin, is, that the public will pay the sum expressed in the security, to the first holder, or his *assignee*. The *intent*, in making the security assignable, is, that the proprietor may be able to make use of his property, by selling it for as much as it *may be worth in the market*, and that the buyer may be *safe* in the purchase.

Every buyer therefore stands exactly in the place of the seller, has the same right with him to the identical sum expressed in the security, and having acquired that right, by fair purchase, and in conformity to the original *agreement* and *intention* of the government, his claim cannot be disputed, without manifest injustice.

That he is to be considered as a fair purchaser, results from this: Whatever necessity the seller may have been under, was occasioned by the government, in not making a proper provision for its debts. The buyer had no agency in it, and therefore ought not to suffer. He is not even chargeable with having taken an undue advantage. He paid what the commodity was worth in the market, and took the risks of reimbursement upon himself. He of course gave a fair equivalent, and ought to reap the benefit of his hazard; a hazard which was far from inconsiderable, and which, perhaps, turned on little less than a revolution in government.

That the case of those, who parted with their securities from necessity, is a hard one, cannot be denied. But whatever complaint of injury, or claim of redress, they may have, respects the government solely. They have not only nothing to object to the persons who relieved their necessities, by giving them the current price of their property, but they are even under an implied condition to contribute to the reimbursement of those persons. They knew, that by the terms of the contract with themselves, the public were bound to pay to those, to whom they should convey their title, the sums stipulated to be paid to them; and, that as citizens of the United States, they were to bear their proportion of the contribution for that purpose. This, by the act of assignment, they tacitly engage to do; and if they had an option, they could not, with integrity or good faith, refuse to do it, without the consent of those to whom they sold.

But though many of the original holders sold from necessity, it does not follow, that this was the case with all of them. It may well be supposed, that some of them did it either through want of confidence in an eventual provision, or from the allurements of some profitable speculation. How shall these different classes be discriminated from each other? How shall it be ascertained, in any case, that the money, which the original holder obtained for his security, was not more beneficial to him, than if he had held it to the pressent time, to avail himself of the provision which shall be made? How shall it be known, whether if the purchaser had employed his money in some other way, he would not be in a better situation, than by having applied it in the purchase of securities, though he should now receive their full amount? And if neither of these things can be known, how shall it be determined whether a discrimination, independent of the breach of contract, would not do a real injury to purchasers; and if it included a compensation to the primitive proprietors, would not give them an advantage, to which they had no equitable pretension.

It may well be imagined, also, that there are not wanting instances, in which individuals, urged by a present necessity, parted with the securities received by them from the public, and shortly after replaced them with others, as an indemnity for their first loss. Shall they be deprived of the indemnity which they have endeavoured to secure by so provident an arrangement?

Questions of this sort, on a close inspection, multiply themselves without end, and demonstrate the injustice of a discrimination, even on the most subtile calculations of equity, abstracted from the obligation of contract.

The difficulties too of regulating the details of a plan for that purpose, which would have even the semblance of equity, would be found immense. It may well be doubted whether they would not be insurmountable, and replete with such absurd, as well as inequitable consequences, as to disgust even the proposers of the measure.

As a specimen of its capricious operation, it will be sufficient to notice the effect it would have upon two persons, who may be supposed two years ago to have purchased, each, securities at three shillings in the pound, and one of them to retain those bought by him, till the discrimination should take place; the other to have parted with those bought by him, within a month past, at nine shillings. The former, who had had most confidence in the government, would in this case only receive at the rate of three shillings and the interest; while the latter, who had had less confidence would receive *for what cost him the same money* at the rate of nine shillings, and his representative, *standing in his place*, would be entitled to a like rate.

The impolicy of a discrimination results from two considerations; one, that it proceeds upon a principle destructive of that *quality* of the public debt, or the stock of the nation, which is essential to its capacity for answering the purposes of money—that is the *security* of *transfer*; the other, that as well on this account, as because it includes a breach of faith, it renders property in the funds less valuable; consequently induces lenders to demand a higher premium for what they lend, and produces every other inconvenience of a bad state of public credit.

It will be perceived at first sight, that the transferable quality of stock is essential to its operation as money, and that this depends on the idea of complete security to the transferree, and a firm persuasion, that no distinction can in any circumstances be made between him and the original proprietor.

The precedent of an invasion of this fundamental principle, would of course tend to deprive the community of an advantage, with which no temporary saving could bear the least comparison.

And it will as readily be perceived, that the same cause would operate a diminution of the value of stock in the hands of the first, as well as of every other holder. The price, which any man, who should incline to purchase, would be willing to give for it, would be in a compound ratio to the immediate profit it afforded, and to the chance of the continuance of his profit. If there was supposed to be any hazard of the latter, the risk would be taken into the calculation, and either there would be no purchase at all, or it would be at a proportionably less price.

For this diminution of the value of stock, every person, who should be about to lend to the government, would demand a compensation; and would add to the actual difference, between the nominal and the market value, and equivalent for the chance of greater decrease; which, in a precarious state of public credit, is always to be taken into the account.

Every compensation of this sort, it is evident, would be an absolute loss to the government.

In the preceding discussion of the impolicy of a discrimination, the injurious tendency of it to those, who continue to be the holders of the securities, they received from the government, has been explained. Nothing need be added, on this head, except that this is an additional and interesting light, in which the injustice of the measure may be seen. It would not only divest present proprietors by purchase, of the rights they had acquired under the sanction of public faith, but it would depreciate the property of the remaining original holders.

It is equally unnecessary to add any thing to what has been already said to demonstrate the fatal influence, which the principle of discrimination would have on the public credit.

But there is still a point in view in which it will appear perhaps even more exceptionable, than in either of the former. It would be repugnant to an express provision of the Constitution of the United States. This provision is, that "all debts contracted and engagements entered into before the adoption of that Constitution shall be as valid against the United States under it, as under the confederation," which amounts to a constitutional ratification of the contracts respecting the debt, in the state in which they existed under the confederation. And resorting to that standard, there can be no doubt, that the rights of assignees and original holders, must be considered as equal.

In exploding thus fully the principle of discrimination, the Secretary is happy in reflecting, that he is the only advocate of what has been already sanctioned by the formal and express authority of the government of the Union, in these emphatic terms—"The remaining class of creditors (say Congress in their circular address to the states, of the 26th of April 1783) is composed, partly of such of our fellow-citizens as originally lent to the public the use of their funds, or have since manifested *most confidence* in their country, by receiving transfers from the lenders; and partly of those, whose property has been either advanced or assumed for the public service. To *discriminate* the merits of these several descriptions of creditors, would be a task equally unnecessary and invidious. If the voice of humanity plead more loudly in favor of some than of others, the voice of policy, no less than of justice, pleads in favor of all. A WISE NATION will never permit those who relieve the wants of their country, or who *rely most* on its *faith*, its *firmness*, and its *resources*, when either of them is distrusted, to suffer by the event."

The Secretary concluding, that a discrimination, between the different classes of creditors of the United States, cannot with propriety be *made*, proceeds to examine whether a difference ought to be permitted to *remain* between them, and another description of public creditors—Those of the states individually.

The Secretary, after mature reflection on this point, entertains a full conviction, that an assumption of the debts of the particular states by the union, and a like provision for them, as for those of the union, will be a measure of sound policy and substantial justice.

It would, in the opinion of the Secretary, contribute, in an eminent degree, to an orderly, stable and satisfactory arrangement of the national finances.

Admitting, as ought to be the case, that a provision must be made in some way or other, for the entire debt; it will follow, that no greater revenues will be required, whether that provision be made wholly by the United States, or partly by them, and partly by the states separately.

The principal question then must be, whether such a provision cannot be more conveniently and effectually made, by one general plan issuing from one authority, than by different plans originating in different authorities.

In the first case there can be no competition for resources; in the last, there must be such a competition. The consequences of this, without the greatest caution on both sides, might be interfering regulations, and thence collision and confusion. Particular branches of industry might also be oppressed by it. The most productive objects of revenue are not numerous. Either these must be wholly engrossed by one side, which might lessen the efficacy of the provisions by the other; or both must have recourse to the same objects in different modes, which might occasion an accumulation upon them, beyond what they could properly bear. If this should not happen, the caution requisite to avoiding it, would prevent the revenue's deriving the full benefit of each object. The danger of interference and of excess would be apt to impose restraints very unfriendly to the complete command of those resources, which are the most convenient; and to compel the having recourse to others, less eligible in themselves, and less agreeable to the community.

The difficulty of an effectual command of the public resources, in case of separate provisions for the debt, may be seen in another, and perhaps more striking light. It would naturally happen that different states, from local considerations, would in some instances have recourse to different objects, in others, to the same objects, in different degrees, for procuring the funds of which they stood in need. It is easy to conceive how this diversity would affect the aggregate revenue of the country. By the supposition, articles which yielded a full supply in some states, would yield nothing, or an insufficient product, in others. And hence the public revenue would not derive the full benefit of those articles, from state regulations. Neither could the deficiencies be made good by those of the union. It is a provision of the national constitution, that "all duties, imposts and excises, shall be uniform throughout the United States." And as the general government would be under a necessity from motives of policy, of paying regard to the duty, which may have been previously imposed upon any article, though but in a single state, it would be constrained, either to refrain wholly from any further imposition, upon such article, where it had been already rated as high as was proper, or to confine itself to the difference between the existing rate, and what the article would reasonably bear. Thus the pre-occupancy of an article by a single state, would tend to arrest or abridge the impositions of the union on that article. And as it is supposeable, that a great variety of articles might be placed in this situation, by dissimilar arrangements of the particular states, it is evident, that the aggregate revenue of the country would be likely to be very materially contracted by the plan of separate provisions.

If all the public creditors receive their dues from one source, distributed with an equal hand, their interest will be the same. And having the same interests, they will unite in the support of the fiscal arrangements of the government: As these, too, can be made with more convenience, where there is no competition: These circumstances combined will insure to the revenue laws a more ready and more satisfactory execution.

If on the contrary there are distinct provisions, there will be distinct interests, drawing different ways. That union and concert of views, among the creditors, which in every government is of great importance to their security, and to that of public credit, will not only not exist, but will be likely to give place to mutual jealousy and opposition. And from this cause, the operation of the systems which may be adopted, both by the particular states, and by the union, with relation to their respective debts, will be in danger of being counteracted.

There are several reasons, which render it probable, that the situation of the state creditors would be worse, than that of the creditors of the union, if there be not a national assumption of the state debts. Of these it will be sufficient to mention two; one, that a principal branch of revenue is exclusively vested in the union; the other, that a state must always be checked in the imposition of taxes on articles of consumption, from the want of power to extend the same regulation to the other states, and from the tendency of partial duties to injure its industry and commerce. Should the state creditors stand upon a less eligible footing than the others, it is unnatural to expect they would see with pleasure a provision for them. The influence which their dissatisfaction might have, could not but operate injuriously, both for the creditors, and the credit, of the United States.

Hence it is even the interest of the creditors of the union, that those of the individual states should be comprehended in a general provision. Any attempt to secure to the former either exclusive or peculiar advantages, would materially hazard their interests.

Neither would it be just, that one class of the public creditors should be more favoured than the other. The objects for which both descriptions of the debt were contracted, are in the main the same. Indeed a great part of the particular debts of the States has arisen from assumptions by them on account of the union. And it is most equitable, that there should be the same measure of retribution for all.

There is an objection, however, to an assumption of the state debts, which deserves particular notice. It may be supposed, that it would increase the difficulty of an equitable settlement between them and the United States.

The principles of that settlement, whenever they shall be discussed, will require all the moderation and wisdom of the government. In the opinion of the Secretary, that discussion, till further lights are obtained, would be premature.

All therefore which he would now think adviseable on the point in question, would be, that the amount of the debts assumed and provided for, should be charged to the respective states, to abide an eventual arrangement. This, the United States, as assignees to the creditors, would have an indisputable right to do.

Opinion on the Constitutionality
of an Act to Establish a Bank

The Secretary of the Treasury having perused with attention the papers containing the opinions of the Secretary of State and Attorney General concerning the constitutionality of the bill for establishing a National Bank proceeds according to the order of the President to submit the reasons which have induced him to entertain a different opinion.

It will naturally have been anticipated that, in performing this task he would feel uncommon solicitude. Personal considerations alone arising from the reflection that the measure originated with him would be sufficient to produce it: The sense which he has manifested of the great importance of such an institution to the successful administration of the department under his particular care; and an expectation of serious ill consequences to result from a failure of the measure, do not permit him to be without anxiety on public accounts. But the chief solicitude arises from a firm persuasion, that principles of construction like those espoused by the Secretary of State and the Attorney General would be fatal to the just & indispensible authority of the United States.

In entering upon the argument it ought to be premised, that the objections of the Secretary of State and Attorney General are founded on a general denial of the authority of the United States to erect corporations. The latter indeed expressly admits, that if there be any thing in the bill which is not warranted by the constitution, it is the clause of incorporation.

Now it appears to the Secretary of the Treasury, that this *general principle* is *inherent* in the very *definition* of *Government* and *essential* to every step of the progress to be made by that of the United States; namely—that every power vested in a Government is in its nature *sovereign*, and includes by *force* of the *term*, a right to employ all the *means* requisite, and fairly *applicable* to the attainment of the *ends* of such power; and which are not precluded by restrictions & exceptions specified in the constitution; or not immoral, or not contrary to the essential ends of political society.

This principle in its application to Government in general would be admitted as an axiom. And it will be incumbent upon those, who may incline to deny it, to *prove* a distinction; and to shew that a rule which in the general system of things is essential to the preservation of the social order is inapplicable to the United States.

The circumstances that the powers of sovereignty are in this country divided between the National and State Governments, does not afford the distinction required. It does not follow from this, that each of the *portions* of powers delegated to the one or to the other is not sovereign *with regard to its proper objects*. It will only *follow* from it, that each has sovereign power as to *certain things*, and not as to *other things*. To deny that the Government of the United States has sovereign power as to its declared purposes & trusts, because its power does not extend to all cases, would be equally to deny, that the State Governments have sovereign power in any case; because their power does not extend to every case. The tenth section of the first article of the constitution exhibits a long list of very important things which they may not do. And thus the United States would furnish the singular spectacle of a *political society* without *sovereignty*, or of a people *governed* without *government*.

If it would be necessary to bring proof to a proposition so clear as that which affirms that the powers of the fœderal government, *as to its objects*, are sovereign, there is a clause of its constitution which would be decisive. It is that which declares, that the constitution and the laws of the United States made in pursuance of it, and all treaties made or which shall be made under their authority shall be the supreme law of the land. The power which can create the *Supreme law* of the land, in any case, is doubtless sovereign *as to such case*.

This general & indisputable principle puts at once an end to the *abstract* question—Whether the United States have power to *erect a corporation?* that is to say, to give a *legal* or *artificial* capacity to one or more persons, distinct from the natural. For it is unquestionably incident to *sovereign power* to erect corporations, and consequently to *that* of the United States, in *relation to the objects* intrusted to the management of the government. The difference is this—where the authority of the government is general, it can create corporations in *all cases*; where it is confined to certain branches of legislation, it can create corporations only in those cases.

Here then as far as concerns the reasonings of the Secretary of State & the Attorney General, the affirmative of the constitutionality of the bill might be permitted to rest. It will occur to the President that the principle here advanced has been untouched by either of them.

For a more complete elucidation of the point nevertheless, the arguments which they have used against the power of the government to erect corporations, however foreign they are to the great & fundamental rule which has been stated, shall be particularly examined. And after shewing that they do not tend to impair its force, it shall also be shewn, that the power of incorporation incident to the government in certain cases, does fairly extend to the particular case which is the object of the bill.

The first of these arguments is, that the foundation of the constitution is laid on this ground "that all powers not delegated to the United States by the Constitution nor prohibited to it by the States are reserved to the States or to the people", whence it is meant to be inferred, that congress can in no case exercise any power not included in those enumerated in the constitution. And it is affirmed that the power of erecting a corporation is not included in any of the enumerated powers.

The main proposition here laid down, in its true signification is not to be questioned. It is nothing more than a consequence of this republican maxim, that all government is a delegation of power. But how much is delegated in each case, is a question of fact to be made out by fair reasoning & construction upon the particular provisions of the constitution—taking as guides the general principles & general ends of government.

It is not denied, that there are *implied*, as well as *express* powers, and that the former are as effectually delegated as the latter. And for the sake of accuracy it shall be mentioned, that there is another class of powers, which may be properly denominated *resulting* powers. It will not be doubted that if the United States should make a conquest of any of the territories of its neighbours, they would possess sovereign jurisdiction over the conquered territory. This would rather be a result from the whole mass of the powers of the government & from the nature of political society, than a consequence of either of the powers specially enumerated.

But be this as it may, it furnishes a striking illustration of the general doctrine contended for. It shews an extensive case, in which a power of erecting corporations is either implied in, or would result from some or all of the powers, vested in the National Government. The jurisdiction acquired over such conquered territory would certainly be competent to every species of legislation.

To return—It is conceded, that implied powers are to be considered as delegated equally with express ones.

Then it follows, that as a power of erecting a corporation may as well be *implied* as any other thing; it may as well be employed as an *instrument* or *mean* of carrying into execution any of the specified powers, as any other instrument or mean whatever. The only question must be, in this as in every other case, whether the mean to be employed, or in this instance the corporation to be erected, has a natural relation to any of the acknowledged objects or lawful ends of the government. Thus a corporation may not be erected by congress, for superintending the police of the city of Philadelphia because they are not authorised to *regulate* the *police* of that city; but one may be erected in relation to the collection of the taxes, or to the trade with foreign countries, or to the trade between the States, or with the Indian Tribes, because it is the province of the fœderal government to regulate those objects & because it is incident to a general *sovereign* or *legislative power* to *regulate* a thing, to employ all the means which relate to its regulation to the *best* & *greatest advantage*.

A strange fallacy seems to have crept into the manner of thinking & reasoning upon the subject. Imagination appears to have been unusually busy concerning it. An incorporation seems to have been regarded as some great, independent, substantive thing—as a political end of peculiar magnitude & moment; whereas it is truly to be considered as a *quality*, *capacity*, or *mean* to an end. Thus a mercantile company is formed with a certain capital for the purpose of carrying on a particular branch of business. Here the business to be prosecuted is the *end*; the association in order to form the requisite capital is the primary mean. Suppose that an incorporation were added to this; it would only be to add a new *quality* to that association; to give it an artificial capacity by which it would be enabled to prosecute the business with more safety & convenience.

That the importance of the power of incorporation has been exaggerated, leading to erroneous conclusions, will further appear from tracing it to its origin. The roman law is the source of it, according to which a *voluntary* association of individuals at *any time* or *for any purpose* was capable of producing it. In England, whence our notions of it are immediately borrowed, it forms a part of the executive authority, & the exercise of it has been often *delegated* by that authority. Whence therefore the ground of the supposition, that it lies beyond the reach of all those very important portions of sovereign power, legislative as well as executive, which belong to the government of the United States?

To this mode of reasoning respecting the right of employing all the means requisite to the execution of the specified powers of the Government, it is objected that none but *necessary* & proper means are to be employed, & the Secretary of State maintains, that no means are to be considered as *necessary*, but those without which the grant of the power would be *nugatory*. Nay so far does he go in his restrictive interpretation of the word, as even to make the case of *necessity* which shall warrant the constitutional exercise of the power to depend on *casual* & *temporary* circumstances, an idea which alone refutes the construction. The *expediency* of exercising a particular power, at a particular time, must indeed depend on *circumstances*; but the constitutional right of exercising it must be uniform & invariable— the same to day, as to morrow.

All the arguments therefore against the constitutionality of the bill derived from the accidental existence of certain State-banks: institutions which *happen* to exist to day, & for ought that concerns the government of the United States, may disappear to morrow, must not only be rejected as fallacious, but must be viewed as demonstrative, that there is a *radical* source of error in the reasoning.

It is essential to the being of the National government, that so erroneous a conception of the meaning of the word *necessary*, should be exploded.

It is certain, that neither the grammatical, nor popular sense of the term requires that construction. According to both, *necessary* often means no more than *needful, requisite, incidental, useful,* or *conducive to*. It is a common mode of expression to say, that it is *necessary* for a government or a person to do this or that thing, when nothing more is intended or understood, than that the interests of the government or person require, or will be promoted, by the doing of this or that thing. The imagination can be at no loss for exemplifications of the use of the word in this sense.

And it is the true one in which it is to be understood as used in the constitution. The whole turn of the clause containing it, indicates, that it was the intent of the convention, by that clause to give a liberal latitude to the exercise of the specified powers. The expressions have peculiar comprehensiveness. They are—"to make *all laws*, necessary & proper for *carrying into execution* the foregoing powers & all *other powers* vested by the constitution in the *government* of the United States, or in any *department* or *officer* thereof." To understand the word as the Secretary of State does, would be to depart from its obvious & popular sense, and to give it a *restrictive* operation; an idea never before entertained. It would be to give it the same force as if the word *absolutely* or *indispensibly* had been prefixed to it.

Such a construction would beget endless uncertainty & embarassment. The cases must be palpable & extreme in which it could be pronounced with certainty, that a measure was absolutely necessary, or one without which the exercise of a given power would be nugatory. There are few measures of any government, which would stand so severe a test. To insist upon it, would be to make the criterion of the exercise of any implied power a *case of extreme necessity*; which is rather a rule to justify the overleaping of the bounds of constitutional authority, than to govern the ordinary exercise of it.

It may be truly said of every government, as well as of that of the United States, that it has only a right, to pass such laws as are necessary & proper to accomplish the objects intrusted to it. For no government has a right to do *merely what it pleases*. Hence by a process of reasoning similar to that of the Secretary of State, it might be proved, that neither of the State governments has a right to incorporate a bank. It might be shewn, that all the public business of the State, could be performed without a bank, and inferring thence that it was unnecessary it might be argued that it could not be done, because it is against the rule which has been just mentioned. A like mode of reasoning would prove, that there was no power to incorporate the Inhabitants of a town, with a view to a more perfect police: For it is certain, that an incorporation may be dispensed with, though it is better to have one. It is to be remembered, that there is no *express* power in any State constitution to erect corporations.

The *degree* in which a measure is necessary, can never be a test of the *legal* right to adopt it. That must ever be a matter of opinion; and can only be a test of expediency. The *relation* between the *measure* and the *end*, between the *nature* of *the mean* employed towards the execution of a power and the object of that power, must be the criterion of constitutionality not the more or less of *necessity* or *utility*.

The practice of the government is against the rule of construction advocated by the Secretary of State. Of this the act concerning light houses, beacons, buoys & public piers, is a decisive example. This doubtless must be referred to the power of regulating trade, and is fairly relative to it. But it cannot be affirmed, that the exercise of that power, in this instance, was strictly necessary; or that the power itself would be *nugatory* without that of regulating establishments of this nature.

This restrictive interpretation of the word *necessary* is also contrary to this sound maxim of construction namely, that the powers contained in a constitution of government, especially those which concern the general administration of the affairs of a country, its finances, trade, defence &c ought to be construed liberally, in advancement of the public good. This rule does not depend on the particular form of a government or on the particular demarkation of the boundaries of its powers, but on the nature and objects of government itself. The means by which national exigencies are to be provided for, national inconveniencies obviated, national prosperity promoted, are of such infinite variety, extent and complexity, that there must, of necessity, be great latitude of discretion in the selection & application of those means. Hence consequently, the necessity & propriety of exercising the authorities intrusted to a government on principles of liberal construction.

The Attorney General admits the *rule*, but takes a distinction between a State, and the fœderal constitution. The latter, he thinks, ought to be construed with greater strictness, because there is more danger of error in defining partial than general powers.

But the reason of the *rule* forbids such a distinction. This reason is—the variety & extent of public exigencies, a far greater proportion of which and of a far more critical kind, are objects of National than of State administration. The greater danger of error, as far as it is supposeable, may be a prudential reason for caution in practice, but it cannot be a rule of restrictive interpretation.

In regard to the clause of the constitution immediately under consideration, it is admitted by the Attorney General, that no *restrictive* effect can be ascribed to it. He defines the word necessary thus. "To be necessary is to be *incidental*, and may be denominated the natural means of executing a power."

But while, on the one hand, the construction of the Secretary of State is deemed inadmissible, it will not be contended on the other, that the clause in question gives any *new* or *independent* power. But it gives an explicit sanction to the doctrine of *implied* powers, and is equivalent to an admission of the proposition, that the government, *as to its specified powers* and *objects*, has plenary & sovereign authority, in some cases paramount to that of the States, in others coordinate with it. For such is the plain import of the declaration, that it may pass *all laws* necessary & proper to carry into execution those powers.

It is no valid objection to the doctrine to say, that it is calculated to extend the powers of the general government throughout the entire sphere of State legislation. The same thing has been said, and may be said with regard to every exercise of power by *implication* or *construction*. The moment the literal meaning is departed from, there is a chance of error and abuse. And yet an adherence to the letter of its powers would at once arrest the motions of the government. It is not only agreed, on all hands, that the exercise of constructive powers is indispensible, but every act which has been passed is more or less an exemplification of it. One has been already mentioned, that relating to light houses &c. That which declares the power of the President to remove officers at pleasure, acknowlidges the same truth in another, and a signal instance.

The truth is that difficulties on this point are inherent in the nature of the fœderal constitution. They result inevitably from a division of the legislative power. The consequence of this division is, that there will be cases clearly within the power of the National Government; others clearly without its power; and a third class, which will leave room for controversy & difference of opinion, & concerning which a reasonable latitude of judgment must be allowed.

But the doctrine which is contended for is not chargeable with the consequence imputed to it. It does not affirm that the National government is sovereign in all respects, but that it is sovereign to a certain extent: that is, to the extent of the objects of its specified powers.

It leaves therefore a criterion of what is constitutional, and of what is not so. This criterion is the *end* to which the measure relates as a *mean*. If the end be clearly comprehended within any of the specified powers, & if the measure have an obvious relation to that end, and is not forbidden by any particular provision of the constitution—it may safely be deemed to come within the compass of the national authority. There is also this further criterion which may materially assist the decision. Does the proposed measure abridge a preexisting right of any State, or of any individual? If it does not, there is a strong presumption in favour of its constitutionality; & slighter relations to any declared object of the constitution may be permitted to turn the scale.

The general objections which are to be inferred from the reasonings of the Secretary of State and of the Attorney General to the doctrine which has been advanced, have been stated and it is hoped satisfactorily answered. Those of a more particular nature shall now be examined.

The Secretary of State introduces his opinion with an observation, that the proposed incorporation undertakes to create certain capacities properties or attributes which are *against* the laws of *alienage*, *descents*, *escheat* and *forfeiture*, *distribution* and *monopoly*, and to confer a power to make laws paramount to those of the States. And nothing says he, in another place, but a *necessity invincible by other means* can justify such a *prostration* of *laws* which constitute the pillars of our whole system of jurisprudence, and are the foundation laws of the State Governments.

If these are truly the foundation laws of the several states, then have most of them subverted their own foundations. For there is scarcely one of them which has not, since the establishment of its particular constitution, made material alterations in some of those branches of its jurisprudence especially the law of descents. But it is not conceived how any thing can be called the fundamental law of a State Government which is not established in its constitution unalterable by the ordinary legislature. And with regard to the question of necessity it has been shewn, that this can only constitute a question of expediency, not of right.

To erect a corporation is to substitute a *legal* or *artificial* to a *natural* person, and where a number are concerned to give them *individuality*. To that legal or artificial person once created, the common law of every state of itself *annexes* all those incidents and attributes, which are represented as a prostration of the main pillars of their jurisprudence. It is certainly not accurate to say, that the erection of a corporation is *against* those different *heads* of the State laws; because it is rather to create a kind of person or entity, to which *they* are inapplicable, and to which the general rule of those laws assign a different regimen. The laws of alienage cannot apply to an artificial person, because it can have no country. Those of descent cannot apply to it, because it can have no heirs. Those of escheat are foreign from it for the same reason. Those of forfeiture, because it cannot commit a crime. Those of distribution, because, though it may be dissolved, it cannot die. As truly might it be said, that the exercise of the power of prescribing the rule by which foreigners shall be naturalised, is *against* the law of alienage; while it is in fact only to put them in a situation to cease to be the subject of that law. To do a thing which is *against* a law, is to do something which it forbids or which is a violation of it.

But if it were even to be admitted that the erection of a corporation is a direct alteration of the State laws in the enumerated particulars; it would do nothing towards proving, that the measure was unconstitutional. If the government of the United States can do no act, which amounts to an alteration of a State law, all its powers are nugatory. For almost every new law is an alteration, in some way or other of an old *law*, either *common*, or *statute*.

There are laws concerning bankruptcy in some states—some states have laws regulating the values of foreign coins. Congress are empowered to establish uniform laws concerning bankruptcy throughout the United States, and to regulate the values of foreign coins. The exercise of either of these powers by Congress necessarily involves an alteration of the laws of those states.

Again: Every person by the common law of each state may export his property to foreign countries, at pleasure. But Congress, in pursuance of the power of regulating trade, may prohibit the exportation of commodities: in doing which, they would alter the common law of each state in abridgement of individual rights.

It can therefore never be good reasoning to say—this or that act is unconstitutional, because it alters this or that law of a State. It must be shewn, that the act which makes the alteration is unconstitutional on other accounts, not *because* it makes the alteration.

There are two points in the suggestions of the Secretary of State which have been noted that are peculiarly incorrect. One is, that the proposed incorporation is against the laws of monopoly, because it stipulates an exclusive right of banking under the national authority. The other that it gives power to the institution to make laws paramount to those of the states.

But with regard to the first point, the bill neither prohibits any State from erecting as many banks as they please, nor any number of

Individuals from associating to carry on the business: & consequently is free from the charge of establishing a monopoly: for monopoly implies a *legal impediment* to the carrying on of the trade by others than those to whom it is granted.

And with regard to the second point, there is still less foundation. The bye-laws of such an institution as a bank can operate only upon its own members; can only concern the disposition of its own property and must essentially resemble the rules of a private mercantile partnership. They are expressly not to be contrary to law; and law must here mean the law of a State as well as of the United States. There never can be a doubt, that a law of the corporation, if contrary to a law of a state, must be overruled as void; unless the law of the State is contrary to that of the United States; and then the question will not be between the law of the State and that of the corporation, but between the law of the State and that of the United States.

Another argument made use of by the Secretary of State, is, the rejection of a proposition by the convention to empower Congress to make corporations, either generally, or for some special purpose.

What was the precise nature or extent of this proposition, or what the reasons for refusing it, is not ascertained by any authentic document, or even by accurate recollection. As far as any such document exists, it specifies only canals. If this was the amount of it, it would at most only prove, that it was thought inexpedient to give a power to incorporate for the purpose of opening canals, for which purpose a special power would have been necessary; except with regard to the Western Territory, there being nothing in any part of the constitution respecting the regulation of canals. It must be confessed however, that very different accounts are given of the import of the proposition and of the motives for rejecting it. Some affirm that it was confined to the opening of canals and obstructions in rivers; others, that it embraced banks; and others, that it extended to the power of incorporating generally. Some again alledge, that it was disagreed to, because it was thought improper to vest in Congress a power of erecting corporations—others, because it was thought unnecessary to *specify* the power, and inexpedient to furnish an additional topic of objection to the constitution. In this state of the matter, no inference whatever can be drawn from it.

But whatever may have been the nature of the proposition or the reasons for rejecting it concludes nothing in respect to the real merits of the question. The Secretary of State will not deny, that whatever may have been the intention of the framers of a constitution, or of a law, that intention is to be sought for in the instrument itself, according to the usual & established rules of construction. Nothing is more common than for laws to *express* and *effect*, more or less than was intended. If then a power to erect a corporation, in any case, be deducible by fair inference from the whole or any part of the numerous provisions of the constitution of the United States, arguments drawn from extrinsic circumstances, regarding the intention of the convention, must be rejected.

Most of the arguments of the Secretary of State which have not been considered in the foregoing remarks, are of a nature rather to apply to the expediency than to the constitutionality of the bill. They will however be noticed in the discussions which will be necessary in reference to the particular heads of the powers of the government which are involved in the question.

Those of the Attorney General will now properly come under review.

His first observation is, that the power of incorporation is not *expressly* given to congress. This shall be conceded, but in *this sense* only, that it is not declared in *express terms* that congress may erect a *corporation*. But this cannot mean, that there are not certain *express* powers, which *necessarily* include it.

For instance, Congress have express power "to exercise exclusive legislation in all cases whatsoever, over such *district* (not exceeding ten miles square) as may by cession of particular states, & the acceptance of Congress become the seat of the government of the United states; and to exercise *like authority* over all places purchased by consent of the legislature of the State in which the same shall be for the erection of forts, arsenals, dock yards & other needful buildings."

Here then is express power to exercise *exclusive legislation in all cases whatsoever over certain places*; that is to do in respect to those places, all that any government whatever may do: For language does not afford a more complete designation of sovereign power, than in those comprehensive terms. It is in other words a power to pass all laws whatsoever, & consequently to pass laws for erecting corporations, as well as for any other purpose which is the proper object of law in a free government. Surely it can never be believed, that Congress with *exclusive power of legislation in all cases whatsoever*, cannot erect a corporation within the district which shall become the seat of government, for the better regulation of its police. And yet there is an unqualified denial of the power to erect corporations in every case on the part both of the Secretary of State and of the Attorney General. The former indeed speaks of that power in these emphatical terms, that it is *a right remaining exclusively with the states*.

As far then as there is an express power to do any *particular act of legislation*, there is an express one to erect corporations in the cases above described. But accurately speaking, no *particular power* is more than *implied* in a *general one*. Thus the power to lay a duty on a *gallon of rum*, is only a particular *implied* in the general power to lay and collect taxes, duties, imposts and excises. This serves to explain in what sense it may be said, that congress have not an express power to make corporations.

This may not be an improper place to take notice of an argument which was used in debate in the House of Representatives. It was there urged, that if the constitution intended to confer so important a power as that of erecting corporations, it would have been expressly mentioned. But the case which has been noticed is clearly one in which such a power exists, and yet without any specification or express grant of it, further than as every *particular implied* in a general power, can be said to be so granted.

But the argument itself is founded upon an exaggerated and erroneous conception of the nature of the power. It has been shewn, that it is not of so transcendent a kind as the reasoning supposes; and that viewed in a just light it is a mean which ought to have been left to *implication*, rather than an end which ought to have been *expressly* granted.

Having observed, that the power of erecting corporations is not expressly granted to Congress, the Attorney General proceeds thus . . .

"If it can be exercised by them, it must be

1. because the nature of the fœderal government implies it.
2. because it is involved in some of the specified powers of legislation or
3. because it is necessary & proper to carry into execution some of the specified powers."

To be implied in the *nature of the fœderal government*, says he, would beget a doctrine so indefinite, as to grasp every power.

This proposition it ought to be remarked is not precisely, or even substantially, that, which has been relied upon. The proposition relied upon is, that the *specified powers* of Congress are in their nature sovereign—that it is incident to sovereign power to erect corporations; & that therefore Congress have a right within the *sphere* & *in relation to the objects of their power, to erect corporations.*

It shall however be supposed, that the Attorney General would consider the two propositions in the same light, & that the objection made to the one, would be made to the other.

To this objection an answer has been already given. It is this; that the doctrine is stated with this express *qualification*, that the right to erect corporations does *only* extend to *cases* & *objects* within the *sphere* of the *specified powers* of the government. A general legislative authority implies a power to erect corporations *in all cases*—a particular legislative power implies authority to erect corporations, in relation to cases arising under that power only. Hence the affirming, that as an *incident* to sovereign power, congress may erect a corporation in relation to the *collection* of their taxes, is no more than to affirm that they may do whatever else they please; than the saying that they have a power to regulate trade would be to affirm that they have a power to regulate religion: or than the maintaining that they have sovereign power as to taxation, would be to maintain that they have sovereign power as to every thing else.

The Attorney General undertakes, in the next place, to shew, that the power of erecting corporations is not involved in any of the specified powers of legislation confided to the National government.

In order to this he has attempted an enumeration of the particulars which he supposes to be comprehended under the several heads of the *powers* to lay & collect taxes &c—to borrow money on the credit of the United States—to regulate commerce with foreign nations—between the states, and with the Indian Tribes—to dispose of and make all needful rules & regulations respecting the territory or other property belonging to the United States; the design of which enumeration is to shew *what is* included under those different heads of power, & *negatively*, that the power of erecting corporations is not included.

The truth of this inference or conclusion must depend on the accuracy of the enumeration. If it can be shewn that the enumeration is *defective*, the inference is destroyed. To do this will be attended with no difficulty.

The heads of the power to lay & collect taxes, he states to be

1. To ascertain the subject of taxation &c
2. to declare the quantum of taxation &c
3. to prescribe the *mode* of *collection*.
4. to ordain the manner of accounting for the taxes &c

The defectiveness of this enumeration consists in the generality of the third division "*to prescribe the mode* of collection"; which is in itself an immense chapter. It will be shewn hereafter, that, among a vast variety of particulars, it comprises the very power in question; namely to *erect corporations*.

The heads of the power to borrow money are stated to be

1. to stipulate the sum to be lent.
2. an interest or no interest to be paid.
3. the time & manner of repaying, unless the loan be placed on an irredeemable fund.

This enumeration is liable to a variety of objections. It omits, in the first place, the *pledging* or *mortgaging* of a fund for the security of the money lent, an usual and in most cases an essential ingredient.

The idea of a stipulation of *an interest or no interest* is too confined. It should rather have been said, to stipulate the *consideration* of the loan. Individuals often borrow upon considerations other than the payment of interest. So may government; and so they often find it necessary to do. Every one reCollects the lottery tickets & other douceurs often given in Great Britain, as collateral inducements to the lending of money to the Government.

There are also frequently collateral conditions, which the enumeration does not contemplate. Every contract which has been made for monies borrowed in Holland includes stipulations that the sum due shall be *free from taxes*, and from sequestration in time of war, and mortgages all the land & property of the United States for the reimbursement.

It is also known, that a lottery is a common expedient for borrowing money, which certainly does not fall under either of the enumerated heads.

The heads of the power to regulate commerce with foreign nations are stated to be

1. to prohibit them or their commodities from our ports.
2. to impose duties on *them* where none existed before, or to increase existing duties on them.

3. to subject *them* to any species of custom house regulation
4. to grant *them* any exemptions or privileges which policy may suggest.

This enumeration is far more exceptionable than either of the former. It omits *every thing* that relates to the *citizens vessels* or *commodities* of the United States. The following palpable omissions occur at once.

1. Of the power to prohibit the exportation of commodities which not only exists at all times, but which in time of war it would be necessary to exercise, particularly with relation to naval and warlike stores.
2. Of the power to prescribe rules concerning the *characteristics* & *priviledges* of an american bottom—how she shall be navigated, as whether by citizens or foreigners, or by a proportion of each.
3. Of the power of regulating the manner of contracting with seamen, the police of ships on their voyages &c of which the act for the government & regulation of seamen in the merchants service is a specimen.

That the three preceding articles are omissions, will not be doubted. There is a long list of items in addition, which admit of little, if any question; of which a few samples shall be given.

1. The granting of bounties to certain kinds of vessels, & certain species of merchandise. Of this nature is the allowance on dried & pickled fish & salted provisions.
2. The prescribing of rules concerning the *inspection* of commodities to be exported. Though the states individually are competent to this regulation, yet there is no reason, in point of authority at least, why a general system might not be adopted by the United States.
3. The regulation of policies of insurance; of salvage upon goods found at sea, and the disposition of such goods.
4. The regulation of pilots.
5. The regulation of bills of exchange drawn by a merchant of *one state* upon a merchant of *another state*. This last rather belongs to the regulation of trade between the states, but is equally omitted in the specification under that head.

The last enumeration relates to the power "to dispose of & make *all needful rules and regulations* respecting the territory *or other property* belonging to the United States."

The heads of this power are said to be

1. to exert an ownership over the territory of the United States, which may be properly called the property of the United States, as in the Western Territory, and to *institute a government therein*: or

2. to exert an ownership over the other property of the United States.

This idea of exerting an ownership over the Territory or other property of the United States, is particularly indefinite and vague. It does not at all satisfy the conception of what must have been intended by a power, to make all needful *rules* and *regulations*; nor would there have been any use for a special clause which authorised nothing more. For the right of exerting an ownership is implied in the very definition of property.

It is admitted that in regard to the western territory some thing more is intended—even the institution of a government; that is the creation of a body politic, or corporation of the highest nature; one, which in its maturity, will be able itself to create other corporations. Why then does not the same clause authorise the erection of a corporation in respect to the regulation or disposal of any other of the property of the United States? This idea will be enlarged upon in another place.

Hence it appears, that the enumerations which have been attempted by the Attorney General are so imperfect, as to authorise no conclusion whatever. They therefore have no tendency to disprove, that each and every of the powers to which they relate, includes that of erecting corporations; which they certainly do, as the subsequent illustrations will more & more evince.

It is presumed to have been satisfactorily shewn in the course of the preceding observations

1. That the power of the government, *as to* the objects intrusted to its management, is in its nature sovereign.

2. That the right of erecting corporations is one, inherent in & inseparable from the idea of sovereign power.

3. That the position, that the government of the United States can exercise no power but such as is delegated to it by its constitution, does not militate against this principle.

4. That the word *necessary* in the general clause can have no

restrictive operation, derogating from the force of this principle, indeed, that the degree in which a measure is, or is not necessary, cannot be a *test* of *constitutional* right, but of expediency only.

5. That the power to erect corporations is not to be considered, as an *independent* & *substantive* power but as an *incidental* & *auxiliary* one; and was therefore more properly left to implication, than expressly granted.

6. that the principle in question does not extend the power of the government beyond the prescribed limits, because it only affirms a power to *incorporate* for *purposes within the sphere of the specified powers*.

And lastly that the right to exercise such a power, in certain cases, is unequivocally granted in the most *positive* & *comprehensive* terms.

To all which it only remains to be added that such a power has actually been exercised in two very eminent instances: namely in the erection of two governments, One, northwest of the river Ohio, and the other south west—*the last, independent of any antecedent compact*.

And there results a full & complete demonstration, that the Secretary of State & Attorney General are mistaken, when they deny generally the power of the National government to erect corporations.

It shall now be endeavoured to be shewn that there is a power to erect one of the kind proposed by the bill. This will be done, by tracing a natural & obvious relation between the institution of a bank, and the objects of several of the enumerated powers of the government; and by shewing that, *politically* speaking, it is necessary to the effectual execution of one or more of those powers. In the course of this investigation, various instances will be stated, by way of illustration, of a right to erect corporations under those powers.

Some preliminary observations maybe proper.

The proposed bank is to consist of an association of persons for the purpose of creating a joint capital to be employed, chiefly and essentially, in loans. So far the object is not only lawful, but it is the mere exercise of a right, which the law allows to every individual. The bank of New York which is not incorporated, is an example of such an association. The bill proposes in addition, that the government shall become a joint proprietor in this undertaking, and that it shall permit the bills of the company payable on demand to be receivable in its revenues & stipulates that it shall not grant privileges similar to those which are to be allowed to this company, to any others. All this is in controvertibly within the compass of the discretion of the government. The only question is, whether it has a right to incorporate this company, in order to enable it the more effectually to accomplish *ends*, which are in themselves lawful.

To establish such a right, it remains to shew the relation of such an institution to one or more of the specified powers of the government.

Accordingly it is affirmed, that it has a relation more or less direct to the power of collecting taxes; to that of borrowing money; to that of regulating trade between the states; and to those of raising, supporting & maintaining fleets & armies. To the two former, the relation may be said to be *immediate*.

And, in the last place, it will be argued, that it is, *clearly*, within the provision which authorises the making of all *needful* rules & *regulations* concerning the *property* of the United States, as the same has been practiced upon by the Government.

A Bank relates to the collection of taxes in two ways; *indirectly*, by increasing the quantity of circulating medium & quickening circulation, which facilitates the means of paying—*directly*, by creating a *convenient species* of *medium* in which they are to be paid.

To designate or appoint the money or *thing* in which taxes are to be paid, is not only a proper, but a necessary *exercise* of the power of collecting them. Accordingly congress in the law concerning the collection of the duties on imports & tonnage, have provided that they shall be payable in gold & silver. But while it was an indispensible part of the work to say in what they should be paid, the choice of the specific thing was mere matter of discretion. The payment might have been required in the commodities themselves. Taxes in kind, however ill judged, are not without precedents, even in the United States. Or it might have been in the paper money of the several states; or in the bills of the bank of North America, New York and Massachusetts, all or either of them: or it might have been in bills issued under the authority of the United States.

No part of this can, it is presumed, be disputed. The appointment, then, of the *money* or *thing*, in which the taxes are to be paid, is an incident to the power of collection. And among the expedients which may be adopted, is that of bills issued under the authority of the United States.

Now the manner of issuing these bills is again matter of discretion. The government might, doubtless, proceed in the following manner. It might provide, that they should be issued under the direction of certain officers, payable on demand; and in order to support their credit & give them a ready circulation, it might, besides giving them a currency in its taxes, set apart out of any monies in its Treasury, a given sum and appropriate it under the direction of those officers as a fund for answering the bills as presented for payment.

The constitutionality of all this would not admit of a question. And yet it would amount to the institution of a bank, with a view to the more convenient collection of taxes. For the simplest and most precise idea of a bank, is, a deposit of coin or other property, as a fund for *circulating* a *credit* upon it, which is to answer the purpose of money. That such an arrangement would be equivalent to the establishment of a bank would become obvious, if the place where the fund to be set apart was kept should be made a receptacle of the monies of all other persons who should incline to deposit them there for safe keeping; and would become still more so, if the Officers charged with the direction of the fund were authorised to make discounts at the usual rate of interest, upon good security. To deny the power of the government to add these ingredients to the plan, would be to refine away all government.

This process serves to exemplify the natural & direct relation which may subsist between the institution of a bank and the collection of taxes. It is true that the species of bank which has been designated, does not include the idea of incorporation. But the argument intended to be founded upon it, is this: that the institution comprehended in the idea of a bank being one immediately relative to the collection of taxes, *in regard to the appointment* of *the money or thing* in which they are to be paid; the sovereign power of providing for the collection of taxes necessarily includes the right of granting a corporate capacity to such an institution, as a requisite to its greater security, utility and more convenient management.

A further process will still more clearly illustrate the point. Suppose, when the species of bank which has been described was about to be instituted, it were to be urged, that in order to secure to it a due degree of confidence the fund ought not only to be set apart & appropriated generally, but ought to be specifically vested in the officers who were to have the direction of it, and in their *successors* in office, to the end that it might acquire the character of *private property* incapable of being resumed without a violation of the sanctions by which the rights of property are protected & occasioning more serious & general alarm, the apprehension of which might operate as a check upon the government—such a proposition might be opposed by arguments against the expediency of it or the solidity of the reason assigned for it, but it is not conceivable what could be urged against its constitutionality.

And yet such a disposition of the thing would amount to the erection of a corporation. For the true definition of a corporation seems to be this. It is a *legal* person, or a person created by act of law, consisting of one or more natural persons authorised to hold property or a franchise in succession in a legal as contradistinguished from a natural capacity.

Let the illustration proceed a step further. Suppose a bank of the nature which has been described with or without incorporation, had been instituted, & that experience had evinced as it probably would, that being wholly under public direction it possessed not the confidence requisite to the credit of its bills—Suppose also that by some of those adverse conjunctures which occasionally attend nations, there had been a very great drain of the specie of the country, so as not only to cause general distress for want of an adequate medium of circulation, but to produce, in consequence of that circumstance, considerable defalcations in the public revenues—suppose also, that there was no bank instituted in any State—in such a posture of things, would it not be most manifest that the incorporation of a bank, like that proposed by the bill, would be a measure immediately relative to the *effectual collection* of the taxes and completely within the province of the sovereign power of providing by all laws necessary & proper for that collection?

If it be said, that such a state of things would render that necessary & therefore constitutional, which is not so now—the answer to this, and a solid one it doubtless is, must still be, that which has been already stated—Circumstances may affect the expediency of the measure, but they can neither add to, nor diminish its constitutionality.

A Bank has a direct relation to the power of borrowing money, because it is an usual and in sudden emergencies an essential instrument in the obtaining of loans to Government.

A nation is threatened with a war. Large sums are wanted, on a sudden, to make the requisite preparations. Taxes are laid for the purpose, but it requires time to obtain the benefit of them. Anticipation is indispensible. If there be a bank, the supply can, at once be had; if there be none loans from Individuals must be sought. The progress of these is often too slow for the exigency: in some situations they are not practicable at all. Frequently when they are, it is of great consequence to be able to anticipate the product of them by advances from a bank.

The essentiality of such an institution as an instrument of loans is exemplified at this very moment. An Indian expedition is to be prosecuted. The only fund out of which the money can arise consistently with the public engagements, is a tax which will only begin to be collected in July next. The preparations, however, are instantly to be made. The money must therefore be borrowed. And of whom could it be borrowed; if there were no public banks?

It happens, that there are institutions of this kind, but if there were none, it would be indispensible to create one.

Let it then be supposed, that the necessity existed, (as but for a casualty would be the case) that proposals were made for obtaining a loan; that a number of individuals came forward and said, we are willing to accommodate the government with this money; with what we have in hand and the credit we can raise upon it we doubt not of being able to furnish the sum required: but in order to this, it is indispensible, that we should be incorporated as a bank. This is essential towards putting it in our power to do what is desired and we are obliged on that account to make it the *consideration* or condition of the loan.

Can it be believed, that a compliance with this proposition would be unconstitutional? Does not this alone evince the contrary? It is a necessary part of a power to borrow to be able to stipulate the consideration or conditions of a loan. It is evident, as has been remarked elsewhere, that this is not confined to the mere stipulation of a sum of money by way of interest—why may it not be deemed to extend, where a government is the contracting party, to the stipulation of a *franchise*? If it may, & it is not perceived why it may not, then the grant of a corporate capacity may be stipulated as a consideration of the loan? There seems to be nothing unfit, or foreign from the nature of the thing in giving individuality or a corporate capacity to a number of persons who are willing to lend a sum of money to the government, the better to enable them to do it, and make them an ordinary instrument of loans in future emergencies of the state.

But the more general view of the subject is still more satisfactory.

The legislative power of borrowing money, & of making all laws necessary & proper for carrying into execution that power, seems obviously competent to the appointment of the *organ* through which the abilities and wills of individuals may be most efficaciously exerted, for the accommodation of the government by loans.

The Attorney General opposes to this reasoning, the following observation. "To borrow money presupposes the accumulation of a fund to be lent, and is secondary to the creation of an ability to lend." This is plausible in theory, but it is not true in fact. In a great number of cases, a previous accumulation of a fund equal to the whole sum required, does not exist. And nothing more can be actually presupposed, than that there exist resources, which put into activity to the greatest advantage by the nature of the operation with the government, will be equal to the effect desired to be produced. All the provisions and operations of government must be presumed to contemplate things as they *really* are.

The institution of a bank has also a natural relation to the regulation of trade between the States: in so far as it is conducive to the creation of a convenient medium of *exchange* between them, and to the keeping up a full circulation by preventing the frequent displacement of the metals in reciprocal remittances. Money is the very hinge on which commerce turns. And this does not mean merely gold & silver, many other things have served the purpose with different degrees of utility. Paper has been extensively employed.

It cannot therefore be admitted with the Attorney General, that the regulation of trade between the States, as it concerns the medium of circulation & exchange ought to be considered as confined to coin. It is even supposeable in argument, that the whole, or the greatest part of the coin of the country, might be carried out of it.

The Secretary of State objects to the relation here insisted upon, by the following mode of reasoning—"To erect a bank, says he, & to regulate commerce, are very different acts. He who erects a bank, creates a subject of commerce, so does he, who makes a bushel of wheat, or digs a dollar out of the mines. Yet neither of these persons regulates commerce thereby. To make a thing which may be bought & sold is not to *prescribe* regulations for *buying* & *selling*: thus making the regulation of commerce to consist in prescribing rules for *buying* & *selling*.

This indeed is a species of regulation of trade; but is one which falls more aptly within the province of the local jurisdictions than within that of the general government, whose care must be presumed to have been intended to be directed to those general political arrangements concerning trade on which its aggregate interests depend, rather than to the details of buying and selling.

Accordingly such only are the regulations to be found in the laws of the United States; whose objects are to give encouragement to the entreprise of our own merchants, and to advance our navigation and manufactures.

And it is in reference to these general relations of commerce, that an establishment which furnishes facilities to circulation and a convenient medium of exchange & alienation, is to be regarded as a regulation of trade.

The Secretary of State further argues, that if this was a regulation of commerce, it would be void, *as extending as much to the internal commerce of every state as to its external.* But what regulation of commerce does not extend to the internal commerce of every state? What are all the duties upon imported articles amounting to prohibitions, but so many bounties upon domestic manufactures affecting the interests of different classes of citizens in different ways? What are all the provisions in the coasting act, which relate to the trade between district and district of the same State? In short what regulation of trade between the States, but must affect the internal trade of each State? What can operate upon the whole but must extend to every part!

The relation of a bank to the execution of the powers, that concern the common defence, has been anticipated. It has been noted, that at this very moment the aid of such an institution is essential to the measures to be pursued for the protection of our frontier.

It now remains to shew, that the incorporation of a bank is within the operation of the provision which authorises Congress to make all needful rules & regulations concerning the property of the United States. But it is previously necessary to advert to a distinction which has been taken by the Attorney General.

He admits, that the word *property* may signify personal property however acquired. And yet asserts, that it cannot signify money arising from the sources of revenue pointed out in the constitution; because, says he, "the disposal & regulation of money is the final cause for raising it by taxes."

But it would be more accurate to say, that the *object* to which money is intended to be applied is the *final cause* for raising it, than that the disposal and regulation of it is *such*. The support of Government; the support of troops for the common defence; the payment of the public debt, are the true *final causes* for raising money. The disposition & regulation of it when raised, are the steps by which it is applied to the *ends* for which it was raised, not the ends themselves. Hence therefore the money to be raised by taxes as well as any other personal property, must be supposed to come within the meaning as they certainly do within the letter of the authority, to make all needful rules & regulations concerning the property of the United States.

A case will make this plainer: suppose the public debt discharged, and the funds now pledged for it liberated. In some instances it would be found expedient to repeal the taxes, in others, the repeal might injure our own industry, our agriculture and manufactures. In these cases they would of course be retained. Here then would be monies arising from the authorised sources of revenue which would not fall within the rule by which the Attorney General endeavours to except them from other personal property, & from the operation of the clause in question.

The monies being in the coffers of the government, what is to hinder such a disposition to be made of them as is contemplated in the bill or what an incorporation of the parties concerned under the clause which has been cited.

It is admitted that with regard to the Western territory they give a power to erect a corporation—that is to institute a government. And by what rule of construction can it be maintained, that the same words in a constitution of government will not have the same effect when applied to one species of property, as to another, as far as the subject is capable of it? or that a legislative power to make all needful rules & regulations, or to pass all laws necessary & proper concerning the public property which is admitted to authorise an incorporation in one case will not authorise it in another? will justify the institution of a government over the western territory & will not justify the incorporation of a bank, for the more useful management of the money of the nation? If it will do the last, as well as the first, then under this provision alone the bill is constitutional, because it contemplates that the United States shall be joint proprietors of the stock of the bank.

There is an observation of the secretary of state to this effect, which may require notice in this place. Congress, says he, are not to lay taxes *ad libitum for any purpose they please*, but only to pay the debts, or provide for the *welfare* of the Union. Certainly no inference can be drawn from this against the power of applying their money for the institution of a bank. It is true, that they cannot without breach of trust, lay taxes for any other purpose than the general welfare but so neither can any other government. The welfare of the community is the only legitimate end for which money can be raised on the community. Congress can be considered as under only one restriction, which does not apply to other governments—They cannot rightfully apply the money they raise to any purpose *merely* or purely local. But with this exception they have as large a discretion in relation to the *application* of money as any legislature whatever. The constitutional *test* of a right application must always be whether it be for a purpose of *general* or *local* nature. If the former, there can be no want of constitutional power. The quality of the object, as how far it will really promote or not the welfare of the union, must be matter of conscientious discretion. And the arguments for or against a measure in this light, must be arguments concerning expediency or inexpediency, not constitutional right. Whatever relates to the general order of the finances, to the general interests of trade &c being general objects are constitutional ones for *the application* of *money*.

A Bank then whose bills are to circulate in all the revenues of the country, is *evidently* a general object, and for that very reason a constitutional one as far as regards the appropriation of money to it. Whether it will really be a beneficial one, or not, is worthy of careful examination, but is no more a constitutional point, in the particular referred to; than the question whether the western lands shall be sold for twenty or thirty cents ℔ acre.

A hope is entertained, that it has by this time been made to appear, to the satisfaction of the President, that a bank has a natural relation to the power of collecting taxes; to that of borrowing money; to that of regulating trade; to that of providing for the common defence: and that as the bill under consideration contemplates the government in the light of a joint proprietor of the stock of the bank, it brings the case within the provision of the clause of the constitution which immediately respects the property of the United States.

Under a conviction that such a relation subsists, the Secretary of the Treasury, with all deference conceives, that it will result as a necessary consequence from the position, that all the specified powers of the government are sovereign as to the proper objects; that the incorporation of a bank is a constitutional measure, and that the objections taken to the bill, in this respect, are ill founded.

But from an earnest desire to give the utmost possible satisfaction to the mind of the President, on so delicate and important a subject, the Secretary of the Treasury will ask his indulgence while he gives some additional illustrations of cases in which a power of erecting corporations may be exercised, under some of those heads of the specified powers of the Government, which are alledged to include the right of incorporating a bank.

1. It does not appear susceptible of a doubt, that if Congress had thought proper to provide in the collection law, that the bonds to be given for the duties should be given to the collector of each district in the name of the collector of the district A. or B. as the case might require, to enure to him & his successors in office, in trust for the United States, that it would have been consistent with the constitution to make such an arrangement. And yet this it is conceived would amount to an incorporation.

2. It is not an unusual expedient of taxation to farm particular branches of revenue, that is to mortgage or sell the product of them for certain definite sums, leaving the collection to the parties to whom they are mortgaged or sold. There are even examples of this in the United States. Suppose that there was any particular branch of revenue which it was manifestly expedient to place on this footing, & there were a number of persons willing to engage with the Government, upon condition, that they should be incorporated & the funds vested in them, as well for their greater safety as for the more convenient recovery & management of the taxes. Is it supposeable, that there could be any constitutional obstacle to the measure? It is presumed that there could be none. It is certainly a mode of collection which it would be in the discretion of the Government to adopt; though the circumstances must be very extraordinary, that would induce the Secretary to think it expedient.

3. suppose a new & unexplored branch of trade should present itself with some foreign country. Suppose it was manifest, that, to undertake it with advantage, required an union of the capitals

of a number of individuals; & that those individuals would not be disposed to embark without an incorporation, as well to obviate that consequence of a private partnership, which makes every individual liable in his whole estate for the debts of the company to their utmost extent, as for the more convenient management of the business—what reason can there be to doubt, that the national government would have a constitutional right to institute and incorporate such a company? None.

They possess a general authority to regulate trade with foreign countries. This is a mean which has been practiced to that end by all the principal commercial nations; who have trading companies to this day which have subsisted for centuries. Why may not the United States *constitutionally* employ the means usual in other countries for attaining the ends entrusted to them?

A power to make all needful rules & regulations concerning territory has been construed to mean a power to erect a government. A power to *regulate* trade is a power to make all needful rules & regulations concerning trade. Why may it not then include that of erecting a trading company as well as in the other case to erect a Government?

It is remarkable, that the State Conventions who have proposed amendments in relation to this point, have most, if not all of them, expressed themselves nearly thus—"Congress shall not grant monopolies, nor *erect any company* with exclusive advantages of commerce;" thus at the same time expressing their sense, that the power to erect trading companies or corporations, was inherent in Congress, & objecting to it no further, than as to the grant of *exclusive* priviledges.

The Secretary entertains all the doubts which prevail concerning the utility of such companies; but he cannot fashion to his own mind a reason to induce a doubt, that there is a constitutional authority in the United States to establish them. If such a reason were demanded, none could be given unless it were this—that congress cannot erect a corporation; which would be no better than to say they cannot do it, because they cannot do it: first presuming an inability, without reason, & then assigning that *inability* as the cause of itself.

Illustrations of this kind might be multiplied without end. They shall however be pursued no further.

There is a sort of evidence on this point, arising from an aggregate view of the constitution, which is of no inconsiderable weight. The very general power of laying & collecting taxes & appropriating their proceeds—that of borrowing money indefinitely—that of coining money & regulating foreign coins—that of making all needful rules and regulations respecting the property of the United States—these powers combined, as well as the reason & nature of the thing speak strongly this language: That it is the manifest design and scope of the constitution to vest in congress all the powers requisite to the effectual administration of the finances of the United States. As far as concerns this object, there appears to be no parsimony of power.

To suppose then, that the government is precluded from the employment of so usual as well as so important an instrument for the administration of its finances as that of a bank, is to suppose, what does not coincide with the general tenor & complexion of the constitution, and what is not agreeable to impressions that any mere spectator would entertain concerning it. Little less than a prohibitory clause can destroy the strong presumptions which result from the general aspect of the government. Nothing but demonstration should exclude the idea, that the power exists.

In all questions of this nature the practice of mankind ought to have great weight against the theories of Individuals.

The fact, for instance, that all the principal commercial nations have made use of trading corporations or companies for the purposes of *external commerce*, is a satisfactory proof, that the Establishment of them is an incident to the regulation of that commerce.

This other fact, that banks are an usual engine in the administration of national finances, & an ordinary & the most effectual instrument of loans & one which in this country has been found essential, pleads strongly against the supposition, that a government clothed with most of the most important prerogatives of sovereignty in relation to the revenues, its debts, its credit, its defence, its trade, its intercourse with foreign nations—is forbidden to make use of that instrument as an appendage to its own authority.

It has been stated as an auxiliary test of constitutional authority, to try, whether it abridges any preexisting right of any state, or any Individual. The proposed incorporation will stand the most severe examination on this point. Each state may still erect as many banks as it pleases; every individual may still carry on the banking business to any extent he pleases.

Another criterion may be this, whether the institution or thing has a more direct relation as to its uses, to the objects of the reserved powers of the State Governments, than to those of the powers delegated by the United States. This rule indeed is less precise than the former, but it may still serve as some guide. Surely a bank has more reference to the objects entrusted to the national government, than to those, left to the care of the State Governments. The common defence is decisive in this comparison.

It is presumed, that nothing of consequence in the observations of the Secretary of State and Attorney General has been left unnoticed.

There are indeed a variety of observations of the Secretary of State designed to shew that the utilities ascribed to a bank in relation to the collection of taxes and to trade, could be obtained without it, to analyse which would prolong the discussion beyond all bounds. It shall be forborne for two reasons—first because the report concerning the Bank may speak for itself in this respect; and secondly, because all those observations are grounded on the erroneous idea, that the *quantum* of necessity or utility is the test of a constitutional exercise of power.

One or two remarks only shall be made: one is that he has taken no notice of a very essential advantage to trade in general which is mentioned in the report, as peculiar to the existence of a bank circulation equal, in the public estimation to Gold & silver. It is this, that it renders it unnecessary to *lock* up the money of the country to accumulate for months successively in order to the periodical payment of interest. The other is this; that his arguments to shew that treasury orders & bills of exchange from the course of trade will prevent any considerable displacement of the metals, are founded on a partial view of the subject. A case will prove this: The sums collected in a state may be small in comparison with the debt due to it. The balance of its trade, direct & circuitous, with the seat of government may be even or nearly so. Here then without bank bills, which in that state answer the purpose of coin, there must be a displacement of the coin, in proportion to the difference between the sum collected in the State and that to be paid in it. With bank bills no such displacement would take place, or, as far as it did, it would be gradual & insensible. In many other ways also, would there be at least a temporary & inconvenient displacement of the coin, even where the course of trade would eventually return it to its proper channels.

The difference of the two situations in point of convenience to the Treasury can only be appreciated by one, who experiences the embarassments of making provision for the payment of the interest on a stock continually changing place in thirteen different places.

One thing which has been omitted just occurs, although it is not very material to the main argument. The Secretary of State affirms, that the bill only contemplates a re-payment, not a loan to the government. But here he is, certainly mistaken. It is true, the government invests in the stock of the bank a sum equal to that which it receives on loan. But let it be remembered, that it does not, therefore, cease to be a proprietor of the stock; which would be the case, if the money received back were in the nature of a repayment. It remains a proprietor still, & will share in the profit, or loss, of the institution, according as the dividend is more or less than the interest it is to pay on the sum borrowed. Hence that sum is manifestly, and, in the strictest sense, a loan.

Philadelphia February 23d. 1791.

To Philip A. Hamilton

Philadelphia December 5
1791

I received with great pleasure My Dear Philip the letter which you wrote me last week. Your Mama and myself were very happy to learn that you are pleased with your situation and content to stay as long as shall be thought for your good. We hope and believe that nothing will happen to alter this disposition.

Your Master also informs me that you recited a lesson the first day you began, very much to his satisfaction. I expect every letter from him will give me a fresh proof of your progress. For I know that you can do a great deal, if you please, and I am sure you have too much spirit not to exert yourself, that you may make us every day more and more proud of you.

Your Mama has got an Ovid for you and is looking up your Mairs introduction. If it cannot be found tomorrow another will be procured and the books with the other articles she promised to send you will be forwarded in two or three days.

You remember that I engaged to send for you next Saturday and I will do it, unless you request me to put it off. For a promise must never be broken; and I never will make you one, which I will not fulfil as far as I am able. But it has occurred to me that the Christmas holidays are near at hand, and I suppose your school will then break up for some days and give you an opportunity of coming to stay with us for a longer time than if you should come on Saturday. Will it not be best for you, therefore, to put off your journey till the holidays? But determine as you like best and let me know what will be most pleasing to you.

A good night to my darling son. Adieu

A HAMILTON

To Edward Carrington

Philadelphia May 26th, 1792

MY DEAR SIR

Believing that I possess a share of your personal friendship and confidence and yielding to that which I feel towards you—persuaded also that our political creed is the same on *two essential points*, 1st the necessity of *Union* to the respectability and happiness of this Country and 2 the necessity of an *efficient* general government to maintain that Union—I have concluded to unbosom myself to you on the present state of political parties and views. I ask no reply to what I shall say. I only ask that you will be persuaded, the representations I shall make are agreable to the real and sincere impressions of my mind. You will make the due allowances for the influence of circumstances upon it—you will consult your own observations and you will draw such a conclusion as shall appear to you proper.

When I accepted the Office, I now hold, it was under a full persuasion, that from similarity of thinking, conspiring with personal goodwill, I should have the firm support of Mr. Madison, in the *general course* of my administration. Aware of the intrinsic difficulties of the situation and of the powers of Mr. Madison, I do not believe I should have accepted under a different supposition.

I have mentioned the similarity of thinking between that Gentleman and myself. This was relative not merely to the general principles of National Policy and Government but to the leading points which were likely to constitute questions in the administration of the finances. I mean 1 the expediency of *funding* the debt 2 the inexpediency of *discrimination* between original and present holders   3 The expediency of *assuming* the state Debts.

As to the first point, the evidence of Mr. Madisons sentiments at one period is to be found in the address of Congress of April 26th 1783, which was planned by him in conformity to his own ideas and without any previous suggestions from the Committee and with his hearty cooperation in every part of the business. His conversations upon various occasions since have been expressive of a continuance in the same sentiment, nor indeed, has he yet contradicted it by any part of his official conduct. How far there is reason to apprehend a change in this particular will be stated hereafter.

As to the second part, the same address is an evidence of Mr. Madison's sentiments at the same period. And I had been informed that at a later period he had been in the Legislature of Virginia a strenuous and successful opponent of the principle of discrimination. Add to this that a variety of conversations had taken place between him and myself respecting the public debt down to the commencement of the New Government in none of which had he glanced at the idea of a change of opinion. I wrote him a letter after my appointment in the recess of Congress to obtain his sentiments on the subject of the Finances. In his answer there is not a lisp of his new system.

As to the third point, the question of an assumption of the state Debts by the U States was in discussion when the Convention that framed the present Government was sitting at Philadelphia; and in a long conversation, which I had with Mr. Madison in an afternoon's walk I well remember that we were perfectly agreed in the expediency and propriety of such a measure, though we were both of opinion that it would be more adviseable to make it a measure of administration than an article of constitution; from the impolicy of multiplying obstacles to its reception on collateral details.

Under these circumstances, you will naturally imagine that it must have been matter of surprize to me, when I was apprised, that it was Mr. Madison's intention to oppose my plan on both the last mentioned points.

Before the debate commenced, I had a conversation with him on my report, in the course of which I alluded to the calculation I had made of his sentiments and the grounds of that calculation. He did not deny them, but alledged in his justification that the very considerable alienation of the debt, subsequent to the periods at which he had opposed a discrimination, had essentially changed the state of the question—and that as to the assumption, he had contemplated it to take place *as matters stood at the peace*.

While the change of opinion avowed on the point of discrimination diminished my respect for the force of Mr. Madison's mind and the soundness of his judgment—and while the idea of reserving and setting afloat a vast mass of already extinguished debt as the condition of a measure the leading objects of which were an accession of strength to the National Government and an assurance of order and vigour in the national finances by doing away the necessity of thirteen complicated and conflicting systems of finance—appeared to me somewhat extraordinary: Yet my previous impressions of the fairness of Mr. Madison's character and my reliance on his good will towards me disposed me to believe that his suggestions were sincere; and even, on the point of an assumption of the debts of the States as they stood at the peace, to lean towards a cooperation in his view; 'till on feeling the ground I found the thing impracticable, and on further reflection I thought it liable to immense difficulties. It was tried and failed with little countenance.

At this time and afterwards repeated intimations were given to me that Mr. Madison, from a spirit of rivalship or some other cause had become personally unfriendly to me; and one Gentleman in particular, whose honor I have no reason to doubt, assured me, that Mr. Madison in a conversation with him had made a pretty direct attempt to insinuate unfavourable impressions of me.

Still I suspended my opinion on the subject. I knew the malevolent officiousness of mankind too well to yield a very ready acquiescience to the suggestions which were made, and resolved to wait 'till time and more experience should afford a solution.

It was not 'till the last session that I became unequivocally convinced of the following truth—*"That Mr. Madison cooperating with Mr. Jefferson is at the head of a faction decidedly hostile to me and my administration, and actuated by views in my judgment subversive of the principles of good government and dangerous to the union, peace and happiness of the Country."*

These are strong expressions; they may pain your friendship for one or both of the Gentlemen whom I have named. I have not lightly resolved to hazard them. They are the result of a *Serious alarm* in my mind for the public welfare, and of a full conviction that what I have alledged is a truth, and a truth, which ought to be told and well attended to, by all the friends of Union and efficient National Government. The suggestion will, I hope, at least awaken attention, free from the byass of former prepossessions.

This conviction in my mind is the result of a long train of circumstances; many of them minute. To attempt to detail them all would fill a volume. I shall therefore confine myself to the mention of a few.

First—As to the point of opposition to me and my administration.

Mr. Jefferson with very little reserve manifests his dislike of the funding system generally; calling in question the expediency of funding a debt at all. Some expressions which he has dropped in my own presence (sometimes without sufficient attention to delicacy) will not permit me to doubt on this point, representations, which I have had from various respectable quarters. I do not mean, that he advocates directly the undoing of what has been done, but he censures the whole on principles, which if they should become general, could not but end in the subversion of the system.

In various conversations with *foreigners* as well as citizens, he has thrown censure on my *principles* of government and on my measures of administration. He has predicted that the people would not long tolerate my proceedings & that I should not long maintain my ground. Some of those, whom he *immediately* and *notoriously* moves, have *even* whispered suspicions of the rectitude of my motives and conduct. In the question concerning the Bank he not only delivered an opinion in writing against its constitutionality & expediency; but he did it *in a stile and manner* which I felt as partaking of asperity and ill humour towards me. As one of the trustees of the sinking fund, I have experienced in almost every leading question opposition from him. When any turn of things in the community has threatened either odium or embarrassment to me, he has not been able to suppress the satisfaction which it gave him.

A part of this is of course information, and might be misrepresentation. But it comes through so many channels and so well accords with what falls under my own observation that I can entertain no doubt.

I find a strong confirmation in the following circumstances. *Freneau* the present Printer of the National Gazette, who was a journeyman with Childs & Swain at New York, was a known anti-federalist. It is reduced to a certainty that he was brought to Philadelphia by Mr. Jefferson to be the conductor of a News Paper. It is notorious that cotemporarily with the commencement of his paper he was a Clerk in the department of state for foreign languages. Hence a clear inference that his paper has been set on foot and is conducted under the patronage & not against the views of Mr. Jefferson. What then is the complexion of this paper? Let any impartial man peruse all the numbers down to the present day; and I never was more mistaken, if he does not pronounce that it is a paper devoted to the subversion of me & the measures in which I have had an Agency; and I am little less mistaken if he do not pronounce that it is a paper of a tendency *generally unfriendly* to the Government of the U States.

It may be said, that a News Paper being open to all the publications, which are offered to it, its complexion may be influenced by other views than those of the Editor. But the fact here is that wherever the Editor appears it is in a correspondent dress. The paragraphs which appear as his own, the publications, not original which are selected for his press, are of the same malignant and unfriendly aspect, so as not to leave a doubt of the temper which directs the publication.

Again *Brown*, who publishes an Evening paper called *The Federal Gazette* was originally a zealous federalist and personally friendly to me. He has been employed by Mr. Jefferson as a Printer to the Government for the publication of the laws; and for some time past 'till lately the complexion of his press was equally bitter and unfriendly to me & to the Government.

Lately, Col Pickering in consequence of certain attacks upon him, got hold of some instances of malconduct of his which have served to hold him in Check and seemed to have varied his tone a little. I dont lay so much stress on this last case as on the former. There, I find an internal evidence which is as conclusive as can be expected in any similar case. Thus far, as to Mr. Jefferson.

With regard to Mr. Madison—the matter stands thus. I have not heard, but in the one instance to which I have alluded, of his having held language unfriendly to me in private conversation. But in his public conduct there has been a more uniform & persevering opposition than I have been able to resolve into a sincere difference of opinion. I cannot persuade myself that Mr. Madison and I, whose politics had formerly so much the *same point of departure*, should now diverge so widely in our opinions of the measures which are proper to be pursued. The opinion I once entertained of the candour and simplicity and fairness of Mr. Madisons character has, I acknowledge, given way to a decided opinion that *it is one of a peculiarly artificial and complicated kind*.

For a considerable part of the last session, Mr. Madison lay in a great measure *perdu*. But it was evident from his votes & a variety of little movements and appearances, that he was the prompter of Mr. Giles & others, who were the open instruments of opposition. Two facts occurred, in the course of the session, which I view as unequivocal demonstrations of his disposition towards me. In one, a direct and decisive blow was aimed. When the department of the Treasury was established Mr. Madison was an unequivocal advocate of the principles which prevailed in it and of the powers and duties which were assigned by it to the head of the department. This appeared both from his private and public discourses; and I will add, that I have personal evidence that Mr. Madison is as well convinced as any man in the U States of the necessity of the arrangement which characterizes that establishment to the orderly conducting of the business of the Finances.

Mr. Madison nevertheless opposed directly a reference to me to report *ways* & *means* for the Western expedition, & combatted *on principle* the propriety of such references.

He well knew, that, if he had prevailed, a certain consequence was, my *resignation*—that I would not be fool enough to make pecuniary sacrifices and endure a life of extreme drudgery without opportunity either to do material good or to acquire reputation; and frequently with a responsibility in reputation for measures in which I had no hand, and in respect to which, the part I had acted, if any, could not be known.

To accomplish this point, an effectual train, as was supposed, was laid. Besides those who ordinarily acted under Mr. Madison's banners, several, who had generally acted with me from various motives, vanity, self importance, &c. &c. were enlisted.

My overthrow was anticipated as certain and Mr. Madison, *laying aside his wonted caution*, boldly led his troops as he imagined to a certain victory. He was disappointed. Though, *late* I became apprized of the danger. Measures of counteraction were adopted, & when the Question was called, Mr. Madison was confounded to find characters voting against him, whom he had counted upon as certain.

Towards the close of the Session, another, though a more covert, attack was made. It was in the shape of a proposition to insert in the supplementary Act respecting the public Debt something by way of instruction to the Trustees "to make their purchases of the debt at the *lowest* market price." In the course of the discussion of this point, Mr. Madison dealt much in *insidious insinuations* calculated to give an impression that the public money under my particular direction had been unfaithfully applied to put undue advantages in the pockets of speculators, & to support the debt at an *artificial* price for their benefit. The whole manner of this transaction left no doubt in any ones mind that Mr. Madison was actuated by *personal* & political animosity.

As to this last instance, it is but candid to acknowledge, that Mr. Madison had a better right to act the enemy than on any former occasion. I had some short time before, subsequent to his conduct respecting the reference, declared openly my opinion of the views, by which he was actuated towards me, & my determination to consider & treat him as a political enemy.

An intervening proof of Mr. Madisons unfriendly intrigues to my disadvantage is to be found in the following incident which I relate to you upon my honor but from the nature of it, you will perceive in the *strictest confidence*. The president having prepared his speech at the commencement of the ensuing session communicated it to Mr. Madison for his remarks. It contained among other things a *clause* concerning weights & measures, hinting the advantage of an invariable standard, which *preceded*, in the original state of the speech, a clause concerning the Mint. Mr. Madison suggested a transposition of these clauses & the addition of certain words, which I now forget importing an *immediate connection* between the two subjects. You may recollect that Mr. Jefferson proposes that the *unit of weight* & the *unit in the coins* shall be the same, & that my propositions are to preserve the Dollar as the Unit, adhering to its present quantity of Silver, & establishing the same proportion of alloy in the silver as in the gold Coins. The evident design of this manoeuvre was to connect the Presidents opinion in favour of Mr. Jefferson's idea, in contradiction to mine, &, the worst of it is, *without his being aware of the tendency of the thing*. It happened, that the President shewed me the Speech, altered in conformity to Mr. Madisons suggestion, just before it was copied for the purpose of being delivered. I remarked to him the tendency of the alteration. *He*

*declared that he had not been aware of it & had no such intention; & without
hesitation agreed to expunge the words which were designed to connect the
two subjects.*

This transaction, in my opinion, not only furnishes a proof of Mr.
Madisons *intrigues*, in opposition to my measures, but charges him with
an *abuse* of the Presidents confidence in him, by endeavouring to make
him, without his knowledge, take part with one officer against another,
in a case in which they had given different opinions to the Legislature of
the Country. *I forbore to awaken the President's mind to this last inference*;
but it is among the circumstances which have convinced me that Mr.
Madisons true character is the reverse of that *simple, fair, candid one*,
which he has assumed.

I have informed you, that Mr. Freneau was brought to Philadelphia,
by Mr. Jefferson, to be the Conductor of a News Paper. My information
announced Mr. Madison as the mean of negotiation while he was at
New York last summer. This and the general coincidence & close
intimacy between the two Gentlemen leave no doubt that their views
are substantially the same.

Secondly As to the tendency of the views of the two Gentlemen
who have been named.

Mr. Jefferson is an avowed enemy to a funded debt. Mr. Madison
disavows in public any intention to *undo* what has been done; but
in a private conversation with Mr. Charles Carroll (Senator), this
Gentlemans name I mention confidentially though he mentioned the
matter to Mr. King & several other Gentlemen as well as myself; & if
any chance should bring you together you would easily bring him to
repeat it to you, he favoured the sentiment in Mr. Mercers speech that
a Legislature had no right to *fund* the debt by mortgaging permanently
the public revenues because they had no right to bind posterity. The
inference is that what has been unlawfully done may be undone.

The discourse of partizans in the Legislature & the publications in
the party news-papers direct their main battery against the *principle* of a
funded debt, & represent it in the most odious light as a perfect *Pandoras
box*.

If Mr. Barnewell of St. Carolina, who appears to be a man of nice
honor, may be credited, Mr. Giles declared in a conversation with him
that if there was a question for reversing the funding system on the
abstract point of the right of pledging & the futility of preserving

public faith, he should be for reversal; merely to demonstrate his sense of the defect of right & the inutility of the thing. If positions equally extravagant were not publicly advanced by some of the party & secretly countenanced by the most guarded & *discreet* of them, one would be led, from the absurdity of the declaration, to suspect misapprehension. But from what is *known* any thing may be *believed*.

Whatever were the original merits of the funding system, after having been so solemly adopted, & after so great a transfer of property under it, what would become of the Government should it be reversed? What of the National Reputation? Upon what system of morality can so atrocious a doctrine be maintained? In me, I confess it excites *indignation* & *horror*!

What are we to think of those maxims of Government by which the power of a Legislature is denied to bind the Nation by a *Contract* in an affair of *property* for twenty four years? For this is precisely the case of the debt. What are to become of all the legal rights of property, of all charters to corporations, nay, of all grants to a man his heirs & assigns for ever, if this doctrine be true? What is the term for which a government is in capacity to *contract*? Questions might be multiplied without end to demonstrate the perniciousness & absurdity of such a doctrine.

In almost all the questions great & small which have arisen, since the first session of Congress, Mr. Jefferson & Mr. Madison have been found among those who were disposed to narrow the Federal authority. The question of a National Bank is one example. The question of bounties to the Fisheries is another. Mr. Madison resisted it on the ground of constitutionality, 'till it was evident, by the intermediate questions taken, that the bill would pass & he then under the wretched subterfuge of a change of a single word "bounty" for "allowance" went over to the Majority & voted for the bill. In the Militia bill & in a variety of minor cases he has leaned to abridging the exercise of foederal authority, & leaving as much as possible to the States & he has lost no opportunity of *sounding the alarm* with great affected solemnity at encroachments meditated on the rights of the States, & of holding up the bugbear of a faction in the Government having designs unfriendly to Liberty.

This kind of conduct has appeared to me the more extraordinary on the part of Mr. Madison as I know for a certainty it was a primary article in his Creed that the real danger in our system was the subversion of the

National authority by the preponderancy of the State Governments. All his measures have proceeded on an opposite supposition.

I recur again to the instance of Freneaus paper. In matters of this kind one cannot have direct proof of men's latent views; they must be inferred from circumstances. As the coadjutor of Mr. Jefferson in the establishment of this paper, I include Mr. Madison in the consequences imputable to it.

In respect to our foreign politics the views of these Gentlemen are in my judgment equally unsound & dangerous. *They have a womanish attachment to France and a womanish resentment against Great Britain.* They would draw us into the closest embrace of the former & involve us in all the consequences of her politics, & they would risk the peace of the country in their endeavours to keep us at the greatest possible distance from the latter. This disposition goes to a length particularly in Mr. Jefferson of which, till lately, I had no adequate Idea. Various circumstances prove to me that if these Gentlemen were left to pursue their own course there would be in less than six months *an open War between the U States & Great Britain.*

I trust I have a due sense of the conduct of France towards this Country in the late Revolution, & that I shall always be among the foremost in making her every suitable return; but there is a wide difference between this & implicating ourselves in all her politics; between bearing good will to her, & hating and wranggling with all those whom she hates. The Neutral & the Pacific Policy appear to me to mark the true path to the U States.

Having now delineated to you what I conceive to be the true complexion of the politics of these Gentlemen, I will now attempt a solution of these strange appearances.

Mr. Jefferson, it is known, did not in the first instance cordially acquiesce in the new constitution for the U States; he had many doubts & reserves. He left this Country before we had experienced the imbicillities of the former.

In France he saw government only on the side of its abuses. He drank deeply of the French Philosophy, in Religion, in Science, in politics. He came from France in the moment of a fermentation which he had had a share in exciting, & in the passions and feelings of which he shared both from temperament and situation.

He came here probably with a too partial idea of his own powers, and with the expectation of a greater share in the direction of our councils than he has in reality enjoyed. I am not sure that he had not peculiarly marked out for himself the department of the Finances.

He came electrified *plus* with attachment to France and with the project of knitting together the two Countries in the closest political bands.

Mr. Madison had always entertained an exalted opinion of the talents, knowledge and virtues of Mr. Jefferson. The sentiment was probably reciprocal. A close correspondence subsisted between them during the time of Mr. Jefferson's absence from this country. A close intimacy arose upon his return.

Whether any peculiar opinions of Mr. Jefferson concerning the public debt wrought a change in the sentiments of Mr. Madison (for it is certain that the former is more radically wrong than the latter) or whether Mr. Madison seduced by the expectation of popularity and possibly by the calculation of advantage to the state of Virginia was led to change his own opinion—certain it is, that a very material change took place, & that the two Gentlemen were united in the new ideas. Mr. Jefferson was indiscreetly open in his approbation of Mr. Madison's principles, upon his first coming to the seat of Government. I say indiscreetly, because a Gentleman in the administration in one department ought not to have taken sides against another, in another department.

The course of this business & a variety of circumstances which took place left Mr. Madison a very discontented & chagrined man and begot some degree of ill humour in Mr. Jefferson.

Attempts were made by these Gentlemen in different ways to produce a Commercial Warfare with Great Britain. In this too they were disappointed. And as they had the liveliest wishes on the subject their dissatisfaction has been proportionally great; and as I had not favoured the project, I was comprehended in their displeasure.

These causes and perhaps some others created, much sooner than I was aware of it, a systematic opposition to me on the part of those Gentlemen. My subversion, I am now satisfied, has been long an object with them.

Subsequent events have encreased the Spirit of opposition and the feelings of personal mortification on the part of these Gentlemen.

A mighty stand was made on the affair of the Bank. There was much *commitment* in that case. I prevailed.

On the Mint business I was opposed from the same Quarter, & with still less success. In the affair of ways & means for the Western expedition—on the supplementary arrangements concerning the debt except as to the additional assumption, my views have been equally prevalent in opposition to theirs. This current of success on one side & defeat on the other have rendered the Opposition furious, & have produced a disposition to subvert their Competitors even at the expence of the Government.

Another circumstance has contributed to widening the breach. 'Tis evident beyond a question, from every movement, that Mr Jefferson aims with ardent desire at the Presidential Chair. This too is an important object of the party-politics. It is supposed, from the nature of my former personal & political connexions, that I may favour some other candidate more than Mr. Jefferson when the Question shall occur by the retreat of the present Gentleman. My influence therefore with the Community becomes a thing, on ambitious & personal grounds, to be resisted & destroyed.

You know how much it was a point to establish the Secretary of State as the Officer who was to administer the Government in defect of the President & Vice President. Here I acknowledge, though I took far less part than was supposed, I run counter to Mr. Jefferson's wishes; but if I had had no other reason for it, I had already *experienced opposition* from him which rendered it a measure of *self defence.*

It is possible too (for men easily heat their imaginations when their passions are heated) that they have by degrees persuaded themselves of what they may have at first only sported to influence others—namely that there is some dreadful combination against State Government & republicanism; which according to them, are convertible terms. But there is so much absurdity in this supposition, that the admission of it tends to apologize for their hearts, at the expence of their heads.

Under the influence of all these circumstances, the attachment to the Government of the U States originally weak in Mr Jeffersons mind has given way to something very like dislike; in Mr. Madisons, it is so counteracted by personal feelings, as to be more an affair of the head than of the heart—more the result of a conviction of the necessity of Union than of cordiality to the thing itself. I hope it does not stand worse than this with him.

In such a state of mind, both these Gentlemen are prepared to hazard a great deal to effect a change. Most of the important measures of every Government are connected with the Treasury. To subvert the present head of it they deem it expedient to risk rendering the Government itself odious; perhaps foolishly thinking that they can easily recover the lost affections & confidence of the people, and not appreciating as they ought to do the natural resistance to Government which in every community results from the human passions, the degree to which this is strengthened by the *organised rivality* of State Governments, & the infinite danger that the National Government once rendered odious will be kept so by these powerful & indefatigable enemies.

They forget an old but a very just, though a coarse saying—That it is much easier to raise the Devil than to lay him.

Poor *Knox* has come in for a share of their persecution as a man who generally thinks with me & who has a portion of the Presidents good Will & confidence.

In giving you this picture of political parties, my design is I confess, to awaken your attention, if it has not yet been awakened to the conduct of the Gentlemen in question. If my opinion of them is founded, it is certainly of great moment to the public weal that they should be understood. I rely on the strength of your mind to appreciate men as they merit—when you have a clue to their real views.

A word on another point. I am told that serious apprehensions are disseminated in your state as to the existence of a Monarchical party meditating the destruction of State & Republican Government. If it is possible that so absurd an idea can gain ground it is necessary that it should be combatted. I assure you on my *private faith* and *honor* as a Man that there is not in my judgment a shadow of foundation of it. A very small number of men indeed may entertain theories less republican than Mr Jefferson & Mr. Madison; but I am persuaded there is not a Man among them who would not regard as both *criminal* & *visionary* any attempt to subvert the republican system of the Country. Most of these men rather *fear* that it may not justify itself by its fruits, than feel a predilection for a different form; and their fears are not diminished by the factions & fanatical politics which they find prevailing among a certain set of Gentlemen and threatening to disturb the tranquillity and order of the Government.

As to the destruction of State Governments, the *great* and *real* anxiety is to be able to preserve the National from the too potent and counteracting influence of those Governments. As to my own political Creed, I give it to you with the utmost sincerity. I am *affectionately* attached to the Republican theory. I desire *above all things* to see the *equality* of political rights exclusive of all *hereditary* distinction firmly established by a practical demonstration of its being consistent with the order and happiness of society.

As to State Governments, the prevailing byass of my judgment is that if they can be circumscribed within bounds consistent with the preservation of the National Government they will prove useful and salutary. If the States were all of the size of Connecticut, Maryland or New Jersey, I should decidedly regard the local Governments as both safe & useful. As the thing now is, however, I acknowledge the most serious apprehensions that the Government of the U States will not be able to maintain itself against their influence. I see that influence already penetrating into the National Councils & preverting their direction.

Hence a disposition on my part towards a liberal construction of the powers of the National Government and to erect every fence to guard it from depredations, which is, in my opinion, consistent with constitutional propriety.

As to any combination to prostrate the State Governments I disavow and deny it. From an apprehension lest the Judiciary should not work efficiently or harmoniously I have been desirous of seeing some rational scheme of connection adopted as an amendment to the constitution, otherwise I am for maintaining things as they are, though I doubt much the possibility of it, from a tendency in the nature of things towards the preponderancy of the State Governments.

I said, that I was *affectionately* attached to the Republican theory. This is the real language of my heart which I open to you in the sincerity of friendship; & I add that I have strong hopes of the success of that theory; but in candor I ought also to add that I am far from being without doubts. I consider its success as yet a problem.

It is yet to be determined by experience whether it be consistent with that *stability* and *order* in Government which are essential to public strength & private security and happiness. On the whole, the only enemy which Republicanism has to fear in this Country is in the Spirit of faction and anarchy. If this will not permit the ends of Government to be attained under it—if it engenders disorders in the community, all regular & orderly minds will wish for a change—and the demagogues who have produced the disorder will make it for their own aggrandizement. This is the old Story.

If I were disposed to promote Monarchy & overthrow State Governments, I would mount the hobby horse of popularity—I would cry out usurpation—danger to liberty &c. &c—I would endeavour to prostrate the National Government—raise a ferment—and then "ride in the Whirlwind and direct the Storm." That there are men acting with Jefferson & Madison who have this in view I verily believe. I could lay my finger on some of them. That Madison does *not* mean it I also verily believe, and I rather believe the same of Jefferson; but I read him upon the whole thus—"A man of profound ambition & violent passions."

You must be by this time tired of my epistle. Perhaps I have treated certain characters with too much severity. I have however not meant to do them injustice—and from the bottom of my soul believe I have drawn them truly and that it is of the utmost consequence to the public weal they should be viewed in their true colors. I yield to this impression. I will only add that I make no clandestine attacks on the gentlemen concerned. They are both apprized indirectly from myself of the opinion I entertain of their views. With the truest regard and esteem.

An American No. I

For the Gazette of the United States

Mr. Fenno

It was easy to foresee, when the hint appeared in your Gazette of [   ] that the Editor of the National Gazette received a salary from the General Government, advantage would be taken of its want of explicitness and particularity to make the circumstance matter of merit in Mr. Freneau and an argument of his independent disinterestedness. Such a turn of the thing cannot be permitted to succeed. It is now necessary that the whole truth should be told, and that the real state of the affair should be well understood.

Mr. Freneau before he came to this City to conduct the National Gazette was employed by Childs & Swaine Printers of the Dayly Advertiser in the City of New York in capacity of [   ]. A paper more devoted to the views of a certain party of which Mr. Jefferson is the head than any to be found in this City was wanted. Mr. Freneau was thought a fit instrument. His talents for invective and abuse had before been tried as Conductor of the Freemans Journal in this City. A negotiation was opened with him, which ended in the establishment of the National Gazette under his direction. There is good ground to believe that Mr. Madison while in New York in the summer of [   ] was the medium of that Negotiation.

Mr. Freneau came here at once Editor of the National Gazette and Clerk for foreign languages in the department of Mr. Jefferson, Secretary of State; an experiment somewhat new in the history of political manœvres in this Country; a news paper instituted by a public officer, and the Editor of it regularly pensioned with the public money, in the disposal of that officer; an example savouring not a little of that spirit, which in the enumeration of European abuses is the continual theme of declamatory censure with the party whose leader is the author of it; an example which could not have been set by any other head of a department without having long since rung throughout the UStates.

Mr. Freneau is not then, as he would have supposed, the Independent Editor of a News Paper, who though receiving a salary from Government has firmness enough to expose its maladministration. He is the faithful and devoted servant of the head of a party, from whose hand he receives the boon. The whole complexion of his paper is an exact copy of the politics of his employer foreign and domestic, and exhibits a decisive internal evidence of the influence of that patronage under which he acts.

Whether the services rendered by him are an equivalent for the compensation he receives is best known to his employer and himself. There is however some room for doubt. Tis well known that his employer is himself well acquainted with the French language; the only one of which he is the translator; and it may be a question how often his aid is necessary.

It is somewhat singular too that a man acquainted with but one foreign language engaged in a particular trade, which it may be presumed occupies his whole time and attention, the Editor of a News Paper, should be the person selected as the Clerk for foreign languages, in the department of the United States for foreign affairs. Could no person have been found acquainted with more than one foreign language, and who, in so confidential a trust, could have been regularly attached to, in the constant employ of the department and immediately under the eye of the head of it?

But it may be asked—Is it possible that Mr. Jefferson, the head of a principal department of the Government can be the Patron of a Paper, the evident object of which is to decry the Government and its measures? If he disapproves of the Government itself and thinks it deserving of opposition, could he reconcile to his own personal dignity and the principles of probity to hold an office under it and employ the means of official influence in that opposition? If he disapproves of the leading measures, which have been adopted in the course of its administration, could he reconcile it with the principles of delicacy and propriety to continue to hold a place in that administration, and at the same time to be instrumental in vilifying measures which have been adopted by majorities of both branches of the Legislature and *sanctionned by the Chief Magistrate of the Union*?

These questions would certainly be natural. An answer to them might be left to the facts which establish the relation between the Secretary of State and the Editor of the National Gazette, as the text, and to the general tenor of that paper as the Commentary. Let any intelligent man read the paper, from the commencement of it, and let him determine for himself, whether it be not a paper virulently hostile both to the Government and to its measures. Let him then ask himself, whether considering the connection which has subsisted between the Secretary of State and the Editor of that Paper, cœval with its first establishment, it be probable that the complexion of the paper is contrary to the views of that officer.

If he wishes a confirmation of the inference, which he cannot fail to draw, as a probable one, let him be informed in addition—

1 That while the Constitution of the United States was depending before the People of this Country, for their consideration and decision, Mr. Jefferson, being in France, was opposed to it, in some of its most important feautures, and wrote his objections to some of his friends in Virginia. That he, at first, went so far as to discountenance its adoption; though he afterwards recommended it, on the ground of expediency, in certain contingencies.

2 That he is the declared opponent of almost all the important measures which have been devised by the Government; more especially the provision which has been made for the public Debt, the institution

of the Bank of the United States, and such other measures as relate to the Public Credit and the Finances of the UStates.

It is proper that these facts should be known. If the People of the UStates believe, that their happiness and their safety are connected with the existence and maintenance of an efficient National or Fœderal Government—if they continue to think that, which they have created and established, worthy of their confidence, if they are willing, that the powers they have granted to it should be exercised with sufficient latitude to attain the ends they had in view in granting them and to do the essential business of the Nation—If they feel an honest pride in seeing the Credit of their country, so lately prostrate, elevated to an equal station with that of any Nation upon earth—if they are conscious that their own importance is increased by the increased respectability of their Country, which from an abject and degraded state, owing to the want of government, has, by the establishment of a wise constitution and by the measures which have been pursued under it, become a theme for the praise and admiration of mankind—if they experience that their own situation is improved and improving—that commerce and navigation have advanced—that manufactures are progressing—that agriculture is thriving—that property is more secure than it was—industry more certain of real not nominal reward, personal liberty perfectly protected—that notwithstanding the unavoidable demands upon them to satisfy the justice retrieve the reputation and answer the exigencies of the Country they are either less burthened than they were or more equal to the burthen which they have to sustain—if these are their opinions and their experience, let them know and understand, that the sentiments of the officer who has been mentioned, both as to the principles and the practice of the Constitution, which was framed by them and has been administered by their representatives, freely chosen, are essentially different from theirs.

If on the contrary—The People of the United States are of opinion that they erred in adopting their present constitution—that it contains pernicious principles and dangerous powers—that is has been administered injudiciously and wickedly—that men whose abilities and patriotism were tried in the worst of times have entered into a league to betray and oppress them—that they are really oppressed and ruined or in imminent danger of being so—If they think the preservation of National Union a matter of no or small consequence—if they are willing to return to the situation, from which they have just escaped, and to strip the government of some of the most necessary powers with which they have cloathed it—if they are desirous that those which are permitted to remain should be frittered away by a narrow timid and feeble exercise of them—If they are disposed to see the National Government transformed into the skeleton of Power—and the separate omnipotence of the state Governments exalted upon its ruins—If they are persuaded that Nations are under no ties of moral obligation that public Credit is useless or something worse—that public debts may be paid or cancelled at pleasure; that when a provision is not likely to be made for them, the discontents to be expected from the omission may honestly be transferred from a Government able to vindicate its rights to the breasts of Individuals who may first be encouraged to become the Substitutes to the Original Creditor, and afterwards defrauded without danger.* If to National Union, national respectability Public Order and public Credit they are willing to substitute National disunion, National insignificance, Public disorder and discredit—then let them unite their acclamations and plaudits in favour of Mr. Jefferson: Let him be the toast of every political club, and the theme of every popular huzza. For to those points, without examining his motives do assuredly tend the political tenets, real or pretended, of that Gentleman.

These strictures are made from a Conviction, that it is important to the People to know the characters intrusted with their public affairs.

As Mr. Jefferson is emulous of being the head of a party, whose politics have constantly aimed at elevating State-power, upon the ruins of National Authority—Let him enjoy all the glory and all the advantage of it. But Let it at the same time be understood by those, who are persuaded that the real and permanent welfare of the Country is to be promoted by other means that such are the views by which he is actuated.

AN AMERICAN
August 4, 1792

---

* Such was the advice given by Mr. Jefferson, when Minister Plenipotentiary to the Court of France, to Congress, respecting the debt due to France. The precise terms are not recollected but the substance may be depended upon. The poor Hollanders were to be the victims.

To George Washington

Philadelphia September 9
1792

SIR

I have the pleasure of your private letter of the 26th of August.

The feelings and views which are manifested in that letter are such as I expected would exist. And I most sincerely regret the causes of the uneasy sensations you experience. It is my most anxious wish, as far as may depend upon me, to smooth the path of your administration, and to render it prosperous and happy. And if any prospect shall open of healing or terminating the differences which exist, I shall most chearfully embrace it; though I consider myself as the deeply injured party. The recommendation of such a spirit is worthy of the moderation and wisdom which dictated it; and if your endeavours should prove unsucessful, I do not hesitate to say that in my opinion the period is not remote when the public good will require *substitutes* for the *differing members* of your administration. The continuance of a division there must destroy the energy of Government, which will be little enough with the strictest Union. On my part there will be a most chearful acquiescence in such a result.

I trust, Sir, that the greatest frankness has always marked and will always mark every step of my conduct towards you. In this disposition, I cannot conceal from you that I have had some instrumentality of late in the retaliations which have fallen upon certain public characters and that I find myself placed in a situation not to be able to recede *for the present.*

I considered myself as compelled to this conduct by reasons public as well as personal of the most cogent nature. I know that I have been an object of uniform opposition from Mr. Jefferson, from the first moment of his coming to the City of New York to enter upon his present office. I know, from the most authentic sources, that I have been the frequent subject of the most unkind whispers and insinuating from the same quarter. I have long seen a formed party in the Legislature, under his auspices, bent upon my subversion. I cannot doubt, from the evidence I possess, that the National Gazette was instituted by him for political purposes and that one leading object of it has been to render me and all the measures connected with my department as odious as possible.

Nevertheless I can truly say, that, except explanations to confidential friends, I never directly or indirectly retaliated or countenanced retaliation till very lately. I can even assure you, that I was instrumental in preventing a very severe and systematic attack upon Mr. Jefferson, by an association of two or three individuals, in consequence of the persecution, which he brought upon the Vice President, by his indiscreet and light letter to the Printer, transmitting *Paine's* pamphlet.

As long as I saw no danger to the Government, from the machinations which were going on, I resolved to be a silent sufferer of the injuries which were done me. I determined to avoid giving occasion to any thing which could manifest to the world dissentions among the principal characters of the government; a thing which can never happen without weakening its hands, and in some degree throwing a stigma upon it.

But when I no longer doubted, that there was a formed party deliberately bent upon the subversion of measures, which in its consequences would subvert the Government—when I saw, that the undoing of the funding system in particular (which, whatever may be the original merits of that system, would prostrate the credit and the honor of the Nation, and bring the Government into contempt with that description of Men, who are in every society the only firm supporters of government) was an avowed object of the party; and that all possible pains were taking to produce that effect by rendering it odious to the body of the people—I considered it as a duty, to endeavour to resist the torrent, and as an essential mean to this end, to draw aside the veil from the principal Actors. To this strong impulse, to this decided conviction, I have yielded. And I think events will prove that I have judged rightly.

Nevertheless I pledge my honor to you Sir, that if you shall here-after form a plan to reunite the members of your administration, upon some steady principle of cooperation, I will faithfully concur in executing it during my continuance in office. And I will not directly or indirectly say or do a thing, that shall endanger a feud.

I have had it very much at heart to make an excursion to Mount Vernon, by way of the Fœderal City in the course of this Month—and have been more than once on the point of asking your permission for it. But I now despair of being able to effect it. I am nevertheless equally obliged by your kind invitation.

The subject mentioned in the Postscript of your letter shall with great pleasure be carefully attended to. With the most faithful and affectionate attachment I have the honor to remain

Sir Your most Obed & humble servant

A HAMILTON

P.S I had written you two letters on public business, one of which will go with this; but the other will be witheld, in consequence of a slight indisposition of the Attorney General, to be sent by express sometime in the course of tomorrow.

Letter to an Unknown Correspondent

Philadelphia Sept. 26.
1792

MY DEAR SIR

Some days since, I was surprised with the following intelligence, in a letter from Mr. King (whose name I disclose to you in confidence).

"*Burr* is industrious in his Canvass and his object is well understood by our Antis. Mr. Edwards is to make interest for him in Connecticut and Mr. Dallas, who is here, and quite in the circle of the Governor and the party informs us, that Mr. Burr will be supported as Vice President in Pensylvania. Nothing which has hereto-fore happened so decisively proves the inveteracy of the opposition. Should they succeed much would be to be apprehended"

Though in my situation I deem it most proper to avoid interference in any matter relating to the elections for Members of the Government— Yet I feel reasons of sufficient force to induce a departure from that rule in the present instance.

Mr. Burr's integrity as an Individual is not unimpeached. As a public man he is one of the worst sort—a friend to nothing but as it suits his interest and ambition. Determined to climb to the highest honours of State, and as much higher as circumstances may permit—he cares nothing about the means of effecting his purpose. Tis evident that he aims at putting himself at the head of what he calls the "popular party" as affording the best tools for an ambitious man to work with. Secretly turning Liberty into ridicule, he knows as well as most men how to make use of the name. In a word, if we have an embryo-Cæsar in the United States 'tis Burr.

Defense of the President's Neutrality Proclamation

1. It is a melancholy truth, which every new political occurrence more and more unfolds, that there is a discription of men in this country, irreconcileably adverse to the government of the United States; whose exertions, whatever be the springs of them, whether infatuation or depravity or both, tend to disturb the tranquillity order and prosperity of this now peaceable flourishing and truly happy land. A real and enlightened friend to public felicity cannot observe new confirmations of this fact, without feeling a deep and poignant regret, that human nature should be so refractory and perverse; that amidst a profusion of the bounties and blessings of Providence, political as well as natural, inviting to contentment and gratitude, there should still be found men disposed to cherish and propagate disquietude and alarm; to render suspected and detested the instruments of the felicity, in which they partake; to sacrifice the most substantial advantages, that ever fell to the lot of a people at the shrine of personal envy rivalship and animosity, to the instigations of a turbulent and criminal ambition, or to the treacherous phantoms of an ever craving and never to be satisfied spirit of innovation; a spirit, which seems to suggest to its votaries that the most natural and happy state of Society is a state of continual revolution and change—that the welfare of a nation is in exact ratio to the rapidity of the political vicissitudes, which it undergoes—to the frequency and violence of the tempests with which it is agitated.

2. Yet so the fact unfortunately is—such men there certainly are— and it is essential to our dearest interests to the preservation of peace and good order to the dignity and independence of our public councils— to the real and permanent security of liberty and property—that the Citizens of the UStates should open their eyes to the true characters and designs of the men alluded to—should be upon their guard against their insidious and ruinous machinations.

3. At this moment a most dangerous combination exists. Those who for some time past have been busy in undermining the constitution and government of the UStates, by indirect attacks, by labouring to render its measures odious, by striving to destroy the confidence of the people in its administration—are now meditating a more direct and destructive war against it—and embodying and arranging their forces and systematising their efforts. Secret clubs are formed and private consultations held. Emissaries are dispatched to distant parts of the United States to effect a concert of views and measures, among the members and partisans of the disorganising corps, in the several states. The language in the confidential circles is that the constitution of the United States is too complex a system—that it savours too much of the pernicious doctrine of "ballances and checks" that it requires to be simplified in its structure, to be purged of some monarchical and aristocratic ingredients which are said to have found their way into it and to be stripped of some dangerous prerogatives, with which it is pretended to be invested.

4. The noblest passion of the human soul, which no where burns with so pure and bright a flame, as in the breasts of the people of the UStates, is if possible to be made subservient to this fatal project. That zeal for the liberty of mankind, which produced so universal a sympathy in the cause of France in the first stages of its revolution, and which, it is supposed, has not yet yielded to the just reprobation, which a sober temperate and humane people, friends of religion, social order, and justice, enemies to tumult and massacre, to the wanton and lawless shedding of human blood cannot but bestow upon those extravagancies excesses and outrages, which have sullied and which endanger that cause—that laudable, it is not too much to say that holy zeal is intended by every art of misrepresentation and deception to be made the instrument first of controuling finally of overturning the Government of the Union.

5. The ground which has been so wisely taken by the Executive of the UStates, in regard to the present war of Europe against France, is to be the pretext of this mischievous attempt. The people are if possible to be made to believe, that the Proclamation of neutrality issued by the President of the US was unauthorised illegal and officious—inconsistent with the treaties and plighted faith of the Nation—inconsistent with a due sense of gratitude to France for the services rendered us in our late

contest for independence and liberty—inconsistent with a due regard for the progress and success of republican principles. Already the presses begin to groan with invective against the Chief Magistrate of the Union, for that prudent and necessary measure; a measure calculated to manifest to the World the pacific position of the Government and to caution the citizens of the UStates against practices, which would tend to involve us in a War the most unequal and calamitous, in which it is possible for a Country to be engaged—a war which would not be unlikely to prove pregnant with still greater dangers and disasters, than that by which we established our existence as an Independent Nation.

6. What is the true solution of this extraordinary appearance? Are the professed the real motives of its authors? They are not. The true object is to disparage in the opinion and affections of his fellow citizens that man who at the head of our armies fought so successfully for the Liberty and Independence, which are now our pride and our boast—who during the war supported the hopes, united the hearts and nerved the arm of his countrymen—who at the close of it, unseduced by ambition & the love of power, soothed and appeased the discontents of his suffering companions in arms, and with them left the proud scenes of a victorious field for the modest retreats of private life—who could only have been drawn out of these favourite retreats, to aid in the glorious work of ingrafting that liberty, which his sword had contributed to win, upon a stock of which it stood in need and without which it could not flourish—endure—a firm adequate national Government—who at this moment sacrifices his tranquillity and every favourite pursuit to the peremptory call of his country to aid in giving solidity to a fabric, which he has assisted in rearing—whose whole conduct has been one continued proof of his rectitude moderation disinterestedness and patriotism, who whether the evidence of a uniform course of virtuous public actions be considered, or the motives likely to actuate a man placed precisely in his situation be estimated, it may safely be pronounced, can have no other ambition than that of doing good to his Country & transmitting his fame unimpaired to posterity. For what or for whom is he to hazard that rich harvest of glory, which he has acquired that unexampled veneration and love of his fellow Citizens, which he so eminently possesses?

7. Yet the men alluded to, while they contend with affected zeal for gratitude towards a foreign Nation, which in assisting us was and ought

to have been influenced by considerations relative to its own interest—forgetting what is due to a fellow Citizen, who at every hazard rendered essential services to his Country from the most patriotic motives—insidiously endeavour to despoil him of that precious reward of his services, the confidence and approbation of his fellow Citizens.

8. The present attempt is but the renewal in another form of an attack some time since commenced, and which was only dropped because it was perceived to have excited a general indignation. Domestic arrangements of mere convenience, calculated to reconcile the œconomy of time with the attentions of decorum and civility were then the topics of malevolent declamation. A more serious article of charge is now opened and seems intended to be urged with greater earnestness and vigour. The merits of it shall be examined in one or two succeeding papers, I trust in a manner, that will evince to every candid mind to futility.

9. To be an able and firm supporter of the Government of the Union is in the eyes of the men referred to a crime sufficient to justify the most malignant persecution. Hence the attacks which have been made and repeated with such persevering industry upon more than one public Character in that Government. Hence the effort which is now going on to depreciate in the eyes and estimation of the People the man whom their unanimous suffrages have placed at the head of it.

10. Hence the pains which are taking to inculcate a discrimination between *principles* and *men* and to represent an attachment to the one as a species of war against the other; an endeavour, which has a tendency to stifle or weaken one of the best and most useful feelings of the human heart—a reverence for merit—and to take away one of the strongest incentives to public virtue—the expectation of public esteem.

11. A solicitude for the character who is attacked forms no part of the motives to this comment. He has deserved too much, and his countrymen are too sensible of it to render any advocation of him necessary. If his virtues and services do not secure his fame and ensure to him the unchangeable attachment of his fellow Citizens, twere in vain to attempt to prop them by anonymous panygeric.

12. The design of the observations which have been made is merely to awaken the public attention to the views of a party engaged in a dangerous conspiracy against the tranquillity and happiness of their country. Aware that their hostile aims against the Government can never succeed til they have subverted the confidence of the people in its present

Chief Magistrate, they have at length permitted the suggestions of their enmity to betray them into this hopeless and culpable attempt. If we can destroy his popularity (say they) our work is more than half completed.

13. In proportion as the Citizens of the UStates value the constitution on which their union and happiness depend, in proportion as they tender the blessings of peace and deprecate the calamities of War— ought to be their watchfulness against this success of the artifices which will be employed to endanger that constitution and those blessings. A mortal blow is aimed at both.

14. It imports them infinitely not to be deceived by the protestations which are made—that no harm is meditated against the Constitution— that no design is entertained to involve the peace of the Country. These appearances are necessary to the accomplishment of the plan which has been formed. It is known that the great body of the People are attached to the constitution. It would therefore defeat the intention of destroying it to avow that it exists. It is also known that the People of the UStates are firmly attached to peace. It would consequently frustrate the design of engaging them in the War to tell them that such an object is in contemplation.

15. A more artful course has therefore been adopted. Professions of good will to the Constitution are made without reserve: But every possible art is employed to render the administration and the most zealous and useful friends of the Government odious. The reasoning is obvious. If the people can be persuaded to dislike all the measures of the Government and to dislike all or the greater part of those who have been most conspicuous in establishing or conducting it—the passage from this to the dislike and change of the constitution will not be long nor difficult. The abstract idea of regard for a constitution on paper will not long resist a thorough detestation of its practice.

16. In like manner, professions of a disposition to preserve the peace of the Country are liberally made. But the means of effecting the end are condemned; and exertions are used to prejudice the community against them. A proclamation of neutrality in the most cautious form is represented as illegal—contrary to our engagements with and our duty towards one of the belligerent powers. The plain inference is that in the opinion of these characters the UStates are under obligations which do not permit them to be neutral. Of course they are in a situation to become a party in the War from duty.

17. Pains are likewise taken to inflame the zeal of the people for the cause of France and to excite their resentments against the powers at War with her. To what end all this—but to beget if possible a temper in the community which may overrule the moderate or pacific views of the Government.

c. May 1793

Pacificus No. 1

As attempts are making very dangerous to the peace, and it is to be feared not very friendly to the constitution of the UStates—it becomes the duty of those who wish well to both to endeavour to prevent their success.

The objections which have been raised against the Proclamation of Neutrality lately issued by the President have been urged in a spirit of acrimony and invective, which demonstrates, that more was in view than merely a free discussion of an important public measure; that the discussion covers a design of weakening the confidence of the People in the author of the measure; in order to remove or lessen a powerful obstacle to the success of an opposition to the Government, which however it may change its form, according to circumstances, seems still to be adhered to and pursued with persevering Industry.

This Reflection adds to the motives connected with the measure itself to recommend endeavours by proper explanations to place it in a just light. Such explanations at least cannot but be satisfactory to those who may not have leisure or opportunity for pursuing themselves an investigation of the subject, and who may wish to perceive that the policy of the Government is not inconsistent with its obligations or its honor.

The objections in question fall under three heads—

1 That the Proclamation was without authority

2 That it was contrary to our treaties with France

3 That it was contrary to the gratitude, which is due from this to that country; for the succours rendered us in our own Revolution.

4 That it was out of time & unnecessary.

In order to judge of the solidity of the first of these objections, it is necessary to examine what is the nature and design of a proclamation of neutrality.

The true nature & design of such an act is—to *make known* to the powers at War and to the Citizens of the Country, whose Government does the Act that such country is in the condition of a Nation at Peace with the belligerent parties, and under no obligations of Treaty, to become an *associate in the war* with either of them; that this being its situation its intention is to observe a conduct conformable with it and to perform towards each the duties of neutrality; and as a consequence of this state of things, to give warning to all within its jurisdiction to abstain from acts that shall contravene those duties, under the penalties which the laws of the land (of which the law of Nations is a part) annexes to acts of contravention.

This, and no more, is conceived to be the true import of a Proclamation of Neutrality.

It does not imply, that the Nation which makes the declaration will forbear to perform to any of the warring Powers any stipulations in Treaties which can be performed without rendering it an *associate* or *party* in the War. It therefore does not imply in our case, that the UStates will not make those distinctions, between the present belligerent powers, which are stipulated in the 17th and 22d articles of our Treaty with France; because these distinctions are not incompatible with a state of neutrality; they will in no shape render the UStates an *associate* or *party* in the War. This must be evident, when it is considered, that even to furnish *determinate* succours, of a certain number of Ships or troops, to a Power at War, in consequence of *antecedent treaties having no particular reference to the existing war*, is not inconsistent with neutrality; a position well established by the doctrines of Writers and the practice of Nations.*

But no special aids, succours or favors having relation to war, not positively and precisely stipulated by some Treaty of the above description, can be afforded to either party, without a breach of neutrality.

In stating that the Proclamation of Neutrality does not imply the non performance of any stipulations of Treaties which are not of a nature to make the Nation an associate or party in the war, it is conceded that an execution of the clause of Guarantee contained in the 11th article of our Treaty of Alliance with France would be contrary to the sense and spirit of the Proclamation; because it would engage us with our whole

* See Vatel Book III Chap. VI § 101.

force as an *associate* or *auxiliary* in the War; it would be much more than the case of a definite limited succour, previously ascertained.

It follows that the Proclamation is virtually a manifestation of the sense of the Government that the UStates are, *under the circumstances of the case, not bound* to execute the clause of Guarantee.

If this be a just view of the true force and import of the Proclamation, it will remain to see whether the President in issuing it acted within his proper sphere, or stepped beyond the bounds of his constitutional authority and duty.

It will not be disputed that the management of the affairs of this country with foreign nations is confided to the Government of the UStates.

It can as little be disputed, that a Proclamation of Neutrality, where a Nation is at liberty to keep out of a War in which other Nations are engaged and means so to do, is a *usual* and a *proper* measure. *Its main object and effect are to prevent the Nation being immediately responsible for acts done by its citizens, without the privity or connivance of the Government, in contravention of the principles of neutrality.* *

An object this of the greatest importance to a Country whose true interest lies in the preservation of peace.

The inquiry then is—what department of the Government of the UStates is the proper one to make a declaration of Neutrality in the cases in which the engagements of the Nation permit and its interests require such a declaration.

A correct and well informed mind will discern at once that it can belong neither to the Legislative nor Judicial Department and of course must belong to the Executive.

The Legislative Department is not the *organ* of intercourse between the UStates and foreign Nations. It is charged neither with *making* nor *interpreting* Treaties. It is therefore not naturally that Organ of the Government which is to pronounce the existing condition of the Nation, with regard to foreign Powers, or to admonish the Citizens of their obligations and duties as founded upon that condition of things. Still less is it charged with enforcing the execution and observance of these obligations and those duties.

It is equally obvious that the act in question is foreign to the Judiciary Department of the Government. The province of that Department is

* See Vatel Book III Chap. VII § 113.

to decide litigations in particular cases. It is indeed charged with the interpretation of treaties; but it exercises this function only in the litigated cases; that is where contending parties bring before it a specific controversy. It has no concern with pronouncing upon the external political relations of Treaties between Government and Government. This position is too plain to need being insisted upon.

It must then of necessity belong to the Executive Department to exercise the function in Question—when a proper case for the exercise of it occurs.

It appears to be connected with that department in various capacities, as the *organ* of intercourse between the Nation and foreign Nations— as the interpreter of the National Treaties in those cases in which the Judiciary is not competent, that is in the cases between Government and Government—as that Power, which is charged with the Execution of the Laws, of which Treaties form a part—as that Power which is charged with the command and application of the Public Force.

This view of the subject is so natural and obvious—so analogous to general theory and practice—that no doubt can be entertained of its justness, unless such doubt can be deduced from particular provisions of the Constitution of the UStates.

Let us see then if cause for such doubt is to be found in that constitution.

The second Article of the Constitution of the UStates, section 1st, establishes this general Proposition, That "The EXECUTIVE POWER shall be vested in a President of the United States of America."

The same article in a succeeding Section proceeds to designate particular cases of Executive Power. It declares among other things that the President shall be Commander in Cheif of the army and navy of the UStates and of the Militia of the several states when called into the actual service of the UStates, that he shall have power by and with the advice of the senate to make treaties; that it shall be his duty to receive ambassadors and other public Ministers and to take care that the laws be faithfully executed.

It would not consist with the rules of sound construction to consider this enumeration of particular authorities as derogating from the more comprehensive grant contained in the general clause, further than as it may be coupled with express restrictions or qualifications; as in regard to the cooperation of the Senate in the appointment of Officers and the making of treaties; which are qualifications of the general executive powers of appointing officers and making treaties: Because the difficulty of a complete and perfect specification of all the cases of Executive authority would naturally dictate the use of general terms—and would render it improbable that a specification of certain particulars was designd as a substitute for those terms, when antecedently used. The different mode of expression employed in the constitution in regard to the two powers the Legislative and the Executive serves to confirm this inference. In the article which grants the legislative powers of the Governt. the expressions are—*"All Legislative powers herein granted shall be vested in a Congress of the UStates;"* in that which grants the Executive Power the expressions are, as already quoted "The EXECUTIVE POWER shall be vested in a President of the UStates of America."

The enumeration ought rather therefore to be considered as intended by way of greater caution, to specify and regulate the principal articles implied in the definition of Executive Power; leaving the rest to flow from the general grant of that power, interpreted in conformity to other parts of the constitution and to the principles of free government.

The general doctrine then of our constitution is, that the EXECUTIVE POWER of the Nation is vested in the President; subject only to the *exceptions* and *qualifications* which are expressed in the instrument.

Two of these have been already noticed—the participation of the Senate in the appointment of Officers and the making of Treaties. A third remains to be mentioned the right of the Legislature "to declare war and grant letters of marque and reprisal."

With these exceptions the EXECUTIVE POWER of the Union is completely lodged in the President. This mode of construing the Constitution has indeed been recognized by Congress in formal acts, upon full consideration and debate. The power of removal from office is an inportant instance.

And since upon general principles for reasons already given, the issuing of a proclamation of neutrality is merely an Executive Act; since also the general Executive Power of the Union is vested in the President, the conclusion is, that the step, which has been taken by him, is liable to no just exception on the score of authority.

It may be observed that this Inference would be just if the power of declaring war had not been vested in the Legislature, but that this power naturally includes the right of judging whether the Nation is under obligations to make war or not.

The answer to this is, that however true it may be, that the right of the Legislature to declare war includes the right of judging whether the Nation be under obligations to make War or not—it will not follow that the Executive is in any case excluded from a similar right of Judgment, in the execution of its own functions.

If the Legislature have a right to make war on the one hand—it is on the other the duty of the Executive to preserve Peace till war is declared; and in fulfilling that duty, it must necessarily possess a right of judging what is the nature of the obligations which the treaties of the Country impose on the Government; and when in pursuance of this right it has concluded that there is nothing in them inconsistent with a state of neutrality, it becomes both its province and its duty to enforce the laws incident to that state of the Nation. The Executive is charged with the execution of all laws, the laws of Nations as well as the Municipal law, which recognises and adopts those laws. It is consequently bound, by faithfully executing the laws of neutrality, when that is the state of the Nation, to avoid giving a cause of war to foreign Powers.

This is the direct and proper end of the proclamation of neutrality. It declares to the UStates their situation with regard to the Powers at war and makes known to the Community that the laws incident to that situation will be enforced. In doing this, it conforms to an established usage of Nations, the operation of which as before remarked is to obviate a responsibility on the part of the whole Society, for secret and unknown violations of the rights of any of the warring parties by its citizens.

Those who object to the proclamation will readily admit that it is the right and duty of the Executive to judge of, or to interpret, those articles of our treaties which give to France particular privileges, in order to the enforcement of those privileges: But the necessary consequence of this is, that the Executive must judge what are the proper bounds of those privileges—what rights are given to other nations by our treaties with them—what rights the law of Nature and Nations gives and our treaties permit, in respect to those Nations with whom we have no treaties; in fine what are the reciprocal rights and obligations of the United States & of all & each of the powers at War.

The right of the Executive to receive ambassadors and other public

Ministers may serve to illustrate the relative duties of the Executive and Legislative Departments. This right includes that of judging, in the case of a Revolution of Government in a foreign Country, whether the new rulers are competent organs of the National Will and ought to be recognised or not: And where a treaty antecedently exists between the UStates and such nation that right involves the power of giving operation or not to such treaty. For until the new Government is *acknowleged*, the treaties between the nations, as far at least as regards *public* rights, are of course suspended.

This power of determining virtually in the case supposed upon the operation of national Treaties as a consequence, of the power to receive ambassadors and other public Ministers, is an important instance of the right of the Executive to decide the obligations of the Nation with regard to foreign Nations. To apply it to the case of France, if there had been a Treaty of alliance *offensive* and defensive between the UStates and that Country, the unqualified acknowlegement of the new Government would have put the UStates in a condition to become an associate in the War in which France was engaged—and would have laid the Legislature under an obligation, if required, and there was otherwise no valid excuse, of exercising its power of declaring war.

This serves as an example of the right of the Executive, in certain cases, to determine the condition of the Nation, though it may consequentially affect the proper or improper exercise of the Power of the Legislature to declare war. The Executive indeed cannot control the exercise of that power—further than by the exercise of its general right of objecting to all acts of the Legislature; liable to being overruled by two thirds of both houses of Congress. The Legislature is free to perform its own duties according to its own sense of them— though the Executive in the exercise of its constitutional powers, may establish an antecedent state of things which ought to weigh in the legislative decisions. From the division of the Executive Power there results, in referrence to it, a *concurrent* authority, in the distributed cases.

Hence in the case stated, though treaties can only be made by the President and Senate, their activity may be continued or suspended by the President alone.

No objection has been made to the Presidents having acknowleged the Republic of France, by the Reception of its Minister, without having consulted the Senate; though that body is connected with him in the making of Treaties, and though the consequence of his act of reception is to give operation to the Treaties heretofore made with that Country: But he is censured for having declared the UStates to be in a state of peace & neutrality, with regard to the Powers at War; because the right of *changing* that state & *declaring war* belongs to the Legislature.

It deserves to be remarked, that as the participation of the senate in the making of Treaties and the power of the Legislature to declare war are exceptions out of the general "Executive Power" vested in the President, they are to be construed strictly—and ought to be extended no further than is essential to their execution.

While therefore the Legislature can alone declare war, can alone actually transfer the nation from a state of Peace to a state of War— it belongs to the "Executive Power," to do whatever else the laws of Nations cooperating with the Treaties of the Country enjoin, in the intercourse of the UStates with foreign Powers.

In this distribution of powers the wisdom of our constitution is manifested. It is the province and duty of the Executive to preserve to the Nation the blessings of peace. The Legislature alone can interrupt those blessings, by placing the Nation in a state of War.

But though it has been thought adviseable to vindicate the authority of the Executive on this broad and comprehensive ground—it was not absolutely necessary to do so. That clause of the constitution which makes it his duty to "take care that the laws be faithfully executed" might alone have been relied upon, and this simple process of argument pursued.

The President is the constitutional EXECUTOR of the laws. Our Treaties and the laws of Nations form a part of the law of the land. He who is to execute the laws must first judge for himself of their meaning. In order to the observance of that conduct, which the laws of nations combined with our treaties prescribed to this country, in reference to the present War in Europe, it was necessary for the President to judge for himself whether there was any thing in our treaties incompatible with an adherence to neutrality. Having judged that there was not, he had a right, and if in his opinion the interests of the Nation required it, it was his duty, as Executor of the laws, to proclaim the neutrality of the Nation, to exhort all persons to observe it, and to warn them of the penalties which would attend its non observance.

The Proclamation has been represented as enacting some new law.

This is a view of it entirely erroneous. It only proclaims a *fact* with regard to the *existing state* of the Nation, informs the citizens of what the laws previously established require of them in that state, & warns them that these laws will be put in execution against the Infractors of them.

Gazette of the United States,
June 29, 1793

To Andrew G. Fraunces

Contemptible as you are, what answer could I give to your last letter?

The enclosed is a copy of what will shortly appear in one of the Gazettes of the city of New-York.

A. HAMILTON

Albany, October 1, 1793.

One Andrew G. Fraunces, lately a clerk in the treasury department, has been endeavoring to have it believed, that he is possessed of some facts, of a nature to criminate the official conduct of the Secretary of the Treasury; an idea to which, for obvious reasons, an extensive circulation has been given, by a certain description of persons. The Public may be assured, that the said Fraunces has been regularly and repeatedly called upon, to declare the grounds of his suggestion; that he has repeatedly evaded the enquiry; that he possesses no facts of the nature pretended; and that he is a dispicable calumniator.

To Angelica Hamilton

I was very glad to learn, my dear daughter, that you were going to begin the study of the French language. We hope you will in every respect behave in such a manner as will secure to you the good-will and regard of all those with whom you are. If you happen to displease any of them, be always ready to make a frank apology. But the best way is to act with so much politeness, good manners, and circumspection, as never to have occasion to make any apology. Your mother joins in best love to you. Adieu, my very dear daughter.

c. November 1793

Tully No. III

For the American Daily Advertiser.
To the PEOPLE of the UNITED STATES.

LETTER III.

If it were to be asked, What is the most sacred duty and the greatest source of security in a Republic? the answer would be, An inviolable respect for the Constitution and Laws—the first growing out of the last. It is by this, in a great degree, that the rich and powerful are to be restrained from enterprises against the common liberty—operated upon by the influence of a general sentiment, by their interest in the principle, and by the obstacles which the habit it produces erects against innovation and encroachment. It is by this, in a still greater degree, that caballers, intriguers, and demagogues are prevented from climbing on the shoulders of faction to the tempting seats of usurpation and tyranny.

Were it not that it might require too lengthy a discussion, it would not be difficult to demonstrate, that a large and well organized Republic can scarcely lose its liberty from any other cause than that of anarchy, to which a contempt of the laws is the high road.

But, without entering into so wide a field, it is sufficient to present to your view a more simple and a more obvious truth, which is this—that a sacred respect for the constitutional law is the vital principle, the sustaining energy of a free government.

Government is frequently and aptly classed under two descriptions, a government of FORCE and a government of LAWS; the first is the definition of despotism—the last, of liberty. But how can a government of laws exist where the laws are disrespected and disobeyed? Government supposes controul. It is the power by which individuals in society are kept from doing injury to each other and are bro't to co-operate to a common end. The instruments by which it must act are either the AUTHORITY of the Laws or FORCE. If the first be destroyed, the last must be substituted; and where this becomes the ordinary instrument of government there is an end to liberty.

Those, therefore, who preach doctrines, or set examples, which undermine or subvert the authority of the laws, lead us from freedom to slavery; they incapacitate us for a GOVERNMENT OF LAWS, and consequently prepare the way for one of FORCE, for mankind MUST HAVE GOVERNMENT OF ONE SORT OR ANOTHER.

There are indeed great and urgent cases where the bounds of the constitution are manifestly transgressed, or its constitutional authorities so exercised as to produce unequivocal oppression on the community, and to render resistance justifiable. But such cases can give no colour to the resistance by a comparatively inconsiderable part of a community, of constitutional laws distinguished by no extraordinary features of rigour or oppression, and acquiesced in by the BODY OF THE COMMUNITY.

Such a resistance is treason against society, against liberty, against every thing that ought to be dear to a free, enlightened, and prudent people. To tolerate were to abandon your most precious interests. Not to subdue it, were to tolerate it. Those who openly or covertly dissuade you from exertions adequate to the occasion are your worst enemies. They treat you either as fools or cowards, too weak to perceive your interest and your duty, or too dastardly to pursue them. They therefore merit, and will no doubt meet your contempt.

To the plausible but hollow harangues of such conspirators, ye cannot fail to reply, How long, ye Catilines, will you abuse our patience.

TULLY.

Dunlap and Claypoole's American Daily Advertiser,
August 28, 1794

To Angelica Church

Bedford Pensylvania
October 23. 1794
205 Miles Westward of
Philadelphia

I am thus far my dear Angelica on my way to attack and subdue the wicked insurgents of the West. But you are not to promise yourself that I shall have any trophies to lay at your feet. A large army has cooled the courage of those madmen & the only question seems now to be how to guard best aganst the return of the phrenzy.

You must not take my being here for a proof that I continue a quixot. In popular governments 'tis useful that those who propose measures should partake in whatever dangers they may involve. Twas very important there should be no mistake in the management of the affair—and I *might* contribute to prevent one. I wish to have every thing well settled for Mr. Church & you, that when you come, you may tread on safe ground. Assure him that the insurrection will do us a great deal of good and add to the solidity of every thing in this country. Say the same to Mr Jay to whom I have not time to write & to Mr Pinkney.

God bless You Dear Sister & make you as happy as I wish you. Love to Mr. Church.

A HAMILTON

To Angelica Church

Philadelphia, December 8, 1794.

You say I am a politician, and good for nothing. What will you say when you learn that after January next, I shall cease to be a politician at all? So is the fact. I have formally and definitely announced my intention to resign at that period, and have ordered a house to be taken for me at New York.

My dear Eliza has been lately very ill. Thank God, she is now quite recovered, except that she continues somewhat weak. My absence on a certain expedition was the cause (with army to suppress the whisky insurrection in Pennsylvania). You will see, notwithstanding your disparagement of me, I am still of consequence to her.

Liancourt has arrived, and has delivered your letter. I pay him the attentions due to his misfortunes and his merits. I wish I was a Croesus; I might then afford solid consolations to these children of adversity, and how delightful it would be to do so. *But now*, sympathy, kind words, and *occasionally a dinner, are all I can contribute.*

Don't let Mr. Church be alarmed at my retreat—all is well with the public. Our insurrection is most happily terminated. Government has gained by it reputation and strength, and our finances are in a most flourishing condition. *Having contributed to place those of the Nation on a good footing, I go to take a little care of my own; which need my care not a little.*

Love to Mr. Church. Betsy will add a line or two. Adieu.

The French Revolution

In the early periods of the French Revolution, a warm zeal for its success was in this Country *a sentiment truly universal*. The love of Liberty is here the ruling passion *of the Citizens of the UStates* pervading every class animating every bosom. As long therefore as the Revolution of France bore the marks of being the cause of liberty it united all hearts concentered all opinions. But this unanimity of approbation has been for a considerable time decreasing. The excesses which have constantly multiplied, with greater and greater aggravations have successively though slowly detached reflecting men from their partiality for an object which has appeared less and less to merit their regard. Their reluctance to abandon it has however been proportioned to the ardor and fondness with which they embraced it. They were willing to overlook many faults—to apologise for some enormities—to hope that better justifications existed than were seen—to look forward to more calm and greater moderation, after the first shocks of the political earthquake had subsided. But instead of this, they have been witnesses to one volcano succeeding another, the last still more dreadful than the former, spreading ruin and devastation far and wide—subverting the foundations of right security and property, of order, morality and religion—sparing neither sex nor age, confounding innocence with guilt, involving the old and the young, the sage and the madman, the long tried friend of virtue and his country and the upstart pretender to purity and patriotism—the bold projector of new treasons with the obscure in indiscriminate and profuse destruction. They have found themselves driven to the painful alternative of renouncing an object dear to their wishes or of becoming by the continuance of their affection for it accomplices with Vice Anarchy Depotism and Impiety.

But though an afflicting experience has materially lessened the number of the admirers of the French Revolution among us and has served to chill the ardor of many more, who profess still to retain their attachment to it, from what they suppose to be its ultimate tendency; yet the effect of Experience has been thus far much less than could reasonably have been expected. The predilection for it still continues extensive and ardent. And what is extraordinary it continues to comprehend men who are able to form a just estimate of the information which destroys its title to their favour.

It is not among the least perplexing phœnomina of the present times, that a people like that of the UStates—exemplary for humanity and moderation surpassed by no other in the love of order and a knowlege of the true principles of liberty, distinguished for purity of morals and a just reverence for Religion should so long perservere in partiality for a state of things the most cruel sanguinary and violent that ever stained the annuals of mankind, a state of things which annihilates the foundations of social order and true liberty, confounds all moral distinctions and *substitutes to* the mild & beneficent religion of the Gospel a gloomy persecuting and desolating atheism. To the eye of a wise man, this partiality is the most inauspicious circumstance, that has appeared in the affairs of this country. It leads involuntarily and irresistibly to apprehensions concerning the soundness of our principles and the stability of our welfare. It is natural to fear that the transition may not be difficult from the approbation of bad things to the imitation of them; a fear which can only be mitigated by a careful estimate of the extraneous causes that have served to mislead the public judgment.

But though we may find in these causes a solution of the fact calculated to abate our solicitude for the consequences; yet we can not consider the public happiness as out of the reach of danger so long as our principles continue to be exposed to the debauching influence of admiration for an example which, it will not be too strong to say, presents the caricature of human depravity. And the pride of national character at least can find no alleviation for the wound which must be inflicted by so ill-judged so unfortunate a partiality.

If there be any thing solid in virtue—the time must come when it will have been a disgrace to have advocated the Revolution of France in its late stages.

This is a language to which the ears of the people of this country have not been accustommed. Every thing has hitherto conspired to confirm the pernicious fascination by which they are enchained. There has been a positive and a negative conspiracy against the truth which has served to shut out its enlightening ray. Those who always float with the popular gale perceiving the prepossession of the people have administered to it by all the acts in their power—endeavouring to recommend themselves by an exaggerated zeal for a favourite object. Others through timidity caution or an ill-judged policy unwilling to expose themselves to the odium of resisting the general current of feeling have betrayed by silence that Truth which they were unable not to perceive. Others, whose sentiments have weight in the community have been themselves the sincere dupes of [   ]. Hence the voice of reason has been stifled and the Nation has been left unadmonished to travel on in one of the most degrading delusions that ever disparaged the understandings of an enlightened people.

To recal them from this dangerous error—to engage them to dismiss their prejudices & consult dispassionately their own good sense—to lead them to an appeal from their own enthusiasm to their reason and humanity would be the most important service that could be rendered to the UStates at the present juncture. The error entertained is not on a mere speculative question. The French Revolution is a political convulsion that in a great or less degree shakes the whole civilized world and it is of real consequence to the principles and of course to the happiness of a Nation to estimate it rightly.

1794

To George Washington

Philadelphia February 3. 1795

SIR

My particular acknowlegements are due for your very kind letter of yesterday. As often as I may recall the vexations I have endured, your approbation will be a great and precious consolation.

It was not without a struggle, that I yielded to the very urgent motives, which impelled me to relinquish a station, in which I could hope to be in any degree instrumental in promoting the success of an administration under your direction; a struggle which would have been far greater, had I supposed that the prospect of future usefulness was proportioned to the sacrifices to be made.

Whatsoever may be my destination hereafter, I entreat you to be persuaded (not the less for my having been sparing in professions) that I shall never cease to render a just tribute to those eminent and excellent qualities which have been already productive of so many blessings to your country—that you will always have my fervent wishes for your public and personal felicity, and that it will be my pride to cultivate a continuance of that esteem regard and friendship, of which you do me the honor to assure me. With true respect and affectionate attachment I have the honor to be

Sir Your obliged & obedt servt

A HAMILTON

To Rufus King

Kingston Feby. 21. 1795

MY DEAR KING

The unnecessary capricious & abominable assassination of the National honor by the rejection of the propositions respecting the unsubscribed debt in the House of Representatives haunts me every step I take, and afflicts me more than I can express. To see the character of the Government and the country so sported with, exposed to so indelible a blot puts my heart to the Torture. Am I then more of an American than those who drew their first breath on American Ground? Or What is it that thus torments me at a circumstance so calmly viewed by almost every body else? Am I a fool—a Romantic quixot—Or is there a constitutional defect in the American Mind? Were it not for yourself and a few others, I could adopt the reveries of De Paux as substantial truths, and would say with him that there is something in our climate which belittles every Animal human or brute.

I conjure you, my friend, Make a vigorous stand for the honor of your Country. Rouse all the energies of your mind, and measure swords in the Senate with the great Slayer of public faith—the hacknied *Veteran* in the violation of public engagements. Prevent him if possible from triumphing a second time over the prostrate credit* and injured interests of his Country. Unmask his false and horrid hypothesis. Display the immense difference between an able statesman and the *Man of subtilties*. Root out the distempered and noisome *weed* which is attempted to be planted in our political garden—to choak and wither in its infancy the fair plant of public credit.

I disclose to you without reserve the state of my mind. It is

* Witness the 40 for 1 scheme a most unskilful measure, to say the best of it.

discontented and gloomy in the extreme. I consider the cause of good government as having been put to an issue & the verdict against it.

Introduce I pray you into the Senate, when the bill comes up the clause which has been rejected freed from embarrassment by the bills of Credit bearing interest on the nominal value. Press its adoption in this the most unexceptionable shape & let the *yeas* & *nays* witness the result.

Among other reasons for this is my wish that the true friends of public credit may be distinguished from its enemies. The question is too great a one not to undergo a thorough examination before the Community. It would pain me not to be able to distinguish. Adieu.

God bless you

A HAMILTON

P.S. Do me the favour to revise carefully the course of the bill respecting the unsubscribed Debt & let me know the particulars. I wish to be able to judge more particularly of the under plot I suspect.

To Robert Troup

Albany April 13. 1795

I should want feeling & friendship were I not penetrated by the affectionate concern you so repeatedly manifest for my interest.

Without knowing the particulars of the plan to which you refer I ought not to decide finally against it. But I very much believe that it will not comport with my general system which is to avoid large or complicated speculations especially where foreigners are concerned.

Tis not my Dear Friend that I think there is any harm or even indelicacy in the thing—I am now in no situation that restrains me—But 'tis because I think there is at present a great crisis in the affairs of mankind which may in its consequences involve this country in a sense most affecting to every true friend to it—because concerns of the nature alluded to, though very harmless in the *saints*, who may even fatten themselves on the opportunities or if you please spoils of office, as well as profit by every good thing that is going—who may [   ] agents & tools of foreign *Governments* without hazarding their popularity yet those who are not of the *regenerating* tribe may not do the most unexceptionable things without its being thundered in their ears—without being denounced as speculators peculators British Agents &c. &c. Because there must be some *public fools* who sacrifice private to public interest at the certainty of ingratitude and obloquy—because my *vanity* whispers I ought to be one of those fools and ought to keep myself in a situation the best calculated to render service—because I dont want to be rich and if I cannot live *in splendor* in Town, with a moderate fortune moderately acquired, I can at least live *in comfort* in the country and I am content to do so.

The game to be played may be a most important one. It may be for nothing less than true liberty, property, order, religion and of course *heads*. I will try Troupe if possible to guard yours & mine.

You are good enough to offer to stand between me and ostensibility. I thank you with all my soul. You cannot doubt that I should have implicit confidence in you but it has been the rule of my life to do nothing for my own emolument *undercover*—what I would not promulge I would avoid. This may be too great refinement. I know it is pride. But this pride makes it part of my plan to *appear truly what I am*.

God bless you. Always Affectionately Yrs.

A HAMILTON

Design for a Seal for the United States

A Globe with Europe and part of Africa on one side—America on the other—the Atlantic Ocean between. The portion occupied by America to be larger than that occupied by Europe. A COLOSSUS to be placed on this Globe, with one foot on Europe, the other extending partly over the Atlantic towards America, having on his head a *quintuple* crown in his right hand an *Iron*-Sceptre projected but broken in the middle—in his left hand a *Pileus* reversed, the staff intwined by a snake with its head downward having the staff in its mouth and folding in its tail (as if in the act of strangling) a label with these words "Rights of Man."

Upon a base, supported by fifteen columns, erected on the Continent of America, to be placed the *Genius* of America, represented by *Pallas*—a female figure with a firm composed countenance, in an attitude of defiance, cloathed in armour with a golden breast plate, a spear in her right hand and an *Ægis* or shield in her left, decorated with the scales of Justice instead of the Medusa's head—her helmet incircled with wreaths of Olive—her spear striking upon the Sceptre of the Colussus and breaking it obliquely over her head a radiated Crown or *Glory*.

EXPLANATION

The Globe is an antient symbol of universal Dominion. This, with the Colossus alluding to the Directory, will denote the project of acquiring it—the position of one leg of the colussus will signify the *attempt* to extend it to America. The Columns will represent the American States. Pallas, as the Genius of America will denote, that though loving Peace (of which the Olive wreath is the emblem) yet guided by *Wisdom*, or an enlightened sense of her own rights and interests, she is determined to exert and does successfully exert her *valour*, in breaking the sceptre of the Tyrant. The *Glory* is the usual type of Providential interposition.

It would improve it if it did not render it too complicated to represent the Ocean in Tempest & Neptune striking with his Trident the projected leg of the Colussus.

But perhaps instead of all this it may suffice to have the figure of Pallas on horse back the harp placed on the Columns these on a small mount—her spear breaking a Sceptre projected by a *Herculean Arm*.

c. May 1796

To George Washington

New York July 30. 1796

SIR

I have the pleasure to send you herewith a certain draft which I have endeavoured to make as perfect as my time and engagements would permit. It has been my object to render this act *importantly* and *lastingly* useful, and avoiding all just cause of present exception, to embrace such reflections and sentiments as will wear well, progress in approbation with time, & redound to future reputation. How far I have succeeded you will judge.

I have begun the second part of the task—the digesting the supplementary remarks to the first address which in a fortnight I hope also to send you—yet I confess the more I have considered the matter the less eligible this plan has appeared to me. There seems to me to be a certain awkwardness in the thing—and it seems to imply that there is a doubt whether the assurance without the evidence would be believed. Besides that I think that there are some ideas which will not wear well in the former address, & I do not see how any part can be omitted, if it is to be given as the thing formerly prepared. Nevertheless when you have both before you you can better judge.

If you should incline to take the draft now sent—and after perusing and noting any thing that you wish changed & will send it to me I will with pleasure shape it as you desire. This may also put it in my power to improve the expression & perhaps in some instances condense.

I rejoice that certain clouds have not lately thickened & that there is a prospect of a brighter horison.

With affectionate & respectful attachment I have the honor to be Sir Yr. Very Obed Serv

A Hamilton

Enclosure: Draft of Washington's Farewell Address

The period for a new election of a Citizen to administer the Executive Gov of the U States being not very distant and the time actually arrived when your thoughts must be employed in designating the person who is to be cloathed with that important trust for another term, it appears to me proper, and especially as it may conduce to a more distinct expression of the public voice, that I should now apprize you of the resolution I have formed to decline being considered among the number of those out of whom a choice is to be made.

I beg you nevertheless at the same time to be assured that the resolution, which I announce, has not been taken without a strict regard to all the considerations attached to the relation which as a dutiful Citizen I bear to my Country; and that in withdrawing the tender of my service, which silence in my situation might imply, I am influenced by no diminution of zeal for its future interest nor by any deficiency of grateful respect for its past kindness, but by a full conviction that such a step is compatible with both.

The acceptance of and continuance hitherto in the office to which your suffrages have twice called me has been a uniform sacrifice of private inclination to the opinion of public duty coinciding with what appeared to be your wishes. I had constantly hoped that it would have been much earlier in my power consistently with motives which I was not at liberty to disregard to return to that retirement from which they those motives had reluctantly drawn me.

The strength of my desire to withdraw previous to the last election had even led to the preparation of an address to declare it to you—but deliberate reflection on the very critical and perplexed posture of our affairs with foreign nations and the unanimous advice of men of every way intitled to my confidence obliged me to abandon the idea.

I rejoice that the state of your national Concerns external as well as internal no longer renders the pursuit of my inclination incompatible with the sentiment of duty or propriety, and that whatever partiality any portion of You may still retain for my services, they, under the existing circumstances of our Country, will not disapprove the resolution I have formed.

The impressions under which I first accepted the arduous trust of chief Magistrate of the U States were explained on the proper occasion. In the discharge of this trust I can only say that I have with pure intentions contributed towards the organisation and administration of the Government the best exertions of which a very fallible judgment was capable. Not unconscious at the outset of the inferiority of my qualifications for the station, experience in my own eyes and perhaps still more in those of others has not diminished in me the diffidence of myself—and every day the increasing weight of years admonishes me more and more that the shade of retirement is as necessary to me as it will be welcome to me. Satisfied that if any circumstances have given a peculiar value to my services they were temporary, I have the consolation to believe that while inclination and prudence urge me to recede from the political scene patriotism does not forbid it—May I also have that of perceiving in my retreat that the involuntary errors which I have probably committed have been the causes of no serious or lasting mischief to my Country and thus be spared the anguish of regrets which would disturb the repose of my retreat and embitter the remnant of my life! I may then expect to realize without alloy the purest enjoyment of partaking, in the midst of my fellow citizens of the benign influence of good laws under a free Government; the ultimate object of all my wishes and to which

I look as the happy reward I hope of our mutual cares labours and dangers.

In looking forward to the moment which is to terminate the carreer of my public life, my sensations do not permit me to suspend the deep acknowlegements required by that debt of gratitude which I owe to my beloved country for the many honors it has conferred upon me still more for the distinguished and steadfast confidence it has reposed in me and for the opportunities it has thus afforded me of manifesting my inviolable attachment by services faithful and persevering—however the inadequateness of my faculties may have ill seconded my zeal. If benefits have resulted to you my fellow Citizens from these services, let it always be remembered to your praise and as an instructive example in our annals that the constancy of your support amidst appearances sometimes dubious vicissitudes of fortune often discouraging and in situations in which not infrequently want of success has seconded the criticisms of malevolence was the essential prop of the efforts and the guarantee of the measures by which they were atchieved. Profoundly penetrated with this idea, I shall carry it with me to my retirement and to my grave as a lively incitement to unceasing vows (the only returns I can henceforth make) that Heaven may continue to You the choicest tokens of the beneficence merited by national piety and morality—that your union and brotherly affection may be perpetual—that the free constitution, which is the work of your own hands may be sacredly maintained—that its administration in every department may be stamped with wisdom and virtue—that in fine the happiness of the People of these States under the auspices of liberty may be made complete by so careful a preservation & so prudent a use of this blessing as will acquire them the glorious satisfaction of recommending it to the affection the praise—and the adoption of every nation which is yet a stranger to it.

Here perhaps I ought to stop. But a solicitude for your welfare, which cannot end but with my life, and the fear that there may exist projects unfriendly to it against which it may be necessary you should be guarded, urge me in taking leave of you to offer to your solemn consideration and frequent review some sentiments the result of mature reflection confirmed by observation & experience which appear to me essential to the permanency of your felicity as a people. These will be offered with the more freedom as you can only see in them the disinterested advice of a parting friend who can have no personal motive to tincture or byass his counsel.

Interwoven as is the love of Liberty with every fibre of your hearts no recommendation is necessary to fortify your attachment to it. Next to this that unity of Government which constitutes you one people claims your vigilant care & guardianship—as a main pillar of your real independence of your peace safety freedom and happiness.

This being the point in your political fortress against which the batteries of internal and external enemies will be most constantly and actively however covertly and insidiously levelled, it is of the utmost importance that you should appreciate in its full force the immense value of your political Union to your national and individual happiness—that you should cherish towards it an affectionate and immoveable attachment and that you should watch for its presservation with jealous solicitude.

For this you have every motive of sympathy and interest. Children for the most part of a common country, that country claims and ought to concentrate your affections. The name of American must always gratify and exalt the just pride of patriotism more than any denomination which can be derived from local discrimination. You have with slight shades of difference the same religion manners habits & political institutions & principles. You have in a common cause fought and triumphed to gether. The independence and liberty you enjoy are the work of joint councils efforts—dangers sufferings & successes. By your Union you atchieved them, by your union you will most effectually maintain them.

The considerations which address themselves to your sensibility are greatly strengthened by those which apply to your interest. Here every portion of our Country will find the most urgent and commanding motives for guarding and preserving the Union of the Whole.

The North in a free & unfettered intercourse with the South under the equal laws of one Government will in the production of the latter many of them peculiar find vast additional resources of maritime and commercial enterprise and precious materials of their manufacturing industry. The South in the same intercourse will share in the benefits of the Agency of the North will find its agriculture promoted and its commerce extended by turning into its own channels means of Navigation which the North more abundantly affords and while it contributes to extend the national navigation will participate in the protection of a maritime strength to which itself is unequally adapted. The East in a like intercourse with the West finds and in the progressive improvement of internal navigation will more & more find, a valuable vent for the commodities which it brings from abroad or manufactures at home. The West derives through this Channel an essential supply of its wants—and what is far more important to it, it must owe the secure and permanent enjoyment of the indispensable outlets for its own productions to the weight influence & maritime resources of the Atlantic States directed by an indissoluble community of interest. The tenure by which it could hold this advantage either from its own separate strength or by an apostate and unnatural connection with any foreign Nation must be intrinsically & necessarily precarious at every moment liable to be disturbed by the fluctuating combinations of those primary European interests which constantly regulate the conduct of every portion of Europe—And where every part finds a particular interest in the Union All the parts of our Country will find in their Union greater independence from the superior abundance & variety of production incident to the diversity of soil & climate, all the parts of it must find in the aggregate assemblage & reaction of their mutual population production greater strength, proportional security from external danger, less frequent interruption of their peace with foreign nations and what is far more valuable an exemption from those broils & wars between the parts if disunited which their own rivalships fomented by foreign intrigue, or the opposite alliances with foreign nations engendered by their mutual jealousies would inevitably produce—a consequent exemption from the necessity of those military establishments upon a large scale which bear in every country so menacing an aspect toward Liberty.

These considerations speak a conclusive language to every virtuous and considerate mind. They place the continuance of our Union among the first objects of patriotic desire. Is there a doubt whether a common government can long embrace so extensive a sphere? Let Time & Experience decide the question. Speculation in such a case ought not to be listened to—And tis rational to hope that the auxiliary agency of the governments of the subdivisions, with a proper organisation of the whole will secure a favourable issue to the Experiment. Tis allowable to believe that the spirit of party the intrigues of foreign nations, the corruption & the ambition of Individuals are likely to prove more formidable adversaries to the unity of our Empire than any inherent difficulties in the scheme. Tis against these that the guards of national opinion national sympathy national prudence & virtue are to be erected. With such obvious motives to Union there will be always cause from the fact itself to distrust the <u>patriotism</u> of those who in any quarter may endeavour to weaken its bands. And by all the love I bear you My fellow Citizens I conjure you as often as it appears to frown upon the attempt.

Besides the more serious causes which have been hinted at, as endangering our Union there is another less dangerous but against which it is necessary to be on our guard. I mean the petulance collisions & disgusts of party differences of Opinion. It is not uncommon to hear the irritations which these excite vent themselves in declarations that the different parts of the Union are ill assorted and cannot remain together—in menaces from the inhabitants of one part to those of another that it will be dissolved by this or that measure. Intimations of the kind are as indiscreet as they are intemperate. Though frequently made with levity and without being in earnest they have a tendency to produce the consequence which they indicate. They teach the minds of men to consider the Union as precarious as an object to which they are not to attach their hopes and fortunes and thus weaken the sentiment in its favour. By rousing the resentment and alarming the pride of those to whom they are addressed they set ingenuity to work to depreciate the value of the object and to discover motives of Indifference to it. This is not wise. Prudence demands that we should habituate ourselves in all our words and actions to reverence the Union as a sacred and inviolable palladium of our happiness—and should discountenance whatever can lead to a suspicion that it can in any event be abandonned.

Tis matter of serious concern that parties in this Country for some time past have been too much characterised by geographical discriminations—Northern and Southern States Atlantic and Western Country. These discriminations of party which are the mere artifice of the spirit of party (always dexterous to avail itself of every source of sympathy of every handle by which the passions can be taken hold of and which has been careful to turn to account the circumstance of territorial vicinity) have furnished an argument against the Union as evidence of a real difference of local interests and views and serve to hazard it by organising large districts of country under the direction of the leaders of different factions whose passions & prejudices rather than the true interests of the Country, will be too apt to regulate the use of their influence. If it be possible to correct <u>this poison</u> in the affairs of our Country it is worthy the best endeavours of moderate & virtuous men to effect it.

One of the expedients which the partisans of Faction employ towards strengthening their influence by local discriminations is to misrepresent the opinions and views of rival districts—The People at large cannot be too much on their guard against the jealousies which grow out of these misrepresentations. They tend to render aliens to each other those who ought to be tied together by fraternal affection. The Western Country have lately had a useful lesson on this subject. They have seen in the negotiation by the Executive & in the unanimous ratification of the Treaty with Spain by the Senate & in the universal satisfaction at that event in all parts of the Country a decisive proof how unfounded have been the suspicions that have been instilled inpropagated among them of a policy in the Atlantic States & in the different departments of the General Government hostile to their interests in relation to the Mississipian. They have seen two treaties formed which secure to them every thing that they could desire to confirm their prosperity. Will they not henceforth rely for the preservation of these advantages on that union by which they were procured? Will they not reject those counsellors who would render them alien to their brethren & connect them with Aliens?

To the duration and efficacy of your Union a Government extending over the whole is indispensable. No alliances however strict between the parts could be an adequate substitute. These could not fail to be liable to the infractions and interruptions which all alliances in all times have suffered. Sensible of this important truth you have lately established a Constitution of General Government, better calculated than the former for an intimate union and more adequate to the direction of your common concerns. This Government the offspring of your own choice uninfluenced and unawed, completely free in its principles, in the distribution of its powers uniting energy with safety and containing in itself a provision for its own amendment is well entitled to your confidence and support—Respect for its authority, compliance with its laws, acquiescence in its measures, are duties dictated by the fundamental maxims of true Liberty. The basis of our political systems is the right of the people to make and to alter their constitutions of Government. But the constitution for the time, and until changed by an explicit and authentic act of the whole people, is sacredly binding upon all. The very idea of the right and power of the people to establish Government presupposes the duty of every individual to obey the established Government.

All obstructions to the execution of the laws—all <u>combinations</u> and <u>associations</u> under whatever plausible character with the real design to direct counteract countroul influence or awe the regular deliberation or action of the constituted authorities are contrary to this fundamental principle & of the most fatal tendency. They serve to organise Faction to give it an artificial force; and to put in the stead of the delegated will of the whole nation the will of a party. often a small but artful & enterprising minority of the community—and according to the alternate triumphs of different parties to make the public administration reflect the ill concerted schemes and projects of faction rather than the wholesome plans of common councils and deliberations. However combinations or associations of this description may occasionally promote popular ends and purposes they are likely to produce in the course of time and things the most effectual engines by which artful ambitious and unprincipled men will be enabled to subvert the power of the people and usurp the reins of Government.

Towards the preservation of your government and the permanency of your present happy state, it is not only requisite that you steadily discountenance irregular oppositions to its authority but that you should be upon your guard against the spirit of innovation upon its principles however specious the pretexts. One method of assault may be to effect alterations in the forms of the constitution tending to impair the energy of the system and so to undermine what cannot be directly overthrown. In all the changes to which you may be invited remember that time and habit are as necessary to fix the true character of governments as of any other human institutions, that experience is the surest standard by which the real tendency of existing constitutions of government can be tried—that changes upon the credit of mere hypothesis and opinions exposes you to perpetual change from the successive and endless variety of hypothesis and opinion—and remember also that for the efficacious management of your common interests in a country so extensive as ours a Government of as much force and strength as is consistent with the perfect security of liberty is indispensable. Liberty itself will find in such a Government, with powers properly distributed and arranged, its surest guardian—and protector. In my opinion the real danger in our system is that the General Government organised as at present will prove too weak rather than too powerful.

I have already observed the danger to be apprehended from founding our parties on Geographical discriminations. Let me now enlarge the view of this point and caution you in the most solemn manner against the baneful effects of party spirit in general. This spirit unfortunately is inseperable from human nature and has its root in the strongest passions of the human heart.—It exists under different shapes in all governments but in different degrees stifled controuled or repressed in those of the popular form it is always seen in its utmost vigour & rankness and it is their worst enemy. In republics of narrow extent, it is not difficult for those who at any time possess the reins of administration, or even for partial combinations of men, who from birth riches and other sources of distinction have an extraordinary influence by possessing or acquiring the direction of the military force or by sudden efforts of partisans & followers to overturn the established order of things and effect a usurpation. But in republics of large extent the one or the other is scarcely possible. The powers and opportunities of resistance of a numerous and wide extended nation defy the successful efforts of the ordinary military force or of any collections which wealth and patronage may call to their aid—especially if there be no city of overbearing force resources and influence. In such Republics it is perhaps safe to assert that the conflict of popular faction offer the only avenues to tyranny & usurpation. The domination of one faction over another stimulated by that spirit of Revenge which is apt to be gradually engendered and which in different ages and countries have produced the greatest enormities is itself a frightful despotism. But this leads at length to a more formal and permanent despotism. The disorders and miseries which result predispose the minds of men to seek repose & security in the absolute power of a single man. And some leader of a prevailing faction more able or more fortunate than his competitors turns this disposition to the purpose of an ambitious and criminal self aggrandisement.

Without looking forward to such an extremity (which however ought not to be out of sight) the ordinary and continual mischief of the spirit of party make it the interest and the duty of a wise people to discountenance and repress it.

It serves always to distract the Councils & enfeeble the administration of the Government. It agitates the community with ill founded jealousies and false alarms embittering one part of the community against another, & producing occasionaly riot & insurrection. It opens inlets for foreign corruption and influence—which find an easy access through the channels of party passions—and cause the true policy & interest of our own country to be made subservient to the policy and interest of one and another foreign Nation; sometimes enslaving our own Government to the will of a foreign Government.

There is an opinion that parties in free countries are salutary checks upon the administration of the Government & serve to invigorate the spirit of Liberty. This within certain limits is true and in governments of a monarchical character or byass patriotism may look with some favour on the spirit of party. But in those of the popular kind in those purely elective it is a spirit not to be fostered or encouraged. From the natural tendency of such governments, it is certain there will always be enough of it for every salutary purpose and there being constant danger of excess the effort ought to be by force of public opinion to mitigate & correct it. Tis a fire which cannot be quenched but demands a uniform vigilance to prevent its bursting into a flame—lest it should not only warm but consume.

It is important likewise that the habits of thinking of the people should tend to produce caution in their agents in the several departments of Government, to retain each within its proper sphere and not to permit one to encroach upon another—that every attempt of the kind from whatever quarter should meet with the discountenance of the community, and that in every case in which a precedent of encroachment shall have been given, a corrective be sought in (revocation be effected by) a careful attention to the next choice of public Agents. The spirit of encroachment tends to absorb & consolidate the powers of the several branches and departments into one, and thus to establish under whatever forms a despotism. A just knowlege of the human heart, of that love of power which predominates in it, is alone sufficient to establish this truth. Experiments ancient and modern—some in our own country and under our own eyes serve to confirm it. If in the public opinion the distribution of the constitutional powers be in any instance wrong or inexpedient—let it be corrected by the authority of the people in a legitimate constitutional course—Let there be no change by usurpation, for though this may be the instrument of good in one instance, it is the ordinary and natural instrument of the destruction of free Government—and the influence of the precedent is always infinitely more pernicious than any thing which it may atchieve can be beneficial.

To all those dispositions which promote political happiness prosperity, Religion and Morality are essential props. In vain does that man claim the praise of patriotism who labours to subvert or undermine these great pillars of human happiness these firmest foundations of the duties of men and citizens. The mere politician equally with the pious man ought to respect and cherish them. A volume could not trace all their connections with private and public happiness. Let it simply be asked where is the security for property for reputation for life if the sense of moral and religious obligation deserts the oaths which are administered in the instruments of Investigation Courts of Justice? Nor ought we to flatter ourselves that morality can be separated from religion. Concede as much as may be asked to the effect of refined education in minds of a peculiar structure—can we believe—can we in prudence suppose that national morality can be maintained in exclusion of religious principles? Does it not require the aid of a generally received and divinely authoritative Religion?

Tis essentially true that virtue or morality is a main & necessary spring of popular or republican Governments. The rule indeed extends with more or less force to all free Governments. Who that is a prudent & sincere friend to them can look with indifference on the ravages which are making in the foundation of the Fabric? Religion? The uncommon means which of late have been directed to this fatal end seem to make it in a particular of manner the duty of the Retiring Chief of a nation to warn his country against tasting of the poisonous draught.

Cultivate also industry and frugality. They are auxiliaries of good morals and great sources of private and national prosperity. Is there not room for regret that our propensity to expence exceeds the maturity of our Country for expense? Is there not more luxury among us, in various classes, than suits the actual period of our national progress? Whatever may be the apology for luxury in a Country mature in all the arts which are its ministers and the means of national opulence—can it promote the advantage of a young agricultural Country little advanced in manufactures and not much advanced in wealth?

Cherish public Credit as a mean of strength and security. As one method of preserving it, use it as little as possible. Avoid occasions of expence by cultivating peace—remembering always that the preparation against danger by timely and provident disbursements is often a mean of avoiding greater disbursements to repel it. Avoid the accumulation of debt by avoiding occasions of expence and by vigorous exertions in time of peace to discharge the debts which unavoidable wars may have occasionned—not transferring to posterity the burthen which we ought to bear ourselves. Recollect that towards the payment of debts there must be Revenue, that to have revenue there must be taxes, that it is impossible to devise taxes which are not more or less inconvenient and unpleasant—that they are always a choice of difficulties—that the intrinsic embarrassment which never fails to attend a selection of objects ought to be a motive for a candid construction of the conduct of the Government in making it—and that a spirit of acquiescence in those measures for obtaining revenue which the public exigencies dictate is in an especial manner the duty and interest of the citizens of every State.

Cherish good faith and Justice towards, and peace and harmony with all nations. Religion and morality enjoins this conduct And It cannot be, but that true policy equally demands it. It will be worthy of a free enlightened and at no distant period a great nation to give to mankind the magnanimous and too novel example of a people invariably governed by those exalted views. Who can doubt that in a long course of time and events the fruits of such a conduct would richly repay any temporary advantages which might be lost by a steady adherence to the plan? Can it be that Providence has not connected the permanent felicity of a nation with its virtue? The experiment is recommended by every sentiment which ennobles human nature. Alas! is it rendered impossible by its vices?

Toward the execution of such a plan nothing is more essential than that antipathies against particular nations and passionate attachments for others should be avoided—and that instead of them we should cultivate just and amicable feelings towards all. That nation, which indulges towards another a habitual hatred or a habitual fondness is in some degree a slave. It is a slave to its animosity or to its affection—

either of which is sufficient to lead it astray from its duty and interest. Antipathy against one nation which never fails to beget a similar sentiment in the other disposes each more readily to offer injury and insult to the other—to lay hold of slight causes of umbrage and to be haughty and intractable when accidental or trifling differences arise. Hence frequent quarrels and bitter and obstinate contests. The nation urged by resentment and rage sometimes impels the Government to War contrary to its own calculations of policy. The Government sometimes participates in this propensity & does through passion what reason would forbid—at other times it makes the animosity of the nations subservient to hostile projects which originate in ambition & other sinister motives. The peace often and sometimes the liberty of Nations has been the victim of this cause.

In like manner a passionate attachment of one nation to another produces multiplied ills. Sympathy for the favourite nations, promoting facilitating the illusion of a supposed common interest in cases where it does not exist and communicating to one the enmities of the one betrays into a participation in its quarrels & wars without adequate inducements or justifications. It leads to the concession of privileges to one nation and to the denial of them to others—which is apt doubly to injure the nation making the concession by an unnecessary yielding of what ought to have been retained and by exciting jealousy ill will and retaliation in the party from whom an equal privilege is witheld. And it gives to ambitious corrupted or deluded citizens, who devote themselves to the views of the favourite foreign power, facility in betraying or sacrificing the interests of their own country without odium & even with popularity gilding with the appearance of a virtuous impulse the base yieldings of ambition or corruption.

As avenues to foreign influence in innumerable Ways such attachments are peculiarly alarming to the enlightened independent Patriot. How many opportunities do they afford to intrigue with domestic factions to practice with success the arts of seduction—to mislead public opinion—to influence or awe the public Councils! Such an attachment of a small or weak towards a great & powerful Nation destines the former to revolve round the latter as its satellite.

Against the Mischiefs of Foreign Influence all the Jealousy of a free people ought to be constantly continually exerted. All History & Experience prove that foreign influence is one of the most baneful foes of republican Governt—but that jealousy of it to be useful must be impartial else it becomes an instrument—of the very influence to be avoided instead of a defence against it.

Excessive partiality for one foreign nation & excessive dislike of another, leads to see danger only on one side and serves to viel & second the arts of influence on the other. Real Patriots who resist the intrigues of the favorite become suspected & odious. Its tools & dupes usurp the applause & confidence of the people to betray their interests.

The great rule of conduct for us in regard to foreign Nations ought to be to have as little political connection with them as possible—so far as we have already formed engagements let them be fulfilled—with circumspection indeed but with perfect good faith. Here let us stop.

Europe has a set of primary interests which have none or a very remote relation to us. Hence she must be involved in frequent contests the causes of which will be essentially foreign to us. Hence therefore it must necessarily be unwise on our part to implicate ourselves by an artificial connection in the ordinary vicissitudes of European politics— in the combination, & collisions of her friendships or enmities.

Our detached and distant situation invites us to a different course & enables us to pursue it. If we remain a united people under an efficient Government the period is not distant when we may defy material injury from external annoyance—when we may take such an attitude as will cause the neutrality we shall at any time resolve to observe to be violated with caution—when it will be the interest of belligerent nations under the impossibility of making acquisitions upon us to be very careful how either forced us to throw our weight into the opposite scale—when we may choose peace or war as our interest guided by justice shall dictate.

Why should we forego the advantages of so felicitous a situation? Why quit our own ground to stand upon Foreign ground? Why by interweaving our destiny with any part of Europe should we intangle our prosperity and peace in the nets of European Ambition rivalship interest or Caprice?

Permanent alliance, intimate connection with any part of the foreign world is to be avoided. so far (I mean) as we are now at liberty to do it: for let me never be understood as patronising infidelity to preexisting engagements. These must be observed in their true and genuine sense. But tis not necessary nor will it be prudent to extend them. Tis our true policy as a general principle to avoid permanent or close alliance—Taking care always to keep ourselves by suitable establishments in a respectably defensive posture we may safely trust to occasional alliances for extraordinary emergencies.

Harmony liberal intercourse and commerce with all nations are recommended by justice humanity & interest. But even our commercial policy should hold an equal hand—neither seeking nor granting exclusive favours or preferences—consulting the natural course of things—<u>diffusing</u> and <u>diversifying</u> by gentle means the streams of Commerce but forcing nothing—establishing with powers so disposed in order to give to Trade a stable course, to define the rights of our Merchants and enable the Government to support them—conventional rules of intercourse the best that present circumstances and mutual opinion of interest will permit but temporary—and liable to be abandonned or varied as time experience & future circumstances may dictate—remembering alway that tis folly in one nation to expect disinterested favour in another—that to accept any thing under that character is to part with a portion of its independence—and that it may find itself in the condition of having given equivalents for nominal favours and of being reproached with ingratitude in the bargain. There can be no greater error in national policy than to desire expect or calculate upon real favours. Tis an illusion that experience must cure, that a just pride ought to discard.

In offering to you My Countrymen! these counsels of an old and affectionate friend—counsels suggested by labourious reflection and matured by a various experience—I dare not hope that they will make the strong and lasting impressions I wish—that they will controul the current of the passions or prevent our nation from running the course which has hitherto marked the destiny of all nations. But if I may flatter myself that they even produce some partial benefit, some occasional good—that they sometimes recur to moderate the violence of party spirit—to warn against the evils of foreign intrigue—to guard against the impositions of pretended patriotism—the having offered them must always afford me a precious consolation.

How far in the execution of my present Office I have been guided by the principles which have been inculcated the public records & the external evidences of my conduct must witness. My conscious assures me that I have at least believed myself to be guided by them.

In reference to the present War of Europe my Proclamation of the 22d of April 1793 is the key to my plan. Sanctioned by your approving voice and that of your representatives in Congress the spirit of that measure has continually governed me uninfluenced and unawed by the attempts of any of the warring powers their agents or partizans to deter or divert from it.

After deliberate consideration and the best lights I could obtain (and from men who did not agree in their views of the origin progress & nature of that war) I was satisfied that our Country, under all the circumstances of the case, had a right and was bound in propriety and interest to take a neutral position—And having taken it, I determined as far as should depend on me to maintain it steadily and firmly.

Though in reviewing the incidents of my administration I am unconscious of intentional error—I am yet too sensible of my own deficiencies not to think it probable that I have committed many errors. I deprecate the evils to which they may tend—and fervently implore the Almighty to avert or mitigate them. I shall carry with me nevertheless the hope that my motives will continue to be viewed by my Country with indulgence & that after forty five years of my life devoted with an upright zeal to the public service the faults of inadequate abilities will be consigned to oblivion as myself must soon be to the mansions of rest.

Neither Ambition nor interest has been the impelling cause of my actions. I never designedly misused any power confided to me. The fortune with which I came into office is not bettered otherwise than by that improvement in the value of property which the natural progress and peculiar prosperity of our country have produced. I retire without cause for a blush—with a pure heart with no alien sentiment to the ardor of those vows for the happiness of his Country which is so natural to a Citizen who sees in it vows for the native soil of himself and progenitors for four generations.

To William Hamilton

Albany State of New York
May the 2d. 1797

MY DEAR SIR

Some days since I received with great pleasure your letter of the 10th. of March. The mark, it affords, of your kind attention, and the particular account it gives me of so many relations in Scotland are extremely gratifying to me. You no doubt have understood that my fathers affairs at a very early day went to wreck; so as to have rendered his situation during the greatest part of his life far from eligible. This state of things occasionned a separation between him and me, when I was very young, and threw me upon the bounty of my mothers relations, some of whom were then wealthy, though by vicissitudes to which human affairs are so liable, they have been since much reduced and broken up. Myself at about sixteen came to this Country. Having always had a strong propensity to literary pursuits, by a course of steady and laborious exertion, I was able, by the age of Nineteen to qualify myself for the degree of Batchelor of Arts in the College of New York, and to lay a foundation, by preparatory study, for the future profession of the law.

The American Revolution supervened. My principles led me to take part in it. At nineteen I entered into the American army as Captain of Artillery. Shortly after, I became by his invitation Aide De Camp to General Washington, in which station, I served till the commencement of that Campaign which ended with the seige of York, in Virginia, and the Capture of Cornwallis's Army. This Campaign I made at the head of a corps of light infantry, with which I was present at the seige of York and engaged in some interesting operations.

At the period of the peace with Great Britain, I found myself a member of Congress by appointment of the legislature of this state.

After the peace, I settled in the City of New York in the practice of the law; and was in a very lucrative course of practice, when the derangement of our public affairs, by the feebleness of the general confederation, drew me again reluctantly into public life. I became a member of the Convention which framed the present

Constitution of the U States; and having taken part in this measure, I conceived myself to be under an obligation to lend my aid towards putting the machine in some regular motion. Hence I did not hesitate to accept the offer of President Washington to undertake the office of Secretary of the Treasury.

In that office, I met with many intrinsic difficulties, and many artificial ones proceeding from passions, not very worthy, common to human nature, and which act with peculiar force in republics. The object, however, was effected, of establishing public credit and introducing order into the finances.

Public Office in this Country has few attractions. The pecuniary emolument is so inconsiderable as too amount to a sacrifice to any man who can employ his time with advantage in any liberal profession. The opportunity of doing good, from the jealousy of power and the spirit of faction, is too small in any station to warrant a long continuance of private sacrifices. The enterprises of party had so far succeeded as materially to weaken the necessary influence and energy of the Executive Authority, and so far diminish the power of doing good in that department as greatly to take the motives which a virtuous man might have for making sacrifices. The prospect was even bad for gratifying in future the love of Fame, if that passion was to be the spring of action.

The Union of these motives, with the reflections of prudence in relation to a growing family, determined me as soon as my plan had attained a certain maturity to withdraw from Office. This I did by a resignation about two years since; when I resumed the profession of the law in the City of New York under every advantage I could desire.

It is a pleasing reflection to me that since the commencement of my connection with General Washington to the present time, I have possessed a flattering share of his confidence and friendship.

Having given you a brief sketch of my political career, I proceed to some further family details.

In the year 1780 I married the second daughter of General Schuyler, a Gentleman of one of the best families of this Country; of large fortune and no less personal and public consequence. It is impossible to be happier than I am in a wife and I have five Children, four sons and a daughter, the eldest a son somewhat passed fifteen, who all promise well, as far as their years permit and yield me much satisfaction. Though I have been too much in public life to be wealthy, my situation is extremely comfortable and leaves me nothing to wish but a continuance of health. With this blessing, the profits of my profession and other prospects authorise an expectation of such addition to my resources as will render the eve of life, easy and agreeable; so far as may depend on this consideration.

It is now several months since I have heared from my father who continued at the Island of St Vincents. My anxiety at this silence would be greater than it is, were it not for the considerable interruption and precariousness of intercourse, which is produced by the War.

I have strongly pressed the old Gentleman to come to reside with me, which would afford him every enjoyment of which his advanced age is capable. But he has declined it on the ground that the advice of his Physicians leads him to fear that the change of Climate would be fatal to him. The next thing for me is, in proportion to my means to endeavour to increase his comforts where he is.

It will give me the greatest pleasure to receive your son Robert at my house in New York and still more to be of use to him; to which end my recommendation and interest will not be wanting, and, I hope, not unavailing. It is my intention to embrace the Opening which your letter affords me to extend intercourse with my relations in your Country, which will be a new source of satisfaction to me.

The "Reynolds Pamphlet"

Observations on Certain Documents Contained in No. V & VI of "The History of the United States for the Year 1796," In Which the Charge of Speculation against Alexander Hamilton, Late Secretary of the Treasury, is Fully Refuted. Written by Himself

The spirit of jacobinism, if not entirely a new spirit, has at least been cloathed with a more gigantic body and armed with more powerful weapons than it ever before possessed. It is perhaps not too much to say, that it threatens more extensive and complicated mischiefs to the world than have hitherto flowed from the three great scourges of mankind, WAR, PESTILENCE and FAMINE. To what point it will ultimately lead society, it is impossible for human foresight to pronounce; but there is just ground to apprehend that its progress may be marked with calamities of which the dreadful incidents of the French revolution afford a very faint image. Incessantly busied in undermining all the props of public security and private happiness, it seems to threaten the political and moral world with a complete overthrow.

A principal engine, by which this spirit endeavours to accomplish its purposes is that of calumny. It is essential to its success that the influence of men of upright principles, disposed and able to resist its enterprises, shall be at all events destroyed. Not content with traducing their best efforts for the public good, with misrepresenting their purest motives, with inferring criminality from actions innocent or laudable, the most direct falsehoods are invented and propagated, with undaunted effrontery and unrelenting perseverance. Lies often detected and refuted are still revived and repeated, in the hope that the refutation may have been forgotten or that the frequency and boldness of accusation may supply the place of truth and proof. The most profligate men are encouraged, probably bribed, certainly with patronage if not with money, to become informers and accusers. And when tales, which their characters alone ought to discredit, are refuted by evidence and facts which oblige the patrons of them to abandon their support, they still continue in corroding whispers to wear away the reputations which they could not directly subvert. If, luckily for the conspirators against honest fame, any little foible or folly can be traced out in one, whom they desire to persecute, it becomes at once in their hands a two-edged sword, by which to wound the public character and stab the private felicity of the person. With such men, nothing is sacred. Even the peace of an unoffending and amiable wife is a welcome repast to their insatiate fury against the husband.

In the gratification of this baleful spirit, we not only hear the jacobin news-papers continually ring with odious insinuations and charges against many of our most virtuous citizens; but, not satisfied with this, a measure new in this country has been lately adopted to give greater efficacy to the system of defamation—periodical pamphlets issue from the same presses, full freighted with misrepresentation and falsehood, artfully calculated to hold up the opponents of the FACTION to the jealousy and distrust of the present generation and if possible, to transmit their names with dishonor to posterity. Even the great and multiplied services, the tried and rarely equalled virtues of a WASHINGTON, can secure no exemption.

How then can I, with pretensions every way inferior expect to escape? And if truly this be, as every appearance indicates, a conspiracy of vice against virtue, ought I not rather to be flattered, that I have been so long and so peculiarly an object of persecution? Ought I to regret, if there be any thing about me, so formidable to the Faction as to have made me worthy to be distinguished by the plentitude of its rancour and venom?

It is certain that I have had a pretty copious experience of its malignity. For the honor of human nature, it is to be hoped that the examples are not numerous of men so greatly calumniated and persecuted, as I have been, with so little cause.

I dare appeal to my immediate fellow citizens of whatever political party for the truth of the assertion, that no man ever carried into public life a more unblemished pecuniary reputation, than that with which I undertook the office of Secretary of the Treasury; a character marked by an indifference to the acquisition of property rather than an avidity for it.

With such a character, however natural it was to expect criticism and opposition, as to the political principles which I might manifest or be supposed to entertain, as to the wisdom or expediency of the plans, which I might propose, or as to the skill, care or diligence with which the business of my department might be executed, it was not natural to expect nor did I expect that my fidelity or integrity in a pecuniary sense would ever be called in question.

But on his head a mortifying disappointment has been experienced. Without the slightest foundation, I have been repeatedly held up to the suspicions of the world as a man directed in his administration by the most sordid views; who did not scruple to sacrifice the public to his private interest, his duty and honor to the sinister accumulation of wealth.

Merely because I *retained* an opinion once common to me and the most influencial of those who opposed me, *That the public debt ought to be provided for on the basis of the contract upon which it was created*, I have been wickedly accused with wantonly increasing the public burthen many millions, in order to promote a stock-jobbing interest of myself and friends.

Merely because a member of the House of Representatives entertained a different idea from me, as to the legal effect of appropriation laws, and did not understand accounts, I was exposed to the imputation of having committed a deliberate and criminal violation of the laws and to the suspicion of being a defaulter for millions; so as to have been driven to the painful necessity of calling for a formal and solemn inquiry.

The inquiry took place. It was conducted by a committee of fifteen members of the House of Representatives—a majority of them either my decided political enemies or inclined against me, some of them the most active and intelligent of my opponents, without a single man, who being known to be friendly to me, possessed also such knowledge and experience of public affairs as would enable him to counteract injurious intrigues. Mr. Giles of Virginia who had commenced the attack was of the committee.

The officers and books of the treasury were examined. The transactions between the several banks and the treasury were scrutinized. Even my *private accounts* with those institutions were laid open to the committee; and every possible facility given to the inquiry. The result was a complete demonstration that the suspicions which had been entertained were groundless.

Those which had taken the fastest hold were, that the public monies had been made subservient to loans, discounts and accommodations to myself and friends. The committee in reference to this point reported thus: "It appears from the affidavits of the Cashier and several officers of the bank of the United States and several of the directors, the Cashier, and other officers of the bank of New York, that the Secretary of the Treasury never has either *directly* or *indirectly*, for himself or any other person, procured any discount or credit from either of the said banks upon the basis of any public monies which at any time have been deposited therein under his direction: And the committee are *satisfied*, that *no monies* of the United States, whether *before* or *after* they have passed to the credit of the Treasurer have ever been *directly* or *indirectly* used for or applied to *any purposes* but those of the government, except so far as all monies deposited in a bank are concerned in the *general operations* thereof."

The report, which I have always understood was unanimous, contains in other respects, with considerable detail the materials of a complete exculpation. My enemies, finding no handle for their malice, abandoned the pursuit.

Yet unwilling to leave any ambiguity upon the point, when I

determined to resign my office, I gave early previous notice of it to the House of Representatives, for the declared purpose of affording an opportunity for legislative crimination, if any ground for it had been discovered. Not the least step towards it was taken. From which I have a right to infer the universal conviction of the House, that no cause existed, and to consider the result as a complete vindication.

On another occasion, a worthless man of the name of Fraunces found encouragement to bring forward to the House of Representatives a formal charge against me of unfaithful conduct in office. A Committee of the House was appointed to inquire, consisting in this case also, partly of some of my most intelligent and active enemies. The issue was an unanimous exculpation of me as will appear by the following extract from the Journals of the House of Representatives of the 19th of February 1794.

"The House resumed the consideration of the report of the Committee, to whom was referred the memorial of Andrew G. Fraunces: whereupon,

"*Resolved*, That the reasons assigned by the secretary of the treasury, for refusing payment of the warrants referred to in the memorial, are fully sufficient to justify his conduct; and that in the whole course of this transaction, the secretary and other officers of the treasury, have acted a meritorious part towards the public."

"*Resolved*, That the charge exhibited in the memorial, against the secretary of the treasury, relative to the purchase of the pension of Baron de Glaubeck is wholly illiberal and groundless*."

Was it not to have been expected that these repeated demonstrations of the injustice of the accusations hazarded against me would have abashed the enterprise of my calumniators? However natural such an expectation may seem, it would betray an ignorance of the true character of the Jacobin system. It is a maxim deeply ingrafted in that dark system, that no character, however upright, is a match for constantly reiterated attacks, however false. It is well understood by its disciples, that every calumny makes some proselites and even retains some; since justification seldom circulates as rapidly and as widely as slander. The number of those who from doubt proceed to suspicion and thence to belief of imputed guilt is continually augmenting; and

---

* Would it be believed after all this, that Mr. Jefferson Vice President of the United States would write to this Fraunces friendly letters? Yet such is the fact as will be seen in the Appendix, Nos. XLIV & XLV.

the public mind fatigued at length with resistance to the calumnies which eternally assail it, is apt in the end to sit down with the opinion that a person so often accused cannot be entirely innocent.

Relying upon this weakness of human nature, the Jacobin Scandal-Club though often defeated constantly return to the charge. Old calumnies are served up a-fresh and every pretext is seized to add to the catalogue. The person whom they seek to blacken, by dint of repeated strokes of their brush, becomes a demon in their own eyes, though he might be pure and bright as an angel but for the daubing of those wizard painters.

Of all the vile attempts which have been made to injure my character that which has been lately revived in No. V and VI, of the history of the United States for 1796 is the most vile. This it will be impossible for any *intelligent*, I will not say *candid*, man to doubt, when he shall have accompanied me through the examination.

I owe perhaps to my friends an apology for condescending to give a public explanation. A just pride with reluctance stoops to a formal vindication against so despicable a contrivance and is inclined rather to oppose to it the uniform evidence of an upright character. This would be my conduct on the present occasion, did not the tale seem to derive a sanction from the names of three men of some weight and consequence in the society: a circumstance, which I trust will excuse me for paying attention to a slander that without this prop, would defeat itself by intrinsic circumstances of absurdity and malice.

The charge against me is a connection with one James Reynolds for purposes of improper pecuniary speculation. My real crime is an amorous connection with his wife, for a considerable time with his privity and connivance, if not originally brought on by a combination between the husband and wife with the design to extort money from me.

This confession is not made without a blush. I cannot be the apologist of any vice because the ardour of passion may have made it mine. I can never cease to condemn myself for the pang, which it may inflict in a bosom eminently intitled to all my gratitude, fidelity and love. But that bosom will approve, that even at so great an expence, I should effectually wipe away a more serious stain from a name, which it cherishes with no less elevation than tenderness. The public too will I trust excuse the confession. The necessity of it to my defence against a more heinous charge could alone have extorted from me so painful an indecorum.

Before I proceed to an exhibition of the positive proof which repels the charge, I shall analize the documents from which it is deduced, and I am mistaken if with discerning and candid minds more would be necessary. But I desire to obviate the suspicions of the most suspicious.

The first reflection which occurs on a perusal of the documents is that it is morally impossible I should have been foolish as well as depraved enough to employ so vile an instrument as *Reynolds* for such *insignificant ends*, as are indicated by different parts of the story itself. My enemies to be sure have kindly pourtrayed me as another *Chartres* on the score of moral principle. But they have been ever bountiful in ascribing to me talents. It has suited their purpose to exaggerate such as I may possess, and to attribute to them an influence to which they are not intitled. But the present accusation imputes to me as much folly as wickedness. All the documents shew, and it is otherwise matter of notoriety, that Reynolds was an obscure, unimportant and profligate man. Nothing could be more weak, because nothing could be more unsafe than to make use of such an instrument; to use him too without any intermediate agent more worthy of confidence who might keep me out of sight, to write him numerous letters recording the objects of the improper connection (for this is pretended and that the letters were afterwards burnt at my request) to unbosom myself to him with a prodigality of confidence, by very unnecessarily telling him, as he alleges, of a connection in speculation between myself and Mr. Duer. It is very extraordinary, if the head of the money department of a country, being unprincipled enough to sacrifice his trust and his integrity, could not have contrived objects of profit sufficiently large to have engaged the co-operation of men of far greater importance than Reynolds, and with whom there could have been due safety, and should have been driven to the necessity of unkennelling such a reptile to be the instrument of his cupidity.

But, moreover, the scale of the concern with Reynolds, such as it is presented, is contemptibly narrow for a rapacious speculating secretary of the treasury. *Clingman, Reynolds* and his wife were manifestly in very close confidence with each other. It seems there was a free communication of secrets. Yet in clubbing their different items of information as to the supplies of money which Reynolds received from me, what do they amount to? *Clingman* states, that Mrs. Reynolds told him, that at a certain time her husband had received from me upwards of eleven hundred dollars. A note is produced which shews that at one time fifty dollars were sent to him, and another note is produced, by which and the information of Reynolds himself through Clingman, it appears that at another time 300 dollars were asked and refused. Another sum of 200 dollars is spoken of by *Clingman* as having been furnished to Reynolds at some other time. What a scale of speculation is this for the head of a public treasury, for one who in the very publication that brings forward the charge is represented as having procured to be funded at forty millions a debt which ought to have been discharged at ten or fifteen millions for the criminal purpose of enriching himself and his friends? He must have been a clumsy knave, if he did not secure enough of this excess of twenty five or thirty millions, to have taken away all inducement to risk his character in such bad hands and in so huckstering a way—or to have enabled him, if he did employ such an agent, to do it with more means and to better purpose. It is curious, that this rapacious secretary should at one time have furnished his speculating agent with the paltry sum of fifty dollars, at another, have refused him the inconsiderable sum of 300 dollars, declaring upon his honor that it was not in his power to furnish it. This declaration was true or not; if the last the refusal ill comports with the idea of a speculating connection—if the first, it is very singular that the head of the treasury engaged without scruple in schemes of profit should have been destitute of so small a sum. But if we suppose this officer to be living upon an inadequate salary, without any collateral pursuits of gain, the appearances then are simple and intelligible enough, applying to them the true key.

It appears that *Reynolds* and *Clingman* were detected by the then comptroller of the treasury, in the odious crime of suborning a witness to commit perjury, for the purpose of obtaining letters of administration on the estate of a person who was living in order to receive a small sum of money due to him from the treasury. It is certainly extraordinary that the confidential agent of the head of that department should have been in circumstances to induce a resort to so miserable an expedient. It is odd, if there was a speculating connection, that it was not more profitable both to the secretary and to his agent than are indicated by the circumstances disclosed.

It is also a remarkable and very instructive fact, that notwithstanding the great confidence and intimacy, which subsisted between *Clingman, Reynolds* and his wife, and which continued till after the period of the liberation of the two former from the prosecution against them, neither of them has ever specified the objects of the pretended connection in speculation between Reynolds and me. The pretext that the letters which contained the evidence were destroyed is no answer. They could not have been forgotten and might have been disclosed from memory. The total omission of this could only have proceeded from the consideration that detail might have led to detection. The destruction of letters besides is a fiction, which is refuted not only by the general improbability, that I should put myself upon paper with so despicable a person on a subject which might expose me to infamy, but by the evidence of extreme caution on my part in this particular, resulting from the laconic and disguised form of the notes which are produced. They prove incontestibly that there was an unwillingness to trust Reynolds with my hand writing. The true reason was, that I apprehended he might make use of it to impress upon others the belief of some pecuniary connection with me, and besides implicating my character might render it the engine of a false credit, or turn it to some other sinister use. Hence the disguise; for my conduct in admitting at once and without hesitation that the notes were from me proves that it was never my intention by the expedient of disguising my hand to shelter myself from any serious inquiry.

The accusation against me was never heard of 'till Clingman and Reynolds were under prosecution by the treasury for an infamous crime. It will be seen by the document No. 1 (a) that during the endeavours of *Clingman* to obtain relief, through the interposition of Mr. Mughlenberg, he made to the latter the communication of my pretended criminality. It will be further seen by document No. 2 (a) that Reynolds had while in prison conveyed to the ears of Messrs. Monroe and Venable that he could give intelligence of my being concerned in speculation, and that he also supposed that he was kept in prison by a design on my part to oppress him and drive him away. And by his letter to Clingman of the 13 of December, after he was released from prison, it also appears that he was actuated by a spirit of revenge against me; for he declares that he will have *satisfaction* from me *at all events*; adding, as addressed to *Clingman*, "And *you only I trust*."

Three important inferences flow from these circumstances—
one that the accusation against me was an auxiliary to the efforts
of *Clingman* and *Reynolds* to get released from a disgraceful
prosecution—another that there was a vindicative spirit against me at
least on the part of Reynolds—the third, that he confided in *Clingman* as
a coadjutor in the plan of vengeance. These circumstances, according
to every estimate of the credit due to accusers, ought to destroy their
testimony. To what credit are persons intitled, who in telling a story
are governed by the double motive of escaping from disgrace and
punishment and of gratifying revenge? As to Mrs. Reynolds, if she was
not an accomplice, as it is too probable she was, her situation would
naturally subject her to the will of her husband. But enough besides
will appear in the sequel to shew that her testimony merits no attention.

The letter which has been just cited deserves a more
particular attention. As it was produced by Clingman, there is a chasm
of three lines, which lines are manifestly essential to explain the sense.
It may be inferred from the context, that these deficient lines would
unfold the cause of the resentment which is expressed. 'Twas from
them that might have been learnt the true nature of the transaction.
The expunging of them is a violent presumption that they would have
contradicted the purpose for which the letter was produced. A witness
offering such a mutilated piece descredits himself. The mutilation is
alone satisfactory proof of contrivance and imposition. The manner of
accounting for it is frivolous.

The words of the letter are strong—satisfaction is to be had *at all
events, per fas et nefas*, and *Clingman* is the chosen confidential agent
of the laudable plan of vengeance. It must be confessed he was not
wanting in his part.

Reynolds, as will be seen by No. II (a) alleges that a merchant came to
him and offered as a volunteer to be his bail, who he suspected had been
instigated to it by me, and after being decoyed to the place the merchant
wished to carry him to, he refused being his bail, unless he would
deposit a sum of money to some considerable amount which he could
not do and was in consequence committed to prison. Clingman (No.
IV a) tells the same story in substance though with some difference in
form leaving to be implied what Reynolds expresses and naming *Henry
Seckel* as the merchant. The deposition of this respectable citizen (No.
XXIII) gives the lie to both, and shews that he was in fact the agent

of *Clingman*, from motives of good will to him, as his former book-keeper, that he never had any communication with me concerning either of them till after they were both in custody, that when he came as a messenger to me from one of them, I not only declined interposing in their behalf, but informed Mr. Seckel that they had been guilty of a crime and advised him to have nothing to do with them.

This single fact goes far to invalidate the whole story. It shews plainly the disregard of truth and the malice by which the parties were actuated. Other important inferences are to be drawn from the transaction. Had I been conscious that I had any thing to fear from *Reynolds* of the nature which has been pretended, should I have warned Mr. *Seckel* against having any thing to do with them? Should I not rather have encouraged him to have come to their assistance? Should I not have been eager to promote their liberation? But this is not the only instance, in which I acted a contrary part. *Clingman* testifies in No. V. that I would not permit *Fraunces* a clerk in my office to become their bail, but signified to him that if he did it, he must quit the department.

Clingman states in No. IV. (a) that my note in answer to Reynolds' application for a loan towards a subscription to the *Lancaster Turnpike* was in his possession from about the time it was written (June 1792.) This circumstance, apparently trivial, is very explanatory. To what end had *Clingman* the custody of this note all that time if it was not part of a project to lay the foundation for some false accusation?

It appears from No. V. that *Fraunces* had said, or was stated to have said, something to my prejudice. If my memory serves me aright, it was that he had been my agent in some speculations. When *Fraunces* was interrogated concerning it, he absolutely denied that he had said any thing of the kind. The charge which this same *Fraunces* afterwards preferred against me to the House of Representatives, and the fate of it, have been already mentioned. It is illustrative of the nature of the combination which was formed against me.

There are other features in the documents which are relied upon to constitute the charge against me, that are of a nature to corroborate the inference to be drawn from the particulars which have been noticed. But there is no need to be over minute. I am much mistaken if the view which has been taken of the subject is not sufficient, without any thing further, to establish my innocence with every discerning and fair mind.

I proceed in the next place to offer a frank and plain solution of the enigma, by giving a history of the origin and progress of my connection with Mrs. Reynolds, of its discovery, real and pretended by the husband, and of the disagreeable embarrassments to which it exposed me. This history will be supported by the letters of Mr. and Mrs. Reynolds, which leave no room for doubt of the principal facts, and at the same time explain with precision the objects of the little notes from me which have been published, shewing clearly that such of them as have related to money had no reference to any concern in speculation. As the situation which will be disclosed, will fully explain every ambiguous appearance, and meet satisfactorily the written documents, nothing more can be requisite to my justification. For frail indeed will be the tenure by which the most blameless man will hold his reputation, if the assertions of three of the most abandoned characters in the community, two of them stigmatized by the discrediting crime which has been mentioned, are sufficient to blast it. The business of accusation would soon become in such a case, a regular trade, and men's reputations would be bought and sold like any marketable commodity.

Some time in the summer of the year 1791 a woman called at my house in the city of Philadelphia and asked to speak with me in private. I attended her into a room apart from the family. With a seeming air of affliction she informed that she was a daughter of a Mr. Lewis, sister to a Mr. G. Livingston of the State of New-York, and wife to a Mr. Reynolds whose father was in the Commissary Department during the war with Great Britain, that her husband, who for a long time had treated her very cruelly, had lately left her, to live with another woman, and in so destitute a condition, that though desirous of returning to her friends she had not the means—that knowing I was a citizen of New-York, she had taken the liberty to apply to my humanity for assistance.

I replied, that her situation was a very interesting one—that I was disposed to afford her assistance to convey her to her friends, but this at the moment not being convenient to me (which was the fact) I must request the place of her residence, to which I should bring or send a small supply of money. She told me the street and the number of the house where she lodged. In the evening I put a bank-bill in my pocket and went to the house. I inquired for Mrs. Reynolds and was shewn up stairs, at the head of which she met me and conducted me into a bed room. I took the bill out of my pocket and gave it to her. Some conversation ensued from which it was quickly apparent that other than pecuniary consolation would be acceptable.

After this, I had frequent meetings with her, most of them at my own house; Mrs. Hamilton with her children being absent on a visit to her father. In the course of a short time, she mentioned to me that her husband had solicited a reconciliation, and affected to consult me about it. I advised to it, and was soon after informed by her that it had taken place. She told me besides that her husband had been engaged in speculation, and she believed could give information respecting the conduct of some persons in the department which would be useful. I sent for Reynolds who came to me accordingly.

In the course of our interview, he confessed that he had obtained a list of claims from a person in my department which he had made use of in his speculations. I invited him, by the expectation of my friendship and good offices, to disclose the person. After some affectation of scruple, he pretended to yield, and ascribed the infidelity to Mr. Duer from whom he said he had obtained the list in New-York, while he (Duer) was in the department.

As Mr. Duer had resigned his office some time before the seat of government was removed to Philadelphia; this discovery, if it had been true, was not very important—yet it was the interest of my passions to appear to set value upon it, and to continue the expectation of friendship and good offices. Mr. Reynolds told me he was going to Virginia, and on his return would point out something in which I could serve him. I do not know but he said something about employment in a public office.

On his return he asked employment as a clerk in the treasury department. The knowledge I had acquired of him was decisive against such a request. I parried it by telling him, what was true, that there was no vacancy in my immediate office, and that the appointment of clerks in the other branches of the department was left to the chiefs of the respective branches. Reynolds alleged, as *Clingman* relates No. IV (a) as a topic of complaint against me that I had promised him *employment* and had *disappointed* him. The situation with the wife would naturally incline me to conciliate this man. It is possible I may have used vague expressions which raised expectation; but the more I learned of the person, the more inadmissible his employment in a public office became. Some material reflections will occur here to a discerning mind. Could I have preferred my private gratification to the public interest, should I not have found the employment he desired for a man, whom it was so convenient to me, on my own statement, to lay under obligations. Had I had any such connection with him, as he has since pretended, is it likely that he would have wanted other employment? Or is it likely that wanting it, I should have hazarded his resentment by a persevering refusal? This little circumstance shews at once the delicacy of my conduct, in its public relations, and the impossibility of my having had the connection pretended with Reynolds.

The intercourse with Mrs. Reynolds, in the mean time, continued; and, though various reflections, (in which a further knowledge of Reynolds' character and the suspicion of some concert between the husband and wife bore a part) induced me to wish a cessation of it; yet her conduct, made it extremely difficult to disentangle myself. All the appearances of violent attachment, and of agonizing distress at the idea of a relinquishment, were played off with a most imposing art. This, though it did not make me entirely the dupe of the plot, yet kept me in a state of irresolution. My sensibility, perhaps my vanity, admitted the possibility of a real fondness; and led me to adopt the plan of a gradual discontinuance rather than of a sudden interruption, as least calculated to give pain, if a real partiality existed.

Mrs. Reynolds, on the other hand, employed every effort to keep up my attention and visits. Her pen was freely employed, and her letters were filled with those tender and pathetic effusions which would have been natural to a woman truly fond and neglected.

One day, I received a letter from her, which is in the appendix (No. I. b) intimating a discovery by her husband. It was matter of doubt with me whether there had been really a discovery by accident, or whether the time for the catastrophe of the plot was arrived.

The same day, being the 15th of December 1791, I received from Mr. Reynolds the letter (No. II. b) by which he informs me of the detection of his wife in the act of writing a letter to me, and that he had obtained from her a discovery of her connection with me, suggesting that it was the consequence of an undue advantage taken of her distress.

In answer to this I sent him a note, or message desiring him to call upon me at my office, which I think he did the same day.

He in substance repeated the topics contained in his letter, and concluded as he had done there, that he was resolved to have satisfaction.

I replied that he knew best what evidence he had of the alleged connection between me and his wife, that I neither admitted nor denied it—that if he knew of any injury I had done him, intitling him to satisfaction, it lay with him to name it.

He travelled over the same ground as before, and again concluded with the same vague claim of satisfaction, but without specifying the kind, which would content him. It was easy to understand that he wanted money, and to prevent an explosion, I resolved to gratify him. But willing to manage his delicacy, if he had any, I reminded him that I had at our first interview made him a promise of service, that I was disposed to do it as far as might be proper, and in my power, and requested him to consider in what manner I could do it, and to write to me. He withdrew with a promise of compliance.

Two days after, the 17th of December, he wrote me the letter (No. III. b). The evident drift of this letter is to exaggerate the injury done by me, to make a display of sensibility and to magnify the atonement, which was to be required. It however comes to no conclusion, but proposes a meeting at the George Tavern, or at some other place more agreeable to me, which I should name.

On receipt of this letter, I called upon Reynolds, and assuming a decisive tone, told him, that I was tired of his indecision, and insisted upon his declaring to me explicitly what it was he aimed at. He again promised to explain by letter.

On the 19th, I received the promised letter (No. IV. b) the essence of which is that he was willing to take a thousand dollars as the plaister of his wounded honor.

I determined to give it to him, and did so in two payments, as per receipts (No. V and VI) dated the 22d of December and 3d of January. It is a little remarkable, that an avaricious speculating secretary of the treasury should have been so straitened for money as to be obliged to satisfy an engagement of this sort by two different payments!

On the 17th of January, I received the letter No. V. by which Reynolds invites me to *renew my visits to his wife*. He had before requested that I would see her no more. The motive to this step appears in the conclusion of the letter, "*I rely* upon your befriending me, *if there should any thing offer that should be to my advantage*, as you *express a wish to befriend me*." Is the pre-existence of a speculating connection reconcileable with this mode of expression?

If I recollect rightly, I did not immediately accept the invitation, nor 'till after I had received several very importunate letters from Mrs. Reynolds—See her letters No. VIII, (b) IX, X.

On the 24th of March following, I received a letter from *Reynolds*, No. XI, and on the same day one from his wife, No. XII. These letters will further illustrate the obliging co-operation of the husband with his wife to aliment and keep alive my connection with her.

The letters from Reynolds, No. XIII to XVI, are an additional comment upon the same plan. It was a persevering scheme to spare no pains to levy contributions upon my passions on the one hand, and upon my apprehensions of discovery on the other. It is probably to No. XIV that my note, in these words, was an answer; "To-morrow what is requested will be done. 'Twill hardly be possible *to-day*." The letter presses for the loan which is asked for *to-day*. A scarcity of cash, which was not very uncommon, is believed to have modelled the reply.

The letter No. XVII is a master-piece. The husband there forbids my future visits to his wife, chiefly because I was careful to avoid publicity. It was probably necessary to the project of some deeper treason against me that I should be seen at the house. Hence was it contrived, with all the caution on my part to avoid it, that *Clingman* should occasionally see me.

The interdiction was every way welcome, and was I believe, strictly observed. On the second of June following, I received the letter No. XVIII, from Mrs. Reynolds, which proves that it was not her plan yet to let me off. It was probably the prelude to the letter from Reynolds, No. XIX, soliciting a *loan* of 300 dollars towards a subscription to the Lancaster Turnpike. *Clingman's* statement, No. IV (a), admits, on the information of Reynolds, that to this letter the following note from me was an answer—"*It is utterly out of my power I assure you 'pon my honour to comply with your request. Your note is returned.*" The letter itself demonstrates, that here was no concern in speculation on my part—that the money is asked as a *favour* and as a *loan*, to be reimbursed simply and without profit *in less than a fortnight*. My answer shews that even the loan was refused.

The letter No. XX, from *Reynolds*, explains the object of my note in these words, "*Inclosed are 50 dollars, they could not be sent sooner,*" proving that this sum also was begged for in a very apologetic stile as a mere loan.

The letters of the 24th and 30th of August, No. XXI and XXII, furnish the key to the affair of the 200 dollars mentioned by *Clingman* in No. IV, shewing that this sum likewise was asked by way of loan, towards furnishing a small boarding-house which Reynolds and his wife were or pretended to be about to set up.

These letters collectively, furnish a complete elucidation of the nature of my transactions with *Reynolds*. They resolve them into an amorous connection with his wife, detected, or pretended to be detected by the husband, imposing on me the necessity of a pecuniary composition with him, and leaving me afterwards under a duress for fear of disclosure, which was the instrument of levying upon me from time to time *forced loans*. They apply directly to this state of things, the notes which *Reynolds* was so careful to preserve, and which had been employed to excite suspicion.

Four, and the principal of these notes have been not only generally, but particularly explained—I shall briefly notice the remaining two.

"My dear Sir, I expected to have heard the day after I had the pleasure of seeing you." This fragment, if truly part of a letter to *Reynolds*, denotes nothing more than a disposition to be civil to a man, whom, as I said before, it was the interest of my passions to conciliate. But I verily believe it was not part of a letter to him, because I do not believe that I ever addressed him in such a stile. It may very well have been part of a letter to some other person, procured by means of which I am ignorant, or it may have been the beginning of an intended letter, torn off, thrown into the chimney in my office, which was a common practice, and there or after it had been swept out picked up by Reynolds or some coadjutor of his. There appears to have been more than one clerk in the department some how connected with him.

The endeavour shewn by the letter No. XVII, to induce me to render my visits to Mrs. Reynolds more public, and the great care with which my little notes were preserved, justify the belief that at a period, before it was attempted, the idea of implicating me in some accusation, with a view to the advantage of the accusers, was entertained. Hence the motive to pick up and preserve any fragment which might favour the idea of friendly or confidential correspondence.

2dly. "The person Mr. Reynolds inquired for on Friday waited for him all the evening at his house from a little after seven. Mr. R. may see him at any time to-day or to-morrow between the hours of two and three."

Mrs. Reynolds more than once communicated to me, that Reynolds would occasionally relapse into discontent to his situation—would treat her very ill—hint at the assassination of me—and more openly threaten, by way of revenge, to inform Mrs. Hamilton—all this naturally gave some uneasiness. I could not be absolutely certain whether it was artifice or reality. In the workings of human inconsistency, it was very possible, that the same man might be corrupt enough to compound for his wife's chastity and yet have sensibility enough to be restless in the situation and to hate the cause of it.

Reflections like these induced me for some time to use palliatives with the ill humours which were announced to me. Reynolds had called upon me in one of these discontented moods real or pretended. I was unwilling to provoke him by the appearance of neglect—and having failed to be at home at the hour he had been permitted to call, I wrote her the above note to obviate an ill impression.

The foregoing narrative and the remarks accompanying it have prepared the way for a perusal of the letters themselves. The more attention is used in this, the more entire will be the satisfaction which they will afford.

It has been seen that an explanation on the subject was had cotemporarily that is in December 1792, with three members of Congress—F. A. Muhlenberg, J. Monroe, and A. Venable. It is proper that the circumstances of this transaction should be accurately understood.

The manner in which Mr. Muhlenberg became engaged in the affair is fully set forth in the document (No. I. a). It is not equally clear how the two other gentlemen came to embark in it. The phraseology, in reference to this point in the close of (No. I. a) and beginning of (No. II. a) is rather equivocal. The gentlemen, if they please, can explain it.

But on the morning of the 15th of December 1792, the above mentioned gentlemen presented themselves at my office. Mr. Muhlenberg was then speaker. He introduced the subject by observing to me, that they *had discovered a very improper connection* between me and a Mr. Reynolds: extremely hurt by this mode of introduction, I arrested the progress of the discourse by giving way to very strong expressions of indignation. The gentlemen explained, telling me in substance that I had misapprehended them—that they did not intend to take the fact for established—that their meaning was to apprise me that unsought by them, information had been given them of an improper pecuniary connection between Mr. Reynolds and myself; that they had thought it their duty to pursue it and had become possessed of some documents of a suspicious complexion—that they had contemplated the laying the matter before the President, but before they did this, they thought it right to apprise me of the affair and to afford an opportunity of explanation; declaring at the same time that their agency in the matter was influenced solely by a sense of public duty and by no motive of personal ill will. If my memory be correct, the notes from me in a disguised hand were now shewn to me which without a moment's hesitation I acknowledged to be mine.

I replied, that the affair was now put upon a different footing—that I always stood ready to meet fair inquiry with frank communication—that it happened, in the present instance, to be in my power by written documents to remove all doubt as to the real nature of the business, and fully to convince, that nothing of the kind imputed to me did in fact exist. The same evening at my house was by mutual consent appointed for an explanation.

I immediately after saw Mr. Wolcott, and for the first time informed him of the affair and of the interview just had; and delivering into his hands for perusal the documents of which I was possessed, I engaged him to be present at the intended explanation in the evening.

In the evening the proposed meeting took place, and Mr. Wolcott according to my request attended. The information, which had been received to that time, from *Clingman, Reynolds* and his wife was communicated to me and the notes were I think again exhibited.

I stated in explanation, the circumstances of my affair with Mrs. Reynolds and the consequences of it and in confirmation produced the documents (No. I. b, to XXII.) One or more of the gentlemen (Mr. Wolcott's certificate No. XXIV, mentions one, Mr. Venable, but I think the same may be said of Mr. Muhlenberg) was struck with so much conviction, before I had gotten through the communication that they delicately urged me to discontinue it as unnecessary. I insisted upon going through the whole and did so. The result was a full and unequivocal acknowlegement on the part of the three gentlemen of perfect satisfaction with the explanation and expressions of regret at the trouble and embarrassment which had been occasioned to me. Mr. Muhlenberg and Mr. Venable, in particular manifested a degree of sensibility on the occasion. Mr. Monroe was more cold but intirely explicit.

One of the gentlemen, I think, expressed a hope that I also was satisfied with their conduct in conducting the inquiry. I answered, that they knew I had been hurt at the opening of the affair—that this excepted, I was satisfied with their conduct and considered myself as having been treated with candor or with fairness and liberality, I do not now pretend to recollect the exact terms. I took the next morning a memorandum of the substance of what was said to me, which will be seen by a copy of it transmitted in a letter to each of the gentlemen No. XXV.

I deny absolutely, as alleged by the editor of the publication in question, that I intreated a suspension of the communication to the President, or that from the beginning to the end of the inquiry, I asked any favour or indulgence whatever, and that I discovered any symptom different from that of a proud consciousness of innocence.

Some days after the explanation I wrote to the three gentlemen the letter No. XXVI already published. That letter evinces the light in which I considered myself as standing in their view.

I received from Mr. Muhlenberg and Mr. Monroe in answer the letters No. XXVII and XXVIII.

Thus the affair remained 'till the pamphlets No. V and VI of the history of the U. States for 1796 appeared; with the exception of some dark whispers which were communicated to me by a friend in Virginia, and to which I replied by a statement of what had passed.

When I saw No. V though it was evidence of a base infidelity somewhere, yet firmly believing that nothing more than a want of due care was chargeable upon either of the three gentlemen who had made the inquiry, I immediately wrote to each of them a letter of which No. XXV is a copy in full confidence that their answer would put the whole business at rest. I ventured to believe, from the appearances on their part at closing our former interview on the subject, that their answers would have been both cordial and explicit.

I acknowledge that I was astonished when I came to read in the pamphlet No. VI the conclusion of the document No. V, containing the equivocal phrase *"We left him under an impression our suspicions were removed,"* which seemed to imply that this had been a mere piece of management, and that the impression given me had not been reciprocal.

The appearance of duplicity incensed me; but resolving to proceed with caution and moderation, I thought the first proper step was to inquire of the gentlemen whether the paper was genuine. A letter was written for this purpose the copy of which I have mislaid.

I afterwards received from Messrs. Muhlenberg and Venable the letters No. XXIX, XXX, and XXXI.

Receiving no answer from Mr. Monroe, and hearing of his arrival at New-York I called upon him. The issue of the interview was that an answer was to be given by him, in conjunction with Mr. Muhlenberg and Mr. Venable on his return to Philadelphia, he thinking that as the agency had been joint it was most proper the answer should be joint, and informing me that Mr. Venable had told him he would wait his return.

I came to Philadelphia accordingly to bring the affair to a close; but on my arrival I found Mr. Venable had left the city for Virginia.

Mr. Monroe reached Philadelphia according to his appointment. And the morning following wrote me the note No. XXXII. While this note was on its way to my lodgings I was on my way to his. I had a conversation with him from which we separated with a repetition of the assurance in the note. In the course of the interviews with Mr. Monroe, the equivoque in document No. V, (a) and the paper of January 2d, 1793, under his signature were noticed.

I received the day following the letter No. XXXIII, to which I returned the answer No. XXXIV,—accompanied with the letter No. XXXV. which was succeeded by the letters No. XXXVI—XXXVII—XXXVIII—XXXIX—XL. In due time the sequel of the correspondence will appear.

Though extremely disagreeable to me, for very obvious reasons, I at length determined in order that no cloud whatever might be left on the affair, to publish the documents which had been communicated to Messrs. Monroe, Muhlenberg and Venable, all which will be seen in the appendix from No. I, (b) to No. XXII, inclusively.

The information from *Clingman* of the 2d January 1793, to which the signature of Mr. Monroe is annexed, seems to require an observation or two in addition to what is contained in my letter to him No. XXXIX.

Clingman first suggests that he had been apprized of my vindication through Mr. Wolcott a day or two after it had been communicated. It did not occur to me to inquire of Mr. Wolcott on this point, and he being now absent from Philadelphia, I cannot do it at this moment.

Though I can have no doubt of the friendly intention of Mr. Wolcott, if the suggestion of Clingman in this particular be taken as true; yet from the condition of secrecy which was annexed to my communication, there is the strongest reason to conclude it is not true. If not true, there is besides but one of two solutions, either that he obtained the information from one of the three gentlemen who made the inquiry, which would have been a very dishonourable act in the party, or that he conjectured what my defence was from what he before knew it truly could be. For there is the highest probability, that through Reynolds and his wife, and as an accomplice, he was privy to the whole affair. This last method of accounting for his knowledge would be conclusive on the sincerity and genuineness of the defence.

But the turn which *Clingman* gives to the matter must necessarily fall to the ground. It is, that Mrs. Reynolds denied her amorous connection with me, and represented the suggestion of it as a mere contrivance between *her husband* and *myself* to cover me, alleging that there had been a fabrication of letters and receipts to countenance it. The plain answer is, that Mrs. Reynolds' own letters contradict absolutely this artful explanation of hers; if indeed she ever made it, of which *Clingman's* assertion is no evidence whatever. These letters are proved by the affidavit No. XLI, though it will easily be conceived that the proof of them was rendered no easy matter by a lapse of near five years. They shew explicitly the connection with her, the discovery of it by her husband and the pains she took to prolong it when I evidently wished to get rid of it. This cuts up, by the root, the pretence of a contrivance between the husband and myself to fabricate the evidences of it.

The variety of shapes which this woman could assume was endless. In a conversation between her and a gentleman whom I am not at liberty publicly to name, she made a voluntary confession of her belief and even knowledge, that I was innocent of all that had been laid to my charge by *Reynolds* or any other person of her acquaintance, spoke of me in exalted terms of esteem and respect, declared in the most solemn manner her extreme unhappiness lest I should suppose her accessary to the trouble which had been given me on that account, and expressed her fear that the resentment of Mr. Reynolds on *a particular score*, might have urged him to improper lengths of revenge—appearing at the same time extremely agitated and unhappy. With the gentleman who gives this information, I have never been in any relation personal or political that could be supposed to bias him. His name would evince that he is an impartial witness. And though I am not permitted to make a public use of it, I am permitted to refer any gentleman to the perusal of his letter in the hands of William Bingham, Esquire; who is also so obliging as to permit me to deposit with him for similar inspection all the original papers which are contained in the appendix to this narrative. The letter from the gentleman above alluded to has been already shewn to *Mr. Monroe.*

Let me now, in the last place, recur to some comments, in which the hireling editors of the pamphlets No. V and VI has thought fit to indulge himself.

The first of them is that the *soft* language of one of my notes addressed to a man in the habit of threatening me with disgrace, is incompatible with the idea of innocence. The threats alluded to must be those of being able to hang the Secretary of the Treasury. How does it appear that Reynolds was in such a *habit?* No otherwise than by the declaration of *Reynolds* and *Clingman.* If the assertions of these men are to condemn me, there is an end of the question. There is no need, by elaborate deductions from *parts* of their assertions, to endeavour to establish what their assertions collectively affirm in express terms. If they are worthy of credit I am guilty; if they are not, all wire-drawn inferences from parts of their story are mere artifice and nonsense. But no man, not as debauched as themselves, will believe them, independent of the positive disproof of their story in the written documents.

As to the affair of threats (except those in Reynolds letters respecting the connection with his wife, which it will be perceived were very gentle for the occasion) not the least idea of the sort ever reached me 'till after the imprisonment of Reynolds. Mr. Wolcott's certificate shews my conduct in that case—notwithstanding the powerful motives I may be presumed to have had to desire the liberation of Reynolds, on account of my situation with his wife, I cautioned Mr. Wolcott not to facilitate his liberation, till the affair of the threat was satisfactorily cleared up. The solemn denial of it in Reynold's letter No. XLII was considered by Mr. Wolcott as sufficient. This is a further proof, that though in respect to my situation with his wife, I was somewhat in Reynolds's power. I was not disposed to make any improper concession to the apprehension of his resentment.

As the threats intimated in his letters, the nature of the cause will shew that the soft tone of my note was not only compatible with them, but a natural consequence of them.

But it is observed that the dread of the disclosure of an amorous connection was not a sufficient cause for my humility, and that I had nothing to lose as to my reputation for chastity concerning which the world had fixed a previous opinion.

I shall not enter into the question what was the previous opinion entertained of me in this particular—nor how well founded, if it was indeed such as it is represented to have been. It is sufficient to say that there is a wide difference between vague rumours and suspicions and the evidence of a positive fact—no man not indelicately unprincipled, with the state of manners in this country, would be willing to have a conjugal infidelity fixed upon him with positive certainty. He would know that it would justly injure him with a considerable and respectable portion of the society—and especially no man, tender of the happiness of an excellent wife could without extreme pain look forward to the affliction which she might endure from the disclosure, especially a *public disclosure*, of the fact. Those best acquainted with the interior of my domestic life will best appreciate the force of such a consideration upon me.

The truth was, that in both relations and especially the last, I dreaded extremely a disclosure—and was willing to make large sacrifices to avoid it. It is true, that from the acquiescence of Reynolds, I had strong ties upon his secrecy, but how could I rely upon any tie upon so base a character. How could I know, but that from moment to moment he might, at the expence of his own disgrace, become the *mercenary* of a party, with whom to blast my character in *any way* is a favorite object!

Strong inferences are attempted to be drawn from the release of *Clingman* and *Reynolds* with the consent of the Treasury, from the want of communicativeness of Reynolds while in prison—from the subsequent disappearance of Reynolds and his wife, and from their not having been produced by me in order to be confronted at the time of the explanation.

As to the first, it was emphatically the transaction of Mr. Wolcott the then Comptroller of the Treasury, and was bottomed upon a very adequate motive—and one as appears from the document No. I, (a) early contemplated in this light by that officer. It was certainly of more consequence to the public to detect and expel from the bosom of the Treasury Department an unfaithful Clerk to prevent future and extensive mischief, than to disgrace and punish two worthless individuals. Besides that a powerful influence foreign to me was exerted to procure indulgence to them—that of Mr. Muhlenberg and Col. Burr—that of Col. Wadsworth, which though insidiously placed to my account was to the best of my recollection utterly unknown to me at the time, and according to the confession of Mrs. Reynolds herself, was put in motion by her entreaty. Candid men will derive strong evidence of my innocence and delicacy, from the reflection, that under circumstances so peculiar, the culprits were compelled to give a real and substantial equivalent for the relief which they obtained from a department, *over which I presided*.

The backwardness of Reynolds to enter into detail, while in jail, was an argument of nothing but that conscious of his inability to communicate any particulars which could be supported, he found it more convenient to deal in generals, and to keep up appearances by giving promises for the future.

As to the disappearance of the parties after the liberation, how am I answerable for it? Is it not presumable, that the instance discovered at the Treasury was not the only offence of the kind of which they were guilty? After one detection, is it not very probable that Reynolds fled to avoid detection in other cases? But exclusive of this, it is known and might easily be proved, that Reynolds was considerably in debt! What more natural for him than to fly from his creditors after having been once exposed by confinement for such a crime? Moreover, atrocious as his conduct had been towards me, was it not natural for him to fear that my resentment might be excited at the discovery of it, and that it might have been deemed a sufficient reason for retracting the indulgence, which was shewn by withdrawing the prosecution and for recommending it?

One or all of these considerations will explain the disappearance of Reynolds without imputing it to me as a method of getting rid of a dangerous witness.

That disappearance rendered it impracticable, if it had been desired to bring him forward to be confronted. As to *Clingman* it was not pretended that he knew any thing of what was charged upon me, otherwise than by the notes which he produced, and the information of Reynolds and his wife. As to Mrs. Reynolds, she in fact appears by *Clingman's* last story to have remained, and to have been accessible through him, by the gentlemen who had undertaken the inquiry. If they supposed it necessary to the elucidation of the affair, why did not they bring her forward? There can be no doubt of the sufficiency of Clingman's influence, for this purpose, when it is understood that Mrs. Reynolds and he afterwards lived together as man and wife. But to what purpose the confronting? What would it have availed the elucidation of truth, if Reynolds and his wife had impudently made allegations which I denied. Relative character and the written documents must still determine These could decide without it, and they were relied upon. But could it be expected, that I should so debase myself as to think it necessary to my vindication to be confronted with a person such as Reynolds? Could I have borne to suffer my veracity to be exposed to the humiliating competition?

For what?—why, it is said, to tear up the last twig of jealousy—but when I knew that I possessed written documents which were decisive, how could I foresee that any twig of jealousy would remain? When the proofs I did produce to the gentlemen were admitted by them to be completely satisfactory, and by some of them to be more than sufficient, how could I dream of the expediency of producing more—how could I imagine that every twig of jealousy was not plucked up?

If after the recent confessions of the gentlemen themselves, it could be useful to fortify the proof of the full conviction, my explanation had wrought, I might appeal to the total silence concerning this charge, when at a subsequent period, in the year 1793, there was such an active legislative persecution of me. It might not even perhaps be difficult to establish, that it came under the eye of Mr. Giles, and that he discarded it as the plain case of a private amour unconnected with any thing that was the proper subject of a public attack.

Thus has my desire to destroy this slander, completely, led me to a more copious and particular examination of it, than I am sure was necessary. The bare perusal of the letters from Reynolds and his wife is sufficient to convince my greatest enemy that there is nothing worse in the affair than an irregular and indelicate amour. For this, I bow to the just censure which it merits. I have paid pretty severely for the folly and can never recollect it without disgust and self condemnation. It might seem affectation to say more.

To unfold more clearly the malicious intent, by which the present revival of the affair must have been influenced—I shall annex an affidavit of Mr. Webster tending to confirm my declaration of the utter falsehood of the assertion, that a menace of publishing the papers which have been published had arrested the progress of an attempt to hold me up as a candidate for the office of President. Does this editor imagine that he will escape the just odium which awaits him by the miserable subterfuge of saying that he had the information from a respectable citizen of New-York? Till he names the author the inevitable inference must be that he has fabricated the tale.

ALEXANDER HAMILTON.

Philadelphia, July, 1797.

To Elizabeth Hamilton

Philadelphia
Nov 1798

I am always very happy My Dear Eliza when I can steal a few moments to sit down and write to you. You are my good genius; of that kind which the ancient Philosophers called a *familiar;* and you know very well that I am glad to be in every way as familiar as possible with you. I have formed a sweet project, of which I will make you my confident when I come to New York, and in which I rely that you will cooperate with me chearfully.

> "You may guess and guess and guess again
> Your guessing will be still in vain."

But you will not be the less pleased when you come to understand and realize the scheme.

Adieu best of wives & best of mothers. Heaven ever bless you & me in you

A H

To Theodore Sedgwick

New York Feby 2. 1799

What, My Dear Sir, are you going to do with Virginia? This is a very serious business, which will call for all the wisdom and firmness of the Government. The following are the ideas which occur to me on the occasion.

The first thing in all great operations of such a Government as ours is to secure the opinion of the people. To this end, the proceedings of Virginia and Kentucke with the two laws complained of should be referred to a special Committee. That Committee should make a report exhibiting with great luminousness and particularity the reasons which support the constitutionality and expediency of those laws— the tendency of the doctrines advanced by Virginia and Kentucke to destroy the Constitution of the UStates—and, with calm dignity united with pathos, the full evidence which they afford of a regular conspiracy to overturn the government. And the Report should likewise dwell upon the inevitable effect and probably the intention of these proceedings to encourage a hostile foreign power to decline accommodation and proceed in hostility. The Government must not merely defend itself but must attack and arraign its enemies. But in all this, there should be great care to distinguish the people of Virginia from the legislature and even the greater part of those who may have concurred in the legislature from the Chiefs; manifesting indeed a strong confidence in the good sense and patriotism of the people, that they will not be the dupes of an insidious plan to disunite the people of America to break down their constitution & expose them to the enterprises of a foreign power.

This Report should conclude with a declaration that there is no cause for a Repeal of the laws. If however on examination any modifications consistent with the general design of the laws, but instituting better guards, can be devised it may be well to propose them as a bridge for those who may incline to retreat over. Concessions of this kind adroitly made have a good rather than a bad effect. On a recent though hasty revision of the Alien law it seems to me deficient in precautions against abuse and for the security of Citizens. This should not be.

No pains or expence should be spared to desseminate this Report. A little pamphlet containing it should find its way into every house in Virginia.

This should be left to work and nothing to court a shock should be adopted.

In the mean time the measures for raising the Military force should proceed with activity. Tis much to be lamented that so much delay has attended the execution of this measure. In times like the present not a moment ought to have been lost to secure the Government so powerful an auxiliary. Whenever the experiment shall be made to subdue a *refractory* & powerful *state* by Militia, the event will shame the advocates of their sufficiency. In the expedition against the Western Insurgents I trembled every moment lest a great part of the Militia should take it into their heads to return home rather than go forward.

When a clever force has been collected let them be drawn towards Virginia for which there is an obvious pretext—& then let measures be taken to act upon the laws & put Virginia to the Test of resistance.

This plan will give time for the fervour of the moment to subside, for reason to resume the reins, and by dividing its enemies will enable the Government to triumph with ease.

As an auxiliary measure, it is very desireable that the Provisional Army Bill should pass & that the Executive should proceed to the appointment of the Officers. The tendency of this needs no comment.

Yrs. affecy

A HAMILTON

To James McHenry

New York March 18. 1799

PRIVATE

Beware, my Dear Sir, of magnifying a riot into an insurrection, by employing in the first instance an inadequate force. Tis better far to err on the other side. Whenever the Government appears in arms it ought to appear like a *Hercules*, and inspire respect by the display of strength. The consideration of expence is of no moment compared with the advantages of energy. Tis true this is always a relative question—but tis always important to make no mistake. I only offer a *principle* and a *caution*.

A large corps of auxiliary cavalry may be had in Jersey New York Delaware Maryland without interfering with farming pursuits.

Will it be inexpedient to put under marching Orders a large force provisionally, as in eventual support of the corps to be employed—to awe the disaffected?

Let all be well considered.

Yrs. truly

A HAMILTON

To Charles Cotesworth Pinckney

Philadelphia Decr.
1799

SIR

The death of our beloved commander in Chief was known to you before it was to me. I can be at no loss to anticipate what have been your feelings. I need not tell you what are mine. Perhaps no friend of his has more cause to lament, on personal account, than my self. The public misfortune is one which all the friends of our Government will view in the same light. I will not dwell on the subject. My Imagination is gloomy my heart sad.

Inclosed is an order relative to the occasion which speaks its own object.

With the sincerest esteem and most affectionate regard I remain Sir Yr very Obed ser

To Martha Washington

New York Jany. 12. 1800

I did not think it proper, Madam, to intrude amidst the first effusions of your grief. But I can no longer restrain my sensibility from conveying to you an imperfect expression of my affectionate sympathy in the sorrows you experience. No one, better than myself, knows the greatness of your loss, or how much your excellent heart is formed to feel it in all its extent. Satisfied that you cannot receive consolation, I will attempt to offer none. Resignation to the will of Heaven, which the practice of your life ensures, can alone alleviate the sufferings of so heart-rending an affliction.

There can be few, who equally with me participate in the loss you deplore. In expressing this sentiment, I may without impropriety allude to the numerous and distinguished marks of confidence and friendship, of which you have yourself been a Witness; but I cannot say in how many ways the continuance of that confidence and friendship was necessary to me in future relations.

Vain, however, are regrets. From a calamity, which is common to a mourning nation, who can expect to be exempt? Perhaps it is even a privilege to have a claim to a larger portion of it than others.

I will only add, Madam, that I shall deem it a real and a great happiness, if any future occurrence shall enable me to give you proof of that respectful and cordial attachment with which I have the honor to be

Your obliged & very obedient servant

To John Jay

New York May 7. 1800

DEAR SIR

You have been informed of the loss of our Election in this City. It is also known that we have been unfortunate throughout Long Island & in West Chester. According to the Returns hitherto, it is too probable that we lose our Senators for this District.

The moral certainty therefore is that there will be an Anti-fœderal Majority in the Ensuing Legislature, and this very high probability is that this will bring *Jefferson* into the Chief Magistracy; unless it be prevented by the measure which I shall now submit to your consideration, namely the immediate calling together of the existing Legislature.

I am aware that there are weighty objections to the measure; but the reasons for it appear to me to outweigh the objections. And in times like these in which we live, it will not do to be overscrupulous. It is easy to sacrifice the substantial interests of society by a strict adherence to ordinary rules.

In observing this, I shall not be supposed to mean that any thing ought to be done which integrity will forbid—but merely that the scruples of delicacy and propriety, as relative to a common course of things, ought to yield to the extraordinary nature of the crisis. They ought not to hinder the taking of a *legal* and *constitutional* step, to prevent an *Atheist* in Religion and a *Fanatic* in politics from getting possession of the helm of the State.

You Sir know in a great degree the Antifœderal party, but I fear that you do not know them as well as I do. Tis a composition indeed of very incongruous materials but all tending to mischief—some of them to the overthrow of the Government by stripping it of its due energies others of them to a Revolution after the manner of Buonaparte. I speak from indubitable facts, not from conjectures & inferences.

In proportion as the true character of this party is understood is the force of the considerations which urge to every effort to disappoint it. And it seems to me that there is a very solemn obligation to employ the means in our power.

The calling of the Legislature will have for object the choosing of Electors by the people in Districts. This (as Pennsylvania will do nothing) will insure a Majority of votes in the U States for Fœderal Candidates.

The measure will not fail to be approved by all the Fœderal Party; while it will no doubt be condemned by the opposite. As to its intrinsic nature it is justified by unequivocal reasons for *public safety*.

The reasonable part of the world will I believe approve it. They will see it as a proceeding out of the common course but warranted by the particular nature of the Crisis and the great cause of social order.

If done the motive ought to be frankly avowed. In your communication to the Legislature they ought to be told that Temporary circumstances had rendered it probable that without their interposition the executive authority of the General Government would be transfered to hands hostile to the system heretofore pursued with so much success and dangerous to the peace happiness and order of the Country—that under this impression from facts convincing to your own mind you had thought it your duty to give the existing Legislature an opportunity of deliberating whether it would not be proper to interpose and endeavour to prevent so great an evil by referring the choice of Electors to the People distributed into Districts.

In weighing this suggestion you will doubtless bear in mind that Popular Governments must certainly be overturned & while they endure prove engines of mischief—if one party will call to its aid all the resources which *Vice* can give and if the other, however pressing the emergency, confines itself within all the ordinary forms of delicacy and decorum.

The legislature can be brought together in three weeks. So that there will be full time for the objects; but none ought to be lost.

Think well my Dear Sir of this proposition. Appreciate the extreme danger of the Crisis; and I am unusually mistaken in my view of the matter, if you do not see it right and expedient to adopt the measure.

Respectfully & Affecty Yrs.

A HAMILTON

To Theodore Sedgwick

New York May 10. 1800

DR SIR

I am very sorry for the information contained in your letter of the 7th. But I am not intimate enough with Dexter to put myself upon Paper to him. If on his return I can catch him at New York I shall have a particular conversation with him.

He is I am persuaded much mistaken as to the opinion entertained of Mr Adams by the Fœderal party. Were I to determine from my own observation I should say, *most* of the *most influential men* of that party consider him as a very *unfit* and *incapable* character.

For my individual part my mind is made up. I will never more be responsible for him by my direct support—even though the consequence should be the election of *Jefferson*. If we must have an *enemy* at the head of the Government, let it be one whom we can oppose & for whom we are not responsible, who will not involve our party in the disgrace of his foolish and bad measures. Under *Adams* as under *Jefferson* the government will sink. The party in the hands of whose chief it shall sink will sink with it and the advantage will all be on the side of his adversaries.

Tis a notable expedient for keeping the Fœderal party together to have at the head of it a man who hates and is dispised by those men of it who in time past have been its most efficient supporters.

If the cause is to be sacrificed to a weak and perverse man, I withdraw from the party & act upon my own ground—never certainly against my principles but in pursuance of them in my own way. I am mistaken if others will not do the same.

The only way to prevent a fatal scism in the Fœderal party is to support G Pinckney in good earnest.

If I can be perfectly satisfied that Adams & Pinckney will be upheld in the East with intire good faith, on the ground of conformity I will wherever my influence may extend pursue the same plan. If not I will pursue Mr. Pinkny as my single object.

Adieu Yrs. truly

A H

To John Adams

New York August 1. 1800

SIR

It has been repeatedly mentioned to me that you have, on different occasions, asserted the existence of a *British Faction* in this Country, embracing a number of leading or influential characters of the *Fœderal Party* (as usually denominated) and that you have sometimes named me, at other times plainly alluded to me, as one of this description of persons: And I have likewise been assured that of late some of your warm adherents, for electioneering purposes, have employed a corresponding language.

I must, Sir, take it for granted, that you cannot have made such assertions or insinuations without being willing to avow them, and to assign the reasons to a party who may conceive himself injured by them. I therefore trust that you will not deem it improper that I apply directly to yourself, to ascertain from you, in reference to your own declarations, whether the information, I have received, has been correct or not, and if correct what are the grounds upon which you have founded the suggestion.

With respect I have the honor to be Sir Your obedient servt.

ALEXANDER HAMILTON

To William Jackson

New-York Aug 26 1800.

MY DEAR JACKSON.

Never was there a more ungenerous persecution of any man than of myself.—Not only the worst constructions are put upon my conduct as a public man but it seems my birth is the subject of the most humiliating criticism.

On this point as on most others which concern me, there is much mistake—though I am pained by the consciousness that it is not free from blemish.

I think it proper to confide to your bosom the real history of it, that among my friends you may if you please wipe off some part of the stain which is so industriously impressed.

The truth is that on the question who my parents were, I have better pretensions than most of those who in this Country plume themselves on Ancestry.

My Grandfather by the mothers side of the name of Faucette was a French Huguenot who emigrated to the West Indies in consequence of the revocation of the Edict of Nantz and settled in the Island of Nevis and there acquired a pretty fortune. I have been assured by persons who knew him that he was a man of letters and much of a gentleman. He practiced as a Physician, whether that was his original profession, or one assumed for livelihood after his emigration is not to me ascertained.

My father now dead was certainly of a respectable Scotch Family. His father was, and the son of his Eldest brother now is Laird of Grange. His mother was the sister of an ancient Baronet *Sir Robert Pollock*.

Himself being a younger son of a numerous family was bred to trade. In capacity of merchant he went to St Kitts, where from too generous and too easy a temper he failed in business, and at length fell into indigent circumstances. For some time he was supported by his friends in Scotland, and for several years before his death by me. It was his fault to have had too much pride and two large a portion of indolence—but his character was otherwise without reproach and his manners those of a Gentleman.

So far I may well challenge comparison, but the blemish remains to be unveiled.

A Dane a fortune-hunter of the name of *Lavine* came to Nevis bedizzened with gold, and paid his addresses to my mother then a handsome young woman having a *snug* fortune. In compliance with the wishes of her mother who was captivated by the glitter of the [   ] but against her own inclination she married Lavine. The marriage was unhappy and ended in a separation by divorce. My mother afterwards went to St Kitts, became acquainted with my father and a marriage between them ensued, followed by many years cohabitation and several children.

But unluckily it turned out that the divorce was not absolute but qualified, and thence the second marriage was not lawful. Hence when my mother died the small property which she left went to my half brother Mr Lavine who lived in South Carolina and was for a time partner with Mr Kane. He is now dead.

As to my fathers family Mr McCormick of this city, merchant, can give testimony and will corroborate what I have stated.

Yours truly and affectionately.

ALEXANDER HAMILTON

Rules for Philip Hamilton

Rules for *Mr Philip Hamilton* from the first of April to the first of October he is to rise not later than Six Oclock—The rest of the year not later than Seven. If Earlier he will deserve commendation. Ten will be his hour of going to bed throughout the year.

From the time he is dressed in the morning till nine o clock (the time for breakfast Excepted) he is to read Law.

At nine he goes to the office & continues there till dinner time—he will be occupied partly in the writing and partly in reading law.

After Dinner he reads law at home till five O clock. From this hour till Seven he disposes of his time as he pleases. From Seven to ten he reads and Studies what ever he pleases.

From twelve on Saturday he is at Liberty to amuse himself.

On Sunday he will attend the morning Church. The rest of the day may be applied to innocent recreations.

He must not Depart from any of these rules without my permission.

1800

To Gouverneur Morris

New York 26 Decr. 1800

D<small>R</small> S<small>IR</small>

The post of yesterday gave me the pleasure of a letter from you. I thank you for the communication. I trust that a letter which I wrote you the day before the receipt of yours will have duly reached you as it contains some very free & confidential observations ending in two results—1 That The Convention with France ought to be ratified as the least of two evils   2 That *on the same ground Jefferson* ought to be preferred to *Burr*.

I trust the Fœderalists will not finally be so mad as to vote for the *latter*. I speak with an intimate & accurate knowlege of character. His elevation can only promote the purposes of the desperate and proflicate. If there be a man in the world I ought to hate it is Jefferson. With *Burr* I have always been personally well. But the public good must be paramount to every private consideration. My opinion may be freely used with such reserves as you shall think discreet.

Yrs. very truly

A H

To John Rutledge Jr.

Confidential   *New York Jany. 4. 1801*

M<small>Y</small> D<small>EAR</small> S<small>IR</small>

My extreme anxiety about the ensuing election of President by the House of Representatives will excuse to you the liberty I take in addressing you concerning it without being consulted by you. Did you know Mr. *Burr* as well as I do, I should think it unnecessary. With your honest attachment to the Country and correctness of views, it would not then be possible for you to hesitate, *if you now do*, about the course to be taken. You would be clearly of opinion with me that Mr. Jefferson is to be preferred.

As long as the Fœderal party preserve their high ground of integrity and principle, I shall not despair of the public weal. But if they quit it and descend to be the willing instruments of the Elevation of the most unfit and most dangerous man of the Community to the highest station in the Government—I shall no longer see any anchor for the hopes of good men. I shall at once anticipate all the evils that a daring and unprincipled ambition wielding the lever of Jacobinism can bring upon an infatuated Country.

The enclosed paper exhibits a faithful sketch of Mr. Burr's character as I believe it to exist, with better opportunities than almost any other man of forming a true estimate.

The expectation, I know, is, that if Mr. Burr shall owe his elevation to the Fœderal party he will judge it his interest to adhere to that party. But it ought to be recollected, that he will owe it in the first instance to the Antifoederal party; that among these, though perhaps not in the House of Representatives, a numerous class prefers him to Mr. Jefferson as best adapted by the boldness and cunning of his temper to fulfill their mischievous views; and that it will be the interest of his Ambition to preserve and cultivate these friends.

Mr. Burr will doubtless be governed by his interest as he views it. But *stable* power and Wealth being his objects—and there being no prospect that the respectable and sober fœderalists will countenance the projects of an irregular Ambition or prodigal Cupidity, he will not long lean upon them—but selecting from among them men suited to his purpose he will seek with the aid of those and of the most unprincipled of the opposite party to accomplish his ends. At least such ought to be our calculation. From such a man as him, who practices all the maxims of a Catiline, who, while despising, has played the whole game of, democracy, what better is to be looked for. Tis not to a Chapter of Accidents, that we ought to trust the Government peace and happiness of our Country. Tis enough for us to know that Mr. Burr is one of the most unprincipled men in the UStates in order to determine us to decline being responsible for the precarious issues of his calculations of Interest.

Very different ought to be our plan. Under the uncertainty of the Event we ought to seek to obtain from Mr. Jefferson these assurances 1 That the present Fiscal System will be maintained. 2 That the present neutral plan will be adhered to. 3 That the Navy will be preserved and gradually increased. 4 That Fœderalists now in office, not being heads of the great departments, will be retained. As to the heads of Departments & other matters he ought to be free.

You cannot in my opinion render a greater service to your Country than by exerting your influence to counteract the *impolitic* and *impure* idea of raising Mr. Burr to the Chief Magistracy.

Adieu My Dear Sir   Yrs. with sincere esteem & regard

A HAMILTON

Confidential

A Burr

1 He is in every sense a profligate; a voluptuary in the extreme, with uncommon habits of expence; in his profession extortionate to a proverb; suspected on strong grounds of having *corruptly* served the views of the Holland Company, in the capacity of a member of our legislature*; and understood to have been guilty of several breaches of probity in his pecuniary transactions. His very friends do not insist upon his integrity.

2 He is without doubt insolvent for a large *deficit*. All his visible property is deeply mortgaged, and he is known to owe other large debts, for which there is no specific security. Of the number of these is a Judgment in favour of Mr. Angerstien for a sum which with interest amounts to about 80,000 Dollars.

3 The fair emoluments of any station, under our government, will not equal his expences in that station; still less will they suffice to extricate him from his embarassments & he must therefore from the necessity of his situation have recourse to unworthy expedients. These may be a *bargain* and *sale* with some foreign power, or combinations with public agents in projects of gain by means of the public monies; perhaps and probably, to enlarge the sphere—a *War*.

4 He has no pretensions to the Station from services. He acted in different capacities in the last war finally with the rank of Lt. Col in a Regiment, and gave indications of being a good officer; but without having had the opportunity of performing any distinguished action. At a *critical period* of the War, he resigned his commission, assigning for cause ill-health, and went to reside at *Paramus* in the State of New Jersey. If his health was bad he might without difficulty have obtained a furlough and was not obliged to resign. He was afterwards seen in his usual health. The circumstance excited much jealousy of his motives. In civil life, he has never projected nor aided in producing a single measure of important public utility.

* He cooperated in obtaining a law to permit Aliens to hold & convey lands.

5 He has *constantly* sided with the party hostile to *fœderal* measures before and since the present constitution of the U States. In opposing the adoption of this constitution he was engaged covertly and insidiously; because, as he said at the time "it was too strong and too weak" and he has been uniformly the opposer of the Fœderal Administration.

6 No mortal can tell what his political principles are. He has talked *all round the compass. At times* he has dealt in all the jargon of Jacobinism; at other times he has proclaimed decidedly the total insufficiency of the Fœderal Government and the necessity of changes to one far more energetic. The truth seems to be that he has no plan but that of *getting* power by *any* means and *keeping* it by *all* means. It is probable that if he has any theory 'tis that of a simple *despotism*. He has intimated that he thinks the present French constitution not a bad one.

7 He is of a temper bold enough to think no enterprize too hazardous and sanguine enough to think none too difficult. He has censured the leaders of the Fœderal party as wanting in vigour and enterprise, for not having established a strong Government when they were in possession of the power and influence.

8 Discerning men of all parties agree in ascribing to him an irregular and inordinate ambition. Like *Catiline*, he is indefatigable in courting the *young* and the *profligate*. He knows well the weak sides of human nature, and takes care to play in with the passions of all with whom he has intercourse. By natural disposition, the haughtiest of men, he is at the same time the most creeping to answer his purposes. Cold and collected by nature and habit, he never loses sight of his object and scruples no means of accomplishing it. He is artful and intriguing to an inconceivable degree. In short all his conduct indicates that he has in view nothing less than the establishment of Supreme Power in his own person. Of this nothing can be a surer index than that having in fact high-toned notions of Government, he has nevertheless constantly opposed the *fœderal* and courted the *popular* party. As he never can effect his wish by the aid of good men, he will court and employ able and daring scoundrels of every party, and by availing himself of their assistance and of all the bad passions of the Society, he will in all likelihood attempt an usurpation.

8 Within the last three weeks at his own Table, he drank these toasts successively 1 The French Republic 2 The Commissioners who negotiated the Convention 3 *Buonaparte* 4 *La Fayette*; and he

countenanced and seconded the positions openly advanced by one of his guests that it was the interest of this Country to leave it free to the Belligerent Powers to sell their prizes in our ports and to build and equip ships for their respective uses; a doctrine which evidently aims at turning all the naval resources of the UStates into the channel of France; and which by making these states the most pernicious enemy of G Britain would compel her to go to War with us.

9 Though possessing infinite art cunning and address—he is yet to give proofs of great or solid abilities. It is certain that at the Bar he is more remarkable for ingenuity and dexterity than for sound judgment or good logic. From the character of his understanding and heart it is likely that any innovations which he may effect will be such as to serve the turn of his own power, not such as will issue in establishments favourable to the permanent security and prosperity of the Nation— founded upon the principles of a *strong free* and *regular* Government.

To James A. Bayard

New-York Jany. 16th. 1801.

I was glad to find my dear sir, by your letter, that you had not yet determined to go with the current of the Fœderal Party in the support of Mr *Burr* & that you were resolved to hold yourself disengaged till the moment of final decision. Your resolution to separate yourself, in this instance, from the Fœderal Party if your conviction shall be strong of the unfitness of Mr Burr, is certainly laudable. So much does it coincide with my ideas, that if the Party Shall by supporting Mr Burr as President adopt him for their official Chief—I shall be obliged to consider myself as an *isolated* man. It will be impossible for me to reconcile with my notions of *honor* or policy, the continuing to be of a Party which according to my apprehension will have degraded itself & the country. I am sure nevertheless that the motives of many will be good, and I shall never cease to esteem the individuals, tho' I shall deplore a step which I fear experience will show to be a very fatal one. Among the letters which I receive assigning the reasons *pro* & *con* for prefering Burr to J. I observe no small exaggeration to the prejudice of the latter & some things taken for granted as to the former which are at least questionable. Perhaps myself the first, at some expence of popularity, to unfold the true character of Jefferson, it is too late for me to become his apologist. Nor can I have any disposition to do it. I admit that his politics are tinctured with fanaticism, that he is too much in earnest in his democracy, that he has been a mischevous enemy to the principle measures of our past administration, that he is crafty & persevering in his objects, that he is not scrupulous about the means of success, nor very mindful of truth, and that he is a contemptible hypocrite. But it is not true as is alleged that he is an enemy to the power of the Executive, or that he is for confounding all the powers in the House of Rs. It is a fact which I have frequently mentioned that while we were in the administration together he was generally for a large construction of the Executive authority, & not backward to act upon it in cases which coincided with his views. Let it be added, that in his theoretic Ideas he has considered as improper the participations of the Senate in the Executive Authority. I have more than once made the reflection that viewing himself as the reversioner, he was solicitous to come into possession of a Good Estate. Nor is it true that Jefferson is zealot enough to do anything in pursuance of his principles which will contravene his popularity, or his interest. He is as likely as any man I know to temporize—to calculate what will be likely to promote his own reputation and advantage; and the probable result of such a temper is the preservation of systems, though originally opposed, which being once established, could not be overturned without danger to the person who did it. To my mind a true estimate of Mr J.'s character warrants the expectation of a temporizing rather than a violent system. That Jefferson has manifested a culpable predilection for France is certainly true; but I think it a question whether it did not proceed quite as much from her *popularity* among us, as from sentiment, and in proportion as that popularity is diminished his zeal will cool. Add to this that there is no fair reason to suppose him capable of being corrupted, which is a security that he will not go beyond certain limits. It is not at all improbable that under the change of circumstances Jefferson's Gallicism has considerably abated.

As to Burr these things are admitted and indeed cannot be denied, that he is a man of *extreme* & *irregular* ambition—that he is *selfish* to a degree which excludes all social affections & that he is decidedly *profligate*. But it is said, 1st. that he is *artful* & *dexterous* to accomplish his ends—2nd. that he holds no pernicious theories, but is a mere *matter of fact* man—

3rd. that his very selfishness* is a guard against mischevous foreign predilections. 4th That his *local situation* has enabled him to appreciate the utility of our Commercial & fiscal systems, and the same quality of selfishness will lead him to support & invigorate them. 5th. that he is now disliked by the Jacobins, that his elevation will be a mortal stab to them, breed an invincible hatred to him, & compel him to lean on the Federalists. 6th. That Burr's ambition will be checked by his good sense, by the manifest impossibility of succeeding in any scheme of usurpation, & that if attempted, there is nothing to fear from the attempt. These topics are in my judgment more plausible than solid. As to the 1st point the fact must be admitted, but those qualities are objections rather than recommendations when they are under the direction of bad principles. As to the 2nd point too much is taken for granted. If Burr's conversation is to be credited he is not very far from being a visionary.† It is ascertained in some instances that he has talked perfect *Godwinism*. I have myself heard him speak with applause of the French system as unshackling the mind & leaving it to its natural energies, and I have been present when he has contended against Banking Systems‡ with earnestness & with the same arguments that Jefferson would use. The truth is that *Burr* is a man of a very subtile imagination, and a mind of this make is rarely free from ingenious whimsies. Yet I admit that he has no fixed theory & that his peculiar notions will easily give way to his interest. But is it a recommendation to have *no theory*? Can that man be a systematic or able statesman who has none? I believe not. *No general principles* will hardly work much better than erroneous ones. As to the 3rd. point— it is certain that Burr generally speaking has been as warm a partisan of France as Jefferson—that he has in some instances shewn himself to be so with passion. But if it was from calculation who will say that his calculations§ will not continue him so? His selfishness§ so far from being an obstacle may be a prompter. If corrupt as well as selfish he may be a partisan for gain—if ambitious as well as selfish, he may be a partisan for the sake of aid to his views. No man has trafficked more than he in the floating passions of the multitude. Hatred to G. Britain

* It is always very dangerous to look to the *vices* of men for *Good*.

† He has quoted to me Connecticut as an example of the success of the Democratic theory, and as authority, serious doubts whether it was not a good one.

‡ Yet he has lately by a trick established a *Bank*, a perfect monster in its principles; but a very convenient instrument of *profit* & *influence*.

§ Unprincipled selfishness is more apt to seek rapid gain in disorderly practices than slow advantages from orderly systems.

& attachment to France in the public mind will naturally lead a man of his selfishness, attached to place and power, to favour France & oppose G. Britain. The Gallicism of many of our patriots is to be thus resolved, & in my opinion it is morally certain that Burr will continue to be influenced by this calculation. As to the 4th point the instance I have cited with respect to Banks proves that the argument is not to be relied on. If there was much in it, why does Chancellor Livingston maintain that we ought not to cultivate navigation but ought to let foreigners be our Carriers? France is of this opinion too & Burr for some reason or other, will be very apt to be of the opinion of *France*. As to the 5th point—nothing can be more fallacious. It is demonstrated by recent facts* that Burr is *solicitous* to *keep* upon *Antifœderal ground*, to avoid compromitting himself by any engagements† with the Fœderalists. With or without such engagements he will easily persuade his former friends that he does stand on that ground, & after their first resentment they will be glad to rally under him. In the mean time he will take care not to disoblige them & he will always court those among them who are best fitted for tools. He will never choose to lean on good men because he knows that they will never support his bad projects: but instead of this he will endeavour to disorganize both parties & to form out of them a third composed of men fitted by their characters to be conspirators, & instruments of such projects. That this will be his future conduct may be inferred from his past plan, & from the admitted quality of irregular ambition. Let it be remembered that Mr Burr has never appeared solicitous for fame, & that great Ambition unchecked by principle, or the love of Glory, is an unruly Tyrant which never can keep long in a course which good men will approve. As to the last point—The propostion is against the experience of all times. Ambition without principle never was long under the guidance of good sense. Besides that, really the force of Mr Burrs understanding is much overrated. He is far more *cunning* than *wise*, far more *dexterous* than *able*. In my opinion he is inferior in real ability to Jefferson. There are also facts against the supposition. It is past all doubt that he has blamed me for not having improved the situation I once was in to change the Government. That when answered that this could not have been done without guilt—he replied—"Les grands ames se soucient peu des petits morceaux"—that

---

* My letter to Mr Morris states some of them.
† He trusts to their *prejudices* and *hopes* for support.

when told the thing was never practicable from the genious and situation of the country, he answered, "that depends on the estimate we form of the human passions and of the means of influencing them." Does this prove that Mr Burr would consider a scheme of usurpation as visionary. The truth is with great apparent coldness he is the most sanguine man in the world. He thinks every thing possible to adventure and perseverance. And tho' I believe he will fail, I think it almost certain he will attempt usurpation. And the attempt will involve great mischief.

But there is one point of view which seems to me decisive. If the Antifœderalists who prevailed in the election are left to take their own man, they remain responsible, and the Fœderalists remain *free united* and without *stain*, in a situation to resist with effect pernicious measures. If the Fœderalists substitute Burr, they adopt him and become answerable for him. Whatever may be the theory of the case, abroad and at *home* (for so from the beginning will be taught) Mr Burr will become *in fact* the man of our party. And if he acts ill, we must share in the blame and disgrace. By adopting him we do all we can to reconcile the minds of the Fœderalists to him, and prepare them for the effectual operation of his arts. He will doubtless gain many of them, & the Fœderalists will become a disorganized and contemptible party. Can there be any serious question between the policy of leaving the Antifœderalists to be answerable for the elevation of an exceptionable man, & that of adopting ourselves & becoming answerable for a man who on all hands is acknowledged to be a complete *Cataline* in his practice & principles? 'Tis enough to state the question to indicate the answer, if reason not passion presides in the decision. You may communicate this & my former letter to discreet & confidential friends.

Your's very truly,

A H

To Gouverneur Morris

My Dr. Sir

Your letter of the 22d is the third favour for which I am indebted to you since you left N York.

Your frankness in giving me your opinion as to the expediency of an application of our bar to Congress obliges me. But you know we are not readily persuaded to think we have been wrong. Were the matter to be done over I should pursue the same course. I did not believe the measure would be useful as a preventative, and for the people an expression of an opinion by letter would be as good as in a memorial. It appeared to me best because it saved our delicacy and because in the abstract I am not over fond of the precedent of the bar addressing Congress. But I did what I thought likely to do more good—I induced the Chamber of Commerce to send a memorial.

As to the rest, I should be a very unhappy man, if I left my tranquillity at the mercy of the misinterpretations which friends as well as foes are fond of giving to my conduct.

Mine is an odd destiny. Perhaps no man in the UStates has sacrificed or done more for the present Constitution than myself—and contrary to all my anticipations of its fate, as you know from the very begginning I am still labouring to prop the frail and worthless fabric. Yet I have the murmurs of its friends no less than the curses of its foes for my rewards. What can I do better than withdraw from the Scene? Every day proves to me more and more that this American world was not made for me.

The suggestions with which you close your letter suppose a much sounder state of the public mind than at present exists. Attempts to make a show of a general *popular* dislike of the pending measures of the Government would only serve to manifest the direct reverse. Impressions are indeed making but as yet within a very narrow sphere. The time may ere long arrive when the minds of men will be prepared to make an offer to *recover* the Constitution, but the many cannot now be brought to make a stand for its preservation. We must wait awhile.

I have read your speeches with great pleasure. They are truly worthy of you. Your real friends had many sources of satisfaction on account of them. The conspiracy of Dulness was at work. It chose to misinterpret your moderation in certain transactions of a personal reference. A public energetic display of your talents and principles was requisite to silence the Cavillers. It is now done. You, friend Morris, are by *birth* a native of this Country but by *genius* an exotic. You mistake if you fancy that you are more a favourite than myself or that you are in any sort upon a theatre suited to you.

Adieu   Yrs. ever

A H

Feby 29.

To Benjamin Rush

New York March 29. 1802

DEAR SIR

I felt all the weight of the obligation which I owed to you and to your amiable family, for the tender concern they manifested in an event, beyond comparison, the most afflicting of my life. But I was obliged to wait for a moment of greater calm, to express my sense of the kindness.

My loss is indeed great. The highest as well as the eldest hope of my family has been taken from me. You estimated him rightly—He was truly a fine youth. But why should I repine? It was the will of heaven; and he is now out of the reach of the seductions and calamities of a world, full of folly, full of vice, full of danger—of least value in proportion as it is best known. I firmly trust also that he has safely reached the haven of eternal repose and felicity.

You will easily imagine that every memorial of the goodness of his heart must be precious to me. You allude to one recorded in a letter to your son. If no special reasons forbid it, I should be very glad to have a copy of that letter.

Mrs. Hamilton, who has drank deeply of the cup of sorrow, joins me in affectionate thanks to Mrs. Rush and yourself. Our wishes for your happiness will be unceasing.

Very sincerely & cordially Yrs.

A HAMILTON

To James A. Bayard

New-York April 1802

DEAR SIR.

Your letter of the 12th inst. has relieved me from some apprehension. Yet it is well that it should be perfectly understood by the truly sound part of the Fœderalists, that there do in fact exist intrigues in good earnest, between several individuals not unimportant, of the Fœderal Party, and the person in question; which are bottomed upon motives & views, by no means auspicious to the real welfare of the country. I am glad to find that it is in contemplation to adopt a plan of conduct. It is very necessary; & to be useful it must be efficient & comprehensive in the means which it embraces, at the same time that it must meditate none which are not really constitutional & patriotic. I will comply with your invitation by submitting some ideas which from time to time have passed through my mind. Nothing is more fallacious than to expect to produce any valuable or permanent results, in political projects, by relying merely on the reason of men. Men are rather reasoning than reasonable animals for the most part governed by the impulse of passion. This is a truth well understood by our adversaries who have practised upon it with no small benefit to their cause. For at the very moment they are eulogizing the reason of men & professing to appeal only to that faculty, they are courting the strongest & most active passion of the human heart—*VANITY!*

It is no less true that the Fœderalists seem not to have attended to the fact sufficiently; and that they erred in relying so much on the rectitude & utility of their measures, as to have neglected the cultivation of popular favour by fair & justifiable expedients. The observation has been repeatedly made by me to individuals with whom I particularly conversed & expedients suggested for gaining good will which were never adopted. Unluckily however for us in the competition for the passions of the people our opponents have great advantages over us; for the plain reason, that the vicious are far more active than the good passions, and that to win the latter to our side we must renounce our principles & our objects, & unite in corrupting public opinion till it becomes fit for nothing but mischief. Yet unless we can contrive to take hold of & carry along with us some strong feelings of the mind we shall in vain calculate upon any substantial or durable results. Whatever plan we may adopt, to be successful must be founded on the truth of this proposition. And perhaps it is not very easy for us to give it full effect; especially not without some deviations from what on other occasions we have maintained to be right. But in determining upon the propriety of the deviations, we must consider whether it be possible for us to succeed without in some degree employing the weapons which have been employed against us, & whether the actual state & future prospect of things, be not such as to justify the reciprocal use of them. I need not tell you that I do not mean to countenance the imitation of things intrinsically unworthy, but only of such as may be denominated irregular, such as in a sound & stable order of things ought not to exist. Neither are you to infer that any revolutionary result is contemplated. In my opinion the present Constitution is the standard to which we are to cling. Under its banners, *bona fide* must we combat our political foes—rejecting all changes but through the channel itself provides for amendments. By these general views of the subject have my reflections been guided. I now offer you the outline of the plan which they have suggested. Let an Association be formed to be denominated, "The Christian Constitutional Society." It's objects to be

1st   The support of the Christian Religion.

2nd   The support of the Constitution of the United States.

Its Organization.

1st   A directing council consisting of a President & 12 Members, of whom 4 & the President to be a quorum.

2nd   A sub-directing council in each State consisting of a Vice-President & 12 Members, of whom 4 with the Vice-President to be a quorum & 3rd As many societies in each State, as local circumstances may permit to be formed by the Sub-directing council.

The meeting at Washington to Nominate the *President* & *Vice-President* together with *4 Members of each* of the councils, who *are to complete* their own numbers respectively.

Its Means.

1st   The diffusion of information. For this purpose not only the Newspapers but pamphlets must be largely employed & to do this a fund must be created. 5 dollars annually for 8 years, to be contributed by each member who can really afford it, (taking care not to burden the less able brethren) may afford a competent fund for a competent time. It is essential to be able to disseminate *gratis* useful publications. Whenever it can be done, & there is a press, clubs should be formed to meet once a week, read the newspapers & prepare essays paragraphs &ct.

2nd   The use of all lawful means in concert to promote the election of *fit men*. A lively correspondence must be kept up between the different Societies.

3rd   The promoting of institutions of a charitable & useful nature
in the management of Fœderalists. The populous cities ought
particularly to be attended to. Perhaps it will be well to institute
in such places 1st Societies for the relief of Emigrants—2nd.
Academies each with one professor for instructing the different
Classes of Mechanics in the principles of Mechanics & Elements
of Chemistry. The cities have been employed by the Jacobins
to give an impulse to the country. And it is believed to be an
alarming fact, that while the question of Presidential Election
was pending in the House of Rs. parties were organized in several
of the Cities, in the event of there being no election, to cut off the
leading Fœderalists & sieze the Government.

especially confidential

An Act of association to be drawn up in concise general
terms. It need only designate the "name" "objects" & contain
an engagement to promote the objects by all lawful means, and
particularly by the diffusion of Information. This act to be signed
by every member.

The foregoing to be the principal Engine. In addition let measures
be adopted to bring as soon as possible the repeal of the Judiciary
law before the Supreme Court. Afterwards, if not before, let as many
Legislatures as can be prevailed upon, instruct their Senators to
endeavour to procure a repeal of the repealing law. The body of New-
England speaking the same language will give a powerful impulse. In
Congress our friends to *propose* little, to agree candidly to all good
measures, & to resist & expose all bad. This is a general sketch of what
has occurred to me. It is at the service of my friends for so much as it
may be worth. With true esteem & regard

Dr Sir Yours

AH

To Charles Cotesworth Pinckney

Grange (NY)
Decr. 29. 1802

MY DEAR SIR

A garden, you know, is a very usual refuge of a disappointed
politician. Accordingly, I have purchased a few acres about 9 Miles from

Town, have built a house and am cultivating a Garden. The melons in your country are very fine. Will you have the goodness to send me some seed both of the Water & Muss Melons?

My daughter adds another request, which is for three or four of your peroquets. She is very fond of birds. If there be any thing in this quarter the sending of which can give you pleasure, you have only to name them. As Farmers a new source of sympathy has risen between us; and I am pleased with every thing in which our likings and tastes can be approximated.

Amidst the triumphant reign of Democracy, do you retain sufficient interest in public affairs to feel any curiosity about what is going on? In my opinion the follies and vices of the Administration have as yet made no material impression to their disadvantage. On the contrary, I think the malady is rather progressive than upon the decline in our Northern Quarter. The last *lullaby* message, instead of inspiring contempt, attracts praise. Mankind are forever destined to be the dupes of bold & cunning imposture.

But a difficult *knot* has been twisted by the incident of the cession of Louisian and the interruption of the Deposit at New Orleans. You have seen the soft tun given to this in the message. Yet we are told the President in conversation is very stout. The great embarrassment must be how to carry on war without taxes. The pretty scheme of substituting œconomy to taxation will not do here; and a war would be a terrible comment upon the abandonment of the Internal Revenue. Yet how is popularity to be preserved with the Western partisans if their interests are tamely sacrificed? Will the artifice be for the Chief to hold a bold language and the subalters to act a public part? Time must explain.

You know my general theory as to our Western affairs. I have always held that the Unity of our empire and the best interests of our Nation require that we should annex to the UStates all the territory East of the Mississippia, New Orleans included. Of course I infer that in an emergency like the present, Energy is Wisdom.

Adieu My Dear Sir Ever Yrs

A H

Mrs. H joins me in affectionate Compliments to Mrs. Pinckney.

To Elizabeth Hamilton

March 1803

I thank you My Betsy for your letter from Fish Kill. I hope the subsequent part of your journey has proved less fatiguing than the two first days.

I have anticipated with dread your interview with your father. I hope your prudence and fortitude have been a match for your sensibility. Remember that the main object of visit is to console him; that his own burthen is sufficient, and that it would be too much to have it increased by the sorrows of his Children.

Arm yourself with resignation. We live in a world full of evil. In the later period of life misfortunes seem to thicken round us; and our duty and our peace both require that we should accustom ourselves to meet disasters with christian fortitude.

Kiss Kitty for me & give my love to Angelica, & all the friends & connections round you.

Adieu My excellent wife.

A H

Your Children are all well. I write your father by this oppy.

To Timothy Pickering

New York September 16
1803

MY DEAR SIR

I will make no apology for my delay in answering your inquiry some time since made, because I could offer none which would satisfy myself. I pray you only to believe that it proceeded from any thing rather than want of respect or regard. I shall now comply with your request.

The highest toned propositions, which I made in the Convention, were for a President, Senate and Judges during good behaviour—a house of representatives for three years. Though I would have enlarged the Legislative power of the General Government, yet I never contemplated the abolition of the State Governments; but on the contrary, they were, in some particulars, constituent parts of my plan.

This plan was in my conception comformable with the strict theory of a Government purely republican; the essential criteria of which are that the principal organs of the Executive and Legislative departments be elected by the people and hold their offices by a *responsible* and temporary or *defeasible* tenure.

A vote was taken on the proposition respecting the Executive. Five states were in favour of it; among those Virginia; and though from the manner of voting, by delegations, individuals were not distinguished, it was morally certain, from the known situation of the Virginia members (six in number, two of them *Mason* and *Randolph* possessing popular doctrines) that *Madison* must have concurred in the vote of Virginia. Thus, if I sinned against Republicanism, Mr. Madison was not less guilty.

I may truly then say, that I never proposed either a President, or Senate for life, and that I neither recommended nor meditated the annihilation of the State Governments.

And I may add, that in the course of the discussions in the Convention, neither the propositions thrown out for debate, nor even those voted in the earlier stages of deliberation were considered as evidences of a definitive opinion, in the proposer or voter. It appeared to me to be in some sort understood, that with a view to free investigation, experimental propositions might be made, which were to be received merely as suggestions for consideration.

Accordingly, it is a fact, that my final opinion was against an Executive during good behaviour, on account of the increased danger to the public tranquility incident to the election of a Magistrate of this degree of permanency. In the plan of a Constitution, which I drew up, while the convention was sitting & which I communicated to Mr. Madison about the close of it, perhaps a day or two after, the Office of President has no greater duration than for three years.

This plan was predicated upon these bases— 1 That the political principles of the people of this country would endure nothing but republican Government. 2 That in the actual situation of the Country, it was in itself right and proper that the republican theory should have a fair and full trial— 3 That to such a trial it was essential that the

Government should be so constructed as to give it all the energy and stability reconciliable with the principles of that theory. These were the genuine sentiments of my heart, and upon them I acted.

I sincerely hope, that it may not hereafter be discovered, that through want of sufficient attention to the last idea, the experiment of Republican Government, even in this Country, has not been as complete, as satisfactory and as decisive as could be wished.

Very truly Dear Sir Yr friend & servt

A HAMILTON

From Aaron Burr

Nyork 18 June 1804

SIR,

I send for your perusal a letter signed Ch. D. Cooper which, though apparently published some time ago, has but very recently come to my knowledge. Mr Van Ness who does me the favor to deliver this, will point out to you that Clause of the letter to which I particularly request your attention.

You might perceive, Sir, the necessity of a prompt and unqualified acknowledgment or denial of the use of any expressions which could warrant the assertions of Dr Cooper.

I have the honor to be Your Obt Svt

A. BURR

Enclosure: Charles D. Cooper to Philip Schuyler

SIR,

The malignant attack which my character has sustained in an anonymous hand-bill, to which your letter of the 21st inst. directed to the chairman of the Federal electioneering committee of this city is annexed; and in which you contradict certain facts contained in a letter, said to have been written by me to ANDREW BROWN, Esq. of Bern, will be my apology for repelling the unfounded aspersions which have been thus dishonorably obtruded on the public. My letter to Mr. Brown was committed to the care of JOHAN J. DEITZ, Esq. of Bern; but to this gentleman, I hope, cannot be imputed the embezzling and breaking open of a letter, a crime which in England has met with the most ignominious punishment.

Admitting the letter published to be an exact transcript of the one intended for Mr. BROWN, and which, it seems, instead of being delivered according to promise, was EMBEZZLED and BROKEN OPEN; I aver, that the assertions therein contained are substantially true, and that I can prove them by the most unquestionable testimony. I assert that Gen. HAMILTON and Judge KENT have declared, in substance, that they looked upon Mr. BURR to be a dangerous man, and one who ought not to be trusted with the reins of government. If, Sir, you attended a meeting of federalists, at the city tavern, where Gen. HAMILTON made a speech on the pending election, I might appeal to you for the truth of so much of this assertion as relates to him. I have, however, other evidence to substantiate the fact. With respect to Judge KENT's declaration, I have only to refer to THEODORUS V. W. GRAHAM, Esq. and Mr. JAMES KANE, of this city, whose veracity, I trust, will not be impeached; but should the fact have escaped their recollection, I am not in want of other evidence, equally respectable, to support it. Mr. VAN RENSSELAER, a few days before he left town for New-York, in a conversation with me, declared in substance what I communicated in the letter to Mr. BROWN, as coming from him; and I am perfectly willing to repose myself on his well-known candour for the truth of this declaration.

I asserted, in the letter which has been so disgracefully EMBEZZLED, and the BREAKING OPEN of which must be ranked with the lowest species of villainy, that many of the reflecting federalists would support Judge LEWIS. Will this be considered a rash assertion, when it is known, that two federal gentlemen, high in office in this city, have declared they would vote for him? Judge PENDLETON, of New-York, made the same declaration in this city, under the impression, however, that no federal candidate was to be offered. OLIVER PHELPS, when in this city, on his way to Canandaigua, stated, that Gen. HAMILTON, and about one hundred federalists in New-York, would not vote for Mr. Burr.

It is true, that Judge TAYLER intimated to me, the conversation Mr. VAN RENSSELAER had with him, to which you allude, but it was subsequent to my having written and dispatched the letter for Mr. BROWN.

I beg leave to remark, sir, that the anxiety you discovered, when his Honor the Chancellor was about to be nominated, induced me to believe, that you entertained a bad opinion of Mr. BURR, especially when taken in connection with General HAMILTON's harangue at the city tavern; and although I have never suggested that you would act on the one side or the other in this election—yet, presuming on the correctness of your mind, and the reputation you sustain of an upright and exemplary character, I could not suppose you would support a man whom I had reason to believe, you held in the lowest estimation.

It is sufficient for me, on this occasion, to substantiate what I have asserted. I have made it an invariable rule of my life, to be circumspect in relating what I may have heard from others; and in this affair, I feel happy to think, that I have been unusually cautious—for really sir, I could detail to you a still more despicable opinion which General HAMILTON has expressed of Mr. BURR.

I cannot conclude, without paying some attention to your friend, Dr. STRINGER; I have to regret that this gentleman, so renowned for the Christian virtues, should have consented to dishonour your name, by connecting your letter with an anonymous production, replete with the vilest falsehood and the foulest calumny.

I am, Sir, with due respect,   Your humble servant,

CHARLES D. COOPER.

April 23, 1804.

To Aaron Burr

New York June 20. 1804

SIR

I have maturely reflected on the subject of your letter of the 18th instant; and the more I have reflected the more I have become convinced, that I could not, without manifest impropriety, make the avowal or disavowal which you seem to think necessary.

The clause pointed out by Mr. Van Ness is in these terms "I could detail to you a *still more despicable opinion*, which General Hamilton has expressed of Mr. Burr." To endeavour to discover the meaning of this declaration, I was obliged to seek in the antecedent part of the letter, for the opinion to which it referred, as having been already disclosed. I found it in these words "General Hamilton and Judge Kent have declared, *in substance*, that they looked upon Mr. Burr to be *a dangerous man*, and one who *ought not to be trusted with the reins of Government*". The language of Doctor Cooper plainly implies, that he considered this opinion of you, which he attributes to me, as a *despicable* one; but he affirms that I have expressed some other *still more despicable;* without however mentioning to whom, when, or where. 'Tis evident, that the phrase "still more dispicable" admits of infinite shades, from very light to very dark. How am I to judge of the degree intended? Or how shall I annex any precise idea to language so indefinite?

Between Gentlemen, *despicable* and *more despicable* are not worth the pains of a distinction. When therefore you do not interrogate me, as to the opinion which is specifically ascribed to me, I must conclude, that you view it as within the limits, to which the animadversions of political opponents, upon each other, may justifiably extend; and consequently as not warranting the idea of it, which Doctor Cooper appears to entertain. If so, what precise inference could you draw as a guide for your future conduct, were I to acknowlege, that I had expressed an opinion of you, *still more despicable*, than the one which is particularised? How could you be sure, that even this opinion had exceeded the bounds which you would yourself deem admissible between political opponents?

But I forbear further comment on the embarrassment to which the requisition you have made naturally leads. The occasion forbids a more ample illustration, though nothing would be more easy than to pursue it.

Repeating, that I cannot reconcile it with propriety to make the acknowlegement, or denial, you desire—I will add, that I deem it inadmissible, on principle, to consent to be interrogated as to the justness of the *inferences*, which may be drawn by *others*, from whatever I may have said of a political opponent in the course of a fifteen years competition. If there were no other objection to it, this is sufficient, that it would tend to expose my sincerity and delicacy to injurious imputations from every person, who may at any time have conceived the import of my expressions differently from what I may then have intended, or may afterwards recollect.

I stand ready to avow or disavow promptly and explicitly any precise or definite opinion, which I may be charged with having declared of any Gentleman. More than this cannot fitly be expected from me; and especially it cannot reasonably be expected, that I shall enter into an explanation upon a basis so vague as that which you have adopted. I trust, on more reflection, you will see the matter in the same light with me. If not, I can only regret the circumstance, and must abide the consequences.

The publication of Doctor Cooper was never seen by me 'till after the receipt of your letter.

I have the honor to be Sir Your obed. servt

A HAMILTON

From Aaron Burr

Nyork 21 June 1804

SIR

Your letter of the 20th. inst. has been this day received. Having Considered it attentively I regret to find in it nothing of that sincerity and delicacy which you profess to Value.

Political opposition can never absolve Gentlemen from the necessity of a rigid adherence to the laws of honor and the rules of decorum: I neither claim such priviledge nor indulge it in others.

The Common sense of Mankind affixes to the epithet adopted by Dr Cooper the idea of dishonor: it has been publicly applied to me under the Sanction of your name. The question is not whether he has understood the meaning of the word or has used it according to Syntax and with grammatical accuracy, but whether you have authorised this application either directly or by uttering expressions or opinions derogatory to my honor. The time "when" is in your own knowledge, but no way material to me, as the calumny has now first been disclosed so as to become the Subject of my Notice, and as the effect is present and palpable.

Your letter has furnished me with new reasons for requiring a definite reply.

I have the honor to be sir your obt st

A. BURR

To Aaron Burr

New York June 22d. 1804

Sir

Your first letter, in a style too peremptory, made a demand, in my opinion, unprecedented and unwarrantable. My answer, pointing out the embarrassment, gave you an opportunity to take a less exceptionable course. You have not chosen to do it, but by your last letter, received this day, containing expressions indecorous and improper, you have increased the difficulties to explanation, intrinsically incident to the nature of your application.

If by a "definite reply" you mean the direct avowal or disavowal required in your first letter, I have no other answer to give than that which has already been given. If you mean any thing different admitting of greater latitude, it is requisite you should explain.

I have the honor to be Sir Your obed servt.

A Hamilton

From Aaron Burr

Nyork June 22d. 1804

Sir

Mr. V Ness has this evening reported to me Verbally that you refuse to answer my last letter, that you consider the course I have taken as intemperate and unnecessary and some other conversation which it is improper that I should notice.

My request to you was in the first instance proposed in a form the most simple in order that you might give to the affair that course to which you might be induced by your temper and your knowledge of facts. I relied with unsuspecting faith that from the frankness of a Soldier and the Candor of a gentleman I might expect an ingenuous declaration; that if, as I had reason to believe, you had used expressions derogatory to my honor, you would have had the Spirit to Maintain or the Magnanimity to retract them, and, that if from your language injurious inferences had been improperly drawn, Sincerity and delicacy would have pointed out to you the propriety of correcting errors which might thus have been widely diffused.

With these impressions, I was greatly disappointed in receiving from you a letter which I could only consider as evasive and which in manner, is not altogether decorus. In one expectation however, I was not wholly deceived, for at the close of your letter I find an intimation, that if I should dislike your refusal to acknowledge or deny the charge, you were ready to meet the consequences. This I deemed a sort of defiance, and I should have been justified if I had chosen to make it the basis of an immediate message: Yet, as you had also said something (though in my opinion unfounded) of the indefiniteness of my request; as I believed that your communication was the offspring, rather of false pride than of reflection, and, as I felt the utmost reluctance to proceed to extremities while any other hope remained, my request was repeated in terms more definite. To this you refuse all reply, reposing, as I am bound to presume on the tender of an alternative insinuated in your letter.

Thus, Sir, you have invited the course I am about to pursue, and now by your silence impose it upon me. If therefore your determinations are final, of which I am not permitted to doubt, Mr. Van Ness is authorised to communicate my further expectations either to yourself or to such friend as you may be pleased to indicate.

I have the honor to be Your Ob st

A. BURR

Remarks on a Letter from
William P. Van Ness

Whether the observations in this letter are designed merely to justify the result, which is indicated in the close of the letter, or may be intended to give an opening for rendering any thing explicit which may have been deemed vague heretofore can only be judged of by the sequel. At any rate it appears to me necessary not to be misunderstood. Mr. Pendleton is therefore authorised to say that in the course of the present discussion, whether written or verbal, there has been no intention to evade defy or insult, but a sincere disposition to avoid extremities, if it could be done with propriety. With this view G H—— has been ready to enter into a frank and free explanation on any and every object of a specific nature; but not to answer a general and abstract enquiry, embracing a period too long for any accurate recollection, and exposing him to unpleasant criticisms from or unpleasant discussions with any and every person, who may have understood him in an unfavourable sense. This (admitting that he could answer in a manner the most satisfactory to Col Burr) he should deem inadmissible, in principle and precedent, and humiliating in practice. To this therefore he can never submit. Frequent allusion has been made to slanders said to be in circulation. Whether this be openly or in whispers they have a form and shape and might be specified.

If the alternative alluded to in the close of the letter is definitively tendered, it must be accepted, the time place and manner to be afterwards regulated. I should not think it right in the midst of a circuit Court to withdraw my services from those who may have confided important interests to me and expose them to the embarrassment of seeking other counsel who may not have time to be sufficiently instructed in their causes. I shall also want a little time to make some arrangements respecting my own affairs.

June 28, 1804

Alexander Hamilton's Explanation of His Financial Situation

New York, July 1, 1804

Herewith is a general statement of my pecuniary affairs; in which there can be no material error. The result is that calculating my property at what it stands me in, I am now worth about Ten thousand pounds, and that estimating according to what my lands are now selling for and are likely to fetch, the surplus beyond my debts may fairly be stated at nearly double that sum. Yet I am pained to be obliged to entertain doubts whether, if an accident should happen to me, by which the sales of my property should come to be forced, it would be even sufficient to pay my debts.

In a situation like this, it is perhaps due to my reputation to explain why I have made so considerable an establishment in the country. This explanation shall be submitted.

To men, who have been so much harassed in the busy world as

myself, it is natural to look forward to a comfortable retirement, in the sequel of life, as a principal desideratum. This desire I have felt in the strongest manner; and to prepare for it has latterly been a favourite object. I thought that I might not only expect to accomplish the object, but might reasonably aim at it and pursue the preparatory measures, from the following considerations.

It has been for some time past pretty well ascertained to my mind, that the emoluments of my profession would prove equal to the maintenance of my family and the gradual discharge of my debts, within a period to the end of which my faculties, for business might be expected to extend, in full energy. I think myself warranted to estimate the annual product of those emoluments at Twelve* Dollars at the least. My expences while the first improvements of my country establishment were going on have been great; but they would this summer and fall reach the point, at which it is my intention they should stop, at least 'till I should be better able than at present to add to them; and after a fair examination founded upon an actual account of my expenditures, I am persuaded that a plan I have contemplated for the next and succeeding years would bring my expences of every kind within the compass of four thousand Dollars yearly, exclusive of the interest of my country establishment. To this limit, I have been resolved to reduce them, even though it should be necessary to lease that establishment for a few years.

In the mean time, my lands now in a course of sale & settlement would accelerate the extinguishment of my debt, and in the end leave me a handsome clear property. It was also allowable for me to take into view, collaterally, the expectations of my wife; which have been of late partly realised. She is now intitled to a property of between two and three thousand pounds (as I compute) by descent from her mother; and her father is understood to possess a large estate. I feel all the delicacy of this allusion; but the occasion I trust will plead my excuse. And that venerable father, I am sure, will pardon. He knows well all the nicety of my past conduct.

Viewing the matter in these different aspects, I trust the opinion of candid men will be, that there has been no impropriety in my conduct; especially when it is taken into the calculation that my Country establishment, though costly, promises, by the progressive rise of

* "Thousand" likely omitted in error. —ED.

property on this Island, and the felicity of its situation to become more and more valuable.

My chief apology is due to those friends, who have from mere kindness, indorsed my paper discounted at the Banks. On mature reflection I have thought it justifiable to secure them in preference to other Creditors, lest perchance there should be *a deficit*. Yet while this may save them from eventual loss, it will not exempt them from some present inconvenience. As to this I can only throw myself upon their kindness, and entreat the indulgence of the Banks for them. Perhaps this request may be supposed intitled to some regard.

In the event, which would bring this paper to the public eye, one thing at least would be put beyond a doubt. This is, that my public labours have amounted to an absolute sacrifice of the interests of my family—and that in all pecuniary concerns the delicacy, no less than the probity of my conduct in public stations, has been such as to defy even the shadow of a question.

Indeed, I have not enjoyed the ordinary advantages incident to my military services. Being a member of Congress, while the question of the commutation of the half pay of the army in a sum in gross was in debate, delicacy and a desire to be useful to the army, by removing the idea of my having an interest in the question, induced me to write to the Secretary of War and relinquish my claim to half pay; which, or the equivalent, I have accordingly never received. Neither have I ever applied for the lands allowed by the United States to Officers of my rank. Nor did I ever obtain from this state the allowance of lands made to officers of similar rank. It is true that having served through the latter period of the War on the general staff of the UStates and not in the line of this State. I could not claim that allowance as a matter of course. But having before the War resided in this State and having entered the military career at the head of a company of Artillery raised for the particular defence of this State, I had better pretensions to the allowance than others to whom it was actually made—Yet has it not been extended to me.

A H

To Elizabeth Hamilton

This letter, my very dear Eliza, will not be delivered to you, unless I shall first have terminated my earthly career; to begin, as I humbly hope from redeeming grace and divine mercy, a happy immortality.

If it had been possible for me to have avoided the interview, my love for you and my precious children would have been alone a decisive motive. But it was not possible, without sacrifices which would have rendered me unworthy of your esteem. I need not tell you of the pangs I feel, from the idea of quitting you and exposing you to the anguish which I know you would feel. Nor could I dwell on the topic lest it should unman me.

The consolations of Religion, my beloved, can alone support you; and these you have a right to enjoy. Fly to the bosom of your God and be comforted. With my last idea; I shall cherish the sweet hope of meeting you in a better world.

Adieu best of wives and best of Women. Embrace all my darling Children for me.

Ever yours

A H

July 4. 1804

Statement on Impending Duel with Aaron Burr

On my expected interview with Col Burr, I think it proper to make some remarks explanatory of my conduct, motives and views.

I am certainly desirous of avoiding this interview, for the most cogent reasons.

1   My religious and moral principles are strongly opposed to the practice of Duelling, and it would even give me pain to be obliged to shed the blood of a fellow creature in a private combat forbidden by the laws.

2   My wife and Children are extremely dear to me, and my life is of the utmost importance to them, in various views.

3   I feel a sense of obligation towards my creditors; who in case of accident to me, by the forced sale of my property, may be in some degree sufferers. I did not think my self at liberty, as a man of probity, lightly to expose them to this hazard.

4   I am conscious of no *ill-will* to Col Burr, distinct from political opposition, which, as I trust, has proceeded from pure and upright motives.

Lastly, I shall hazard much, and can possibly gain nothing by the issue of the interview.

But it was, as I conceive, impossible for me to avoid it. There were *intrinsick* difficulties in the thing, and *artificial* embarrassments, from the manner of proceeding on the part of Col Burr.

Intrinsick—because it is not to be denied, that my animadversions on the political principles character and views of Col Burr have been extremely severe, and on different occasions, I, in common with many others, have made very unfavourable criticisms on particular instances of the private conduct of this Gentleman.

In proportion as these impressions were entertained with sincerity and uttered with motives and for purposes, which might appear to me commendable, would be the difficulty (until they could be removed by evidence of their being erroneous), of explanation or apology. The disavowal required of me by Col Burr, in a general and indefinite form, was out of my power, if it had really been proper for me to submit to be so questionned; but I was sincerely of opinion, that this could not be, and in this opinion, I was confirmed by that of a very moderate and judicious friend whom I consulted. Besides that Col Burr appeared to me to assume, in the first instance, a tone unnecessarily peremptory and menacing, and in the second, positively offensive. Yet I wished, as far as might be practicable, to leave a door open to accommodation. This, I think, will be inferred from the written communications made by me and by my direction, and would be confirmed by the conversations between Mr van Ness and myself, which arose out of the subject.

I am not sure, whether under all the circumstances I did not go further in the attempt to accommodate, than a punctilious delicacy will justify. If so, I hope the motives I have stated will excuse me.

It is not my design, by what I have said to affix any odium on the conduct of Col Burr, in this case. He doubtless has heared of animadversions of mine which bore very hard upon him; and it is probable that as usual they were accompanied with some falshoods. He may have supposed himself under a necessity of acting as he has done. I hope the grounds of his proceeding have been such as ought to satisfy his own conscience.

I trust, at the same time, that the world will do me the Justice to believe, that I have not censured him on light grounds, or from unworthy inducements. I certainly have had strong reasons for what I may have said, though it is possible that in some particulars, I may have been influenced by misconstruction or misinformation. It is also my ardent wish that I may have been more mistaken than I think I have been, and that he by his future conduct may shew himself worthy of all confidence and esteem, and prove an ornament and blessing to his Country.

As well because it is possible that I may have injured Col Burr, however convinced myself that my opinions and declarations have been well founded, as from my general principles and temper in relation to similar affairs—I have resolved, if our interview is conducted in the usual manner, and it pleases God to give me the opportunity, to *reserve* and *throw away* my first fire, and I *have thoughts* even of *reserving* my second fire—and thus giving a double opportunity to Col Burr to pause and to reflect.

It is not however my intention to enter into any explanations on the ground. Apology, from principle I hope, rather than Pride, is out of the question.

To those, who with me abhorring the practice of Duelling may think that I ought on no account to have added to the number of bad examples—I answer that my *relative* situation, as well in public as private aspects, enforcing all the considerations which constitute what men of the world denominate honor, impressed on me (as I thought) a peculiar necessity not to decline the call. The ability to be in future useful, whether in resisting mischief or effecting good, in those crises of our public affairs, which seem likely to happen, would probably be inseparable from a conformity with public prejudice in this particular.

AH
c. July 10, 1804

To Theodore Sedgwick

New York July 10. 1804

MY DEAR SIR

I have received two letters from you since we last saw each other—that of the latest date being the 24 of May. I have had in hand for some time a long letter to you, explaining my view of the course and tendency of our Politics, and my intentions as to my own future conduct. But my plan embraced so large a range that owing to much avocation, some indifferent health, and a growing distaste for Politics, the letter is still considerably short of being finished. I write this now to satisfy you, that want of regard for you has not been the cause of my silence.

I will here express but one sentiment, which is, that Dismemberment of our Empire will be a clear sacrifice of great positive advantages, without any counterballancing good; administering no relief to our real Disease; which is DEMOCRACY, the poison of which by a subdivision will only be the more concentered in each part, and consequently the more virulent.

King is on his way for Boston where you may chance to see him, and hear from himself his sentiments.

God bless you

A H

To Elizabeth Hamilton

MY BELOVED ELIZA

Mrs. Mitchel is the person in the world to whom as a friend I am under the greatest Obligations. I have not hitherto done my duty to her. But resolved to repair my omission as much as possible, I have encouraged her to come to this Country and intend, if it shall be in my power to render the Evening of her days comfortable. But if it shall please God to put this out of my power and to inable you hereafter to be of service to her, I entreat you to do it and to treat her with the tenderness of a Sister.

This is my second letter.

The Scruples of a Christian have determined me to expose my own life to any extent rather than subject my self to the guilt of taking the life of another. This must increase my hazards & redoubles my pangs for you. But you had rather I should die innocent than live guilty. Heaven can preserve me and I humbly hope will but in the contrary event, I charge you to remember that you are a Christian. God's Will be done. The will of a merciful God must be good.

Once more Adieu My Darling darling Wife

A H

Tuesday Evening 10 oClock

July 10, 1804

Joint Statement by William P. Van Ness and Nathaniel Pendleton on the Duel

Col: Burr arrived first on the ground as had been previously agreed. When Genl Hamilton arrived the parties exchanged salutations and the Seconds proceeded to make their arrangments. They measured the distance, ten full paces, and cast lots for the choice of positions as also to determine by whom the word should be given, both of which fell to the Second of Genl Hamilton. They then proceeded to load the pistols in each others presence, after which the parties took their stations. The Gentleman who was to give the word, then explained to the parties the rules which were to govern them in firing which were as follows: The parties being placed at their stations The Second who gives the word shall ask them whether they are ready—being answered in the affirmative, he shall say *"present"* after which the parties shall present & fire when they please. If one fires before the other the opposite second shall say one two, three, fire, and he shall fire or loose his fire. And asked if they were prepared, being answered in the affirmative he gave the word *present* as had been agreed on, and both of the parties took aim, & fired in succession, the Intervening time is not expressed as the seconds do not precisely agree on that point. The pistols were discharged within a few seconds of each other and the fire of Col: Burr took effect; Genl Hamilton almost instantly fell. Col: Burr then advanced toward Genl H——n with a manner and gesture that appeared to Genl Hamilton's friend to be expressive of regret, but without Speaking turned about

& withdrew. Being urged from the field by his friend as has been subsequently stated, with a view to prevent his being recognised by the Surgeon and Bargemen who were then approaching. No farther communications took place between the principals and the Barge that carried Col: Burr immediately returned to the City. We conceive it proper to add that the conduct of the parties in that interview was perfectly proper as suited the occasion.

July 17, 1804

Nathaniel Pendleton's Amendments to the Joint Statement

The statement containing the facts that led to the interview between General Hamilton and Col. Burr, published in the Evening Post on Monday, studiously avoided mentioning any particulars of what past at the place of meeting. This was dictated by suitable considerations at the time, and with the intention, that whatever it might be deemed proper to lay before the public, should be made the subject of a future communication. The following is therefore now submitted.

In the interviews that have since taken place between the gentlemen that were present, they have not been able to agree in two important facts that passed there—for which reason nothing was said on those subjects in the paper lately published as to other particulars in which they were agreed.

Mr. P. expressed a confident opinion that General Hamilton did not fire first—and that he did not fire at all *at Col. Burr*. Mr. V. N. seemed equally confident in the opinion that Gen. H. did fire first—and of course that it must have been *at* his antagonist.

General Hamilton's friend thinks it to be a sacred duty he owes to the memory of that exalted man, to his country, and his friends, to publish to the world such facts and circumstances as have produced a decisive conviction in his own mind, that he cannot have been mistaken in the belief he has formed on these points.

1st. Besides the testimonies of Bishop Moore, and the paper containing an express declaration, under General Hamilton's own hand, enclosed to his friend in a packet, not to be delivered but in the event of his death, and which have already been published, General

Hamilton informed Mr. P. at least ten days previous to the affair, that he had doubts whether he would not receive and not return Mr. Burr's first fire. Mr. P. remonstrated against this determination, and urged many considerations against it, as dangerous to himself and not necessary in the particular case, when every ground of accommodation, not humiliating, had been proposed and rejected. He said he would not decide lightly, but take time to deliberate fully. It was incidentally mentioned again at their occasional subsequent conversations, and on the evening preceding the time of the appointed interview, he informed Mr. P. he had made up his mind *not to fire at Col. Burr the first time, but to receive his fire, and fire in the air.* Mr. P. again urged him upon this subject, and repeated his former arguments. His final answer was in terms that made an impression on Mr. P's mind which can never be effaced. "My friend, it is the effect of A RELIGIOUS SCRUPLE, and does not admit of reasoning, it is useless to say more on the subject, as my purpose is definitely fixed."

2d. His last words before he was wounded afford a proof that this purpose had not changed. When he received his pistol, after having taken his position, he was asked if he would have the hair spring set? His answer was, *"Not this time."*

3d. After he was wounded, and laid in the boat, the first words he uttered after recovering the power of speech, were, (addressing himself to a gentleman present, who perfectly well remembers it) *"Pendleton knows I did not mean to fire at Col. Burr the first time."*

4th. This determination had been communicated by Mr. P. to that gentleman that morning, before they left the city.

5th. The pistol that had been used by General Hamilton, lying loose over the other apparatus in the case which was open; after having been some time in the boat, one of the boatmen took hold of it to put it into the case. General Hamilton observing this, said *"Take care of that pistol—it is cocked. It may go off and do mischief."* This is also remembered by the gentleman alluded to.

This shews he was not sensible of having fired at all. If he had fired *previous* to receiving the wound, he would have remembered it, and therefore have known that the pistol could not go off; but if *afterwards* it must have been the effect of an involuntary exertion of the muscles produced by a mortal wound, in which case, he could not have been conscious of having fired.

6. Mr. P. having so strong a conviction that if General Hamilton had fired first, it could not have escaped his attention (all his anxiety being alive for the effect of the first fire, and having no reason to believe the friend of Col. Burr was not sincere in the contrary opinion) he determined to go to the spot where the affair took place, to see if he could not discover some traces of the course of the ball from Gen. Hamilton's pistol.

He took a friend with him the day after General Hamilton died, and after some examination they fortunately found what they were in search of. They ascertained that the ball passed through the limb of a cedar tree, at an elevation of about twelve feet and a half, perpendicularly from the ground, between thirteen and fourteen feet from the mark on which General Hamilton stood, and about four feet wide of the direct line between him and Colonel Burr, on the right side; he having fallen on the left. The part of the limb through which the ball passed was cut off and brought to this city, and is now in Mr. Church's possession.

No inferences are pointed out as resulting from these facts, nor will any comments be made. They are left to the candid judgment and feelings of the public.

July 19, 1804

William P. Van Ness's Amendments to the Joint Statement

The second of G H having considered it proper to subjoin an explanatory note to the statement mutually furnished, it becomes proper for the gentleman who attended Col Burr to state also his impressions with respect to those points on which their exists a variance of opinion. In doing this he pointedly disclaims any idea disrespectful to the memory of G H, or an intention to ascribe any conduct to him that is not in his opinion perfectly honorable & correct.

The parties met as has been above related & took their respective stations as directed: the pistols were then handed to them by the seconds. Gen Hamilton elevated his, as if to try the light, & lowering it said I beg pardon for delaying you but the direction of the light renders it necessary, at the same time feeling his pockets with his left hand, & drawing forth his spectacles put them on. The second then asked if they were prepared which was replied to in the affirmative. The word *present* was then given, on which both parties took aim. The pistol of General Hamilton was first discharged, and Col Burr fired immediately after, only five or six seconds of time intervening. On this point the second of Col Burr has full & perfect reccollection. He noticed particularly the discharge of G H's pistol, & looked to his principal to ascertain whether he was hurt, he then clearly saw Col Bs pistol discharged. At this moment of looking at Col B on the discharge of G H's pistol he perceived a slight motion in his person, which induced the idea of his being struck. On this point he conversed with his principal on their return, who ascribed that circumstance to a small stone under his foot, & observed that the smoke of G Hs pistol obscured him for a moment in the interval of their firing.

When G H fell Col B advanced toward him as stated & was checked by his second who urged the importance of his immediately repairing to the barge, conceiving that G H was mortally wounded, & being desirous to secure his principal from the sight of the surgeon & bargemen who might be called in evidence. Col B complied with his request.

He shortly followed him to the boat, and Col B again expressed a wish to return, saying with an expression of much concern, I must go & speak to him. I again urged the obvious impropriety stating that the G was surrounded by the Surgeon & Bargemen by whom he must not be seen & insisted on immediate departure.

July 21, 1804

Word Cloud Classics

Word Cloud Classics

Les Misérables

Little Women

Madame Bovary

Mansfield Park

*The Merry Adventures of
Robin Hood*

Moby-Dick

My Ántonia

*Narrative of the Life of Frederick
Douglass and Other Works*

Northanger Abbey

Odyssey

Persuasion

Peter Pan

The Phantom of the Opera

The Picture of Dorian Gray

The Poetry of Emily Dickinson

Pride and Prejudice

The Prince and Other Writings

*The Red Badge of Courage
and Other Stories*

The Romantic Poets

The Scarlet Letter

The Secret Garden

*Selected Works of
Alexander Hamilton*

Sense and Sensibility

*Shakespeare's Sonnets and
Other Poems*

*Strange Case of Dr. Jekyll and
Mr. Hyde & Other Stories*

*Tarzan of the Apes &
The Return of Tarzan*

The Three Musketeers

Treasure Island

*Twenty Thousand Leagues
Under the Sea*

*Uncle Tom's Cabin, or Life
Among the Lowly*

*The U.S. Constitution and Other
Key American Writings*

Walden and Civil Disobedience

The Wizard of Oz

Wuthering Heights

permit me, as I intend

left Philadelphia. I ma

it I was desirous of know

with regard to militar

was any thing worth i

of which at the time I co

but I wished to unders

to you, with a view to

to be seriously engaged i

compliment to you to

men who must be in

we shall want new w

but will do it with an

General Gunn